YOU'LL SEE THIS MESSAGE WHEN IT IS TOO LATE

Information Policy Series
Edited by Sandra Braman

The Information Policy Series publishes research on and analysis of significant problems in the field of information policy, including decisions and practices that enable or constrain information, communication, and culture irrespective of the legal siloes in which they have traditionally been located as well as state-law-society interactions. Defining information policy as all laws, regulations, and decision-making principles that affect any form of information creation, processing, flows, and use, the series includes attention to the formal decisions, decision-making processes, and entities of government; the formal and informal decisions, decision-making processes, and entities of private and public sector agents capable of constitutive effects on the nature of society; and the cultural habits and predispositions of governmentality that support and sustain government and governance. The parametric functions of information policy at the boundaries of social, informational, and technological systems are of global importance because they provide the context for all communications, interactions, and social processes.

Virtual Economies: Design and Analysis, Vili Lehdonvirta and Edward Castronova

Traversing Digital Babel: Information, e-Government, and Exchange, Alon Peled

Chasing the Tape: Information Law and Policy in Capital Markets, Onnig H. Dombalagian

Regulating the Cloud: Policy for Computing Infrastructure, edited by Christopher S. Yoo and Jean-François Blanchette

Privacy on the Ground: Driving Corporate Behavior in the United States and Europe, Kenneth A. Bamberger and Deirdre K. Mulligan

How Not to Network a Nation: The Uneasy History of the Soviet Internet, Benjamin Peters

Hate Spin: The Manufacture of Religious Offense and its Threat to Democracy, Cherian George

Big Data Is Not a Monolith, edited by Cassidy R. Sugimoto, Hamid R. Ekbia, and Michael Mattioli

Decoding the Social World: Data Science and the Unintended Consequences of Communication, Sandra González-Bailón

Open Space: The Global Effort for Open Access to Environmental Satellite Data, Mariel John Borowitz

Digital Lifeline? ICTs for Refugees and Displaced Persons, edited by Carleen F. Maitland

YOU'LL SEE THIS MESSAGE WHEN IT IS TOO LATE

The Legal and Economic Aftermath of Cybersecurity Breaches

Josephine Wolff

The MIT Press
Cambridge, Massachusetts
London, England

This book was set in Stone Serif by Westchester Publishing Services. Printed and bound in the United States of America.

Library of Congress Cataloging-in-Publication Data

Names: Wolff, Josephine, author.
Title: You'll see this message when it is too late : the legal and economic
    aftermath of cybersecurity breaches / Josephine Wolff.
Description: Cambridge, MA : MIT Press, [2018] | Series: Information policy |
    Includes bibliographical references and index.
Identifiers: LCCN 2018010219 | ISBN 9780262038850 (hardcover : alk. paper)
Subjects: LCSH: Computer crimes--Prevention.
Classification: LCC HV6773 .W655 2018 | DDC 364.16/8--dc23
    LC record available at https://lccn.loc.gov/2018010219

10 9 8 7 6 5 4 3 2

In memory of Sheila Solomon Klass, who hated computers but loved writing.

Contents

Series Editor's Introduction   ix

Acknowledgments   xiii

1   Introduction: After the Breach   1

I   Lessons from Financially Motivated Cybercrimes   17

2   Operation Get Rich or Die Tryin': How the TJX Breach
    Set the Stage for a Decade of Payment Card Conflict   19

3   "What They Aren't Telling You Is Their Rules Are Archaic":
    The South Carolina Department of Revenue Breach,
    IRS Fraud, and Identity Theft   39

4   The Most Wanted Cybercriminal in the World:
    GameOver ZeuS, Cryptolocker, and the Rise
    of Ransomware   59

II Lessons from Cyberespionage   79

5   Certificates Gone Rogue: The DigiNotar Compromise
    and the Internet's Fragile Trust Infrastructure   81

6   No Doubt to Hack You, Written by UglyGorilla:
    China's PLA Unit 61398 and Economic Espionage   101

7   "Decades in the Making": The Office of Personnel Management
    Breach and Political Espionage   121

III Lessons from Online Acts of Public Humiliation   143

8   Operation Stophaus: The Spamhaus Denial-of-Service Attacks   145

9   "An Epic Nightmare": The Sony Breach and
     Ex-Post Mitigation   165
10   An Imperfect Affair: Ashley Madison and the Economics
     of Embarrassment   185

IV   Who Should Safeguard Our Data? Distributing Responsibility
     and Liability   205

11   "Email the Way It Should Be": The Role of Application Designers
     and Software Developers   207
12   Reasonable Security: The Role of Organizations in Protecting
     Their Data and Networks   225
13   "Happy Talk About Good Ideas": The Role of Policymakers
     in Defending Computer Systems   243
14   Conclusion: "It Will Take All of Us"   269

Notes   281
Bibliography   301
Index   315

Series Editor's Introduction

Sandra Braman

Everyone is talking about cybersecurity. In most of what we hear, whether from media mass, social, or organizational, this is a simple story: someone did or did not do one thing, like click on a link, and financial, or political, or personal mayhem follows in ways that may ultimately affect millions of people. Relying on stories based on this single point of failure fallacy makes it possible to assign blame (or shift it), and to reassure everyone that the problem has been, or could easily be, solved.

Except, of course, that cybersecurity problems have not gone away. Indeed, they are multiplying in number, with effects that are broadening and multiplying. It is dismaying to note that one of the cases in Josephine Wolff's fascinating and valuable book *You'll See This Message When It Is Too Late* involves a political matter very much on our minds as I write in March of 2018, a 2010 incident involving Chinese government intrusion into the U.S. Steel computer and communication system for espionage purposes during a period of tense negotiations over trade tariffs. What this and the other cases analyzed in this book tell us is that the real story of each event is complex, at every stage offering different opportunities to protect against, prevent, or mitigate the effects of a cybersecurity attack but none of them sufficient on its own.

The first distinction to make is between those processes required to get *into* a technical system, and those required to get information *out* of a system and into a form that has value to the attackers and serves their goals. Those goals themselves can be multiple; the nine incidents analyzed in detail by Wolff were driven by, variously, financial, political (espionage), and personal motives (vengeance). She has done a superb job of choosing fascinating cases—these really *do* make good stories—that also illustrate how differences among types of information affect what type of market there may be for it, how the information can be priced, how long that market might remain open and how to operate within it, as well as how long the attacker needs to be within a system to acquire the information to be sold. Certain data may be targeted or, alternatively, those doing it for the lulz can make use of about whatever they find. Attackers differ in their levels of sophistication, and in whether they are self-motivated or representing the interests of a group (although even in the latter cases, powerful individual egos are often still on display).

These differences in the nature of cybersecurity incidents matter because they affect what kinds of technical and social processes are involved and, thus, what types of organizational, legal, and technical interventions might be made. On the way *in* to systems, where most analysis, policy, and public discourse are focused, opportunities are multiple and can change flexibly and radically, whether deliberately or by nature. Thus, even when a technical effort to protect, prevent, or mitigate works, the defense may well still fail because attackers can simply use another route or technique to get in. It is on the way *out* of systems that attackers lose their flexibility and where, therefore, legal and policy interventions can be the most successful. On both sides, the norm has become avoiding organizational responsibility, reference to multiple often mutually contradictory lists of guidelines followed (the effectiveness of which is unknown), and a dogged shifting of liability to someone else, always someone else.

The difficulty in effectively preventing entry into systems arises out of the characteristics of informational meta-technologies that make them qualitatively different from industrial technologies and preindustrial tools. Where industrial technologies accept only one or a small range of resources for processing and yield only one or a small range of products—going through processing steps that are necessarily linear in their sequencing—informational meta-technologies can work with an always-growing and seemingly boundless range of possible inputs, produce an essentially infinite range of potential outputs, and can process information in endlessly flexible ways, creating new paths as they go. It will, by definition, *never* be possible to fully protect against cybersecurity threats as they occur on the way into systems, whether the concerns are of the types discussed in the nine cases Wolff addresses in this book, or those on the military side, analyzed so thoroughly as they are affected by—or cannot be dealt with by—international law in the *Tallinn Manual* and *Tallinn Manual 2.0*.

For decades we have talked about how it is the speed of technological change that makes it so hard for the law to keep up with digital technologies. Speed matters, but *You'll See This Message When It Is Too Late* alerts us to a number of other fundamental problems these technologies raise for governance. Some are little discussed in the literature, if at all: The law assumes causality is discernible, but this may well not be the case. The law strives for perfection that may be unachievable. Laws and regulations typically present single policy tools that may be at best inefficient and at worst utterly inadequate on their own. Some of the difficulties are regularly acknowledged but raise issues that have not yet been solved: The law relies upon cost-oriented analyses of harm when these may not always be available even though harm is genuine and serious. Jurisdictional issues are, of course, endemic. Standards may be set so low as to be meaningless, as in the Third Circuit Court decision in *FTC v. Wyndham Hotel Group*, in which the only bar that had to be met was having any security measures at all.

Wolff brings to light a significant inequity in the kinds of arguments available to geopolitically recognized states and to others. Though preemption is the justification for counter-terrorism measures like surveillance and the government has used possible harms to others to indict, neither preemption nor possible harms to others was considered an acceptable argument for individuals seeking redress for harms caused by cybersecurity incidents in the nine cases discussed here. This imbalance resonates with one of the generalizations that became evident after looking at developments in thirty-two different areas of the law in *Change of State* (Braman 2006)—that the government knows more and more about individuals while individuals know less and less about the state. These two findings together suggest argumentation should be an area in which those doing research on information policy need to focus, going beyond rhetorical, framing, discourse, and content analysis to look specifically at the logics involved. Policy analysis of algorithms must go in this direction in any event, and deciding whether or not particular logics are acceptable is at the heart of efforts to develop defenses against inference and aggregation attacks.

This book suggests, as computer scientists often do, that the legal side of the problem may be easier to solve. That may or may not be so, but Wolff does include several examples of legal and policy interventions that did reduce cybersecurity incidents or the damage resulting from them. And she does make a number of positive policy recommendations that range from the development of conceptual approaches such as kill chain modeling and defense-in-depth to specific and often familiar techniques such as using the law to shift liability for losses when credit card companies are hacked. Regarding the nature of governance itself, Wolff argues, among other things, for centralized control of flows after information has been exfiltrated, clear definition of roles and responsibilities for those involved with cybersecurity, and for more international cooperation on such matters.

Josephine Wolff offers us both a model of how to conduct policy analysis in the exceedingly complex digital environment, and a guide to the suite of types of technical, behavioral, and legal efforts needed to be conjoined in order to combat cybersecurity problems and mitigate their effects. The book will leave the reader who has decision-making responsibilities, in organizations, governments, or households, with ideas about how to improve security online. The researcher will be thinking about methods for approaching long-standing questions (which techniques actually *do* work?)—but also deeply appreciative of new questions that need to be asked about the nature of causality and the possibilities for governance in the digital world. Citizens concerned about the security of their data and the systems with which we all live will hope that Wolff's recommendations will be followed.

Acknowledgments

Diving into the aftermath of cybersecurity incidents involves following many different threads tied to fields ranging from economics and law to journalism, computer science, and politics. As I pursued these individual strands, many people helped me understand materials from each of these disciplines and think through how they fit together in the context of an individual incident's causes and impacts.

The person who started me down the path of trying to map out cybersecurity incident lifecycles was my doctoral adviser David Clark, who guided my first attempts at doing interdisciplinary research with his characteristic patience and insight. Several of my other professors in graduate school also profoundly shaped my interests and research. Ken Oye helped me understand the particular dynamics and challenges of regulating new and emerging technologies. Alan Davidson taught me the nuances of the everchanging landscape of Internet policy. David Autor's class on economics and public policy changed my understanding of what it means to craft effective policies and how to figure out whether they work. Going back even further, to my undergraduate years, I am grateful to Robert Calderbank and Ingrid Daubechies who advised my senior thesis on wavelets and paintings and introduced me to the joys of academic research.

At MIT Press, Sandra Braman, Gita Manaktala, and Marcy Ross provided invaluable feedback and guided me through the publication process with unfailing good humor and enthusiasm. Several friends and colleagues also read portions of this project at various stages and I am deeply appreciative of the thoughtful comments and insights I received from Kendra Albert, David Auerbach, Meredith Broussard, Patrick Gage Kelley, Tommy Leung, Alexis Levinson, Nathan Perkins, Charles Seife, and Alicia Solow-Niederman.

At Rochester Institute of Technology, I have been lucky to find a public policy department with a strong focus on technology policy, as well as a computing security department with a real interest in the legal, political, and ethical dimensions of the field. Many of my colleagues at RIT provided support and encouragement throughout the process of writing this book, especially Sarah Burns, Stephanie Godleski, Lauren Hall, Andrea Hickerson, Eric Hittinger, Priti Kalsi, Qing Miao, Sumita Mishra, Yin Pan, Emily Prud'hommeaux, Sandra Rothenberg, Evan Selinger, Jamie Winebrake, Matthew Wright, and Bo Yuan.

While working on this book, I was also fortunate to be invited to present portions of it to scholars and practitioners who challenged me to approach these incidents in new ways. I am especially grateful to Claire Hill for inviting me to present at the University of Minnesota Law School faculty works in progress series in September 2016, to Ido Kilovaty for giving me the opportunity to talk about ransomware at the Yale Law School Hijacking Information workshop in November 2017, and to Daniel Wood for inviting me to the Federal Trade Commission Informational Injury workshop to talk about the impacts of data breaches in December 2017.

This project was funded by a fellowship from New America, and I am deeply grateful to everyone there, especially Emefa Agawu, Laura Bate, Emily Fritcke, Rob Morgus, Ian Wallace, and Elizabeth Weingarten.

I am also indebted to Microsoft, where I spent three summers during graduate school learning about technology policy on the ground from many talented technologists and policy experts, including Sharon Gillett, Paul Mitchell, and Kevin Sullivan.

Torie Bosch at *Slate* is my role model when it comes to writing about technology for a general audience. She has taught me so much about how to make technical topics clear, engaging, and accessible—even when it comes to certificate authorities.

My grandparents, Bob and Renee Wolff, cheerfully read many articles about cybersecurity and proudly reported to me every email they received asking for their bank information that they did not respond to. My grandmother Sheila Solomon Klass, the most dedicated writer I have known, died in 2014 after a years-long battle with a 27-inch iMac she never trusted and long suspected of secretly deleting her files. The threat of disappearing files notwithstanding, I wrote most of this book on that same iMac, with the little notes in her handwriting listing her account usernames and passwords still taped to the bottom of the screen, in defiance of all recommended security best practices.

When I needed breaks from research, Orlando and Anatol Klass generously allowed me to micromanage their respective job search and graduate school applications. For reasons I have never entirely understood, Orlando has long believed that I do highly classified top-secret research of vital importance to critical national security missions, while Anatol has doubted the seriousness of my research ever since I wrote my senior thesis on what he believes to be the entirely fictitious topic of wavelets. Between them, I like to think they keep my ego well balanced.

Larry Wolff taught me everything I know about academic life and embarking on research projects—and the true meaning of kindness. When I was feeling daunted by the prospect of beginning this project, he sent me an email that still hangs in my office, which says, "remember that you can NOT lay the whole thing out in advance, exactly what you're going to read, write, and show; if you could do that then the research wouldn't really be worth doing." In so many ways, Perri Klass made me who I am—a person who cannot drink coffee or wear shoes with backs, a person who can only write with very particular extra-fine pens in very particular graph-paper notebooks, a person who starts every new year with fresh resolutions to write more and write better. She also, on occasion, asks for help with her computer and phone, and when I (inevitably) fail to fix things to her satisfaction says to me, with some skepticism, "Don't you study the Internet?"

1 Introduction: After the Breach

Cybersecurity incidents have a short shelf life. As I write this, in fall 2017, the breaches of the moment are the theft of 145.5 million Americans' information from the credit bureau Equifax, the compromise of three billion Yahoo user accounts, and the Russian government's theft of sensitive National Security Agency documents from a government contractor's home computer. But by the time you read this those incidents will have long since been eclipsed by dozens of other high-profile breaches. We read about the most recent data breaches in the headlines for a few days, maybe weeks, after they are publicly announced—we learn how many records were stolen, or the most embarrassing secrets revealed in the breach, we find out who will be fired and who will sue—and then these stories typically fade from our consciousness as they are overshadowed by newer, bigger, even more dramatic incidents. The most recent cybersecurity breaches grab our attention not just because they are breaking news, but also because there's a strong sense that the older incidents, the ones that happened a few months ago—or, even worse, a few years ago—have nothing to teach us because they are already hopelessly out-of-date, and our adversaries have moved on to new tactics and technologies. Why waste time and resources learning how to defend against yesterday's attacks in the face of constantly evolving threats?

But not everything about these attacks is changing. Certainly, the technical details and exploits can shift rapidly as attackers adapt their methods to route around defensive upgrades and patches. But many of the nontechnical elements of these breaches have changed relatively little over the course of the past decade since the early days of large-scale data breaches and organized cybercrime. The policies that govern how computer systems may

be used and how they should be defended, the policing and law enforcement efforts aimed at tracking down perpetrators of security breaches, the
motivations driving attackers and their ultimate goals—be those money,
espionage, or publicly humiliating their victims—have all stayed fairly constant. Older security incidents offer a wealth of insight into how the current
policy climate enables attackers' pursuit of their end goals and how non-
technical lines of defense can be better tailored to address cybercrimes.

This book traces the trajectory of a series of significant cybersecurity
incidents between 2005 and 2015, with particular attention focused on the
aftermath of those events. Because cybersecurity incidents typically enjoy
such a brief period of public attention, we often miss what happens after
the perpetrators have successfully gained access to their target systems or
data: who sues whom, who ends up paying whom, who changes their security setup, who attempts to dodge responsibility for future incidents, and
how policymakers respond. While there has been significant work done
on the technical components of the breaches discussed here, this book sets
that technical material alongside a close analysis of the legal and economic
fallout of these breaches. This juxtaposition highlights the ways we conclude breaches were caused by technical failings or simple human error,
often overlooking the extent to which those failings are merely catalysts for
longer-term political fights. Those fights involve a multitude of different
stakeholders with different levers of power and they continue to play out
long after the technology has changed and improved. A poorly encrypted
wireless network at a Marshalls store in Miami gives rise to a lengthy, bitter
battle between retailers, banks, and payment networks about who should
be responsible for covering the costs of fraud and new security technologies. The compromise of Dutch certificate authority DigiNotar yields a
years-long tussle between certificate authorities and browser vendors about
who bears ultimate responsibility for vetting websites and how easily trust
can be bought, sold, and revoked online. Even as our technologies continue
to develop and evolve rapidly, these legal and political machinations follow much older, deeply entrenched templates that significantly impact the
ways we choose to protect our computer systems and data. Studying the
history of these incidents—and especially what follows them—sheds new
light on the questions: What have we learned in the first ten years we as
a society have been seriously grappling with the challenges of large-scale

data insecurity? And why haven't we gotten better at securing data and computer networks during that period?

Surveying the brief history of cybersecurity incidents to identify the relatively more static elements of those breaches can inform our understanding of defender-attacker dynamics. The question of who has the advantage in cyberattacks—defenders or attackers—gives rise to two contradictory viewpoints. The traditional perspective is that attackers have the edge. Ross Anderson, for instance, writes: "Attack is simply easier than defense. Defending a modern information system could also be likened to defending a large, thinly-populated territory like the nineteenth century Wild West: the men in black hats can strike anywhere, while the men in white hats have to defend everywhere."[1] This notion that defending all possible avenues of attack is more difficult than finding a single vulnerability in a computer system's defenses resonates with the technical dimensions of defense. It makes intuitive sense given the diverse, ever-evolving set of possibilities for breaching technologies we rely on every day. However, in proposing their cyberattack "kill chain" model for dividing security breaches into a sequence of progressive stages, Eric Hutchins and his colleagues at Lockheed Martin, Michael Cloppert and Rohan Armin, contend just the opposite: "The adversary must progress successfully through each stage of the chain before it can achieve its desired objective; just one mitigation disrupts the chain and the adversary." Because of this, they argue: "the defender can achieve an advantage over the aggressor."[2]

How to reconcile these competing, contradictory viewpoints? How can it be true both that defenders are always at a disadvantage because they have to defend "everywhere" and that attackers are always at a disadvantage because they have to "progress successfully" through every stage of their planned attack to succeed? Which of these perspectives is applicable to any given incident—or stage of an incident—depends on a more nuanced assessment of the particular facts and structure of a given compromise. In this book, by revisiting major cybersecurity incidents of the early 21st century, we can start to define the circumstances under which each of these two framings of attacker and defender advantage is most useful—which stages and components of cybersecurity incidents are most susceptible to a well-placed intervention by defenders, and which stages require those defenders to block off so many parallel options and attack pathways that the attackers unquestioningly hold the upper hand. Or, put more simply: over the course of the lifecycle of a cybersecurity incident, at what points is it most easily and effectively disrupted or prevented and by whom? A central theme that emerges from this analysis is that the elements of these security incidents that are most susceptible to the kinds of interventions that cut off an entire stage of the attack and thereby halt the "kill chain" are often related to public policy and legal intervention. Meanwhile, the attack stages that, by contrast, most resemble the "Wild West" analogy, and therefore provide attackers with the greatest advantage, are those that relate to technical access to protected computer systems.

Identifying the full range of possible opportunities for defensive intervention requires mapping out the entire sequence of events for a given cybersecurity incident. A 2011 study conducted by Kirill Levchenko and several collaborators looked at the best way to reduce commercial email spam by tracing what the authors called the spam messages' "click trajectory." This trajectory represented the full lifecycle of the spammers' operations beginning with sending spam emails, all the way through the messages being opened, the recipients clicking on the links in them, and the products advertised in them being purchased and shipped to customers.[3] The researchers collected spam messages, visited the websites advertised in those messages, bought some of the pharmaceuticals, replica luxury goods, and counterfeit software sold through those sites, and, at each stage of the "spam value chain," analyzed the feasibility of trying to intervene to cut off the spammers' business. In particular, they looked for what they called "bottlenecks," or "opportunities for disrupting monetization at a stage where the fewest alternatives are available to spammers (and ideally for which switching cost is high as well)."[4]

The researchers ultimately determined that rather than trying to take down the bots being used to send spam emails in bulk, or the hosting infrastructure underlying the websites those messages linked to, the most effective defensive intervention would be to crack down on the handful of banks that provided merchant services for the large majority of these transactions. That would entail encouraging the major global payment networks, such as Visa and MasterCard, not to allow certain types of transactions with the small number of banks known to be supporting spammers' enterprises. This stage of the spammers' process—the stage at which they processed customer credit card transactions—satisfied the characteristics of a bottleneck because so few banks were doing business with spammers (95 percent of the transactions the researchers tracked were settled by the same three banks) and also because the switching cost associated with it was high for spammers since setting up an account with a new bank would take days, or even weeks. The researchers concluded their analysis by returning to the question of when and if the defender is ever at an advantage online, writing:

> [I]f U.S. issuing banks (i.e., banks that provide credit cards to U.S. consumers) were to refuse to settle certain transactions (e.g., card-not-present transactions for a subset of Merchant Category Codes) with the banks identified as supporting spam-advertised goods, then the underlying enterprise would be dramatically demonetized. Furthermore, it appears plausible that such a "financial blacklist" could be updated very quickly (driven by modest numbers of undercover buys, as in our study) and far more rapidly than the turn-around time to acquire new banking resources—a rare asymmetry favoring the anti-spam community.[5]

The analysis of past security incidents in this book is related in spirit to this analysis of the spam value chain: it is an opportunity to revisit these incidents with an eye to mapping out their entire trajectories and locating those "rare asymmetries" in favor of the defenders—the opportunities for intervention that constrain attackers by offering them the fewest, and most costly, alternative paths to achieve their ultimate goals. The subsequent case studies are analyzed with an eye to trying to identify similar bottlenecks in the lifecycles of those incidents, or opportunities for especially effective defensive interventions that would require perpetrators to make expensive, slow adjustments to their original plans.

The ultimate goals—or motives—of the perpetrators of security breaches are a central organizing theme of this analysis in part because they remain relatively static over time and in part because they largely dictate the final stages of such incidents. The three types of motives underlying computer security incidents explored here—financial gain, espionage, and public humiliation of the victims, often for the purposes of revenge or wreaking havoc—recur repeatedly throughout the brief history of cybersecurity breaches. While some incidents clearly belong to one of these categories, these classes of harm are not always clear-cut, nor are they always completely distinct. In particular, the goal of publicly humiliating a victim can take many forms, ranging from publishing all of a victim's internal information and communications, as in the case of Sony Pictures, to exposing a victim's customer base and highlighting their inadequate security, as in the case of adultery website Ashley Madison, to overwhelming their servers with traffic in hopes of driving away their customers, as in the case of Spamhaus. Here, this class of harm—broadly described as public humiliation or revenge, and discussed in the third section of the book—is used to encompass incidents that do not have a clear financial or espionage-related motive. Even then, these categories still sometimes overlap. A breach perpetrated primarily for the purposes of public humiliation, such as the breach of Sony Pictures, may still serve some espionage or even financial theft function, either for its perpetrators or for others who piggyback on their crime by exploiting the information that the attackers stole. Similarly, the architects of threats like the Cryptolocker ransomware may be motivated primarily by financial gain, but still sometimes share information they obtain with government officials for the purposes of espionage.

Despite the challenges of assigning a single, clear-cut motivation to any individual incident, this book is organized around these general classes of harm because they dictate the final stages of breaches. These are the stages at which perpetrators have the least flexibility and the fewest options for changing course, the stages which are often most susceptible to political, legal, and social interventions, rather than technical tools and defenses, because they occur after the technical stages of a breach have been completed. Financial gain, espionage, and revenge are by no means the only motivations for cybersecurity incidents. The infamous Stuxnet worm, used to damage uranium enrichment centrifuges in Iran, illustrates yet another class of harm that can be imposed by such incidents—physical service disruption. This type of harm is certainly no less important—but there are too few known cases, beyond Stuxnet, to allow for much comparative or longitudinal analysis at this point. This classification of perpetrator motives is not meant to be exhaustive. Existing work on the mindset and perspective of hackers, especially by Gabriella Coleman, has identified several other motivations underlying cybercrimes beyond those discussed here, including political activism, curiosity, and personal entertainment.[6] The categories used here are chosen not to illustrate the full range of factors that motivate people to commit crimes online, but rather, to be instructive for defensive purposes by highlighting common attacker end goals and the individual stages of incidents that those attackers must complete in order to be successful. The purpose of this classification is to illuminate different possible opportunities for defensive intervention that specifically target perpetrators' ability to achieve their ultimate end goals and this objective also motivates the case selection. The case studies presented here illustrate a range of different attack templates that perpetrators can follow depending on their overarching motivations as well as the variety of economic, legal, and political consequences that can be incurred by individual incidents. The cases were also chosen to span different groups of online stakeholders, from browser manufacturers to payment processors to DNS operators, in order to give a clearer picture of the incentives each group faces when it comes to online security as well as how each set of stakeholders fits into a larger defensive ecosystem.

Just as perpetrators' motives remain relatively constant, so too do the later stages of breaches that occur immediately before they achieve their ultimate goals. This consistency stands in stark contrast to the early, technical phases of cybersecurity breaches, when perpetrators first attempt to gain access to their target computer systems. There is no set order of steps or template for how to go about accessing protected data or networks. Stealing credentials via phishing emails and malicious websites can be a means of stealing sensitive information, or, conversely, attackers may steal sensitive data containing credentials as a means of accessing accounts to send phishing emails and spam. Similarly, stolen credentials can be used to deliver and install malware—or malware can be used to steal credentials. The potential circularity of these access capabilities makes it difficult for defenders to know where they are interfering in an attacker's plan, or, indeed, what that adversary's ultimate intention is. It also grants adversaries considerable freedom to improvise and adjust course during these early stages of a breach when capabilities can be so easily reordered and reassembled in response to defensive interventions. This freedom from a set sequence of steps diminishes, however, as attackers reach the later stages of these incidents and prepare to actually carry out their intended aim. Attackers' options—and, correspondingly, the number of pathways defenders must cover—narrow, as adversaries get closer to their goal. There are many different ways for thieves to initiate the very early stages of a massive breach of payment card numbers, and defending against any one of those access modes individually may do little to hinder their progress, so long as there is another. By contrast, there are relatively fewer different ways to profit from stolen payment card numbers, so defenses aimed at that stage of a breach can be more narrowly focused.

This work, especially where it looks at financially motivated security incidents, owes much to the growing literature on the economics of information security. In a 2012 paper, Anderson and several collaborators provide a thorough breakdown of the different types of costs incurred by cybercrimes and compare the current spending on preemptive defense measures to indirect losses and spending on enforcement.[7] Based on their estimates, they conclude: "we should perhaps spend less in anticipation of computer crime (on antivirus, firewalls etc.)[,] but we should certainly spend an awful lot more on catching and punishing the perpetrators."[8] This important insight that the technical defenses against cybercrimes are overemphasized and receive disproportionate resources as compared to the non-technical mechanisms of law enforcement and policymaking motivates much of this analysis. The case studies analyzed here—which range from large-scale data breaches resulting in financial fraud to state-sponsored espionage to data dumps intended to publicly shame specific companies and victims—examine not just the technical controls that might (or might not) have effectively prevented the incidents from occurring. They also look closely at the range of non-technical defenses that might have been used to interfere with the perpetrators' progress.

Two papers focused on the economics of privacy (both written by Sasha Romanosky and Alessandro Acquisti) also provide crucial background and motivation for this analysis. One of these papers, also co-authored with Rahul Telang, found that the passage of state data breach disclosure laws actually reduces the rate of identity theft by about 6.1 percent.[9] This demonstration of the ability of policies to reduce negative security breach outcomes—one of relatively few attempts to quantify the impact of a computer security-related policy measure—shows the potential of policy measures to help defend against cybersecurity incidents. But it also highlights the many layers of challenges associated with internalizing the externalities of data breaches given the number of different stakeholders involved. "The effectiveness of data breach disclosure laws relies on actions taken by both firms and consumers," the authors point out, noting that in the aftermath of breaches many people affected ignore the letters notifying them of the breach or never bother to sign up for the credit monitoring services offered to them. "Firms can improve their controls; however, once notified, consumers themselves are expected to take responsibility to reduce their own risk of identity theft—something which only a minority appears to be doing," the researchers conclude.[10]

Another article by Romanosky and Acquisti, looking at personal data protection and the costs associated with loss of privacy, classifies policy measures as falling into three categories (ex-ante safety regulations, ex-post liability, and information disclosure) and compares the effectiveness of each type of measure for protecting consumer data.[11] They note that all three mechanisms are inefficient in different ways, arguing, "only in rare and extreme cases will any of these policy approaches be able to achieve the socially optimal outcome." This highlights both the advantages and the drawbacks of each individual type of security policy—from policies that impose baseline protection measures to those that impose liability regimes to those that simply require victims to be notified of breaches of their personal data. Each of these forms of policy, individually, is inadequate and inefficient in some regards. This finding motivates the discussion of these case studies spanning both the preventive measures taken by targeted firms and the ex-post lawsuits and settlements used to distribute costs in their aftermath. Looking at the strengths and weaknesses of each of these types of policy in the context of specific breaches allows for a clearer understanding of how they can be deployed in concert and used to bolster each other.

The theoretical framework used to analyze the cases presented here borrows not just from research on kill chain modeling, the bottleneck stages of cybersecurity incidents, and the need to balance ex-ante and ex-post defenses in these situations, but also from theories drawn from law and international relations scholarship. The analysis of the legal fallout of the incidents examined here and their impact on individuals owes much to the work done by Daniel Solove and Danielle Citron exploring the many different ways that data breaches can harm victims beyond straightforward financial losses.[12] The exploration of espionage incidents and the motivations behind nation-states that conduct cyberespionage for political and economic purposes builds on the impressive body of work by Ronald Deibert, who, together with colleagues at the University of Toronto Citizen Lab, has uncovered details of numerous online espionage and surveillance campaigns and argued persuasively that there is less and less transparency, accountability, and oversight surrounding these sorts of online activities.[13]

Thomas Rid's work on the distinctions between cyber war, cyberespionage, and cyber sabotage has also been invaluable in parsing the various motivations of perpetrators and understanding their political implications.[14] Important work by Martin Libicki,[15] as well as Brandon Valeriano and Ryan Maness,[16] on the international relations dimensions of cyber conflict and the reasons national governments may exercise restraint when it comes to cyber operations has also shaped the discussion of security incidents attributed to state actors, including the DigiNotar compromise, the PLA Unit 61398 espionage attempts, the OPM breach, and the Sony Pictures breach. For thinking about cybersecurity incidents from the perspective of individual, targeted organizations, Scott Shackelford's work on the potential to improve accountability for cybersecurity through polycentric regulation has provided crucial insights on the interplay of economics, law, and policy in an international business context.[17]

Policy and the role it can play in defending against computer-based threats is a central theme of this book, but the Internet spans many nations and is therefore subject to many different, and sometimes contradictory, policy regimes instituted by countries across the world. Each of these countries has its own ideas about what would make the Internet more secure and its own individual set of laws and policy-making processes. While the incidents discussed in this book span several countries—from Iran, to the Netherlands, to Russia, to North Korea—the policy analysis of how lawmakers could help prevent or mitigate such incidents in the future is largely focused on the United States. Many of these recommendations may be relevant or applicable to other countries, but the specific agencies, laws, and court proceedings cited here are drawn, for the most part, from the U.S. system. There are several reasons for this focus on U.S. policy. It would not be practical to tackle every nation's cybersecurity policies in a single book, nor does every nation share a common view of what constitutes "cybersecurity," making it more difficult to draw direct comparisons between their policies. For instance, in both Russia and China there are several cybersecurity policies primarily concerned with ensuring that the national government is capable of accessing information about its citizens' online activities. As a case in point, in July 2017, Russia passed a law banning Virtual Private Networks, often used to protect online users' anonymity, and in June 2016, it passed the so-called Yarovaya law requiring telephone and Internet service providers to store user data for six months and assist intelligence agencies with decrypting that data. In November 2016, China passed a cybersecurity law requiring that information about Chinese citizens be stored on servers in China and not transferred abroad without permission—a measure that might hinder foreign governments from accessing the information but would almost certainly ensure that the Chinese government could access it as needed. The United States also has surveillance laws, but the focus of this book is on policies that govern defense against cybercrimes, not policies that regulate government access to data. While the U.S. government has not always pursued cybercrime policies focused on industry defense initiatives especially aggressively, it has done so to a greater extent than many other countries, making the U.S. a useful starting point for analysis.

In 2016, the European Union passed two policies aimed at strengthening cybersecurity: the General Data Protection Regulation (GDPR) and the Network and Information Security Directive (NISD). Both policies are aimed at setting baseline cybersecurity requirements and instituting new incident reporting requirements for companies, though the former is more focused on giving individuals greater control over their data, while the latter targets the protection of critical IT infrastructure. These are precisely the sorts of policy undertakings examined in this book, but it is still too early to know with any confidence how such measures will play out in practice. As of this writing, the GDPR has not yet gone into effect, and EU member states still have several months to implement the NISD by passing individual national laws that will lay out the specifics of how the directive will be interpreted and enforced in each country and which companies it will apply to within their borders. Clearly, as demonstrated by events in 2016 and 2017, many countries are turning their attention to the question of how to tackle cybersecurity challenges through policy, and, for better or worse, they have few precedents on which to model their efforts besides the United States.

Beyond its potential to shape other countries' policymaking efforts, U.S. cybersecurity policy is also important because it can have a disproportionate global influence on cybercrime given how many major online content providers, payment processors, hardware manufacturers, software companies, and Internet service providers are based in the United States. Regulations aimed at leveraging or incentivizing these entities' defensive capabilities could have significant consequences that reach far beyond the borders of the United States. That does not mean the United States can, on its own, tackle cybercrime any more than any other country—any truly

comprehensive policy approach to dealing with online crime and espionage would, undoubtedly, require extensive international cooperation and
partnership. Certainly, there is no other way to reliably identify and hold
responsible the people perpetrating these crimes who operate irrespective
of national borders. But in the past governments have too often used that
as an excuse for not taking any serious unilateral action, even when carefully crafted, rigorously enforced policies aimed at intermediaries operating
within those governments' own borders might have a profound impact.
Evaluating the existing U.S. policies that aim to do this and where they fall
short provides an opportunity for thinking through both the limitations
of any individual country's ability to regulate the Internet, as well as the
real opportunities afforded to a national government trying to crack down
on cybercrime and espionage within its borders. At a moment when many
governments are interested in the question of how they can better defend
computer systems and data through policymaking, they may all be able to
learn something about what works—and what doesn't—from observing the
efforts of the United States.

By assessing security incidents across their entire lifecycles, this work
incorporates discussion of many different types of defenses (and potential
defenders), not just as they operate in isolation, but also, more significantly,
in terms of their relationship to and interactions with each other. There is
widespread consensus among information security experts that information systems should be secured through a combination of multiple different
controls, a principle sometimes referred to as "defense-in-depth."[18] But the
guidance governing how best to conjoin and layer such controls is often
ambiguous and has focused almost exclusively on the combinations of
technical defense measures that can be implemented by individual actors.
Little attention has been paid to the range of technical and non-technical defenses that can be set up across different types of organizations with
varying capabilities and motivations. Coordinating defenses across different stakeholders introduces significant new logistic challenges, but it also
affords new insights into what it could mean to implement a comprehensive approach to computer security that incorporated every component of
the network and addressed every stage of an attack.

Reconstructing the chain of events for individual cybersecurity incidents
is relatively easier to do for older incidents than more recent ones. When
breaches are first discovered and announced, often little is known about

how they were carried out, or even what motivated them. Moreover, the involved parties may be wary of revealing any more details than absolutely necessary for fear of fueling negative publicity and lawsuits. It takes time for investigators to track down the root causes of major cybersecurity incidents—and it often takes even more time for the people involved in those investigations to be willing to talk publicly about their results, or for those findings to appear in court filings and public records. This is one advantage of revisiting older breaches: It is possible to reconstruct much more detailed timelines and chains of events for attacks and, in doing so, shed light on where attackers had the fewest options for moving forward and which defenders might have been best poised to prevent their success.

Most importantly, revisiting past cybersecurity incidents allows us to trace how all of the different parties involved in the incident—from the targeted organizations to software manufacturers, Internet service providers, banks, web hosts, government agencies, and individuals—divvy up the cleanup costs and the blame afterwards. Tracking who gets held accountable in the aftermath of these incidents allows us to reconceptualize who is capable of being a defender and how. All of the groups and people who play some role in enabling successful cybersecurity incidents—whether that role is opening a phishing email or writing vulnerable code or conveying malicious traffic between computers or settling financial transactions or setting regulatory security guidelines—are potential defenders, in that they are capable of exercising certain types of controls and restrictions over attackers that are not available to anyone else. Often, the fallout of these breaches profoundly shapes the interactions among all these different intermediaries and defenders. It thereby influences the ecosystem of computer system defense long after the breaches themselves have faded from the headlines, the responsible CEOs have been fired, and the lawsuits have been settled.

In large part, what we learn from these breaches is how the dynamics between different defenders—or stakeholders who could potentially serve as defenders in some capacity—have shaped the security landscape we have today. In the aftermath of these incidents, we see how their fallout engenders hostilities between parties who should, ostensibly, be on the same side—and, above all, strengthens the resolve of all involved not to be held responsible for any piece of anyone else's security. Much of what becomes clear in the aftermath of breaches is how complicated and ill-defined the liability regimes for these incidents are—and how that translates into everyone trying to shift blame onto each other and no one being willing to take on even some small piece of the overall defensive posture lest they end up shouldering the entire responsibility alone. The collective action and coordination problems that plague the groups involved in defending against breaches are not unique to cybersecurity incidents, but they are exacerbated by an environment where so many different people and firms are so deeply interconnected—and no data flows through only one party's systems, software, or devices. The interdependence and interrelatedness of the computer systems that are targeted in these breaches adds to the technical complexity of defending them. It also adds to the complexity of non-technical security efforts by broadening the number of people and organizations involved in defense.

Different types of organizations and defenders—from software developers to system administrators to policymakers—are able to influence and intervene at very different stages of security breaches. Each individual defender has a limited scope of control that is crucial for understanding which defensive responsibilities they can reasonably and realistically be expected to assume. When we talk about (and report on and litigate) successful security incidents, too often our inclination is to latch onto the first or the most easily understood point of access—the phishing email, the dictionary attack, the unprotected wireless network—and harp on the simple line defense that seems like it would have made all the difference—two-factor authentication, or rate limiting logins, or better encryption of network traffic. But that perspective oversimplifies the much more complicated narrative of the gradual, escalating capabilities acquired by perpetrators, as well the much more limited and challenging environment in which individual defenders operate. The purpose of this book is to broaden and complicate that picture of who is—and should be—responsible for defending against cybersecurity incidents and to explore why answering that question has proved so difficult and requires more assertive policy-making.

This book is organized in four sections. The first section looks at three case studies of financially motivated cybercrimes and uses them to trace three overlapping waves of economic models: payment card fraud, as seen through the lens of the TJX breach of 2006, identity theft and tax fraud, illustrated by the 2012 South Carolina Department of Revenue Breach, and the rise of ransomware and crimes focused on selling stolen data back to the victims, as viewed through the 2014 takedown of the GameOver

ZeuS botnet, used to distribute the ransomware program Cryptolocker. The second section focuses on three incidents of cyberespionage: the 2011 compromise of Dutch certificate authority DigiNotar to access the email of Iranian individuals, the attempts by Chinese People's Liberation Army Unit 61398 to conduct espionage on U.S.-based companies from 2006 through 2014, and the 2015 breach of the United States Office of Personnel Management (OPM). This section focuses especially on the limited ability of ex-post litigation to settle the costs of breaches when there is no clear financial harm to victims. It also explores the range of other available ex-post mitigations to address espionage harms—from relocating overseas spies, as was done in the case of the OPM breach, to reengineering the responsibilities and transparency of the Internet's global certificate-based trust infrastructure, as in the case of the DigiNotar breach. The third section looks at three incidents motivated by the perpetrators' desire to take revenge on the victims: the large-scale denial-of-service attacks directed against Spamhaus in 2013, the public dump of data stored on Sony Pictures' servers in 2014, and the 2015 breach of the Ashley Madison website owned by Avid Life Media. These incidents provide a window into the opportunities for intermediaries to intervene in non-financial breaches. They also elucidate the considerable challenges associated with trying to defend against the final stages of breaches in which the perpetrators' sole interest with regard to their stolen information or unauthorized access is to make it publicly available as widely as possible rather than exploit it for financial or political purposes. The fourth, and final, section shifts from considering case studies to looking at the capabilities of three groups of stakeholders: application designers, organizations that store and protect data, and policymakers. This section considers the roles each group is equipped to play in defending against such breaches in the future. It closes with recommendations for how they can best leverage their own strengths, both singly and collectively, rather than just working to abdicate responsibility to other parties.

At a superficial level, all of the breaches discussed in this book can be traced back to technical failings—poor encryption, improperly configured firewalls, or out-of-date software—and, in some cases, also to careless users who made the mistake of clicking on a phishing email, or opening an attachment, or failing to change default passwords. But improving computer security is not just a matter of improving technical capabilities and tools, nor is it only about improving user education and awareness—though both of these things are undoubtedly important. It's also, fundamentally, a matter of defining clear roles and responsibilities for the actors positioned to prevent and protect against security breaches, and figuring out how to do that in a way that leverages those "bottleneck" opportunities for effective interventions that offer defenders an edge over attackers. This is every bit as difficult as developing more secure technology—perhaps more difficult in some instances. But it is challenging in very different ways. Figuring out how to apportion responsibility for security across all the different actors involved in developing, maintaining, and providing service to a single computer system requires its own kind of sophisticated engineering and skillful design. Difficult as they may be to implement, these tactics are crucial for defense because they often address the most stable, least rapidly evolving elements of cybersecurity incidents—the ones that don't become immediately obsolete as attackers refine and adapt their methods. Given the understandable reluctance of any private parties to unilaterally shoulder greater security responsibilities, these are challenges that ultimately require the intervention and attention of policymakers, courts, and governments. What the relatively brief but rich history of cybersecurity incidents in the early 21st century teaches us is that, ultimately, these incidents are not failures of our technology but instead failures to craft clear and effective liability regimes, failures to assign responsibility and blame for breaches in ways that appreciate and take advantage of the technical complexity and interconnectedness of the Internet, and failures to accept that cybersecurity is as much a problem of hastily written, out-of-date laws and policies as it is hastily written, out-of-date code.

I Lessons from Financially Motivated Cybercrimes

2 Operation Get Rich or Die Tryin': How the TJX Breach Set the Stage for a Decade of Payment Card Conflict

In July 2005, Albert Gonzalez, Damon Patrick Toey, and Christopher Scott started taking "war driving" expeditions along the South Dixie Highway in Miami. Armed with a laptop and a large radio antenna, the three friends, all in their twenties, tested the wireless signals of the businesses they drove past, looking for vulnerable wireless networks that they could connect to and use to intercept potentially valuable packets.[a] They found what they were looking for at a Marshalls clothing store, part of a chain owned by TJX Companies Inc., the same company that owns T.J. Maxx.[1] Connecting to the wireless network of that Marshalls store in Miami set in motion the lengthy and highly profitable data breach that Gonzalez, Toey, Scott, and their co-conspirators carried out against TJX—a data breach that was revealed in 2007 to have resulted in the compromise of 45.7 million payment card numbers belonging to TJX customers as well as the theft of hundreds of millions of dollars. And that breach, as well as others like it, in turn set in motion an extended and bitter battle over who should bear the costs of payment card fraud and who was responsible for preventing it—a fight that did as much to hinder attempts to reduce financial fraud as it did to hasten the arrival of more secure payment card technologies.

In order to pull off what was, at the time, the largest known data breach in terms of number of records stolen, the team of criminals led by Gonzalez

a. Packets are the units of data transmitted across the Internet. When information is sent between different computers online it is broken into multiple packets, each of which contains information about the source and destination address as well as part of the transmitted content. The packets are individually transmitted across the network to their destination, so, when Gonzalez and his co-conspirators were eavesdropping on wireless networks, they collected lots of packets being sent across those networks and put them together to obtain information.

took advantage of a number of security vulnerabilities and oversights, of which the poor encryption of one retail store's wireless network was only the first. Yet, it was the encryption of that wireless network that drew the greatest scrutiny and criticism in the aftermath of the breach, when several press reports on the incident featured headlines that emphasized the pivotal role of the wireless network, such as "How Credit Card Data Went Out Wireless Door,"[2] and "TJX's failure to secure Wi-Fi could cost $1B,"[3] and "Blame for record-breaking credit card data theft laid at the feet of WEP."[4] WEP, or Wired Equivalent Privacy, was the encryption protocol used to protect the network traffic of the Marshalls store that Gonzalez, Toey, and Scott found while war driving. WEP was known to be vulnerable to attack and less secure than the newer WPA, or Wi-Fi Protected Access, encryption protocol, but TJX had not yet updated the wireless security at that particular Marshalls store at the time of the breach.[b] Undoubtedly, that was a mistake—a serious, important, costly mistake—but it was not the only mistake that enabled the breach and subsequent fraud, nor was it necessarily the critical mistake that, had it not been made, would have averted the breach entirely.

To blame an extended, international, multistage financial fraud operation on a single, poorly protected wireless network is to fundamentally misunderstand how many different steps are involved in carrying out what Gonzalez and his co-conspirators achieved and to vastly oversimplify the task of defending against such breaches. But it was no accident or mere misunderstanding that led to the formulation and dissemination of the enduring lesson of the TJX breach: that businesses should upgrade from WEP to WPA. Rather, it was the result of a concerted payment card industry effort to place blame for the incident squarely on the shoulders of a specific actor (TJX) due to a specific action (failing to update wireless encryption).

Various parties had strong motivations to identify a specific, single locus of blame in the aftermath of the TJX breach. Reporters wanted to offer a satisfying explanation of what had happened to curious readers. The individuals,

---

b. WEP and WPA are both forms of encryption, but, at the time of the TJX compromise, researchers had discovered that WEP encryption could be relatively easily broken. Therefore, WPA was considered preferable, and, in fact, an even more secure version of WPA, called WPA2, was recommended beginning in 2006. However, many older devices could not be configured for WPA or WPA2, so WEP continued to be widely used for years after FBI agents publicly demonstrated its vulnerabilities at an Information Systems Security Association meeting in Los Angeles in 2005.

banks, and payment card networks suing TJX to recoup the fraud losses resulting from the breach wanted to make clear that it was solely the retailer's fault this had happened, not anyone else's. Even TJX itself may have been relieved to be able to pinpoint a specific technical problem so that it could then reassure customers the wireless encryption had been fixed and its systems were now secure. The real legacy of the TJX breach lay not in teaching businesses to update their wireless security, but instead in teaching stakeholders the benefits of rushing to assign blame for a security breach to a particular failed technical mechanism implemented by an individual entity. A closer look at the full timeline of the TJX breach reveals that the episode in fact involved several different technical vulnerabilities and companies, but by singling out one encryption protocol and one organization as fully responsible for the incident the payment card industry was able to effectively shield itself from bearing any of the blame. It was a lesson that would continue to shape the industry for years, long after Gonzalez and several of his co-conspirators had been arrested and imprisoned. In the decade following the TJX breach, the different sectors involved in the payment card industry—from retailers to banks to payment networks—expended tremendous effort and resources in trying to shift liability for security breaches and fraud onto each other, even as they often resisted implementing the newest, most secure versions of payment technologies.

Technical Stages of the TJX Compromise

The Miami Marshalls store's wireless network was vulnerable in two ways that mattered to Gonzalez and his co-conspirators. For one, it allowed Open System Authentication (OSA) instead of shared key authentication, which would have required devices to provide a shared key before they were permitted to join the network.[c] This meant Gonzalez and his co-conspirators were able to join the store's network easily, just by sitting in the parking lot within range of the wireless signal. However, the traffic between devices on those networks was encrypted with WEP. So the thieves could join the network and monitor the encrypted traffic freely, but if they wanted to decrypt and understand it they needed a decryption key. This posed an obstacle

c. Under OSA, anyone can connect any device to a wireless network even without a password or key.

to the intruders—but not an insurmountable one: an attack discovered in 2001 showed that it was possible to derive the key from large volumes of collected WEP wireless traffic.[5] Using a packet sniffer program[d] designed by his friend Stephen Watt to collect the packets on the Marshalls' wireless network, Gonzalez captured the encrypted traffic in bulk and analyzed it in order to discover the decryption key.[6] The decrypted data included store officials' passwords and account information, which enabled the conspirators to access different computer servers containing payment card data within the TJX corporate network, as well as "track 2 data," the information found on the magnetic stripes of credit and debit cards.[7]

Using the employee credentials they had decrypted off the original Miami store's network, Gonzalez's team was then able to connect to the TJX corporate servers in Framingham, Massachusetts. With access to the corporate servers established, Scott and another member of the group, Jonathan James, rented rooms near the Marshalls store and used a six-foot radio antenna to capture the store's signal from their hotel so as not to attract attention by spending hours in the parking lot. (At one point in 2005, James had actually been arrested in Florida for sitting in a car in a retail store parking lot with Scott in the middle of the night with their laptop and antenna.) From their hotel room, the two men could capture not just the bank card information for transactions processed in the single store in Miami, but also the track 2 data for tens of millions of credit and debit cards used in transactions at the thousands of stores operated by TJX worldwide. Card data from transactions prior to 2004 had been stored in clear text (that is, it was not encrypted), but the information relating to more recent transactions was encrypted, due to a change in TJX security practices. Concerned that the older information would be less valuable, since those cards were more likely to have expired, or be closer to expiring, than the ones used to make more recent purchases, Gonzalez enlisted help from accomplices in Eastern Europe to decrypt the newer data.[8]

This encryption added a considerable hurdle. On May 27, 2006, Gonzalez wrote in an online chat: "it took me 2 years to open pins [PIN numbers] from omx [OfficeMax]," adding, "2 years from the time I hack them, to download all data, … to find proper decryption method."[9] Since two years is half the lifespan of an average credit card, this delay would have been a

---

d. Packet sniffers capture the contents of packets traveling across a network.

serious setback for Gonzalez and his team. However, while downloading the encrypted data from the TJX servers, they had discovered that, while a transaction was being processed, for a brief moment between the time when a card was swiped and the moment when the credit card company network approved it, that card's data was available unencrypted on the TJX payment card transaction processing server. So, in May 2006, Gonzalez repurposed Watt's custom packet sniffer to capture the unencrypted card information at this exact moment, obviating the need for time-intensive decryption. The conspirators then began capturing the unencrypted card data and compressing it into files stored on the TJX corporate servers, which they could then download through their access to the Miami Marshalls store. To relieve their dependence on the Marshalls access point, in May 2006 the group established a VPN connection between the TJX corporate payment processing server and a server in Latvia controlled by Gonzalez.[e] During the latter half of 2006, Gonzalez downloaded the unencrypted card data from millions of transactions in TJX stores all over the world directly to his server in Latvia.[10] Gonzalez had successfully acquired tens of millions of credit and debit card details, but he still didn't have what he really wanted: money. Technical tools and capabilities had gotten him this far, but in order to turn stolen information into stolen money Gonzalez had to move beyond the confines of the TJX computer systems.

From Bits to Barrels of Cash

There is little doubt that Gonzalez's primary motivations were financial: he nicknamed the series of credit card theft breaches that included the TJX compromise "Operation Get Rich or Die Tryin'," and told one of his co-conspirators in an online chat on March 7, 2006: "I have a goal … I want to buy a yacht … once I reach my goal I won't be doing anything illegal."[11]

e. A VPN, or virtual private network, is a service that allows users to create a secure, private network while using a public or insecure Internet connection. When connected to a VPN, all of a user's traffic is encrypted and channeled through the VPN provider's servers, so that it is impossible for the operator of a public network (in this case, TJX) to know what that user is doing online when connected to their network. By using a VPN, Gonzalez made it harder for TJX to figure out what was happening on its own servers because they could not directly observe the exfiltration of payment card data to Latvia, since that was happening through the VPN provider.

After Gonzalez was apprehended, Secret Service agents found a barrel containing $1.2 million in cash buried in his parents' backyard.[12] But his desire to profit financially constrained Gonzalez's options following the technical stages of the breach. There were any number of ways Gonzalez might have chosen to exploit technical vulnerabilities in the TJX computer systems to steal payment card data—he happened to take advantage of wireless network encryption, packet sniffers, and VPN access, but similar such breaches have been perpetrated using a range of other tools from phishing emails to malware delivered by USB drive. Once Gonzalez had the data in hand, however, there were only a very limited number of ways to profit from it.

To turn his cache of stolen payment card numbers into hard cash, Gonzalez enlisted the help of Maksym Yastremskiy, a Ukrainian black market card seller, who operated a popular website selling stolen payment cards. Buyers would wire money to Yastremskiy, who would then send them the purchased card information. Yastremskiy paid Gonzalez using ATM cards linked to accounts set up in Latvia. These cards were delivered to "cashers," who were responsible for withdrawing the money from the Latvian accounts and then sending the cash (less a 10 percent commission) to Gonzalez's drop box in Miami. Sometimes, Gonzalez would also send couriers to collect cash directly from Yastremskiy's partners. Humza Zaman, a firewall security specialist at Barclays who acted as both a courier and casher, later testified that he was responsible for laundering approximately $700,000 for Gonzalez.[13]

In December 2006, a credit card company noticed that several compromised cards were linked to TJX stores and alerted the company to a possible breach. On the advice of law enforcement officials, the company waited a month to alert customers in hopes of being able to trace the thieves before scaring them off with a public announcement. TJX hired General Dynamics and IBM to conduct an investigation of the compromise—an investigation that did not go unnoticed by Gonzalez. In fact, he decided to shut down the exfiltration of TJX information when he came close to having his own system infiltrated by General Dynamics. He wrote by way of explanation "after those faggots at general dynamics almost owned me ... while I was owning tjx I don't want to risk anything."[14] The TJX investigation did not succeed in finding the responsible parties, but many of those involved—including Gonzalez, Yastremskiy, Scott, Watt, James, and Zaman—were later identified following Yastremskiy's capture in a nightclub in Turkey in July 2007. In Yastremskiy's chat logs, Secret Service agents found the username of someone who had been supplying many of the stolen card numbers. They could not immediately identify whose username it was, but the same person had asked Yastremskiy to provide a fake passport to help a casher who had recently been arrested leave the country.[15]

The investigators figured out that the anonymous supplier was Jonathan Williams, one of Gonzalez's cashers, who had recently been arrested while carrying $200,000 in cash and eighty blank debit cards. Searching a thumb drive that Williams had on him at the time of his arrest, the Secret Service found a photo of Gonzalez, his credit report, and the address of his sister Maria—materials Williams said were meant to serve as insurance against Gonzalez ever informing on him. The investigators traced the cash Williams was in charge of delivering to a P.O. box in Miami registered to Jonathan James, and then discovered an arrest record for James from 2005, when he had been found late at night in a store parking lot, sitting in a car with another man, named Christopher Scott, along with laptops and a huge radio antenna. Finally, the Secret Service tracked down the registration information for the chat username of Yastremskiy's major supplier, and linked the email address, soupnazi@efnet.ru, to the online alias Gonzalez was known to use: soupnazi. Gonzalez was arrested on May 7, 2008, at the National Hotel in Miami Beach.[16]

The stages of the TJX breach that ultimately led to the identification and arrest of Gonzalez and his conspirators were not technical in nature—they had little to do with how data was stolen from the TJX servers and everything to do with how that data was used to steal money. Not coincidentally, these were the stages of the breach where Gonzalez had the fewest options about how to proceed: while he was stealing data he and his team could improvise and find new ways of accessing the information they wanted (like using the packet sniffer to intercept transaction data in real time), but he had only one way to make money from that information—by selling it. In doing so, he relied not on any technical obfuscation or defense, but rather on the international legal framework he believed would protect Yastremskiy from being apprehended by law enforcement officials. Since Ukraine has no extradition policy with the United States, Gonzalez figured both Yastremskiy and, by extension, he himself, were safe from U.S. investigators. "I never thought [Yastremskiy] would leave Ukraine," Gonzalez told reporter James Verini about his decision to sell the stolen data through Yastremskiy's operation.[17] While the early stages of the TJX breach were enabled by multiple technical vulnerabilities, the later stages—the ones in which money was actually stolen and victims actually suffered—were primarily enabled by policy decisions. Gonzalez's eventual identification and prosecution were similarly only made possible by the policy of extradition between Turkey and the United States that allowed Yastremskiy to be apprehended during his visit to the Turkish seaside resort of Kemer. The role of laws and policies in enabling the TJX breach was not merely incidental. It was an explicit component of Gonzalez's mental calculus—he deliberately chose to sell his stolen card numbers through someone located in a country he believed was beyond the reach of U.S. law enforcement, and it was ultimately Yastremskiy's geographic choices that allowed laws and policies to catch up to him.

Resolving the question of who, or what, is to blame for Gonzalez's success in perpetrating the TJX breach is not nearly so straightforward as simply pointing to the wireless network, or even pointing to TJX. These may have seemed the obvious culprits in the immediate aftermath of the breach's discovery in 2007, but in the months and years that followed, as lawsuits were filed between the involved parties and more details of the incident came to light, it became increasingly clear that there had been several opportunities for interrupting Gonzalez's scheme, both by technical means and through policy measures. Some of these were opportunities that TJX could or should have taken advantage of, but others were not. Indeed, some of the interventions that Gonzalez seemed to view as most threatening to his plans were well beyond the scope of TJX's power, suggesting that the retailer may not even have been in the best strategic position to mitigate the large-scale fraud operation.

Who to Blame?

Undoubtedly, TJX bears significant responsibility for Gonzalez's massive breach of its systems. The company was not completely delinquent when it came to security, however. Communication between devices on store wireless networks was encrypted (though not well), as was all payment card information stored on the corporate servers since 2004 (fairly well, since Gonzalez estimated the decryption process would take two years), and only authenticated users could access those servers. Furthermore, when the breach was brought to their attention, TJX enlisted General Dynamics and IBM, as well as law enforcement officials, to investigate the incident, and their efforts were sufficiently effective to block Gonzalez from continuing his operation. Still, the early stages of the breach indicate several concrete technical measures TJX could have implemented to strengthen its stores' data and network security. These include protecting store networks by eliminating wireless access, or restricting that access to known devices or devices with a shared key, or using stronger WPA encryption, as well as encrypting real-time transaction data, isolating card processing servers, and monitoring exfiltration of data from corporate and store servers.

In the aftermath of the breach, much was made of these missing defenses, and TJX faced enormous criticism for its inadequate security. Lawsuits and media reports alike charged that TJX could have prevented the breach had it only implemented better technical defenses. Class action suits were filed against TJX in state and federal courts in Alabama, California, Massachusetts, and Puerto Rico, and in provincial Canadian courts in Alberta, British Columbia, Manitoba, Ontario, Quebec, and Saskatchewan, on behalf of customers whose transaction data was compromised and financial institutions who issued credit and debit cards used at TJX stores during the breach.[18] The Federal Trade Commission (FTC) also filed a complaint alleging that TJX had failed to appropriately protect the stolen data because the company:

(a) created an unnecessary risk to personal information by storing it on, and transmitting it between and within, in-store and corporate networks in clear text;

(b) did not use readily available security measures to limit wireless access to its networks, thereby allowing an intruder to connect wirelessly to in-store networks without authorization;

(c) did not require network administrators and other users to use strong passwords or to use different passwords to access different programs, computers, and networks;

(d) failed to use readily available security measures to limit access among computers and the Internet, such as by using a firewall to isolate card authorization computers; and

(e) failed to employ sufficient measures to detect and prevent unauthorized access to computer networks or to conduct security investigations, such as by patching or updating antivirus software or following up on security warnings and intrusion alerts.[19]

The FTC complaint does not claim that any one of these decisions, individually, would have constituted inadequate security; instead, it emphasizes that these five practices "taken together" were responsible for the allegations against TJX. The TJX breach is undoubtedly a case of failed security—the protective measures the company had in place were unable to prevent the thieves from stealing and selling millions of dollars' worth of payment card information—but it is not a straightforward story of a company that should have been using WPA encryption or requiring stronger passwords or storing less data. In fact, it's not clear that any of these measures would necessarily have succeeded in stopping Gonzalez's team—some of the practices the FTC mentions, particularly with regard to password strength, seem downright irrelevant.

It's not hard to go down the FTC's list and imagine how Gonzalez and his friends might have bypassed the "reasonable and appropriate" defenses TJX is chastised for not implementing: they could have circumvented WPA encryption by guessing or stealing the password of a store employee; the user passwords they stole from the store's network to access corporate servers would not have been any more difficult to decrypt and use if they were stronger; and much of the card data the team sold was accessed and stolen during current transactions, rather than decrypted from the company's stored, older records. None of that means TJX couldn't—or shouldn't—have done more to defend its customers' data, but it does suggest that the technical controls the FTC and others faulted TJX for failing to implement might well have left the perpetrators room to maneuver and substitute different attack vectors. Clearly, for instance, the encryption of payment card data was not an insurmountable obstacle for the thieves since they were already planning to decrypt and sell the stolen data, even before they realized that the card numbers were briefly available unencrypted. They didn't necessarily need to be able to join an open wireless network or access clear text card numbers in order to achieve their goal; exporting large volumes of data was a more essential capability for the attackers, though it was largely overlooked in the ensuing legal and media reports that focused primarily on TJX's failure to implement WPA encryption or encrypt data stored prior to 2004. For a man saving up for a yacht, however, the most essential element of the breach was the capability to turn those stolen card numbers into cash—a process TJX had no insight into, or control over, whatsoever. These final, monetization stages of the incident had the greatest potential to serve as bottlenecks, in the language of the spam click trajectory study: they were the stages when Gonzalez and his co-conspirators had the fewest alternatives to resort to if their plans were interrupted, and would probably have had to expend considerable resources to switch to a new fence for selling their stolen information, or new money mules.

Gonzalez does not appear to have been particularly worried about TJX interrupting his operation, but there were other parties whom he viewed with greater trepidation. In an online chat with Yastremskiy on March 2, 2006, Gonzalez wrote:

[Gonzalez] I hacked [major retailer] and i'm decrypting pins from their stores

[Gonzalez] visa knows [major retailer] is hacked

[Gonzalez] but they dont know exactly which stores are affected

[Gonzalez] so i decrypt one store and i give to you

[Gonzalez] visa then quickly finds this store and starts killing dumps
[Gonzalez] then i decrypt another one and do the same

[Gonzalez] but i start cashing with my guys

[Gonzalez] visa then finds THAT store and kills all dumps processed by that [major retailer] store

[Gonzalez] understand?

[Gonzalez] its a cycle

[Yastremskiy] yes

[Gonzalez] this is why i'm telling you to sell them fast fast

[Gonzalez] also some banks just said fuck waiting for the fraud to occur, lets just reissue EVERY one of our cardholders which shopped at [major retailer] for the last 4 years[20]

Gonzalez knew that his real challenge was not evading TJX defenses, but rather evading the payment networks, like Visa, that had insight into payment card fraud patterns and could tie those cases back to individual retailers. Setting aside the question of whether TJX could have had stronger technical defenses in place, the company had no means of detecting or monitoring the financial fraud being inflicted on its customers and no visibility into the consequences of its decisions. TJX learned about the breach from a credit card company—which had precisely the perspective TJX itself lacked to piece together the common link across widespread financial fraud cases.

In fact, the defenses implemented by banks, credit card companies, and law enforcement officials in the TJX case were hugely important. It was a credit card company's detection of patterns in fraudulent charges that led to the breach's discovery. Regulations surrounding large international financial transactions forced the perpetrators to repatriate their profits in numerous, smaller increments through use of multiple cashers and couriers. Bank restrictions on maximum ATM withdrawals forced those cashers and couriers to carry suspiciously large numbers of cards (recall that Williams was arrested carrying eighty cards). Credit card expiration policies forced the thieves to discard the older, unencrypted data stored on TJX's servers and instead spend time decrypting more recent data and finding ways to compromise real-time transactions. Banks, payment networks, and law enforcement officers all exercised considerable control over the extent to which credit card fraud could be carried out using the stolen data, as well as the ease with which Gonzalez and his co-conspirators could reap the profits of those sales. While the barriers they imposed did not prevent the large-scale fraud, these defenses likely limited its scope and certainly forced Gonzalez to make some decisions, such as the recruitment of a network of cashers and couriers, which ultimately contributed to his arrest.

The payment card issuers and banks responsible for covering the fraudulent charges and replacing their customers' cards joined the FTC and TJX shoppers in condemning—and suing—the company over its security practices, arguing that TJX had failed to adhere to the Payment Card Industry (PCI) Data Security Standards by using outdated WEP encryption and storing too much data. It's not clear that these PCI standards would have been especially effective lines of defense when it came to thwarting Gonzalez, but that was never the point. The banks and payment networks, faced with the costs of large-scale fraud they had done nothing to cause, understandably wanted to blame someone else for the breach.

Yet, TJX was not the only party that could have done more to mitigate the damage Gonzalez caused. In fact, the line of defense that Gonzalez himself expressed the greatest concern about in his chat logs is the possible preemptive cancelation of all credit cards used at a breached retailer by the issuing company. Other defenses that could have been implemented by non-TJX defenders include issuing chip and PIN credit cards, which would have required the thieves to acquire not just card numbers but also users' PINs. Credit card companies could also have set spending limits on all possibly compromised cards (a less drastic preemptive measure than mass replacement), and banks could have monitored withdrawals from foreign accounts at ATMs in the United States to make repatriation of profits from overseas sales more difficult. No one besides TJX could have stopped the thieves from accessing the payment card data, but lots of other defenders could—and did—play a role in limiting how much harm could be inflicted using that data.

TJX certainly played a large role in enabling the success of Gonzalez and his team, but the security controls it could have implemented—shared key authentication, WPA encryption, and data minimization, for instance— were not the lines of defense that Gonzalez was most concerned about. He could find other stores, other ways into the network, other decryption methods, and real-time data, but he couldn't do anything about the banks that, in his words, "just said fuck waiting for the fraud to occur, lets just reissue EVERY one of our cardholders." The effectiveness of the defensive measures available to these banks and credit card issuing companies depends upon both their broad visibility into incidents of financial fraud—that is, their ability to see patterns across large volumes of transactions—and the specificity of the threat they are responsible for defending against. Payment card fraud may begin with a poorly encrypted wireless network, a compromised point-of-sale terminal, or even a well-worded phishing email—and it is up to firms like TJX to protect against all possible access modes—but, ultimately, these schemes all take on a similar pattern in their later stages as the perpetrators sell their stolen information, relying on the card issuers and processing banks to ensure its value and their profits. In this regard, those card issuers have a significant advantage over TJX when it comes to identifying and stopping financial fraud: they know exactly what the criminals will do because there are a very limited number of ways to profit from stolen payment card information, even though there are many ways to steal it.

Financial theft, and especially payment card fraud, involves an especially consistent and centralized set of third parties as compared to other attacker motivations. Security incidents intended to cause other types of damage may go through other types of intermediaries, but few have the same degree of concentrated control and small number of alternatives as the major payment card issuers. Furthermore, payment card fraud requires a particularly involved and specific sequence of events that need to be successfully undertaken by criminals in order to profit from their activities—a clear example of the kill chain model of cybersecurity incidents. Both of these features give defenders an advantage when it comes to trying to disrupt or mitigate financially motivated breaches.

The TJX breach is primarily remembered as a devastating failure of computer security and justifiably so—the defenses in place did not prevent the loss of hundreds of millions of dollars. But it was also, in its way, an incredible success story about the identification, arrest, and imprisonment of an international ring of cyber criminals who were caught thanks to a series of constraints imposed on them by both technology and policy working in concert. The Marshalls wireless network forced the thieves to sit in a parking lot for long periods with laptops and a radio antenna, attracting the attention of the police, selling the stolen data required the involvement of Yastremskiy, who eventually led investigators to Gonzalez's screen name, and the restrictions on international financial transactions meant Gonzalez had to employ cashers and couriers, one of whom would later reveal his identity to the Secret Service. That process worked but it took years, and, despite the fact that it brought to light the men who were truly to blame for the incident, it had little bearing on the fights playing out in court between TJX, state attorneys general, shoppers, banks, and payment networks, over who was responsible for the breach.

Liability Shift

In the years that followed the TJX breach, a series of massive payment card breaches at other retailers, including Heartland Payment Systems, Target, and Home Depot, made clear that just improving a company's wireless encryption or lengthening their passwords would not be sufficient to combat large-scale breaches of payment card information. But the process set in motion by the TJX breach, in which different third-party "defenders" tried to shift blame and financial responsibility for these breaches onto each other, rather than trying to figure out who was best poised to defend against which stages of these incidents, remained deeply entrenched in the payment card industry. Indeed, the legal disputes that followed the TJX breach between different intermediary organizations, including TJX, payment processors, credit card companies, banks, and individuals, were echoed by the disputes around the implementation of microchip-enabled credit cards in the United States nearly a decade later.

Microchip-enabled EMV cards (named for the payment processors who developed the technology standard: Europay, MasterCard, and Visa) directly address the root cause of breaches like the one that targeted TJX: millions of stored, reusable payment card numbers. The microchips, when inserted into payment terminals, generate a one-time code that is used to process just a single, specific transaction instead of the general card number. So if, later on, a database of those transaction records is breached, the information stored in it is useless to counterfeiters because each transaction code can be used only once (unlike card numbers, which are used again and again). Since these cards are designed to drive down large-scale fraud, and the costs of that fraud are shared among retailers, payment processors, and banks through a complicated process of interchange fees, implementing microchips would seem like an obvious point of agreement for all of the different parties involved in data breaches who were losing money on legal fees and fraud costs in their aftermath. And yet, rather than serving as a way for all these companies to join together to combat criminal activity, the implementation of EMV technology was rife with hostilities and finger-pointing, mirroring the aftermath of the TJX breach. Different firms involved in the transition to EMV cards turned out to be much more interested in how they could push costs onto each other than in how they could best fight fraud.

The costs of transitioning to microchip cards were considerable, in part because the United States had significantly more issuing banks and retailers than many countries that had already made the transition, including Canada, Australia, and most of western Europe. Microchip cards are expensive—so expensive, in fact, that for years banks in the United States had been finding it more convenient (and presumably cheaper) to pay for fraud than to pay to put microchips in all of their customers' cards, a cost estimated at roughly $1.4 billion.[21] And replacing credit cards is only one piece of the overall costs, since, for the cards to be any use, it's also necessary for the retailers and merchants who accept those cards to buy and install new payment terminals that can read those microchips—the cost of replacing some fifteen million payment terminals in the United States was roughly $6.75 billion.[22] Those numbers were a strong motivation for banks and retailers in the United States to stick with magnetic stripe cards, but as the rest of the world pulled ahead in upgrading their cards with EMV technology, and more fraud migrated to the United States as a result, this calculation became increasingly difficult to justify. Most payment cards, even in countries that made the transition to EMV technology long before the United States, still featured magnetic stripes because merchants in the United States still required them. That meant that criminals could still counterfeit those cards relatively easily and use them in the United States, or to make online purchases. "The U.S. became ... a beacon for global criminals," said Jeremy King, the international director for the Payment Card Industry Data Security Standards Council.[23]

As the fraud costs increased and pressure mounted for the United States to make the shift, the tensions between banks, retailers, and payment networks that had played out in the aftermath of the TJX breach again came to a head. Retailers refused to purchase chip terminals before the banks had issued cards with chips, and the banks had no intention of spending the money on new payment cards until they could be sure that retailers would be able to process them. The United States has a unique regulatory landscape when it comes to credit cards, which made it difficult to apply the same tactics that had been used in countries that had previously made the transition. In many of those countries, interchange fees (which help cover fraud costs) are limited by law and EMV transitions were closely overseen and driven forward by the government; but in the United States the payment networks ended up taking the lead in driving the transition. Since the payment networks themselves profited handsomely from interchange fees and sometimes had to help cover fraud costs, they were hardly neutral in how they oversaw the process.

October 1, 2015, marked the beginning of the new "liability shift" for the U.S. payment card industry. As of that day, the payment networks decided, if a fraudulent transaction occurred then whichever party had failed to implement the EMV technology would be responsible for covering the charge. So, if the card that was used to make the fraudulent payment had an EMV chip in it, but the merchant who accepted it didn't have the necessary equipment to read that chip, then it would be the merchant's responsibility to cover the charge. If, however, the merchant did have a terminal that could read chip cards, but the card issuer hadn't bothered to provide its customer with a chip-enabled card, and the merchant therefore was forced to read the magnetic stripe instead, then it would be up to the issuer to cover the fraud costs. From the outset, this liability shift was not so much about reducing fraud as it was about making sure someone else had to pay for it.

Nowhere was the lack of interest in driving down fraud more apparent than in the payment processors approach to chip-and-PIN payment. Banks in most countries that issue EMV cards provide their customers with a PIN they can use to authorize transactions on the card. This provides some greater measure of security than just the microchip alone, especially when it comes to protecting against fraud due to lost or stolen cards, because it means that criminals must not only acquire a card (or a card's information), but also the associated PIN. But in the United States, the 2015 liability shift resulted in a widely accepted chip-and-signature payment mode for EMV cards, in which customers inserted their microchips into the terminals and then authorized the transactions by signing their name, instead of entering a secret PIN. Since a signature scrawled on an electronic terminal screen is significantly easier to forge than a secret PIN, this decision undermined the potential security benefits of microchip credit cards, particularly in instances when a person's physical card was stolen or lost.

The chip-and-signature versus chip-and-PIN fight in the United States played out primarily between the card issuers and merchants, with the payment networks espousing a "chip-and-choice" policy, and deliberately not choosing sides—but also not requiring PINs. U.S. card issuers were reluctant to issue PINs, both because of the expense involved in distributing PINs to all of their customers and building the necessary infrastructure to authenticate those PINs, but also because of the fear that requiring their customers to use PINs would be inconvenient and end up driving customers to use other cards in a "brutally competitive" credit card market.[24] The retailers, meanwhile, lost no time in attacking the issuing banks for their decision not to provide customers with PINs. "Retailers have invested in the technology for chip-and-PIN but banks and issuers have only gone halfway and invested in chip-and-signature," said Jason Brewer, a spokesperson for the Retail Industry Leaders Association.[25] Retailers also accused banks of being reluctant to issue PINs for fear that criminals would start stealing the PINs, by observing people entering them into payment terminals, and then use them to withdraw cash from ATMs with stolen cards—leading to losses that the banks would have to cover themselves. The EMV liability shift was fraught with this kind of complicated calculus centered on the question of how each party could reduce the specific types of fraud that it had to pay for, rather than on bringing down the overall fraud rates. This was entirely logical since no one involved had any incentive to try to mitigate fraud that would be billed to someone else, but it also speaks to the drawbacks of an oversimplified liability regime in which a single entity is held responsible for a cost that could have been prevented or lessened through the involvement of others. This is precisely what makes this kind of fraudulent activity a policy problem—to clarify and expand ideas about who is responsible for defending against cybercrime requires liability regimes that leave everyone involved feeling like they have more at stake when payment card numbers are stolen.

The fights about who should bear responsibility for fraud that were stoked between retailers, banks, and payment networks in the aftermath of the TJX breach culminated in an antitrust lawsuit filed in June 2015 by Home Depot charging Visa and MasterCard with collusion and alleging that the payment networks were not taking necessary steps to reduce fraud.[26] "For years, Visa and MasterCard have been more concerned with protecting their own inflated profits and their dominant market positions than with the security of the payment cards used by American consumers and the health of the United States economy," the lawsuit stated.[27] Cards that use PIN technology typically have to work with multiple competing PIN networks, so those networks can compete for the lowest price to charge retailers for processing the transaction. But because Visa and MasterCard wanted to maintain the high interchange fees that are not subject to regulation in the United States, they resisted the implementation of PIN technology for fear of competition that might force them to lower those fees, Home Depot's suit alleged. The lawsuit argued:

> While U.S. consumers and merchants—like The Home Depot—bear costs related to fraud rates unrivaled in the rest of the industrial world, Visa, MasterCard, and their member banks have acted in concert to prevent the adoption of chip-and-PIN authentication in the United States on a large scale. While chip-and-PIN authentication is proven to be more secure, it is less profitable for Visa, Master-Card, and their member banks, and it provides a greater threat to their market dominance.

Home Depot's lawsuit—a nearly unprecedented hostile act by a retailer toward the payment networks it relies on to process the bulk of its transactions—illustrates the extent to which the legacy of major payment card fraud breaches (like the one directed at TJX) has been to pit the different companies responsible for preventing fraud against each other, rather than against fraudsters. This may be partly due to the challenges of identifying and prosecuting the criminals in many cybercrime cases—the TJX breach is a rare example in which many of the perpetrators were ultimately brought to justice—that fuel the victims' desire to find someone else to blame and hold accountable. But it also speaks to a broader issue related to the complexity of cybercrimes, which, like the Internet itself, often involve a complex sequence of many different intermediaries and third parties, each with its own specific scope of visibility into and ability to prevent certain stages of those incidents. In this environment, there is no shortage of other intermediaries for each to shift blame onto, sue, or cast as the enemy. Often, rather than defending themselves against actual criminals, the parties caught up in these incidents appear more intent on doing battle with each other.

3 "What They Aren't Telling You Is Their Rules Are Archaic": The South Carolina Department of Revenue Breach, IRS Fraud, and Identity Theft

On August 13, 2012, an employee at the South Carolina Department of Revenue (SCDOR) received an email with a link embedded in the message. She clicked on the link and, in doing so, unknowingly downloaded malware onto her work computer in the state government. Two weeks later, someone used her username and password—presumably collected by means of that malware program—to log into her SCDOR work account remotely. It looked like a completely innocuous, routine login—an employee connecting to work from home or a hotel room—but, in fact, it was the first step in what would turn out to be a month-long operation to steal more than three-and-a-half million tax records dating back as far as 1998 and affecting more than 75 percent of the population of South Carolina. The SCDOR breach was significant not just because it targeted a major state government agency and affected millions of people, but also because it signaled a shift in how criminals were using stolen data to profit financially. While previously criminals like Gonzalez had relied primarily on payment card data to commit fraud, now they were increasingly interested in information that, unlike payment card numbers, could not be canceled or easily replaced but could still be used to set up bank accounts, take out loans, or file for tax refunds.

Stealing credit card numbers could certainly be profitable—after all, it earned Gonzalez millions—but credit cards expire, adding an element of time pressure to their resale, and with payment networks monitoring for large-scale fraud, customers could easily cancel stolen numbers. The information found in the South Carolina tax returns—Social Security numbers, addresses, phone numbers, income, employers, birthdays—was, to a large extent, immune from these vulnerabilities. It could be exploited years after it was stolen, reused indefinitely, and sold over and over again to different buyers.

In the aftermath of the SCDOR breach's discovery in October 2012, blame would be cast in several different directions by investigators, reporters, government officials, and victims arguing over what, specifically, had gone wrong and who was responsible for failing to stop the breach. In fighting about what specific technical measures should have been in place at the SCDOR and whose job it was to ensure that they were implemented, the South Carolina government and its critics quickly lost sight of the larger context and chain of events leading up to the breach, focusing almost exclusively on one or two technical fixes they believed would have made all the difference. They ignored myriad other opportunities for defensive intervention, as well as the range of potential stakeholders who could have played a role in preventing this particular breach.

When it comes to data breach postmortems, breached entities are often more eager to deflect blame than investigate root causes, and the state of South Carolina was no exception. Shortly after the incident was revealed, then-Governor of South Carolina, Nikki Haley, told other state officials on a conference call: "There wasn't anything where anyone in state government could have done anything to avoid it."[1] Later, when South Carolina hired security firm Mandiant to investigate the incident, Haley's claim turned out—unsurprisingly—to be misguided. There were, indeed, many things people in the state government could have done that might have helped prevent or mitigate the breach—beginning with not clicking on the link in the phishing email, or perhaps even filtering the email so it never reached the inboxes of its intended recipients in the first place. And yet, even after it became clear that this incident was far from unavoidable, the lawmakers investigating the breach quickly fell into another trap, one arguably even more insidious than denying all culpability—namely, pointing to one particular technical measure and insisting that it would have prevented everything that happened and would, therefore, be sufficient to rely on for security moving forward. To understand why both of these assertions—that there was nothing anyone in the South Carolina state government could have done to defend against the breach and that it could have been easily prevented by the implementation of one silver bullet security technology—are so profoundly misleading, it is helpful to walk through what actually happened in South Carolina at the end of the summer of 2012 and consider the many missed defensive opportunities.

Thirty-Two Days to Extract Seventy-Five GBs

The saga of the SCDOR breach began with the August 13 phishing email that likely allowed the intruder to steal an employee's login credentials, but that was only the first step in a multistage theft. Even just looking at that first step, it's already clear there were opportunities for more aggressive defensive interventions. The SCDOR could have implemented better phishing protections, including employee trainings and email filtering systems, which *might* have averted the breach—just as stronger Wi-Fi encryption *might* have averted the TJX compromise—or South Carolina could have blocked state employees from downloading any software that had not been preapproved by the Department, preventing the email from installing its malware when a recipient clicked on the link it contained. But even had all of these protections been in place, it would still have been possible for the intruder to acquire an employee's login credentials by other means, including guessing common passwords, purchasing stolen credentials from other websites in hopes that employees had reused passwords at work, or even intercepting network traffic, as Gonzalez and his co-conspirators did outside the Miami Marshalls stores. In other words, the success of the phishing email was not central to the SCDOR intruder's ultimate aim—it was just one of many possible tools open to him for stealing credentials. Blocking that step might have stopped him in his tracks—but it might also have simply forced him to shift course slightly.

On August 27, 2012, two weeks after the phishing email was opened by a SCDOR employee, someone logged into the SCDOR servers remotely, using the Citrix remote access tool and that same employee's credentials. The intruder used the Citrix portal to log into the user's workstation and then leveraged the employee's credentials to access other Department of Revenue systems and databases.[2] This initial intrusion after the successful phishing of employee credentials suggests yet another set of possible defensive measures. For instance, the SCDOR could have restricted the use of remote access capabilities so that its servers could not be easily accessed from outside the offices. Alternately, it could have instituted more stringent authentication requirements, including two-factor authentication, which requires users to provide an additional code or login factor besides their passwords to complete authentication.[a] Such measures might have proved more effective impediments to the intruders than trying to stop the phishing email from being delivered or opened, but they, too, would have provided no guarantee that the attackers would not find another means of access.

On September 1, the intruder executed code that allowed him to obtain passwords for all Windows users accounts on the system and also installed a backdoor on one SCDOR server that would permit him to regain access to the system in the event that the compromised credentials were changed. The next day, September 2, the intruder interacted with twenty-one SCDOR servers using a compromised account and authenticated to a web server that handled payment maintenance information for the Department of Revenue. The intruder continued to perform reconnaissance on the SCDOR systems over the next several days, probing different servers to establish what information was accessible and where it was stored.

On September 12, the intruder copied database backup files containing old tax return records to a staging directory, from which the perpetrator would later exfiltrate them out of the SCDOR servers. On September 13 and 14, the thief compressed the database backup files into fourteen encrypted compressed archive files that held 74.7 GB of data containing the records of 3.8 million tax filers, their 1.9 million dependents, and 700,000 businesses (in a state with a population of roughly five million people). These compressed files were then sent to another destination over the Internet, after which the perpetrators deleted the backup and archive files they had created on the SCDOR servers to remove all traces of their activity. At this point, the remaining defensive interventions open to the SCDOR were fairly limited. They included monitoring outbound traffic on the network and placing restrictions on how much or what kinds of information could be sent out via the Internet. On the other hand, while there were relatively few options open to defenders at this point, these interventions could potentially have been much more difficult for the intruder to circumvent than earlier stage defenses aimed at blocking phishing or logins

a. Multi-factor authentication systems can take multiple different forms when it comes to what they require users to provide in addition to a standard password. The SCDOR criticisms focused, in particular, on physical tokens that would have provided employees with a code to input along with their passwords as an additional precaution against intruders using stolen passwords. Other possible factors can include a phone call, a smartphone login notification requiring a user's approval, or a one-time code delivered via email, text message, or phone app.

because exfiltration defenses targeted a bottleneck stage of the intrusion. Phishing was not essential to steal tax return information—data exfiltration from the SCDOR servers was.

Over the course of the next month, the intruder continued to periodically connect to the SCDOR servers using the stolen credentials and installed backdoor capability, but there was no evidence of additional data being stolen during these subsequent intrusions. Finally, on October 19 and 20, the SCDOR executed a series of remediation activities recommended by Mandiant, which they had hired to investigate the incident, and removed the intruder's access points.

The investigation by Mandiant was only one component of a multi-pronged strategy by South Carolina to shore up their defenses—both technical and otherwise—in the aftermath of the incident. The total cleanup and mitigation costs for the breach are difficult to calculate precisely, but were estimated at roughly $14 million.[3] By far, the largest portion of that cost was the $12 million contract South Carolina entered into with Experian to provide a year of credit monitoring to all affected taxpayers. This offering was later extended to a lifetime of free credit monitoring and fraud resolution services for affected taxpayers and their children.[4] Other significant costs included $741,000 to notify the 1.5 million out-of-state residents who had filed taxes in South Carolina since 1998, the $500,000 contract with Mandiant to investigate the breach, a $160,000 contract with public relations firm Chernoff Newman, and a $100,000 payment to the law firm Nelson Mullins to provide outside legal advice.[5] Another $500,000 went to funding 24/7 monitoring of state computer systems through South Carolina's Information Technology center. Following the breach, South Carolina also installed a $160,000 program, dubbed "The Hand," which was paid for by the Department of Homeland Security and enabled officials to shut down computers that had been infected with malware.[6]

But none of these mitigation efforts could get back or destroy the stolen information. And in the years that followed, as tax fraud became increasingly common in several states, including South Carolina, those stolen records continued to haunt the victims, even though it was impossible for anyone to conclusively prove that they were the cause of the fraudulent filings. In March 2015, South Carolina announced that they would be sending out tax refunds by paper check to an undisclosed number of taxpayers, even if they had requested a direct deposit, because of rising fraud in the state.[7]

The SCDOR said at the time that the rising fraud rates were unrelated to the 2012 breach, insisting that the incident had yet to be conclusively linked to a single case of identity fraud.[8] But several critics were skeptical of these claims and, indeed, though it is difficult to ever definitively determine the origins of data used for identity theft—especially since, by 2015, many people's personal information had been stolen many times over in several different breaches—it is equally difficult to rule out any particular breach as having been tied to fraud, as the SCDOR claimed to be able to do.[9] In 2015, as the IRS was finally cracking down on federal tax fraud, states began to see up to 3700 percent increases in fraudulent state tax filings.[10] Certainly, the records stolen from the SCDOR were not the source for all of those fraud efforts across the country—but they could have played a role in the wave of fraud overwhelming South Carolina that year. The two-and-a-half year interval since the actual breach would have had little impact on the value and validity of the data, and the intruder might well have decided to give the state and the victims some time to lower their guards, while waiting for the right moment to cash in on the trove of stolen data.

What Really Matters Is the Blame

More than five years after the SCDOR breach, no one has been identified as the perpetrator or arrested, though the South Carolina police, in partnership with federal law enforcement officers, are still investigating the incident.[11] But the lack of a clear culprit in no way stopped victims and state employees from casting about for someone to blame for the incident—indeed, not being able to hold the criminal responsible for his actions seemed even to drive the search for someone else who could be identified and blamed. The obvious target was the SCDOR itself, which had been responsible for storing the data that was stolen. But the story was, in many ways, more complicated than just the SCDOR's poor choices. For instance, the SCDOR had contracted out some of its computer security to a private security firm, Trustwave, which provided the agency with intrusion detection and vulnerability scanning services.[12]

But Trustwave was not the immediate focus of the state's efforts to cast blame on someone else for its breach—though the company was named, along with the SCDOR and Haley, in a class action complaint filed by some of the victims in November 2012.[13] Taken to task by the Mandiant investigators for failing to encrypt the stolen tax filing data—a protection which might have rendered the stolen data useless to the thieves, or at the very least, made it much harder to monetize—South Carolina officials expressed outrage that the IRS had not required them to do so. In fact, the SCDOR had considered purchasing encryption for its computer system in 2006 but ultimately decided to forego it because of the $5 million price tag.[14] Jim Etter, the SCDOR Director at the time of the breach—who resigned shortly afterwards—testified about that decision at a hearing of a special South Carolina Senate Finance subcommittee, emphasizing that the agency relied primarily on IRS security guidelines, which did not require that tax information be encrypted.[15]

Haley picked up on this theme as well, pivoting deftly from her earlier statements that there was nothing anyone in the South Carolina government could possibly have done to prevent the breach, to accept some blame ("I ultimately am saying that South Carolina is at fault," she conceded more than two months after the breach).[16] But even as she began accepting responsibility for the breach, she insisted that the IRS was primarily at fault for what had happened. At a November 2012 meeting of the Republican Governors Association, Haley said at a press conference:

> What I'm going to do is go and educate all my governors and say, "Don't settle for the IRS saying you're compliant, because what they aren't telling you is their rules are archaic," ... They're not saying that being compliant doesn't include actually encrypting those numbers, and no governor knows that right now.[17]

The combination of the SCDOR being IRS-compliant and the agency's out-of-date hardware made for a "cocktail for an attack," Haley argued.[18] She even sent then-IRS Commissioner Steven Miller a letter urging him to "require all states to have stronger security measures for handling federal tax information, particularly encryption of tax information that is stored or 'at rest.'"[19]

Undoubtedly, South Carolina should have been encrypting its stored tax records. And yet, Haley's fixation on it as the sole reason the SCDOR data was insecure—to say nothing of her insistence that it was the job of the IRS to tell states that they had to encrypt tax data—is perplexing, especially given the nature of the theft. Tax records, whether or not they are encrypted when stored on state servers, have to be accessible in their decrypted, clear text to some state employees and auditors. So at least some number of employees must be granted access to the data in its unencrypted form, and the typical means for that access is for them to enter their credentials to decrypt the data. In other words, an intruder who took the phishing approach used in the SCDOR case and accessed stored data by means of stolen credentials might well have been able to use those same stolen credentials to decrypt the data had it in fact been encrypted.

While Haley positioned herself as a champion of stronger federal encryption standards, media reports and the state senate investigation panel were focused on another, cheaper missing safeguard at the SCDOR: a two-factor authentication system that would have required employees to enter both their password and a code transmitted by electronic token in order to log in. If the SCDOR had required all of its employees to use two-factor authentication then, perhaps, when their credentials were phished, the intruder would still have been unable to use them to log in without the electronic token-transmitted codes as well. Of course, as with encryption, there were no guarantees this line of defense would necessarily have worked—there are strains of malware that intercept the second-factor login codes, in addition to passwords, and multi-factor authentication technology has been successfully circumvented by criminals in other cases. But just as Haley latched onto encryption as the cure-all for future breaches, others investigating the breach insisted that it was the lack of two-factor authentication that was primarily to blame. "This could have been prevented by very inexpensive technology," state senator Kevin Bryant said at the hearings on the breach. SCDOR Director Jim Etter testified that following the breach the SCDOR implemented a two-factor system at a cost of $25,000. "We wouldn't be here had somebody made that decision to use the multifactor authentication," Bryant said. "I almost fell out of my chair when I came to that conclusion."[20]

This inclination to pinpoint a particular missing line of defense as the one crucial element that would have prevented a breach is not unique to the aftermath of the SCDOR breach. Media coverage of a 2014 breach of JPMorgan Chase followed a similar narrative, with investigators and reporters focusing on a network server at the bank that had not been upgraded to require two-factor authentication.[21] And failing to implement multi-factor authentication is not the only thing organizations are taken to task for in the wake of breaches that make use of insecure credentials. When several celebrities had naked photos stolen from their Apple iCloud accounts in 2014, critics blamed Apple's failure to rate limit unsuccessful login attempts in order to prevent adversaries from guessing passwords by brute force.[22] These criticisms are not necessarily wrong—it may well have been the case that Apple and JPMorgan and the SCDOR could have interrupted their breaches by implementing some of these relatively straightforward safe-guards. But, importantly, none of these individual defenses would necessar-ily have prevented the breaches that occurred—and blaming the incidents on their absence belies a deep misunderstanding of the many different pathways into computer systems that are open to intruders.

The tenor of this type of criticism, in which people lay blame for a breach on a particular missing technical defense, often implies that these stronger protections would have automatically prevented the attacks, rather than simply rerouting the attackers through different pathways. This single point of failure fallacy assumes that, of the myriad different ways in which an attack like the one perpetrated against South Carolina might have been defended against—phishing protections, remote access restrictions, limits on data exfiltration—it was the absence of multi-factor authentication (or encryption) that most clearly indicated negligence and inadequate security. This tendency to single out institutions' earliest failures in the sequence of attacks, whether those include adequately protecting authentication cre-dentials (as in the case of the SCDOR) or encrypting wireless networks (as in the case of TJX), is a recurring theme of these postmortems. The strongest focus often falls on early-stage preventative measures, such as multi-factor authentication, rather than later-stage harm mitigation and monitoring efforts, such as restricting outbound traffic.

What is most dangerous about this line of thinking is its implication that organizations that do encrypt their sensitive information, or do use multi-factor authentication, are safe from intrusions—or, at the very least, have done their due diligence when it comes to security. The question of what constitutes cybersecurity due diligence (and who gets to define it) is a dif-ficult one. For the purposes of assigning liability, it's important to be able to distinguish between targets who were breached because they were neg-ligent in protecting their computer systems, and those who were breached because they were up against incredibly sophisticated, well-resourced adver-saries who would ultimately have compromised their systems regardless of how many safeguards were in place. The former group would, ideally, bear more responsibility for what happened and face greater penalties than the latter, but it's far from straightforward figuring out where to draw that line.

Should a state department of revenue that complied with IRS requirements for data storage be considered negligent? If so, what exactly would they have had to do to avoid that designation?

The SCDOR, clearly, was not up against the most sophisticated adversaries and had not done everything possible to protect their systems. But the implicit assumption in taking the SCDOR to task specifically for failing to encrypt its data or use stronger authentication methods—or even in taking the IRS to task for failing to mandate encryption—is that there is some commonly accepted set of "best practices" for security that will prevent most breaches and that everyone should know to implement. Company privacy and security policies frequently offer deliberately vague descriptions of security practices that similarly subscribe to this idea, reassuring customers that their data will be protected through the use of "reasonable safeguards" or "appropriate measures," as if these were anything more than entirely subjective, malleable designations. While there are some accepted best practices in this space, there is also considerable disagreement over which of those tools are actually effective. The recommended list of essential security controls varies significantly over time and depends on who is asked to compile it. That lack of consensus, coupled with relatively little empirical data on the impact and effectiveness of different security controls, has made it all too easy to point to any individual missing security control—encryption, for instance, or multi-factor authentication—as the crucial thing that would have prevented a breach, even in the absence of any clear evidence that it would necessarily have done so. At the same time, these subjective, ever-shifting expectations for what organizations ought to be doing to protect their data have contributed to the uncertainty and ambiguity of the lists of security standards put out by government agencies like the IRS, as well as industry consortiums.

The Search for Security Standards

One of the often repeated truisms of computer security is that there is no perfect security—no such thing as vulnerability-free software or an impenetrable network or a completely locked down database. When it comes to hardware and software manufacturers, the U.S. Computer Fraud and Abuse Act grants immunity to those companies so that they cannot be sued when vulnerabilities in their products are discovered and exploited. The reasoning behind this policy is, essentially, that it would be impossible for those companies to find and fix all of the vulnerabilities in their products—since there's no such thing as perfect security. In granting them immunity, Congress reasoned that if the threat of being sued for every vulnerability or security flaw hung over them, then no one would ever manufacture any software or hardware. But for the much larger number of organizations that collect and store data, rather than developing their own technology, the implications of the "no perfect security" maxim are much less clear-cut and reassuring.

For organizations like TJX and the SCDOR that suffer large-scale data breaches, there is no blanket liability protection granted on the assumption that it would be impossible for them to have perfectly guarded their data from intruders. Instead, the question of whether or not they should be held liable for such breaches often hinges on whether or not they are deemed to have failed to implement a reasonable level of security protections as dictated by a variety of competing lists and catalogs of security standards and best practices. These lists range from standards developed by private companies and consortiums, like the Payment Card Industry Data Security Standards that applied to TJX since it accepted credit card payments, to standards developed by government entities like the IRS and the National Institute of Standards and Technology, to those developed by international standards organizations, like the International Organization for Standardization (ISO). The organizations that adopt these standards—sometimes voluntarily, sometimes to comply with industry or legal requirements—rely on them to define what constitutes enough, or reasonable, security, given that their protections will never be perfect.

So, when Haley faulted the "archaic" IRS security standards for the SCDOR breach, she was not just trying to deflect blame for the incident onto a different organization, she was also invoking the broader questions of how much security is enough, and who gets to decide. Without answers to those questions it is almost impossible to assign blame for security incidents in any meaningful or consistent way. Unless there are clear security expectations for organizations, it is impossible to know if they have met those expectations. Merely accusing all breached organizations of having failed in their duty to protect data is both unfair and unproductive. It loses sight of the fact that some skilled adversaries may be able to outwit even quite sophisticated security setups and also encourages companies to hide their breaches, or never start monitoring for them in the first place, for fear of being required to report them and suffer the consequences. And yet, providing meaningful, consistent, concrete information security standards turns out to be extremely difficult—even counterproductive, at times.

In the United States, the task of determining when a company has failed in its duty to secure customer data falls largely to the Federal Trade Commission (FTC), the government agency charged with holding businesses accountable for engaging in "unfair or deceptive" practices (and the same agency that accused TJX of failing to provide reasonable security for its customer data). The umbrella of unfair and deceptive business practices extends far beyond issues of data protection and computer security. For instance, many of the cases the FTC investigates relate to companies that make false claims about their products in advertisements. In a related vein, many of the agency's early forays into issues of data security and privacy hinged largely on investigating whether companies had adhered to the (generally quite vague) claims they made in their own corporate policies. But in the absence of any other enforcement mechanism for companies whose poor data security practices harm their customers, the FTC has extended its broad consumer protection mission to become the de facto regulator of many issues related to digital privacy and security.[23] In one of its most contested security-related cases, the FTC brought a complaint against the Wyndham Hotel Group, after the hotel chain suffered a series of three data breaches in short succession in 2008 and 2009. In 2012, the FTC charged that Wyndham had been deceptive and unfair to its customers because of its "failure to employ reasonable security measures" even though it assured customers that it adhered to "industry standard practices." Wyndham, in turn, insisted that the FTC had never defined what constituted a "reasonable" level of security—much less industry standard practices—and was therefore enforcing a completely arbitrary and subjective set of rules in blaming Wyndham for failing to implement an undefined set of security standards.

When the dispute went before the Court of Appeals for the Third Circuit, the court ruled in favor of the FTC, but, in doing so, suggested just how low the bar might be for other companies trying to figure out how much security they would need to implement to avoid being punished by the FTC. In the ruling, Judge Thomas Ambro addressed Wyndham's argument that they had not been given fair notice of the necessary security standards they should have implemented, writing:

> As the FTC points out in its brief, the complaint does not allege that Wyndham used weak firewalls, IP address restrictions, encryption software, and passwords. Rather, it alleges that Wyndham failed to use any firewall at critical network points, did not restrict specific IP addresses at all, did not use any encryption for certain customer files, and did not require some users to change their default or factory-setting passwords at all ...[24]

In other words, according to the Third Circuit Court of Appeals, Wyndham's security practices were so awful—nonexistent, even—that it didn't really matter that the FTC hadn't defined clear security standards because Wyndham's were so clearly outside the realm of anything that might be considered "reasonable." And yet, in taking Wyndham to task specifically for having no security at all, the Court left open the possibility that a company with weak encryption, weak firewalls, or weak passwords might be able to evade similar complaints from the FTC on the same grounds, namely, that the agency never explicitly required them to put in place stronger protections. For other companies looking to the ruling for guidance, it is clear that making absolutely no attempt to secure sensitive data could lead to consequences from the FTC, but it is not clear what level of security or combination of technical controls, precisely, would meet their expectation of reasonable security.

This ambiguity is partly by design. Both the threat landscape and the controls available to defenders are constantly changing, making it difficult for a government agency to pin down a specific list of what organizations ought to be doing with regard to security. On top of that, there is still relatively little empirical evidence demonstrating the effectiveness of these different types of security controls when it comes to preventing breaches—many security firms publish data on how many connection attempts or probes their products block or detect, but those numbers are not always reliable indicators of the likelihood of actual security breaches occurring. Even in the industry sectors that have the clearest data protection requirements—for instance, the healthcare sector, which is subject to the requirements of the Health Insurance Portability and Accountability Act (HIPAA), it is not clear that having those standards in place has markedly reduced the risk of security breaches. Being able to make data-driven decisions about which security standards are most effective will require much larger, more consistently collected data sets about when breaches occur and what protections are and are not in place when they do. Perhaps most challenging of all for people developing security standards is the fact that different organizations face different threats, store different kinds of data, and may have very different priorities and approaches to securing their computer systems, so it doesn't necessarily make sense to impose a one-size-fits-all set of requirements. There are even security benefits to a diversity of approaches—if everyone used exactly the same security tools, then an adversary who found vulnerabilities in one organization's defenses would likely be able to exploit those same weaknesses in many other companies' networks as well.

Blaming ambiguous, insufficient, and ill-defined security standards for breaches—as both Governor Haley and Wyndham did—can sometimes allow organizations that suffer security breaches to deflect responsibility for their security practices. And that deflection is not always unreasonable— after all, to whom should the SCDOR have looked for guidance on how to secure tax filings, if not the IRS? But the wide variety of available catalogs and lists of security standards adds an extra layer of complication to that question. When the IRS was pressed on its response to Haley's criticisms and its role in enabling the SCDOR breach by not requiring encryption, IRS spokesperson Michelle Eldridge responded:

> We work closely with the states to ensure the protection of federal tax data. We have a long list of requirements for states to handle and protect federal tax information. Just as importantly, we expect the states to follow the standards of the National Institute of Standards and Technology.[25]

Haley shifted blame for the incident onto the IRS by invoking their security standards for states, and the IRS responded by shifting blame back onto South Carolina by invoking yet another catalog of security standards, published by NIST. Maintaining lots of different security standards and controls for organizations to choose among—and keeping those standards somewhat vague—is often a strategic choice on the part of the agencies and organizations issuing them. And there are good reasons not to lock down security requirements too specifically in many cases. However, that ambiguity also allows for a great deal of equivocating and dispute in the aftermath of security incidents about whether the victims met certain standards for data security, whose standards they were expected to meet, and whether those standards were any good in the first place. Even as they aim to provide organizations with some flexible guidance about how to protect data and networks, security standards and the groups issuing them often end up providing cover for breach victims—as well as other standards-setting organizations. These standards can quickly become a vehicle for breached parties, like the SCDOR, to blame someone else for a missing security control and further focus attention on the role of specific, early-stage preventive security controls rather than later-stage mitigation efforts targeted at preventing criminals from successfully monetizing the data they have stolen.

Tax Fraud

Making money from stolen tax records presents a slightly different set of obstacles than does profiting off stolen payment card numbers. Gonzalez and his co-conspirators had only one clear path to disposing of the TJX payment card data—manufacturing fraudulent cards and selling them—and they were racing to do that before the payment networks detected the fraud and preemptively canceled the cards. By contrast, the perpetrator of the SCDOR breach was under no time pressure and had several different possible paths to financial gain, ranging from filing fraudulent tax returns to opening new accounts and loans in the victims' names to initiating direct transfers from the victims' bank accounts using their routing information. Tax records are not the only type of data that offer criminals this range of profitable activities—for instance, health records, which often contain similar information (Social Security numbers, addresses, billing information), can provide comparable opportunities for financial fraud, with the added possibility of health insurance fraud.

Given the flexibility and long-term value of tax returns, medical records, and other types of personal information that are less easily canceled and less well monitored than payment card numbers, it is no surprise that more criminals began to shift their focus to these alternatives to credit card records in the years following the SCDOR breach. In 2015, for instance, the IRS suffered a major breach,[26] as did health insurance companies Anthem[27] and Excellus Blue Cross Blue Shield.[28] Moreover, analysis of online black market forums the previous year indicated that stolen medical records were selling for roughly ten times as much as stolen payment card numbers, suggesting that there were more lucrative opportunities for criminals to use the former type of data.[29] The advantages of stealing more permanent personal information, such as that found in medical and tax records, went beyond just enabling criminals to explore new forms of financial fraud and evade the threat of payment card expiration or cancelation. Financially motivated cybercriminals who dealt in tax and medical records were largely able to distance themselves from the ongoing fights among the major banks, retailers, and payment networks trying to shift breach costs and liability onto each other with microchip-enabled cards. This meant they could evade the formidable fraud detection teams built up by the payment networks in the wake of major payment card breaches. Those teams were often responsible for identifying major data breaches—including the TJX breach—by finding patterns in how and where compromised cards were used and tracing them back to a common source.

This sort of pattern detection requires large, centralized organizations like MasterCard and Visa that have data on hundreds of millions of payment cards and can therefore piece together where they had all been stolen. Being able to determine how large-scale fraud was initiated—and, specifically, who was responsible for protecting the data that was used to perpetrate it—was crucial for being able to play out any of the fights over who was at fault and would bear the costs of that fraud. It was much more difficult to try to determine what fraud—if any—had been perpetrated using the data stolen from the SCDOR, however.

There is no equivalent of the payment card networks to track patterns across reports of tax fraud or identity theft and link them back to particular breaches. The years following the SCDOR breach did see a steep rise in tax fraud with criminals filing returns in other people's names to claim their refunds. In 2015, the IRS even went so far as to issue nearly three million unique six-digit Identity Protection PINs to individuals who had been the victims of identity theft to ensure that no one else could file their returns without the corresponding PINs, but several individuals reported that their PINs had already been compromised when they tried to file their taxes, forcing them to file in person at IRS offices. This may have been because the online tool provided for users to retrieve any lost PINs asked them for information such as their past addresses, birth dates, and Social Security numbers—data that could easily have been retrieved from the breaches that originally made them susceptible to identity theft.[30] It's certainly possible that the data stolen from the SCDOR was used to conduct some identity theft and file some fraudulent tax claims—some analysts speculated as much when South Carolina saw a sharp increase in state tax fraud in 2015[31]—but no one was in a position to determine conclusively how much of the fraud was tied to any particular breach.

Without the ability to link fraud to specific data breaches it becomes nearly impossible to sort out issues of liability. When several people whose tax returns were stolen from the SCDOR tried to file a class action suit against the SCDOR and its security contractor, Trustwave, a district court in Illinois dismissed the suit on the grounds that the plaintiffs could not show clear evidence of having suffered harm due to the breach and therefore did not have standing to sue. Amber Strautins, the primary plaintiff, alleged no fewer than seven different types of injury she and the other members of the class action suit had suffered as a result of the breach of their personal identifying information (PII):

(1) untimely and/or inadequate notification of the Data Breach;

(2) improper disclosure of PII;

(3) loss of privacy;

(4) out-of-pocket expenses incurred to mitigate the increased risk of identity theft and/or identity fraud pressed upon them by the Data Breach;

(5) the value of time spent mitigating identity theft and/or identity fraud and/or the increased risk of identity theft and/or identity fraud;

(6) deprivation of the value of PII; and

(7) violations of rights under the Fair Credit Reporting Act.

The plaintiffs' strategy was apparently to list every possible injury they could think of—from how rapidly they had been notified of the breach to the money they spent mitigating the consequences, to the more ephemeral loss of privacy (and value of their personal information) that they had suffered. But none of these injuries was sufficiently concrete to satisfy the court that the plaintiffs even deserved the opportunity to sue Trustwave, much less that the company owed them anything for its role in the breach.

In dismissing the claim on the grounds that the plaintiffs lacked standing to sue, District Judge John J. Tharp, Jr. wrote:

> These claims of injury … are too speculative to permit the complaint to go forward. … Whether Strautins or other class members actually become victims of identity theft as a result of the data breach depends on a number of variables, such as whether their data was actually taken during the breach, whether it was subsequently sold or otherwise transferred, whether anyone who obtained the data attempted to use it, and whether or not they succeeded … the harm that Strautins fears is contingent on a chain of attenuated hypothetical events and actions by third parties independent of the defendant.[32]

Tharp's decision, which echoes the logic of a 2013 dismissal of a similar suit brought against Barnes & Noble in the wake of a data breach, indicates just how difficult it is to assign financial liability in the aftermath of a data breach, unless the victims can provide clear evidence of specifically how the stolen data was used. Just the loss of privacy and increased risk of identity theft are not sufficient injuries to grant breach victims standing to sue the organizations responsible for protecting their data. But proving a direct link between a breach and specific instances of fraud is no easy task. Criminals can wait for years following a theft before they begin to use stolen information like Social Security numbers or addresses, and given how many breaches of these types of information have occurred and the lack of powerful, centralized monitoring intermediary organizations, it is not always possible to link an individual case of fraud to a specific breach.

This inability to demonstrate the kind of concrete harm required to gain standing to sue is a recurring problem for those concerned about the security and privacy of their data even beyond the context of data breaches. For instance, in a 2013 decision of the case *Clapper v. Amnesty International* the Supreme Court ruled that the plaintiffs did not have standing to sue over surveillance efforts conducted under the Foreign Intelligence Surveillance Act Amendments Act of 2008 that might have allowed for interception of their communications by the U.S. government. The Supreme Court took issue with the fact that the plaintiffs were merely speculating that their communications *might* be intercepted, without knowing for certain whether or not such surveillance was being conducted (as, indeed, they would have no way of knowing, not being themselves members of the U.S. intelligence community).

The Supreme Court majority ruling dismissed this argument as being based on "a speculative chain of possibilities that does not establish that their potential injury is certainly impending,"[33] much as Tharp dismissed the South Carolinians' fears for being based on a "chain of attenuated hypothetical events and actions." In another attempt to claim standing, the plaintiffs in the surveillance case argued that they had been harmed by having to take preemptive security precautions to protect their communications for fear of government interception, much like the plaintiffs in the Trustwave case had argued they had to spend time and money mitigating the increased risk of identity theft they now faced. The Supreme Court, like Tharp, was also unimpressed with this line of reasoning, ruling that the plaintiffs "cannot manufacture standing by choosing to make expenditures based on hypothetical future harm."[34] This notion that the risks posed by the loss of data security or privacy are no more than "hypothetical future harms," and therefore insufficient to grant legal standing to sue, has important consequences for the victims of data breaches perpetrated for the purposes of identity theft. It leaves them with fewer options to pursue in the aftermath of such breaches, disdains the impacts those breaches have on their lives, and most of all, gives organizations like Trustwave and SCDOR little incentive to do a better job protecting their data.

Theft of tax records and tax fraud—like theft of medical records and insurance fraud—emerged largely in the wake of years of large-scale payment card breaches, like the one targeting TJX, as credit card companies got better at detecting fraud and initiating preemptive card cancelations and withdrawal limits. Like the TJX breach, the SCDOR breach involved several stages—from the initial phishing email through the exfiltration of the stolen data to external servers—and there were potential defensive interventions that might have been effective at each stage of the intrusion. Blame for the breach was quickly confined to one or two of these missing interventions—namely, encryption and two-factor authentication—by media reports and state lawmakers, while Haley faulted the IRS data protection standards for the absence of these defenses, and the IRS, in turn, invoked the NIST security standards, which did include encryption. This circular deflection of responsibility to different government and industry guidelines highlights the challenges of trying to assemble a comprehensive set of security standards. Those challenges create a fertile environment for the targets of security breaches to shift blame onto the organizations that they feel have failed to tell them how to protect themselves. The SCDOR breach demonstrated how easily and quickly a breach could come to be blamed on a few specific technical controls and, simultaneously, how incredibly difficult it is to assign financial liability to any of the involved parties in the absence of robust, specific standards or concrete, immediate harm.

4   The Most Wanted Cybercriminal in the World: GameOver ZeuS, Cryptolocker, and the Rise of Ransomware

When it comes to using computers to steal money, not even Albert Gonzalez with his buried barrel of cash has come close to matching the success of Russian hacker Evgeniy Bogachev. The $3 million bounty the FBI has offered for Bogachev's capture is larger than any that has ever been offered for a cybercriminal—but that sum represents only a tiny fraction of the money he has stolen through his botnet GameOver ZeuS.[1] At its height in 2012 and 2013, GameOver ZeuS, or GOZ, comprised between 500,000 and one million compromised computers all over the world that Bogachev could control remotely. For years, Bogachev used these machines to spread malware that allowed him to steal banking credentials and perpetrate online extortion.[2] No one knows exactly how much money Bogachev stole from his thousands of victims using GOZ, but the FBI conservatively estimates that it was well over $100 million.[3] Meanwhile, Bogachev has spent lavishly on a fleet of luxury cars, two French villas, and—showing a kinship of sorts with Gonzalez—a large yacht.[4]

Bogachev lives in the resort town of Anapa on the Black Sea, where Russian officials have declined for years to arrest him or extradite him to the U.S. In fact, the Russian government has benefited from his criminal activity. While Bogachev has leveraged his vast network of compromised computers and credentials for financial gain, officials of the Russian government have also on occasion made use of his network and computer intrusions for espionage purposes of their own.[5] But, while the FBI cannot arrest Bogachev so long as he remains safely in Russia, in the summer of 2014 they partnered with several companies and researchers to try to shut down GOZ and cut Bogachev off from the hundreds of thousands of compromised computers under his control. Dubbed Operation Tovar, the

GOZ takedown effort was an unprecedented law enforcement effort to fight cybercrime in terms of its scope, technical sophistication, and complexity. It included participants from Germany, the United Kingdom, the Netherlands, and New Zealand, as well as the United States, and hinted at the potential for international cooperation and public-private partnerships to strengthen cybersecurity and attack criminal infrastructure.

But the success of Operation Tovar was short lived. Bogachev was still at large, and he quickly began to rebuild GOZ; meanwhile, similar strains of ransomware to those distributed by GOZ soon began appearing, distributed by other, closely related bots. In designing GOZ, Bogachev pioneered a business model combining many technical intermediaries in the bot's infrastructure that made takedowns extremely difficult with the removal of many of the financial intermediaries present in earlier financially motivated cybercrimes that had made policing efforts possible. This model proved to be uniquely lucrative and stubbornly resistant to even the savviest and most aggressive efforts of law enforcement. The success of GOZ heralded a new wave of financial cybercrime focused on extortion rather than credit card fraud or identity theft, a trend that freed criminals from many of the constraints and law enforcement monitoring capabilities attached to traditional currencies and financial institutions.

This shift to extracting payments directly from individual victims marked a dramatic change not just in how financially motivated cybercrimes were carried out but also in who bore the costs of these incidents. The rise of ransomware significantly altered the economics of cybercrime for criminals and victims alike, eliminating the roles of centralized middlemen and fences like Yastremskiy (who had served as the crux of many law enforcement investigations) and broadening dramatically the types of data it was possible for criminals to monetize.

GameOver ZeuS

Criminals who infect users' computers and harness those machines to create botnets typically control those bots through a centralized command and control server that sends messages to the infected machines telling them what to do—for instance, when to send packets to a particular destination as part of a denial-of-service attack, or what emails to send. Since identifying all of the infected machines in a large bot and getting their owners to remove the bot's malware is a slow and largely ineffective process, takedown efforts often center on shutting down these command and control servers, or cutting off their communication channels with the infected computers they are issuing orders to. The genius of the GOZ design lay primarily in its ability to hide and even change this command and control component of the bot, so that law enforcement struggled to identify a centralized control server, and the GOZ operators could quickly and easily shift to a new server in the event that their current one was discovered and cut off. To make it harder for anyone to figure out which servers were controlling the bot, GOZ-infected devices did not all communicate with a single centralized command and control server. Instead, the bot operated on a peer-to-peer architecture, so each new infected device maintained connections to other infected machines, some of which served as intermediate "proxy nodes," relaying commands from GOZ operators and sending encrypted data back to their "master drop" servers.[6] These proxy nodes made it considerably more difficult—though not impossible—to trace the bot back to a single controlling server, since the GOZ operators were not communicating directly with most of the infected machines they controlled.

The peer-to-peer architecture was not the only precaution Bogachev had taken in designing his bot. Just in case law enforcement officials were, eventually, able to trace the servers he was using to control GOZ, he also programmed the GOZ malware to automatically contact a series of one thousand other Internet addresses every week and ask for instructions from any machines at those addresses, in case he ever needed to set up a new command and control server. The GOZ malware included a Domain Generation Algorithm, or DGA, that generated that list of one thousand new domain names every week, each belonging to one of six top-level domains: .com, .net, .org, .biz, .info, or .ru. Every week, each machine infected with GOZ would go through that week's list and try to contact each of the thousand domains. So if Bogachev's servers were ever threatened and he needed to set up a new command and control server, he could use any one of those domains during the appropriate week to reestablish communication with all of the infected machines and regain control of the bot. This meant that any takedown efforts directed at his command and control servers—typically the most vulnerable element of a bot—would be largely useless, since Bogachev would have a thousand opportunities to set up a new such server every week, and there was no way to predict which domains the DGA would come up with for any given week.

Just as Bogachev protected his command and control servers by hiding them behind layers of infected proxy machines, so, too, he shielded his bank accounts by routing stolen funds through other people. The GOZ malware was designed not just to harness the machines it infected to Bogachev's bot, but also to steal banking and payroll credentials from those machines primarily by logging all of the users' keystrokes, so that everything they typed (including passwords) would be captured and sent back to the bot's operators. Using those stolen credentials, Bogachev could then initiate fraudulent wire transfers from his victims, or redirect their paychecks to be directly deposited into accounts of his choosing. Hospital payroll systems with their large numbers of employees and budgets were a common GOZ target; the FBI estimates that Bogachev stole hundreds of thousands of dollars in this manner from hospitals alone.[7] GOZ could even access bank accounts protected with two-factor authentication that required users to enter not just a password but also another one-time code delivered by text message or physical token. (This was the same technology that South Carolina was faulted for not purchasing prior to its breach.) Using a man-in-the-middle attack[a] to intercept messages between the victim and their banking site, GOZ would present its victims with a fake login window that looked identical to their bank's real login webpages. People trying to log in with two-factor authentication would receive their second authentication code over their phones or by token and then enter it directly into the fake login field. The GOZ malware would capture that authentication code and immediately send it back to the servers controlled by the GOZ operators using the instant messaging service Jabber, and the GOZ operators could then combine it with stolen passwords to access the targeted accounts protected by two-factor authentication.[8]

a. Man-in-the-middle attacks occur when attackers insert themselves between two (or more) communicating parties in order to intercept or alter the communications unbeknownst to the people sending and receiving them. In this case, the GOZ operators inserted themselves between users and their bank servers to intercept bank login information that the users believed they were sending directly to their bank.

Bogachev didn't need to repatriate his profits as elaborately as Gonzalez did with a small army of in-person cashers to deliver cash to Miami, but sending direct deposit payments or fraudulent transfers straight to his own accounts would still have been risky for Bogachev. Even if law enforcement officers in the U.S. were unable to arrest him, they would likely have been able to trace his accounts, block, or at least flag, transfers to them, and restrict any money being paid to them from the United States. So instead, Bogachev mirrored the proxy structure of his bot by building a small army of money mules whose accounts he could route money through before the stolen funds ultimately reached his organization. The mules were recruited via spam email campaigns sent out by the GOZ bot itself—"If you are taking a career break, are on a maternity leave, recently retired or simply looking for some part-time job, this position is for you," the emails said. These mules—based in the U.S. so that their accounts and transactions would not attract suspicion—received wire transfers and salary payments directly from the victims, kept a sum as their payment ("Starting salary is $2000 per month plus commission, paid every month"), and sent the rest along to another account, presumably belonging to the GOZ operators.[9]

This network of money mules ensconced safely in their own homes, sitting at their computers, was already significantly less risky for Bogachev than Gonzalez's system of people walking around with large sums of cash and quantities of payment cards. But this set-up did not satisfy Bogachev for long. For one thing, it required collecting specifically financial information and credentials from victims, and, for another, it relied on a vast network of potentially vulnerable or disloyal money mules. So Bogachev's organization tested a ransom scheme, designing another piece of malware called Cryptolocker, which it spread to hundreds of thousands of computers using the GOZ bot infrastructure. Cryptolocker, which first appeared in 2013, was also designed to steal money but in a different manner than the GOZ credential-theft malware. Instead of capturing financial account credentials, Cryptolocker would encrypt the hard drives of computers it infected and then demand that the victims make ransom payments if they ever wanted to be able to access their files again. The Cryptolocker ransomware demanded payments of hundreds of dollars, sometimes as high as $750, and gave its victims a window of 72 hours to pay, using either anonymous prepaid cash vouchers or the difficult-to-trace cryptocurrency Bitcoin, before the victims would receive a decryption key for their devices. (Many victims struggled to figure out how to make Bitcoin payments, so Bogachev and his conspirators helpfully set up a customer service website with step-by-step instructions.) Unlike redirecting a payroll account—which requires providing potentially traceable information about the new destination account payments should be sent to—the nature of these ransom payments meant they could not be easily tied to specific financial accounts that U.S. law enforcement could control or monitor, alleviating the need for money mules and the risk of Bogachev having his accounts identified and frozen. As with all elements of GOZ-directed financial crime, there is no conclusive evidence of how much money Cryptolocker managed to extort from its victims, but one analysis of Bitcoin logs indicated that during just one two-month period in 2013, from October 15 to December 18, the ransomware program raked in roughly $27 million.[10]

Operation Tovar

What made GOZ and Bogachev especially difficult to trace and shut down lay largely in the bot's multilayered, constantly changing infrastructural setup. The criminals' scheme combined intermediate proxy hosts used to control the bot, the DGA's weekly list of new domains (that enabled them to easily shift their command and control servers), and the financial middlemen and anonymous cryptocurrencies they relied on for financial transfers. The law enforcement shutdown of the bot's operations required tremendous investment in Operation Tovar as well as extensive international cooperation, sophisticated technical expertise, and also some old-fashioned sleuthing efforts. But the rapid reemergence of the bot and its signature malware in the months following the takedown spoke to the resilience of ransomware and distributed bot models in simultaneously inserting many layers of infrastructural intermediaries (proxies) that made technical remediation difficult while also excluding almost all of the traditional financial intermediaries (fences and money mules) that had made policing efforts and legal remediations possible.

Operation Tovar began when UK law enforcement authorities provided the FBI with information about a suspicious server in the UK. The server hosted a password-protected website called visitcoastweekend.com with a Frequently Asked Questions page that read (in Russian):

Starting on September we are beginning to work through the panel where you now find yourselves. [Fraudulent] Money transfers and drop [money mule] managers are synchronizing their work through our panel, which enables a much greater optimization of the work process and increase in the productivity of our work. Starting from this moment, all drop [money mule] managers with whom we are working and all [fraudulent] money transferors who work with us are working through this panel. We wish you all successful and productive work.[11]

The site also included a detailed list of hundreds of financial transactions with dates, company names, amounts, and the type of transfer. The FBI undertook the painstaking work of verifying that these transfers were indeed tied to the GOZ virus. Agents interviewed representatives from a composite materials company in the Western District of Pennsylvania to confirm that a $198,234.03 wire transfer on October 21, 2011, from a SunTrust Bank account, the details of which were listed in the visitcoastweekend.com ledger, was, in fact, the result of credentials stolen from a GOZ-infected machine. "For all listed companies with respect to which the FBI manually reviewed information in the ledger and compared it to information from either field interviews or bank fraud reporting, the information was an exact match," FBI special agent Elliott Peterson wrote in a court declaration.[12]

Meanwhile, the FBI found and interviewed several of the money mules recruited by the GOZ operators. Heidi Nelson described how, after losing her job in 2009 and posting her resume online, she was contacted by someone claiming to work for a Russian company who subsequently hired Nelson to receive payments and wire them to Russia. Renee Michelli told the FBI a similar story about being hired by a supposed Russian software company "1C" to receive payments within the United States and then transfer them to Russian accounts.[13]

The evidence provided by the money mules and the visitcoastweekend .com server helped the FBI begin to map out the extensive technical and human infrastructure responsible for spreading GOZ and Cryptolocker, but offered few hints as to who was in charge of the operation. To trace the ringleaders, the FBI turned to analysis done by security firm iDefense about the ability of GOZ to evade two-factor authentication using the Jabber messaging protocol. iDefense found that many of the credentials stolen by GOZ were transmitted via Jabber to the domain incomeet.com, which was hosted at the IP address 66.199.248.195. That particular IP address was associated with a server operated by a company called EZZI.NET, headquartered in Brooklyn, New York. The FBI interviewed an EZZI.NET employee who told them that the server in question had been leased to a customer named "Alexey S." who said he was associated with a company called IP-Server Ltd, located in Moscow. The FBI obtained search warrants for the contents of the incomeet.com server in Brooklyn and found extensive chat logs in which different users (under pseudonyms such as "tank" and "aqua") exchanged links to news articles about their successful thefts from banks. "This is what they damn wrote about me" tank messaged lucky12345 in July 2009, referencing a *Washington Post* article about money stolen from the Bullitt County Fiscal Court in Shepherdsville, Kentucky.[14] Discussing the same article, aqua wrote to tank: "they described the entire scheme. The Bastards. ... I'm really pissed. They exposed the entire deal."

The FBI had found the people responsible for GOZ, but the only thing they knew about them was their pseudonyms. Agents began combing through the online forums where criminals discuss and disseminate malware programs. A search warrant related to another investigation allowed them to seize and search the contents of one such forum, Mazafaka.info, where they found someone sending messages under the username "Lastik," who took credit for writing the GOZ malware. "I'm monster, and not his reincarnation ... I'm the author of Zeus," Lastik wrote in a private message to another user sent through Mazafaka.info on June 5, 2010. In messages to several users on Mazafaka.info, Lastik indicated that he could be contacted at the addresses lucky12345@jabber.cz and bashorg@talking.cc, suggesting that he was also the lucky12345 whose chat transcripts had been found on the incomeet.com server. Furthermore, when registering for his Mazafaka account, Lastik/lucky12345 had provided the email address alexgarbarchuck@yahoo.com as his contact address. With a search warrant, officers were able to retrieve all of the records related to that email address from a service provider. The service provider gave the FBI all of the information that customer had used to set up his account, including a home address in Krasnodar Krai, Russia, and his name: Evgeniy Bogachev.[15]

Cross-referencing the IP addresses used to access Bogachev's email account with those used to access visitcoastweekend.com and a Cryptolocker command-and-control server (traced from the U.S. to the UK to Luxembourg), the investigators found that there was significant overlap and deduced that Bogachev was involved in both schemes. Moreover, he had high-level administrative access to the GOZ server, leading the FBI to believe he was a "leader of the GOZ conspiracy."

The identification of Bogachev was no small feat, as highlighted by the fact that the FBI was able to identify several of his co-conspirators only by their online aliases ("Temp Special," "Ded," "Chingiz 911," and "mr. kyky-pyky"). If Bogachev had been more careful about not using his real name when registering for accounts, or masking his IP address when he accessed the GOZ and Cryptolocker servers, he might not now be the FBI's most wanted cybercriminal—though it's also possible he felt confident that the Russian authorities wouldn't turn him over and therefore didn't go out of his way to hide his identity.

The work of tracking down Bogachev and the servers running GOZ and Cryptolocker was largely low-tech: interviewing money mules and victims, cross-referencing lengthy data logs, combing through websites and Russian hacker forums. By contrast, the actual takedown efforts to remove the hundreds of thousands of infected machines from Bogachev's control involved extensive technical expertise—much of which is redacted from the public records of the incident—to cut off the communications between all of GOZ's complicated layers of peer and proxy nodes while also seizing the servers issuing commands to them, including machines in Canada, Ukraine, and Kazakhstan.

Law enforcement also had to make sure that Bogachev and his associates would be unable to reestablish control over the infected machines through a new server using the domain names generated each week by the DGA. The FBI worked with a number of security researchers to reverse engineer the DGA and figure out how it generated the list of domain names it provided to the infected computers every week. That way, the FBI would know which thousand domains were being selected every week in advance. Then, right before the takedown, they acquired a temporary restraining order that required domain registries in the U.S. to redirect any attempts to contact those thousand domains to a substitute, government-run server. Since the domains generated by the DGA with the .ru top-level domain were not controlled by registries in the US, but rather by companies in Russia, the order also required U.S. service providers to block any connection requests to the .ru domains generated by the DGA.

The culmination of all these efforts—the DGA reverse-engineering and preemptive restrictions on the domains it generated, the seizure of Cryptolocker command and control servers all over the world, and the court orders authorizing redirection of the connection attempts by any GOZ-infected machines—came in June 2014 and the coordinated takedown delivered a significant blow to the bot's operations. Operation Tovar was touted by the FBI as a massive and multilayered strike against every element of the infrastructure underlying GOZ and Cryptolocker, a triumph of international cybercrime fighting and public sector/private industry collaboration, a victory of law enforcement sleuthing and technical ingenuity over the increasingly sophisticated online criminal world. In a statement posted by the FBI on their website on June 2, 2014, FBI Executive Assistant Director Robert Anderson called GOZ "the most sophisticated botnet the FBI and our allies have ever attempted to disrupt," and U.S. Deputy Attorney General James Cole praised the operation's combination of "traditional law enforcement techniques and cutting edge technical measures necessary to combat highly sophisticated cyber schemes targeting our citizens and businesses."[16] One month later, on July 11, 2014, the Justice Department reported that the number of computers infected with GOZ malware had been reduced by 31 percent thanks to law enforcement intervention.[17]

To some extent, all of the FBI's claims were true—Operation Tovar was a triumph of defense over offense, it was an example of U.S. law enforcement partnering effectively with industry and international officials, and it was a very technically sophisticated endeavor. But it also relied largely on the carelessness of GOZ operators and their money mules rather than technical vulnerabilities inherent to the operation Bogachev had established. So even though the FBI had dealt a significant—if temporary—setback to GOZ, Bogachev's criminal model was still solid, and it would only be a matter of time before he, as well as numerous other copycats, would find ways to tweak it, infect more machines, and get back to business.

The Rise of Ransomware

The most enduring legacy of Bogachev's operation was not the decentralized peer-to-peer bot model, which deliberately introduced several layers of intermediaries between the GOZ-infected computers and their command-and-control servers in order to confound takedown attempts, but the economic model of extortion via Cryptolocker, which, just as deliberately, removed many layers of money mules and intermediaries from financial transactions. These financial intermediaries who route transactions or fence stolen data were typically weak spots in large-scale cybercrimes that enabled law enforcement intervention—recall that several of Bogachev's money mules were identified by the police and interviewed during the course of the investigation, and that Gonzalez's entire scheme was brought down by the initial arrest and questioning of Maksym Yastremskiy, who fenced the stolen payment card information online, and Jonathan Williams, a casher carrying $200,000 in cash to Gonzalez and his associates. Law enforcement had new opportunities to track and catch the people involved at each monetization stage of the TJX breach—the sale of the stolen data, the transfer of the profits back to the U.S.—but while there was no getting around those attack stages for Gonzalez, Bogachev figured out a way to get rich without them.

From a criminal's perspective, the most difficult, or riskiest, stages of cybercrimes have typically been the ones that come after the perpetrator has already successfully stolen data from a protected computer. Finding a way into a computer system to steal data is comparatively easy. Finding a way to monetize that data—making sure that credit card companies don't cancel all the cards whose numbers you've stolen before you have a chance to sell them, or identifying buyers willing to pay a good price, or hiding those profits from the police—can be much harder. Financial intermediaries are easy targets for law enforcement because their records often show a clear money trail between the victims and the perpetrators. The system of money mules utilized by Bogachev was slightly less risky than the cashers employed by Gonzalez because it did not require transporting any cash back into the United States, nor did it rely on the sale of stolen information through a centralized and well-known black market dealer like Yastremskiy who was likely to attract the attention of the police.

Indeed, that was part of the point of recruiting unemployed, new mothers looking to earn money at home, and the recently retired to process the transactions—they were unlikely to have the kind of targets on their backs that Yastremskiy did, and they would attract much less attention simply forwarding small transfers than they would by trying to find customers and sell stolen data or deliver large quantities of cash to Florida.

But all the same, employing people like Michelli and Nelson, who were not hardened criminals, and, indeed, professed to be unaware they were involved in any criminal activity, created risks for Bogachev and his organization. Michelli and Nelson likely didn't know much about whom they were working for or what they were doing—but what they did know they were more than willing to pass on to the FBI when questioned. Meanwhile, Cryptolocker's ransomware scheme allowed Bogachev to eliminate most financial intermediaries and collect money directly from his victims by means of anonymous Bitcoin payments and prepaid cash vouchers.

The ransomware model was advantageous for criminals not just because it eliminated the need for hiring and paying money mules—as well as the risk that they might be traced back to the criminals—but also because it generated profits from data that would otherwise have been worthless if sold on the black market. Up until ransomware, financially motivated cybercriminals had to find and steal only certain types of valuable data that other people would pay for (e.g., credit card numbers, health records, Social Security numbers, intellectual property) or that could be used to initiate financial transfers directly (e.g., account numbers, banking credentials). This meant that the vast majority of data was of no use to them—most people's photos, files, and emails are of no value whatsoever on the black market (which may be one reason most people don't bother to protect these types of data). But these same files that would be worthless to other criminals are often of immense value to the people they belong to—Cryptolocker exploited that by selling data specifically back to the only person in the world for whom it had any value.

Bogachev's organization developed this model at a moment when there was more and more stolen data available on the black market because of frequent large-scale data breaches. The value of that stolen data—even to criminals—was rapidly decreasing thanks to the overwhelming supply. From 2011 to 2016, the price of a stolen payment card record dropped from $25 to $6.[18] So not only were financially motivated criminals limited in what types of data they could monetize, but they were making smaller and smaller profits from selling their stolen data. Ransomware solved both those problems—enabling criminals like Bogachev to extract value from all sorts of seemingly worthless data stored on people's devices for much higher fees than they had ever been able to charge on the black market.

Cryptolocker was not the first strain of ransomware and Bogachev was not the first criminal to employ this economic model, but he was one of the first to employ it at large scale with such lucrative results. Ransomware programs date back as early as 1999, but they did not emerge as a popular mode of attack until more than a decade later, when Bitcoin and other anonymous modes of online payment became more mainstream, allowing criminals to shield their profits from being traced or blocked by law enforcement and financial intermediaries.[19] Even today, cryptocurrencies are not routinely used by many of the people targeted by ransomware, who often struggle to figure out how—technically—they can make the demanded ransom payments. The GOZ operators faced many victims who were willing to pay to regain access to their devices, but could not figure out how within the short time window given by Cryptolocker. Around November 2013, they set up a "customer service" site for Cryptolocker victims to walk them through the process of making the payments and help with the decryption process afterwards.[20] This additional infrastructure detracted from the intermediary-free ideal of ransomware's model, however, as did the extensive record-keeping that the GOZ organization did on the visitcoastweekend .com server, where the FBI found records of specific payments and victims.

Law enforcement investigations were not the only threat—perhaps not even the primary threat—to the continued profitability of Cryptolocker and other successful ransomware operations. Ransomware distributors rely on people actually paying the demanded ransoms, and victims are less likely to pay if they suspect they won't actually receive a decryption key for their devices after doing so. After all, they have only the criminal's word that their devices and data really will be restored if they do pay the ransom. For that reason, it's in criminals' best interests to be honest—at least in honoring their promise to decrypt victims' devices after a ransom is received. But as online extortion became an increasingly viable and popular form of online crime in 2014 and 2015, more people began to develop and distribute ransomware programs, and not all of them were the "trustworthy" kind of criminals who bothered to actually reverse the encryption on victims' devices.[21] That was bad news, of course, for the victims who paid up only to find that they were still stuck without their data, but it was also bad news for the other criminals—the ones like Bogachev who mostly did follow through on decrypting victims' data when paid. As word spread that paying ransoms did not always yield the desired results, users' already shaky trust in the criminals behind ransomware schemes weakened further. Victims became less likely to pay up since they had no way of knowing whether they were dealing with a "trustworthy" criminal—that is, someone who would actually decrypt their hard drives when they paid the ransom—or an "untrustworthy" crook who would simply take the money and disappear without bothering to provide a decryption key.

Despite this destabilization of the ransomware markets by an influx of "untrustworthy criminals," ransomware operations continued to thrive even in the wake of the GOZ and Cryptolocker takedown. In 2014, just as Operation Tovar was being completed, a new strain of ransomware, dubbed CryptoWall, appeared and went on to claim roughly $18 million in ransoms, according to FBI estimates. (By comparison, Cryptolocker, over the course of its operation, was believed to have netted at least $3 million). In the fall of 2014, a pair of Cryptolocker copycats, dubbed Cryptolocker 2.0 and Cryptolocker.F, were detected on computers in Australia and soon spread to the rest of the world. These new classes of ransomware were sufficiently different from Cryptolocker in their delivery mechanisms and encryption schemes that many analysts believed Cryptolocker 2.0 and Cryptolocker.F were designed by different people from the ones launched the original Cryptolocker. But whether or not Bogachev and his collaborators actually wrote these new pieces of malware, their influence and legacy in shaping the format and economic model of online crime were clear in the new strains named in tribute to their program. In 2015, the year after the takedown, the FBI reported 2,453 ransomware incidents, with losses totaling over $1.6 million, but it's likely this is a very incomplete tally since individuals and organizations are under no obligation to report ransomware incidents to law enforcement.

Estimates of ransom payments do not always accurately represent the losses incurred by ransomware, and not just because so many of these payments go unreported. As ransomware continued to evolve, it was adopted by new types of attackers and used for purposes beyond mere financial gain. In May 2017, a massive ransomware attack dubbed WannaCry shut down some 200,000 computer systems in hospitals, banks, governments, and companies worldwide, from Russia's Interior Ministry to the United Kingdom's National Health Service to police departments in India. The locked computers displayed messages demanding ransom payments, but by some estimates the attackers made no more than around $50,000 from those demands since many of the affected organizations chose to look for technical fixes rather than pay for each individual infected device.[22] However, the damage the attack caused, both to the affected organizations as well as to their customers, patients, and citizens, was still substantial. Months later, evidence emerged that WannaCry had originated from North Korea, and the United States itself publicly accused the North Korean government of launching the attack.[23] This attribution to a national government rather than a criminal operation cast uncertainty on whether WannaCry had ever been intended primarily as a means for financial profit. North Korea's involvement suggested the attack might instead have been meant more as an attempt to wreak havoc on the country's many enemies with any financial gains serving merely as an added bonus. Ransomware appeared to have transcended its roots as a tool for financially motivated crime and developed into a more general attack model that cost its victims no less even as it brought in smaller sums for its perpetrators.

Learning from ZeuS

GOZ and Cryptolocker taught criminals two very important lessons about how to make money from cybercrime: use lots of confounding proxies and infrastructural intermediaries to throw law enforcement off your trail when infiltrating computers—but extort money by relying on as few financial intermediaries as possible so that law enforcement has minimal opportunities to interrupt the monetization process. For Gonzalez and his conspirators, the infiltration of the TJX servers was relatively quick and easy—but the monetization of that stolen data was slow and convoluted, requiring a number of middlemen and cashers and correspondingly more people for the police to track. Bogachev flipped that process, building up the elaborate GOZ infrastructure to compromise and communicate with machines in a convoluted manner that routed command-and-control instructions through a network of infected machines, but then keeping the financial transactions as fast and straightforward as possible.

Extracting profits directly from victims and their bank accounts not only eliminated criminal financial intermediaries like Yastremskiy who sold data on the black market, it also eliminated many legitimate intermediaries, especially the payment card networks. Part of what makes ransomware so effective—and so difficult to combat—is that individual users and organizations bear the costs directly. The victims of GOZ and Cryptolocker could not turn to their credit card companies or banks to reimburse them for fraudulent charges, and they could not file class action lawsuits against the retailers who had allowed their data to be stolen. The only financial intermediaries regulators and law enforcement could turn to in this space were the cryptocurrency exchanges, which converted Bitcoins and other virtual currencies into non-virtual currencies such as dollars or rubles. These exchanges provided a rare opportunity for defenders to interrupt the monetization of ransomware incidents, assuming that the criminals would, eventually, want to convert their cryptocurrency profits into local currency (a reasonable assumption, especially during the Cryptolocker infections, since Bitcoins were certainly not universally accepted). But cryptocurrency exchanges existed all over the world and U.S. regulations requiring them to obtain identification from customers and keep detailed records had little impact on the foreign exchanges where Bogachev and his conspirators could cash in their profits.

In the absence of centralized financial intermediaries who could be held responsible or forced to bear the costs of ransomware thefts, the financial burden for these incidents fell completely on the individuals and organizations who were targeted. There was a certain justice in that—those victims were the ones who had let their devices become infected and failed to keep adequate backups of their data, and, in the case of Cryptolocker, made the decision to pay for a decryption key.

But in other ways this absence of a powerful intermediary class was detrimental to everyone because it meant there were no well-resourced, centralized companies or institutions (besides the FBI) with any incentive to try to drive down the costs or to invest in better technologies to strengthen security. Ransomware forces individual victims not only to shoulder the costs of a security breach entirely on their own, but also to face the knowledge that if they do give in to a ransom demand they are directly contributing to criminals' profits and thereby encouraging more criminals to undertake similar operations. Choosing whether or not to acquiesce to extortion by ransomware is not just a decision about how much victims trust their adversary to decrypt their data, or how much their data is worth to them. It's also a decision about the extent to which they are comfortable perpetuating ransomware as a profitable enterprise for criminals.

In the years following Operation Tovar, law enforcement organizations struggled to come to grips with the continued growth of ransomware and how much power lay in the hands of individual victims compared to how little control law enforcement officers had over emerging Cryptolocker-like online extortion schemes. This realization led to sometimes perplexing and often conflicting advice for victims as law enforcement organizations wrestled with the limits of their own power. "To be honest, we often advise people just to pay the ransom," FBI agent Joseph Bonavolonta said in a talk in October 2015, stirring controversy with his indirect recommendation to give in to criminals' demands and implicit admission that there was little the FBI could do to help victims in such cases.[24] The FBI later backpedaled on Bonavolonta's remarks, insisting that their official guidance was for victims *not* to pay ransoms, but this guidance was undercut somewhat by numerous examples of police departments across the country acceding to ransomware demands.[25] Faced with the conundrum of not wanting to encourage people to hand over their money to criminal operations but also knowing that that was likely their best shot at recovering their lost data, the FBI and other law enforcement agencies appeared to be conflicted about what they should tell victims to do—and what they should do themselves.

At the heart of this challenge is a deeper question over what the role of law enforcement entities and policymakers should be in a criminal environment based on decentralized infrastructure and extortion. The traditional roles for policymakers and law enforcement officers in this domain— targeting financial intermediaries with regulations and thorough criminal investigations—are far less effective when dealing with cryptocurrencies, which cannot be as easily controlled or monitored as they enter and leave the country. Accordingly, the FBI and its collaborators in Operation Tovar instead targeted the infrastructural intermediaries that composed the GOZ bot, going after the bot's technical architecture, the DGA, the potential command-and-control domains, even the individual compromised computers that had been infected by GOZ. This was moderately effective in taking down Bogachev's operation, at least temporarily, but it is unclear how scalable or sustainable such an approach could be for dealing with ransomware or distributed bots in general. Law enforcement cannot target infrastructure intermediaries the same way they do financial intermediaries, because the so-called "infrastructural intermediaries" are mostly just everyday computer users and their devices rather than powerful banks or payment networks with lots of resources to devote to fraud prevention.

Internet service providers—many of whom were involved in Operation Tovar—have the potential to be a more centralized and useful set of intermediaries than individual users for controlling and restricting bot traffic. ISPs have considerable insight into network traffic patterns and can therefore identify bots and block malicious traffic fairly effectively. But they do not stand to lose money or be held liable for the spread of malware like GOZ or Cryptolocker, so they have little incentive to take action against these threats. In fact, ISPs may fear losing customers (and money) if they *do* block malicious traffic or cut off Internet access to infected machines because their customers who own and operate those devices may be frustrated with the service interruption regardless of whether it's done to force them to remove malware from their computers. Those customers, of course, are the people who truly stand to lose from ransomware—the costs of such incidents falls squarely on their shoulders—yet, individually, there is a limited amount they can do to stem its spread beyond practicing basic computer hygiene and creating regular backups of their data. Moreover, they are unlikely to have much incentive to do even that until their devices are infected and they find themselves personally paying the price for operating unprotected computers. That is what makes ransomware such a difficult type of crime to protect against: large, powerful, centralized intermediaries bear very little liability for it and therefore have almost no reason to try to stop it, while individual, decentralized end users shoulder all the costs but have little power to fight it.

The sole power those users have—besides backing up their files and not clicking on suspicious email links or attachments or online ads—is to refuse to pay the demanded ransoms. That suggests one way in which law enforcement and policymakers could, potentially, make a difference in this fight: by more clearly and urgently advising users not to give in to these demands, or by taking stringent measures to make it more difficult to purchase Bitcoins, more financially onerous to make ransom payments, or even outright illegal to pay ransoms. Yet government officials, faced with a threat that is largely impervious to traditional policing tactics, seem to have drawn the opposite lesson—advising victims to pay ransoms, or otherwise implying that they may have no other choice. But Bogachev's wildly lucrative criminal enterprise, and the ensuing wave of similar crimes, suggests a set of very different lessons. It highlights the importance of policymakers concentrating financial liability for these security incidents on a strong, centralized set of intermediaries, like ISPs, who are well poised to defend against them, so as to give them an incentive to do so. Beyond that, the role of policymakers is in pressuring people by all means possible not to pay these ransoms and thereby to drive the criminals out of business. While the costs are so widely distributed, it is hard to imagine anyone outside of government stakeholders having a strong incentive to tackle ransomware at their own expense.

The evolution of financially motivated cybercrimes, from payment card fraud to identity theft to ransomware, has been guided in large part by criminals' preferences for business models that do not pit them against powerful, centralized intermediaries who can unilaterally monitor or cut off their profits. Payment card fraud of the sort perpetrated by Gonzalez and his co-conspirators took advantage of the complicated web of intermediaries involved in the payment card industry and their ongoing disputes about how best to protect against fraud and who should bear the costs of it. But despite those disputes, the banks, retailers, and payment networks who serve as the primary lines of defense for incidents such as the TJX breach are often well-resourced and able to cut down on some, if not all, of criminals' profits. Furthermore, payment card fraud often creates opportunities for law enforcement to monitor sales of stolen credit card numbers and trace the delivery of those profits back to the perpetrators, as they did with Yastremskiy, Gonzalez, and Bogachev. These powerful, centralized defenders and the necessity of going through them for the essential monetization stages of payment card fraud incidents made these schemes vulnerable to both interruption and prosecution. Identity fraud schemes of the sort that could be perpetrated using the SCDOR stolen data mitigated, but did not entirely overcome, these hurdles from the criminals' perspective. Filing fraudulent IRS returns, for instance, eliminated the need for thieves to use stolen data quickly, before it expired, and also removed the incentives of payment networks and retailers to intervene. But, at the same time, this model also introduced new potential defenders, such as the IRS or medical insurers, and perhaps more importantly, it still relied on the sale of stolen data through centralized online black market forums that could be monitored and shut down. Ransomware schemes like Cryptolocker took criminals even further from the original payment card fraud model by removing the need to exfiltrate data from targeted computers, much less sell it through any online forum. In doing so, perpetrators of ransomware eliminated several key bottleneck stages that defenders might try to interrupt. By storing the encrypted data directly on victims' own computers and selling it directly back to them for virtual currency, criminals like Bogachev were largely able to escape facing powerful third parties with strong incentives to intervene, as well as avoid the sorts of stolen data marketplaces most susceptible to law enforcement observation. Even so, the FBI ultimately identified Bogachev in part through the very same mechanism that led to Gonzalez's downfall: his money mules. Those intermediaries were not essential for spreading or profiting from ransomware, but Bogachev had used GOZ to undertake some other, older forms of financial cybercrime prior to unleashing Cryptolocker, and it was those earlier models that led the FBI to him. Actually, it led the FBI only as close to him as they could get, which, as it turned out, was not very close at all—so long as Bogachev was happy to remain on the Black Sea and Russia was happy to have him. Without Russia's cooperation, the United States could make some progress toward curtailing Bogachev's profits—hunting down his money mules, disrupting his bot, seizing his servers—but could do very little to stop the man himself.

II Lessons from Cyberespionage

5 Certificates Gone Rogue: The DigiNotar Compromise and the Internet's Fragile Trust Infrastructure

The first outward sign that something was wrong came on Saturday, August 27, 2011, and seemed fairly innocuous: a user in Iran couldn't check his Google Mail account. Strangely, when he connected to a Virtual Private Network that disguised his location, the problem disappeared. Whatever was going on, it seemed only to affect computers in Iran. Concerned that the problem might be tied to the Iranian government or his local Internet service provider, the user posted a question about the issue to the Gmail Help Forum under the username alibo. Two days later, Google responded with a public statement about the incident, attributing it to security problems at a Dutch company, DigiNotar. Five days after that, the Dutch government seized control of DigiNotar. On September 20, 2011, less than a month after alibo's post, DigiNotar was declared bankrupt, and the company was liquidated shortly thereafter.

In just over a month, the public disclosure of a cybersecurity incident had not only doomed a well-respected technology company, it had also spurred the Dutch government to take the unprecedented step of taking over that company's operations. Compared to the typical consequences victims face in the aftermath of suffering high-profile security breaches—bad publicity, public apologies, lawsuits—these were pretty extreme penalties. But the DigiNotar compromise was not like other security incidents. For one thing, it was much harder to understand for most Internet users because it did not involve a company that people trusted to keep their data safe failing to protect that information. Rather, it involved a company that Internet users trusted to tell them whom they could trust online failing to do its job, and, in doing so, revealing the fragility of the largely hidden infrastructure that enables computers to make decisions about which websites to load or which software updates to run.

DigiNotar was a certificate authority (CA), meaning it issued digital certificates[a] to its customers, who included many organizations and website owners. These certificates allow web browsers to verify they are loading the correct websites that are actually operated by the owner of a given domain name, and enable encrypted communication with those sites. Digital certificates also help operating systems verify that software updates have really been issued by the companies they claim to come from and are not just malware masquerading as important updates. DigiNotar was well regarded—the Dutch government obtained many of its certificates from them—and that made all the difference in an industry founded entirely on the question of who could be trusted to tell other people and their devices whom to trust. DigiNotar was a "root CA" (root certificate authority) for all of the major browsers and operating systems, which meant that pretty much every popular web browser and operating system trusted all of the certificates issued by DigiNotar by default. Getting on those root lists, or purchasing a certificate from a company that was on those lists, was a key part of being able to participate in the online trust ecosystem.

Anyone can issue certificates, but those certificates are of little value unless web browsers are willing to recognize them as meaningful and valid by adding their issuer to the root list of trusted CAs. So browser and operating system manufacturers screen CAs to decide whose certificates to trust, and CAs, in turn, screen website operators and organizations to decide who is worthy of their seal of approval.

As the central trust brokers of the Internet, CAs tend to take security very seriously. If someone can compromise a root CA's systems and start issuing rogue certificates signed by that CA—as happened in the DigiNotar case—then all of those rogue certificates will automatically be honored

a. Certificate authorities provide website operators with the tools for encrypting communications with their users and confirming to those users, through their browsers, that they are actually communicating with the website associated with the URL displayed in the browser, not some other imposter website. In some cases, websites also ask CAs to vouch that the entity operating the website is who they say they are, for instance, that bankofamerica.com is actually operated by the business Bank of America and not just whoever purchased that domain name. Not all website operators have their identity verified by a CA through a process called "extended validation," but many websites with a high risk of impersonation or attempted fraud, such as banks, choose to pay for the additional service.

as legitimate by browser and software vendors and all of their customers because they carry a trusted CA's signature. In the wrong hands, that signature is a powerful and dangerous tool because it affords criminals the opportunity to co-opt the trust of everyone who puts their faith in their browser or operating system to tell them what websites they should load or what software they should download. Accordingly, certificate-issuing systems at reputable CAs are typically very heavily guarded.

DigiNotar was no exception. The company kept its certificate-issuing computers in rooms that could only be entered after completing biometric scans, its signing keys were stored on physical key cards locked in vaults, and the computer networks were segmented according to how sensitive the functions each part performed were, with no fewer than 157 distinct firewall rules monitoring and restricting traffic between each zone, as well as an intrusion prevention system monitoring incoming Internet traffic. And yet, all that security proved little help in the face of a determined adversary who has never been definitively identified, but does not appear to have been interested in financial profits. The intruder chose instead to spy on the Google accounts of Iranian users, leading many people to conclude that the Iranian government was, in some fashion, behind the incident. That the incident was driven by espionage rather than financial greed made it more difficult to detect, as well as easier for DigiNotar to try to conceal, since the early indications that a security breach has occurred often come in the form of financial clues—fraudulent charges, newly opened accounts, surprise wire transfers, ransom demands. Part of what made the DigiNotar compromise both scary and effective was how few clues the perpetrators left behind to indicate that anything out of the ordinary was happening. That alibo noticed that something serious was awry and was savvy enough to understand it as a problem with the website certificates was nothing short of astonishing.

The DigiNotar incident laid bare the profound interdependence and equally profound public misunderstanding of the Internet's trust infrastructure—that security flaws at a small company in the Netherlands could lead to the compromise of hundreds of thousands of Iranian email accounts came as a shock to many Internet users unfamiliar with digital certificates and how they work. But even after the incident made international headlines, the DigiNotar incident did little to mitigate people's ignorance of certificate authorities and digital certificates. Instead, the significance of this news was ultimately obscured by people's confusion over how this largely invisible infrastructure operates and their inability to understand how it ties into their daily online experience. Outside the small communities of people who worked in browser and CA security, the DigiNotar compromise was significantly underappreciated and misunderstood—precisely because those same small communities had for years so effectively shielded users from the complicated technical underpinnings of how browsers decide which websites to trust.

For the web browser and CA industries, DigiNotar was a warning sign of how much they stood to lose and how vulnerable their industries were. The incident would be referenced in their security discussions and decision-making for years to come and serve as a constant reminder to these firms that their security failures could have serious consequences for people all over the world. Just as the TJX breach stirred long-lasting debates over how responsibility for fraud should be balanced between retailers, banks, and payment networks, the DigiNotar compromise raised crucial issues about the interplay of different companies, especially certificate authorities and web browsers, when it comes to security. In the wake of the DigiNotar incident, many firms found themselves revisiting the key question: how much responsibility does each of those groups have to protect users from deceptive sites and software and to what extent can they—and should they—trust each other?

Through the Firewalls and Past the Sluice Doors

The breach of DigiNotar's security was not noticed publicly until August 2011, but leading up to that moment were months of careful planning and deliberate probing by a perpetrator who gradually wended his way through many, many layers of elaborate security controls. The intruder's first access to the company's network came on June 17, 2011, investigators found, when two web servers on "the outskirts" of DigiNotar's network (that is, the least protected segment, or external demilitarized zone [DMZ], which connected to the outside Internet) were compromised. The two servers were, at the time, running an outdated and vulnerable version of the web content management system DotNetNuke, which enabled the compromise. An Intrusion Prevention System (IPS) monitored traffic that came through the DigiNotar router responsible for Internet connectivity, but it failed to block the initial intrusion. This failure was perhaps due in part to DigiNotar's deciding to run the IPS in its default configuration and position it in front of the company's firewalls where it registered a large number of false positives when perfectly harmless online traffic was flagged as being a possible intrusion.

Once inside the external demilitarized zone portion of DigiNotar's network, however, there were still significant barriers to producing rogue certificates. Firewalls delineated several separate zones of the network, configured such that the external DMZ could only send traffic to an internal DMZ segment of the network. The two DMZ zones, together, were intended to prevent direct connections between the Internet and the internal DigiNotar network used to generate certificates. Neither DMZ could initiate connections to secure-net, where the certificate issuing systems resided. Instead, a secure-net service regularly collected the certificate requests that were sent by customers via the company's website and stored on a server in the internal DMZ. Each request then had to be vetted and approved by two people before being processed by DigiNotar's main production servers, which were located on secure-net and kept in a room protected by numerous physical security measures. A report commissioned by the Dutch government on the incident describes the security measures protecting the room where the DigiNotar certificate production servers were kept:

> This room could be entered only if authorized personnel used a biometric hand recognition device and entered the correct PIN code. This inner room was protected by an outer room connected by a set of doors that opened dependent on each other creating a sluice. These sluice doors had to be separately opened with an electronic door card that was operated using a separate system than for any other door. To gain access to the outer room from a publicly accessible zone, another electronic door had to be opened with an electronic card.[1]

This was not a company that took issues of security—whether virtual or physical—lightly.

Following his initial compromise of the web servers in the external DMZ, the intruder used these servers as "stepping stones" beginning on June 29 to tunnel traffic between that zone of the network and the internal Office-net zone. On July 2, connections from the CA servers in the secure-net segment of the network were also initiated to the compromised servers in the external DMZ. That traffic was then tunneled back to the intruder's IP addresses from the outward-facing external DMZ portion of the network.

The intruder appeared to have bypassed DigiNotar's security zone firewalls by taking advantage of their numerous exceptions; investigators later identified 156 rules in the firewalls detailing which interconnections were allowed and disallowed between zones. The intruder set up a remote desktop connection using port 3389, which was then tunneled through port 443, generally used for HTTPS, so that the traffic could get past the firewall.

Having bypassed the zoning firewalls and accessed the secure-net servers, the intruder still could not issue a certificate from a DigiNotar CA server without activating the corresponding private key in the hardware security module (netHSM) using a physical smartcard. The activation process required an authorized employee to insert a smartcard into the netHSM, which was stored in the same highly secured room as the CA servers, and then enter a PIN code.

However, evidence collected after the incident suggested that some of those smartcards may have been permanently left in the netHSM to allow for automatic generation of Certificate Revocation Lists (CRLs), the lists of serial numbers of certificates that are no longer trusted. Since issuing a CRL also required that the appropriate private key be activated on the netHSM, the private keys of those CA servers that generated CRLs automatically were probably always activated—and the key cards therefore left permanently inserted in them—otherwise the servers would be unable to perform that function. If, as the DigiNotar investigators hypothesized, this was the case then any attempts to issue rogue certificates on those servers would have been successful, even without physical access to the smartcards, because those smartcards would have been left in the netHSM to allow for automatic generation of CRLs.

DigiNotar had many lines of defense in place to prevent intruders from being able to issue rogue certificates: an IPS meant to keep them off the company's network entirely; a set of firewalls intended to further restrict access to the CA servers; a four-eye principle that required certificate requests to be approved by two people before being processed; and physical key cards that had to be activated from within a room protected by many other forms of security. The capabilities that the perpetrator exploited—connecting to an outward-facing web server, compromising the out-of-date DotNetNuke software to connect to other servers, navigating the maze of firewalls to find exceptions that would allow tunneling between the different network zones over specific ports, and using the always activated private keys intended to allow automatic generation of CRLs—seem to stem in large part from a set of overly complex and arcane security measures, rather than too few defensive efforts or negligence.

How the Rogue Certificates Were Used—and Stopped

Having made it past the many layers of DigiNotar security, the intruder was still a long way from being able to access the email accounts of Iranians like alibo. Since the perpetrator has never been apprehended, his motivation for infiltrating DigiNotar and issuing hundreds of certificates remains somewhat unclear, as does the extent to which he was successful in achieving his ultimate aims. The only known significant consequence of the breach, beyond the damage done to DigiNotar, was a man-in-the-middle (MITM) attack that redirected visitors, like alibo, who were trying to access Google websites. The redirection affected users from 298,140 unique IP addresses, 95 percent of which originated from Iran. While any Google service could have been the focus of this redirection, and no specifics about what the users were trying to do or what happened on the websites they were redirected to can be gleaned from the rogue certificate logs, the report commissioned by the Dutch government speculates as to the possible purposes of this attack:

> Most likely the confidentiality of Gmail accounts was compromised and their credentials, the login cookie and the contents of their e-mails could have been intercepted. Using the credentials or the login cookie, an attacker may be able to log in directly to the Gmail mailbox of the victim and read their stored e-mails. Additionally, the MITM attacker may have been able to log into all other services that Google offers to users, such as stored location information from Latitude or documents in GoogleDocs. Once an attacker is able to receive his targets' e-mails, he is also able to reset passwords of others services such as Facebook and Twitter using the lost password functionality.[2]

The security firm Fox-IT investigated the incident for a year following its disclosure. Hans Hoogstraaten, who led the Fox-IT team and was the primary author on the investigation report, said he was astonished as he came to understand the potential impact of the incident had in Iran. "In those days (and today still?) people got killed for hav[ing] a different opinion," Hoogstraaten said in an email recalling his reactions. "The hackers (presumably the state) had access to over 300,000 Gmail accounts. The realization that the ... security of a small company in Holland played a part in the killing or torture of people really shocked me." Hoogstraaten also pointed out that media coverage of the incident was largely focused on the consequences of the compromise for the Dutch government, which had to revoke several of its certificates, even though, to Hoogstraaten's mind, "they [the Dutch government] had suffered only some 'inconvenience' compared with the people of Iran."

But for the media, as well as for Hoogstraaten's investigative team, there was little concrete evidence of what—if anything—had actually happened to the people in Iran who were tricked by the rogue certificates. Clearly, there is some reason to believe that the attacker's objective may have been to gather information about the email, location, and other online activity of Iranians, but there is very little indication of what the perpetrator intended to do with that information. In fact, the only clue left by the intruder—a message saved in a text file left behind on a compromised DigiNotar server—suggests that, for him at least, the compromise was intended primarily to demonstrate his skills rather than to drive any specific malicious mission. The perpetrator boasts in the message:

> I know you are shocked of my skills, how i got access to your network to your internal network from outside
>
> how I got full control on your domain controller how I got logged in into this computer ...
>
> How i bypassed your expensive firewall, firewalls, NetHSM, unbreakable hardware keys
>
> How I did all xUDA programming without 1 line of resource, got this idea, owned your network accesses your domain controlled, got all your passwords, signed my certificates and received them shortly
>
> THERE IS NO ANY HARDWARE OR SOFTWARE IN THIS WORLD EXISTS WHICH COULD STOP MY HEAVY ATTACKS MY BRAIN OR MY SKILLS OR MY WILL OR MY EXPERTISE
>
> That's all ok! EVerything I do is out of imagination of people in world
>
> I know you'll see this message when it is too late, sorry for that[3]

The tone of the message is at odds with the subtlety and discretion of the compromise itself, designed to evade detection or attention for as long as possible. The real threat of a CA compromise is that, if successful, a perpetrator can use rogue certificates to operate under the radar and evade many online security mechanisms for an extended period of time. This is perfectly in keeping with the aims of espionage efforts, but less in keeping with the character of an arrogant, attention-seeking criminal who wants someone to notice his skill and appreciate his genius. And while the intruder was ultimately right, and his message was not found until it was already "too late" for DigiNotar, that outcome was not nearly so inevitable as he assumed. In fact, the events that followed the perpetrator's elaborate intrusion into the DigiNotar network and successful production of rogue certificates indicate there were early warning signs that DigiNotar failed to fully appreciate. The company would not find the intruder's message until it was, decidedly, too late to help them or the Iranian users affected by the compromise. But that was in large part due to their ignoring or overlooking several important clues—and DigiNotar was not alone in missing opportunities to detect or interrupt the scheme. DigiNotar, like TJX and the SCDOR, operated in the context of a large and complicated ecosystem of stakeholders, each of whom could have played a stronger defensive role in catching and preventing the use of rogue certificates.

To Catch a Rogue Certificate

Much of DigiNotar's security was focused on stopping anyone from being able to control its certificate production servers and issue rogue certificates, but the company did employ one security mechanism to check for the creation of rogue certificates after-the-fact. DigiNotar ran regular, automated tests to confirm that it had records of issuing every certificate listed in its database of serial numbers—it was this test that first detected the existence of some rogue certificates in mid-July 2011 and led to their revocation. But while the testing detected several rogue certificate serial numbers for which there were no associated administrative records, it failed to find and revoke many others, probably because the intruder appears to have tampered with the database of serial numbers that the test verified. The incident investigation recovered versions of the serial_no.dbh database from the DigiNotar servers and found they contained additional, unknown serial numbers—several of which corresponded to rogue certificates that were therefore not detected by the automated test.

Using rogue certificates to spy on Iranians—assuming that was, indeed, the end goal—required going through other intermediaries besides DigiNotar.

Digital certificates bind a public encryption key to a particular entity using the digital signature of a trusted third party, such as DigiNotar. These signed certificates may be used for a variety of different purposes, to validate anything from a website to a software package to an individual. Rogue certificates can allow for impersonation of any of these entities, bypassing DigiNotar's vetting and approval process. So malicious websites can masquerade as google.com, malicious individuals can take on the identities of other people, malware can be attributed to legitimate software companies— all with the (unwitting) endorsement of DigiNotar, in the form of its digital signature. That signature ensured, for instance, that many web browsers, operating systems, and document readers—as well as many Dutch government services—would automatically trust the identity of anything bearing a DigiNotar certificate. In other words, the value of the rogue certificates—and their capability to cause damage—derived not from the certificates themselves but rather from the trust placed in them by numerous outside parties. A DigiNotar certificate was valuable to a website owner, for instance, because all of the major web browsers would trust and load any website that had been issued a DigiNotar certificate.

The operating systems and browsers and other applications that rely on certificates present another opportunity for identifying rogue certificates, particularly if those stakeholders have their own means of verifying certificate validity, independent of DigiNotar, as Google Chrome did. Since Google operates both a browser and a number of online services, its browser knows exactly what certificates the company holds for the domain google.com. At the time of the DigiNotar compromise, these certificates were "pinned" in the Chrome browser, meaning that no other certificates for the google.com domain were accepted by Chrome, regardless of whether they were signed by trusted root CAs like DigiNotar. This certificate pinning enabled Chrome to warn users about malicious websites that used the rogue google.com certificate, and subsequently prevent them from accessing those sites. These warnings were what first tipped off alibo—and Google itself—to the existence of the rogue google.com certificate, leading ultimately to DigiNotar's public acknowledgment of the breach, the subsequent investigation, and the discovery of many other previously undetected fraudulent certificates.

At the time of the DigiNotar compromise, certificate pinning was fairly limited. Since Google runs both Chrome and Gmail, it could tell its browser exactly which certificates should be trusted when attempting to access its email service—but it didn't have that information for every website. Since the DigiNotar incident, however, both CAs and browsers have made significant changes to their security. Certificate pinning has become more common and is now available not just to companies who manufacture their own browsers, but to any certificate owner that wants to publish the list of certificates it holds and ensure that no other certificates for its domains will be accepted by browsers. This approach has been adopted by some larger, frequently targeted companies, but it is still not widespread, largely because "it is relatively easy to shoot yourself in the foot with it," according to Rick Andrews, Senior Technical Director for Website Security at Symantec, one of the largest CAs in the world.[4] If a website pins a set of certificates, for instance, then browsers will reject any other certificates associated with that site for the duration of the pinning, so it becomes extremely difficult to start using a new certificate without advance notice.

A savvy user with a well-protected browser containing pinned certificates was ultimately responsible for catching the DigiNotar compromise, but certificate pinning was not the only line of defense beyond the CA itself. The intruder's attempts to conduct espionage on Iranian Google users relied on his being able to convince the users of Google services that they were checking their email (or searching for directions or watching videos) when, in fact, they were actually visiting a malicious site controlled by him. The DigiNotar certificate, trusted by all major browsers, would serve to persuade users that his fraudulent site was legitimately operated by Google—but first he had to get them to his site, otherwise the forged certificate was useless. This meant redirecting Iranian Internet traffic so that users who attempted to visit Google websites were sent instead to the malicious sites without their knowledge, using a man-in-the-middle attack that intercepted their queries before the actual Google sites could load. This process involved yet another group of stakeholders who had the potential to help prevent the perpetrator's success, even after he had completely penetrated DigiNotar's systems and successfully produced rogue certificates.

There are a few different ways to perpetrate a MITM attack that redirects users' online traffic. One is to intercept traffic at users' upstream provider by inspecting their packets and redirecting those intended for certain destinations. In this case, the service provider transmitting the Iranian users' packets would either have to be complicit in the attack or be compromised by the attacker. It is unlikely that this was the approach used by the DigiNotar intruder, however, since 5 percent of the IP addresses that were affected by the rogue google.com certificate originated outside of Iran. If the redirection had been done by (or through) Iranian service providers, these users would likely not have been affected.

If the perpetrators of the DigiNotar breach did not compromise Internet service providers to redirect traffic to their fraudulent websites, then they probably took advantage of the web's addressing directory, the Domain Name System, or DNS, which maintains records of which URLs map to which servers online.[b] These records are stored on high-level DNS servers that send them to other servers further down the DNS hierarchy. Every time a user tries to load a webpage, their computer queries one of these DNS servers to find the specific address where that webpage is stored. So, by altering the contents of these DNS records, the DigiNotar intruder could redirect people trying to get to google.com to any other site of the intruder's choosing simply by changing the addressing information stored in local DNS servers. This is almost certainly the approach taken in the DigiNotar-related redirection. According to subsequent analysis, the rogue certificate's use was extremely "bursty"—that is, at certain times the certificate's use would spike dramatically and then decline, over and over again. This suggested that the MITM attack was most likely carried out by DNS cache poisoning, or flooding low-level DNS servers with forged messages containing incorrect information for google.com and pretending they had been sent by a higher-level DNS server. This technique "poisons" the targeted record for some period of time, since the lower-level DNS server believes the information has come from a higher-level DNS server and updates it accordingly. This poisoning lasts until the responses expire and the DNS server makes another request to a higher-level server. The brief lifetime of these poisoning attacks would explain the erratic up-and-down volume of requests to validate the rogue google.com certificate over time. Redirecting traffic in this manner introduces a new set of defenders who can help protect against the successful exploitation of rogue SSL certificates: DNS operators. For instance, by implementing DNS Security Extensions (DNSSEC) to verify the senders

b. The DNS serves as a sort of address book for the Internet, containing records of which URLs map to which IP addresses and other information associated with those servers. Whenever a user visits a webpage by typing in a domain name, the browser fetches a DNS record associated with that domain that, in turn, tells it which IP address to connect to in order to load the desired webpage for the user.

of DNS records they receive, or disregarding records that are received in the absence of a particular query, DNS operators might reduce the ease with which someone could perpetrate a cache poisoning MITM attack.

Ultimately it was the web browsers, not the DNS operators, who were responsible for mitigating the consequences of the rogue DigiNotar certificates. In the wake of the DigiNotar compromise, the major web browsers removed DigiNotar from their list of trusted root CAs on the grounds that if someone had successfully issued one rogue DigiNotar certificate there might well be more—as indeed there were. As the ultimate arbiters of which CAs to trust, browsers wield significant power in dictating which certificates the general population of web users will accept by default. In the aftermath of the DigiNotar compromise, as it became clear that the much vaunted security procedures of even the most well respected CAs were vulnerable, browser manufacturers became increasingly willing to embrace this role, occasionally courting open conflict with CAs they deemed irresponsible or insecure.

Tensions over Trustworthiness: Browsers versus CAs

In the immediate aftermath of the discovery of the DigiNotar compromise, browser manufacturers were left scrambling to figure out how to deal with a set of active rogue certificates without greatly inconveniencing their users. In a blog post published on September 3, 2011, a member of the response team at Mozilla, Gervase Markham, described Mozilla's attempts to contact DigiNotar and their ultimate decision to remove DigiNotar from their list of trusted root CAs for Mozilla Firefox. "We decided to take this action based on the fact that we no longer had sufficient confidence in [DigiNotar's] trustworthiness," Markham wrote, citing DigiNotar's decision not to notify browsers when it first detected rogue certificates in July, as well as its inadequate logging practices and misleading press statements as factors that contributed to this decision. (Microsoft, Apple, and Google ultimately did the same for their browsers, Internet Explorer, Safari, and Chrome, as well as their operating systems.)

But removing a root CA was not an easy or immediate process for the browser vendors. "We actually needed to push out an update to Firefox because the CA information was hardcoded to the browser," Firefox security lead Richard Barnes said. Additionally, there were many legitimate websites (including some operated by the Dutch government) that still relied on DigiNotar certificates and would have been severely affected if browsers stopped accepting their certificates, so the browser vendors were forced to hold off on a blanket ban. Instead, Mozilla decided to block all DigiNotar certificates issued after July 1, 2011, but allowed users to decide whether or not they wanted to trust certificates issued by the company before that date. That decision gave users some flexibility—but also assumed they would have some understanding of what had happened to DigiNotar and how digital certificates worked in order to make up their minds about which ones they wanted to trust.

While the browsers focused on how to minimize the impact of the breach, other CAs were also alarmed by the incident. "DigiNotar was a real wakeup call for the entire industry," said Symantec's Rick Andrews.[5] It forced both the CA and the browser communities to revisit the question of what appropriate security guidelines and standards were for CAs. A year after the incident, on August 3, 2012, the Certificate Authority/Browser (CAB) Forum, a group of CAs and browser vendors that collaborate to produce security recommendations and information about best practices, adopted a new set of guidelines for how CAs should protect their networks. Andrews, who was involved in the discussions leading up to the development of these security requirements, said they were driven in large part by what had gone wrong in the DigiNotar case: "We were often talking about, 'Is this a mistake that DigiNotar made?' or 'Would this new text prevent a DigiNotar-type event from happening?'"[6]

The CAB Forum is intended to allow browsers and CAs to work together to protect Internet users, but, in fact, these two industries have very different goals and priorities that do not always align with one another's—or even, necessarily, with the security of their users. The business model of a CA is dependent on selling certificates to customers, so a CA always wants to sell as many as possible without alienating any of the major browsers. The major browsers, on the other hand, all compete with each other for users, so they want to give those users the best possible online experience— and are often wary of blocking people from visiting websites they're trying to reach in the name of certificate concerns those users are unlikely to understand. If one browser decides to take a strong stance on blocking sites with invalid or suspicious certificates, it's possible their customers will switch over to one of their competitors with lower security standards that allows users to view whatever they want. "There's a little bit of a race to the bottom within the browser community in terms of making stronger security decisions," explained Daniel Kahn Gillmor, a Senior Staff Technologist with the ACLU's Speech, Privacy, and Technology Project.[7] On top of that, it's not always clear where a CA's responsibility for security ends and a browser's responsibility begins. If a CA is responsible for vetting websites and a browser is responsible for vetting CAs, then when something like the DigiNotar breach occurs who is ultimately to blame—the CA whose systems were breached or the browsers who failed to recognize that one of the CAs they trusted had inadequate security protections in place? This is another variation of the same dilemma that TJX and Visa and Mastercard faced, and that the SCDOR and the IRS and Trustwave grappled with, minus the financial stakes and incentives: When several different organizations are highly interconnected and interdependent, whose fault is it when something goes wrong, and who gets to decide?

Both CAs and browsers have made significant changes to their security practices since DigiNotar. Certificate pinning—the practice responsible for revealing the compromise publicly—has become more common and is now available not just to companies who manufacture their own browsers, but also to any certificate holder that wants to publish the list of certificates it holds and ensure that no other certificates for its domains will be accepted by browsers. Another initiative, called Certificate Transparency, encourages CAs to publish publicly accessible logs listing every valid certificate they have issued, so domain owners can monitor whether any certificates have been issued for their domains without their knowledge. In the aftermath of DigiNotar's demise, when browsers were wary of trusting even the most reputable CAs to make security decisions, Certificate Transparency was heavily pushed on the CA community by browser manufacturers. In 2016, Google announced that it would no longer display the green address bar in Chrome signaling the presence of a valid certificate unless a website's extended validation certificates had also been logged according to the Certificate Transparency protocol.

This sort of back and forth between CAs and browsers is not uncommon, and the browsers often hold the upper hand in these negotiations since they ultimately decide which websites users can load easily and which subtle security signals—green bars, lock and shield icons[c]—are conveyed to those users. On the other hand, browsers are constrained by how little their users know about certificates and the possibility that those users will therefore blame their browser when a webpage doesn't load immediately.

On March 20, 2015, years after the collapse of DigiNotar, Google discovered another set of rogue certificates for Google domains. These certificates had been issued by an Egyptian company, MCS Holdings, which had, in turn, received its certificates from CNNIC, the CA operated by the China Internet Network Information Center, an agency in the Chinese government's Ministry of Industry and Information Technology. Soon afterwards, Mozilla and Google decided to distrust some CNNIC certificates due to concerns that they had been used by a CNNIC customer to conduct MITM attacks and intercept other users' online traffic in a manner similar to that of the DigiNotar intruder.[8] The following year, in August 2016, another Chinese CA, WoSign, was accused of issuing fake certificates for Github and Alibaba and backdating certificates to avoid meeting security requirements that went into effect for CAs at the beginning of 2016. Apple,[9] Mozilla,[10] and Google Chrome[11] subsequently revoked their trust in WoSign-issued certificates in October 2016.

Conflicts like these between American tech companies and Chinese CAs—especially the CNNIC CA operated by the Chinese government—are not just technical; they're also deeply political in nature. The decision to distrust certificates issued, even indirectly or (as CNNIC later claimed) accidentally, by the Chinese government is a fraught one for companies that have users and customers all over the world. Fundamentally, the question of whom a technology is designed to trust reflects a value-laden judgment about whom its designer trusts. Each CA gets to make its own decisions about whom to issue certificates to, and each browser or operating system vendor then makes decisions about which of those CAs to trust—and all of those decisions are influenced by where the people making them live and which government (or governments) they are accountable to. While there are hundreds of CAs operating all over the world, there are only a small

---

c. Many popular browsers use some combination of these signals in their browser bars to indicate to users when they are viewing websites with valid certificates, whether those certificates include additional extended validation verification of the website operators' identities, and when their communications with those websites are being encrypted.

number of popular web browsers, almost all of which are manufactured by U.S.-based companies. So these international conflicts over whom the international community of Internet users should trust can have complicated geopolitical dynamics, in addition to complicated technical dimensions.

Not every CA-browser conflict is international, however. One of the most dramatic disagreements in this space involved a U.S.-based CA rather than an overseas one. In March 2017, Google Chrome threatened to reduce the level of trust it accorded to certificates issued by CA giant Symantec, which issues more than 30 percent of the certificates used online.[12] Chrome engineer Ryan Sleevi explained the decision in a post accusing Symantec of granting "four parties access to their infrastructure in a way to cause certificate issuance" and failing to oversee those parties or respond appropriately when the problem was brought to their attention. Sleevi couched those shortcomings as a failure to uphold the broader "principles" that Google expects of its root CAs. He wrote:

> [R]oot certificate authorities are expected to perform a number of critical functions commensurate with the trust granted to them. This includes properly ensuring that domain control validation is performed for server certificates, to audit logs frequently for evidence of unauthorized issuance, and to protect their infrastructure in order to minimize the ability for the issuance of fraudulent certs.
>
> On the basis of the details publicly provided by Symantec, we do not believe that they have properly upheld these principles, and as such, have created significant risk for Google Chrome users.[13]

Symantec quickly fired back, issuing a statement of its own just days later in which it called Google's accusations "exaggerated and misleading," but the company ultimately caved and agreed to reissue and revalidate the certificates that Chrome had threatened to distrust.[14] That concession indicated just how dramatically power had shifted to the browsers in dictating the terms of certificate issuance and security. After all, Google deciding to distrust Symantec certificates would have caused major headaches for its users given how ubiquitous Symantec certificates are—users might well have decided to abandon the browser for others that would let them view the websites they were trying to visit more easily. On the other hand, of course, Chrome users not being able to reach those sites would have been a huge blow to Symantec's customers, and they might well also have lost business to other websites whose webpages would load for the hundreds of millions of Chrome users. Both companies potentially stood to lose customers if Google followed through on the threat, but Google seemed to feel—and Symantec ultimately appeared to agree—that users would be more likely to blame the websites than the browser for these inconveniences.

The question of who gets blamed in these disputes is complicated by the complexity of the certificate infrastructure, which often makes it difficult for the wider public to understand how their browsers use certificates to decide what websites do and don't load, as well as how to interpret the signals and warnings that their browsers provide. One way to try to overcome this complexity is to focus on the impacts to the user rather than the underlying technology: It's difficult to understand what happened to DigiNotar, but relatively easy to understand that a bunch of people in Iran had their email accounts compromised. Along these lines, as part of a 2015 study by researchers at Google and the University of Pennsylvania, Google altered its warning message to users about websites with suspicious certificates. Originally, Chrome was using a message that began "The site's security certificate is not trusted!" and went on to explain:

> You attempted to reach example.com, but the server presented a certificate issued by an entity that is not trusted by your computer's operating system. This may mean that the server has generated its own security credentials, which Chrome cannot rely on for identity information, or an attacker may be trying to intercept your communications. You should not proceed, especially if you have never seen this warning before for this site.

In the revised message, intended to improve user understanding of what was going on, the researchers showed people a message with the title "Your connection is not private," and the less technical explanation: "Attackers might be trying to steal your information from example.com (for example, passwords, messages, or credit cards)." But the changes in language had only a minimal impact, increasing the number of users who did not continue on to the site by just 1.2 percent.[15]

The challenges of trying to convey to users what's at stake when it comes to suspicious certificates or breaches like DigiNotar's highlight how difficult it is to sort out the different roles and responsibilities of the browsers and CAs when it comes to protecting users. This is especially true since security is neither industry's primary focus or aim: the main goal of CAs is to sell certificates, for browsers it's to attract users. In cases like the DigiNotar compromise, where rogue certificates are used to conduct espionage rather than theft or financial fraud, users have no choice but to look for protection in this web of Internet company intermediaries because the crimes themselves are largely invisible and financial intermediaries—banks, credit card companies, retailers—have no control or incentive to help. There are even fewer opportunities to protect users in the wake of an espionage-motivated breach, as compared to a financially motivated one, and those opportunities mostly lie enshrouded in the mysterious trust infrastructure of the Internet making it harder for anyone to know whom to blame—or whom to hold responsible.

"The CAs are in a position of centralized authority with basically no checks or balances on them," Gillmor said. "The CA ecosystem is hidden technology and this is something technologists tend to do in general—hide all the messy underpinnings. Sometimes hiding technical details from the users can be helpful, but sometimes it can obscure where the positions of power are."[16] Those positions of power are particularly messy when it comes to regulating the use of certificates online. The browser manufacturers want to protect their users—but their primary goal is to beat out the other, competing browsers and one way to do that is to make sure users can access the content they want as quickly and easily as possible, without encountering a lot of irritating, inscrutable warning messages. The CAs also, presumably, want to protect their customers by making sure they maintain their root trust status with the major browsers—but their primary goal is to sell as many certificates as possible, a goal slightly at odds with careful customer vetting, or refusing to provide certificates to less-than-trustworthy applicants. Meanwhile, the CAs and browsers are fundamentally dependent on each other—without browsers, certificates have little value, and without certificates, the browsers have no way of knowing whom to trust. It's a complicated setup largely devoid of any clearly defined expectations about who is ultimately responsible for the protection of online users. The browsers compete with each other and simultaneously try to coordinate their efforts to jointly vet CAs, while the CAs and browsers together negotiate the appropriate standards for issuing online certificates and subtly work to exercise their own power and influence—without assuming responsibility for anyone's security.

6 No Doubt to Hack You, Writed by UglyGorilla: China's PLA Unit 61398 and Economic Espionage

On February 8, 2010, twenty employees of U.S. Steel received an email from the company's Chief Executive Officer, John Surma. The subject line read "Meeting Invitation," and the agenda for the proposed meeting was also included as an attachment, in a file titled simply "agenda.zip." It was not until long after several of the recipients had opened the attachment and installed the contents on their computers that anyone realized the message had not, in fact, been sent by Surma, but instead by Sun Kailiang, an officer in China's People's Liberation Army (PLA) Unit 61398, the branch of the PLA responsible for conducting cyber operations and signals intelligence from a twelve-story building on Datong Road in the Pudong District of Shanghai.[1] In 2010, few civilians in the United States had heard of PLA Unit 61398, but U.S. Steel's IT staff noticed several suspicious emails on their systems—the "Meeting Invitation" was only one of roughly fifty phishing messages that Sun sent during February 2010 to U.S. Steel employees, ostensibly from the company's own high-level executives. Many of those emails featured subject lines like "U.S. Steel Industry Outlook" and included links or attachments that, like the agenda.zip file, installed malware on the recipients' computers when clicked.[2]

In 2010, U.S. Steel was deeply embroiled in international trade disputes with Chinese steel manufacturers. Chinese companies, U.S. Steel had alleged, were receiving unfair subsidies from the Chinese government and dumping billions of dollars of steel pipes into the U.S. market at prices below what those same products were being sold for within China, and much lower than what U.S. steel manufacturers could afford to match. On February 8, when Sun's first phishing emails arrived, the Department of Commerce was just two weeks away from issuing its preliminary determination in one of these trade disputes—a determination that would ultimately lead to the placement of significant duties on Chinese imports of certain types of steel pipes. So when Surma heard about the spate of phishing emails[a]—one of which was even sent directly to him—he mentioned it to his friend David Hickton, a former classmate at Penn State who had gone on to become the U.S. attorney for western Pennsylvania.[3] That conversation launched Hickton on an investigation into Chinese cyberespionage efforts that culminated some four years later, on May 19, 2014, when he filed an indictment charging five PLA Unit 61398 officers, including Sun, with breaking into the computers of American companies. The indictment alleged that the officers had stolen information from U.S. companies' computers that would give an advantage to Chinese companies when it came to business negotiations, setting prices, resolving trade disputes, and developing new technologies. Hickton was not the only one investigating Unit 61398 during this period—on February 19, 2013, more than a year before Hickton filed his indictment of the PLA officers, the security firm Mandiant released a seventy-five-page report titled "APT1: Exposing One of China's Cyber Espionage Units." This report described in detail a series of online espionage activities Mandiant had traced to Unit 61398 while investigating cybersecurity breaches all over the world. (The "APT" of the title refers to China's military being an "Advanced Persistent Threat" when it came to computer security breaches.)

By aggregating information about multiple incidents, Mandiant was able to conceal the identities of its clients, as well as the specific breaches they experienced, and offer an unusually comprehensive step-by-step deconstruction of an actual set of security incidents. This incident aggregation makes it difficult to pinpoint specific motivations driving the perpetrators, or the actual harm they inflicted. But taken together, the incidents investigated by Mandiant made a compelling case that the type of breach experienced by U.S. Steel was no anomaly, but rather part of a broader pattern of behavior on the part of the Chinese government to access sensitive commercial and economic information. These breaches were perpetrated in order "to steal data, including intellectual property, business contracts

a. Phishing emails are messages that purport to be from legitimate, or known, senders, but are instead sent by imposters seeking to elicit useful information from recipients (such as passwords) or to deliver malware to the recipient's computer by means of a malicious attachment or website linked to in the message.

or negotiations, policy papers or internal memoranda" that could be used, generally, to benefit the Chinese government and Chinese businesses, according to Mandiant's analysis.[4] The victims included 141 organizations that had been breached by PLA Unit 61398 since 2006, and the spoils of these intrusions included information related to product development, designs, and manuals, as well as manufacturing procedures, processes, and standards, along with business plans, legal documents, records detailing contract negotiation positions, mergers, and acquisitions, meeting minutes and agendas, staff emails, and user credentials. The targets—primarily U.S.-based organizations—spanned 20 different sectors, though many victims worked in information technology, satellites and telecommunications, aerospace engineering, and public administration.[5]

As with other intrusions motivated by espionage rather than direct financial profit—including the DigiNotar compromise—it's not clear how, specifically, the stolen data acquired by the PLA was used or what concrete harm, if any, its loss may have caused. Given the large number of targets and the variety of different industry sectors they span, this stolen information could have served a number of different functions—revealing anything from how proprietary products were developed to sensitive financial statements—so it is difficult to say precisely what advantage the perpetrators gained by stealing it, or how they may have used it to harm others.

The 2014 indictment filed by Hickton alleges economic espionage and theft of trade secrets—but despite lengthy descriptions in the indictment of significant breaches aimed at six different target companies, those specific allegations refer only to a single archive file stolen from one particular victim, Westinghouse Electric Company. Similarly, the only concrete example of harm included in the Mandiant report is an incident in which China negotiated a significant reduction in the price of a major commodity with a wholesale firm whose networks were compromised at the time. The report notes: "This may be coincidental; however, it would be surprising if [Unit 61398] could continue perpetrating such a broad mandate of cyber espionage and data theft if the results of the group's efforts were not finding their way into the hands of entities able to capitalize on them."[6] But, while the final stages of these breaches—the ones that occurred after the successful theft of information—are sometimes hard to pin down, the early stages, involving the actual compromise of computer systems are laid out clearly in Mandiant's analysis and Hickton's later indictment.

The PLA Intrusion Process

Despite the variety of targets, Mandiant found that the initial access steps took the same form in almost all of the incidents it investigated: phishing emails containing either a malicious attachment or hyperlink. To ensure recipients downloaded these attachments and followed these URLs, the perpetrators sent the emails from accounts created under the names of real employees at the company, like Surma at U.S. Steel. The PLA officers sending these messages also disguised the attachments with appropriate filenames (e.g., 2012ChinaUSAviationSymposium.zip, Employee-Benefitand-Over-head-Adjustment-Keys.zip, and North_Korean_launch.zip), and, in some cases, changed the attachment icons and names, hiding the actual file extensions from the recipient. When downloaded, these files (such as the agenda. zip attachment sent out to U.S. Steel employees) established backdoors in the victims' systems that initiated outbound connections to command and control (C2) servers operated by PLA officers.[b] The indictment explains the multiple different functions of these connections to C2 servers:

> After creating a backdoor, the malware typically attempted to contact other com-puters controlled by the co-conspirators by sending them a short message known as a "beacon." These beacons typically (1) notified the co-conspirators of the suc-cessful penetration of a victim's computer; (2) provided some information about the victim's computer useful for future intrusion activity; and (3) solicited addi-tional instructions from the co-conspirators.[7]

In its report, Mandiant dubbed these first two stages of PLA Unit 61398 intrusions: "initial compromise" and "establish foothold," corresponding to the initial installation of malware, transmitted via phishing emails, and the subsequent connection of the victims' computers to PLA-controlled C2 servers. Even within each of the seven individual stages of compromise that Mandiant identified, there were sometimes multiple steps. For instance, establishing a foothold in a targeted system could require more than just one malware installation. The easiest kind of backdoor malware to deliver via phishing messages was a "beachhead backdoor," which offered minimal functionality to the intruders. When downloaded, these beachhead back-door programs would load a webpage stored on one of the PLA's C2 servers and look for instructions contained in the HTML tags of that webpage that

b. Command and control, or C2, servers are computers used to remotely commu-nicate with, control, and issue instructions to compromised machines by intruders.

it would know to interpret as commands, rather than part of the website's actual content (because it involves communicating with C2 servers via web-pages, this type of malware is also referred to as a WEBC2 backdoor).[c] The simplicity of these WEBC2 backdoors made them extremely difficult for the victims to notice or flag as malware—all they were doing, after all, was retrieving publicly available webpages—but this simplicity also restricted the range of ways they could be used.

Constrained by the limited range of commands that could be input into a public webpage's HTML code, Unit 61398 officers could only use WEBC2 backdoors to perform very basic functions on the infected computers, such as opening a file, or putting an infected machine to sleep for a specified period of time.[8] In order to find and access the sensitive information they were after, the PLA often needed a wider set of capabilities, so they used the initial WEBC2 backdoor to download yet another, more full-featured backdoor on the infected machine. The real value of the WEBC2 backdoor, delivered via phishing email, was enabling the installation of this second backdoor, which could communicate with the C2 servers directly, rather than through HTML tags on websites. In order to disguise these direct com-munications and avoid any detection tools, the Unit 61398 intruders communicated with compromised servers over the common HTTP proto-col or other custom protocols designed to mimic legitimate applications (like Google Calendar and MSN Messenger), so that the malicious traffic was indistinguishable from the other web traffic going into and out of the targeted companies' network.[9]

These backdoors afforded the intruders a wide array of new capabilities to control and manipulate the compromised systems beyond what was possible with a basic WEBC2 backdoor. Indeed, once a standard backdoor had been installed and was directly communicating with a PLA C2 server, there was very little that the PLA could not do to control the infected machines. Man-diant's report lists sixteen things that Unit 61398 could do to infected com-puters following the successful installation of a standard backdoor ranging

---

c. HTML tags are a common form of formatting or labeling web content to indicate how it should be rendered (for instance, as bold or italic, or as a hyperlink). Typically placed between left- and right-facing angle characters (i.e., '<' and '>'), the text inside HTML tags is often not rendered on a webpage for a viewer to see, but it can still be parsed from the site's source code, as it was in these cases to issue instructions to the machines compromised by PLA Unit 61398.

from creating, modifying, deleting, and executing programs to uploading and downloading files, taking screenshots of the user's desktop, capturing the user's keystrokes and mouse movement, launching an interactive command shell, and harvesting passwords stored on the compromised machine.[10] Of these various capabilities, the ones most central to the PLA's operations were those related to harvesting user account credentials and downloading or viewing sensitive files and messages. There is little evidence to indicate that Unit 61398 took advantage of the more aggressive or destructive capabilities on Mandiant's list—shutting down computers, for instance, or deleting directories. Rather, their intrusions were marked by efforts to change as little as possible that would be visible to the computers' users so that they could remain unnoticed and undetected in the compromised systems for as long as possible. Having installed a full-featured backdoor and having made direct contact with the infected machines via C2 servers, the PLA's next steps focused largely on learning more about the systems they had compromised without alerting any of their victims to their presence.

The third Unit 61398 intrusion phase identified by Mandiant, after the initial compromise and foothold stages, was privilege escalation. This involved collecting server information and user credentials so that the intruders could access as much of the compromised network as possible instead of being limited to only the network segments and files accessible to the person who had fallen for their phishing message and installed their backdoor malware. For instance, after Sun Kailiang launched the successful phishing campaign against U.S. Steel employees and installed malware on their machines, another PLA Unit 61398 officer named in the 2014 indictment, Wang Dong (alias "UglyGorilla"), managed to use those initial footholds planted by Sun to steal hostnames and descriptions for more than 1,700 computers across the company.[11] That long list of server names and descriptions helped Wang identify the functions of the different computers at U.S. Steel (some of the compromised machines were used for emergency response, others for network monitoring and security, and still others controlled physical access to the company's buildings), which, in turn, helped him figure out what machines might be vulnerable, or useful, and how best to compromise them.[12]

Escalating access privileges within compromised networks beyond the initial backdoors also involved PLA officers stealing users' passwords and login credentials. This, again, was a tactic aimed at broadening their ability to search and explore the compromised company network beyond a single compromised user or machine. The keystroke logging capabilities of the PLA's malware meant they could easily capture the passwords and usernames of the individuals who fell for their phishing emails, but that only granted the intruders access to the limited number of email accounts or company files accessible to those particular individuals. Since the Unit 61398 phishing campaigns were, on the whole, fairly tailored to their individual recipients and sent out to only small groups of recipients to avoid or delay detection, they did not scale to the full employee population of large companies. Moreover, phishing intrusions are, by nature, effective only against the people who fall for them and download the attachments or click on the included links. So just as the second phase of the PLA intrusions focused on broadening the capabilities afforded by the initial, simple WEBC2 backdoor to manipulate the individual compromised devices, the third phase focused on broadening the user credentials and access capabilities across the company, beyond the individual users and devices that had fallen prey to phishing schemes in the earlier stages.

For instance, in another incident detailed in the 2014 indictment, a third PLA officer defendant, Wen Xinyu (alias "WinXYHappy"), stole usernames and passwords for more than 7,000 employees of Pennsylvania-based specialty metals company Allegheny Technologies Incorporated (ATI). The credential theft occurred on April 13, 2012, the day after ATI held a board meeting to discuss a joint venture in Shanghai with a Chinese state-owned company.[13] Most companies don't store user passwords in plaintext on their servers, instead choosing to "hash" user passwords and generate a number associated with the password according to some mathematical algorithm. When users then enter their passwords, each entry is hashed according to the same algorithm, and, if it matches the stored hash, the login is successful. So what the PLA Unit 61398 officers, such as Wen, were usually stealing during the privilege escalation stage of their intrusions were lists of these scrambled, or hashed, passwords. But even so, they often found ways to make use of the hashes, either by cracking the hashing algorithm so they were able to extract plaintext passwords from the hashes, or by logging into accounts directly by using the hashes themselves to authenticate (a technique known as "passing the hash").[14]

Following the privilege escalation phase, and having substantially broadened their ability to access different networks segments and accounts of the compromised computer system, PLA intruders progressed to "internal reconnaissance," the fourth intrusion stage identified by Mandiant. Internal reconnaissance entailed gathering as much information as possible about the contents and architecture of the penetrated system. This information was typically obtained by running automated scripts on the compromised system that would list such things as the network's accounts, processes, programs, network connections, configuration settings, and administrators in a text file generated for the intruders.[15] Having mapped out the victim's computer systems and acquired credentials to access every segment and server of the network, the Unit 61398 intruders then moved on to the fifth intrusion stage: lateral movement within the compromised system to find the information and files of greatest interest.

Lateral movement in pursuit of high-value information was followed by a sixth intrusion stage—one uniquely essential to espionage-motivated incidents, as opposed to those perpetrated in pursuit of financial gain or revenge: maintaining a long-term presence within the victim's network. According to Mandiant's investigations of companies targeted by PLA Unit 61398, the intruders aimed to establish multiple means of entry in the computer systems they targeted. This way, even if the victim discovered and mitigated the initial backdoor delivered via phishing email, the intruder still had other available means of access and exfiltration. Unit 61398 officers accomplished this by installing additional backdoor malware programs in different places on the compromised systems, and using stolen credentials to log in through the target organizations' own VPNs and web portals.[16] These additional access pathways enabled Unit 61398 officers to conduct espionage campaigns over months, or years. Across ninety-one of the different companies that Mandiant investigated and believed had been compromised by Unit 61398, the average period of compromise was 356 days, and the longest compromise lasted nearly five years.[17] Hickton's investigation also uncovered evidence that Unit 61398's espionage campaigns could last a long time. The indictment alleges that Unit 61398 officers were conducting espionage on the computer systems of Westinghouse Electric Company for two years, from 2010 to 2012, stealing at least 1.4 gigabytes of data (equal to "roughly 700,000 pages of e-mail messages and attachments") during that period.[18] Further evidence also indicated that the defendants were not conducting one-time intrusions—for instance, in the month following Wen's theft of 7,000 ATI account credentials, ATI-owned computers continued to communicate with the same server that was used to steal those credentials, suggesting that Unit 61398 continued to issue instructions to ATI's computers remotely.

The seventh, and final, stage of PLA Unit 61398 intrusions identified by Mandiant was simply "completing the mission." This largely consisted of compressing information the intruders found valuable or interesting into smaller archive files (which ended with the extension .rar), splitting those files into smaller pieces so they wouldn't attract attention when they were exfiltrated out of the victim's network, and then transferring them back to the PLA via backdoors or common file transfer techniques, such as File Transfer Protocol.[19] In a narrow, technical sense, this exfiltration marked the completion of Unit 61398's mission—the desired data had been successfully stolen. But in a broader, political and economic sense, this was presumably only the first step in some larger scheme of the Chinese government's that the stolen information contributed to. Despite the considerable insight they offer into how the PLA stole sensitive and proprietary data, the 2014 indictment and the Mandiant report offer little detail about the ultimate use of the stolen information, making it difficult to analyze how defenders might mitigate the harm inflicted by these incidents even after the exfiltration stage was completed successfully. The circumstances and timing of the intrusions strongly suggest that the PLA was attempting to help Chinese enterprises gain insight into their competitors' commercial strategies, international trade negotiations, and proprietary intellectual property belonging to foreign companies—and the indictment makes the most of these implications, even going so far as to claim that Chinese companies hired Unit 61398 to provide information about their foreign competitors. For instance, the indictment states:

> [A]n Oregon producer of solar panel technology was rapidly losing its market share to Chinese competitors that were systematically pricing exports well below production costs; at the same time, members of the conspiracy stole cost and pricing information from the Oregon producer. And while a Pennsylvania nuclear power plant manufacturer was negotiating with a Chinese company over the construction and operation of four power plants in China, the conspirators stole, among other things, proprietary and confidential technical and design specifications for pipes, pipe supports, and pipe routing for those nuclear power plants that would enable any competitors looking to build a similar plant to save on research and development costs in the development of such designs.[20]

Yet, of the thirty-one crimes that the five Unit 61398 officers were charged with, only two actually relate to what they did with the information they stole—the rest are focused on *how* they stole information. The two counts that address the use of the stolen information—one for economic espionage, one for theft of trade secrets—are confined to the Westinghouse intrusion and the theft of one particular file, wd.rar, that contained "proprietary and confidential technical and design specifications, owned by Westinghouse, which were related to the pipes, pipe supports, and pipe routing within the AP1000 nuclear power plant."[21]

The absence of detailed information about how the stolen information was used is not necessarily surprising—in espionage cases, it's often much easier for victims and the security firms and law enforcement officers they work with to determine how information was stolen than to trace what happened to it after it left their systems. But, all the same, it is striking that so little seems to be known about how the intruders used the information they stole since that usage is often how perpetrators are identified. When it comes to tracing financially motivated cybercrimes, for instance, it is much easier to wait and see who is receiving deliveries of large quantities of cash (e.g., Albert Gonzalez and his co-conspirators in the 2005 TJX data breach) than it is to figure out who is controlling an overseas server housing stolen data. The theft of money using stolen data not only helps investigators identify the responsible parties, it also provides a way to estimate the harm inflicted by a cybercrime: this amount of money was stolen, therefore this amount of damage was done. But the incidents detailed by Mandiant and the 2014 indictment offer no clear way to assess what harm—if any—was inflicted by the Unit 61398 intrusions, much less how to translate that harm into a dollar sum. Furthermore, both Mandiant and Hickton rely on circumstantial, if persuasive, forms of attribution based on clues like who would likely have been interested in the stolen information (Chinese companies), and who was operating the infrastructure used by the intruders. Mandiant also inspected the malware programs used by the intruders to compile a list of grammatically incorrect phrases in the code that indicate they were written by non-native English speakers. Many of the code snippets they cite seem like relatively banal typos or errors—"If use it, key is the KEY," "File no exist," "Doesn't started!," "Exception Catched"—but at least one of them reads as a fairly damning boast by Wang: "No Doubt to Hack You, Writed by UglyGorilla." As with the DigiNotar compromise, intruders—even when they're trying to lay low for the purposes of long-term espionage—sometimes like to take credit for their handiwork.

Intermediaries and Opportunities for Intervention

In the aftermath of financially motivated cybersecurity incidents, the question of who is to blame for failing to prevent the breaches is an urgent one because it so immediately leads to the larger question of who will bear the burden of covering the financial losses. When it comes to espionage incidents, like the DigiNotar breach and the PLA Unit 61398 intrusions, however, the losses are much less clear and therefore much more difficult to transfer to other parties via lawsuits or public pronouncements. For these reasons, the victims of espionage incidents are often satisfied to direct blame at the perpetrators—even though they have little hope of extracting financial compensation for their losses from adversaries like the Chinese military. This allows the victims to avoid the battles over what responsibility they may have had to protect the data that was stolen, as well as what role third-party intermediaries might have played in contributing to that protection. To some extent, this can be a good thing—it focuses blame where it most squarely belongs and avoids the finger pointing and squabbling over who was negligent and who was just unlucky. But viewed from another perspective, this focus on the perpetrators is profoundly unproductive. The way to try to prevent future espionage efforts like those perpetrated by Unit 61398 is to figure out who can better defend against those efforts and how—rather than trying to dissuade the perpetrators by symbolically indicting foreign spies who live safely within their own borders beyond the reach of the U.S. justice system.

Unsurprisingly, the five PLA officers named in the 2014 indictment were never actually arrested. In fact, beyond simply not arresting the named officers, the Chinese government vehemently denied and denounced the charges, claiming they were "based on deliberately fabricated facts" and urging the U.S. to "withdraw the 'indictment'" (China's statement referred to the 2014 indictment in quotation marks, as an "indictment," as if to suggest it was not quite real or legitimate).[22] Responding to the indictment, Foreign Minister Qin Gang said, unequivocally, that China's government

"never engaged or participated in cyber theft of trade secrets." Gang further accused the United States of "large-scale and organized cyber theft as
well as wiretapping and surveillance activities against foreign political leaders, companies and individuals," alluding to the NSA documents leaked by
Edward Snowden in 2013.[23] Filing indictments against the spies employed
by foreign governments did not appear to be a productive means of fostering greater international collaboration or less cyberespionage. In fact,
China officially suspended the US-China Cyber Working Group because of
the indictment—or, as Gang referred to it, the "indictment."

Understanding the role that the Chinese government played in the espionage incidents described by Mandiant and the 2014 indictment, or that
the Iranian government played in the DigiNotar compromise, is important for trying to assess who might have been affected by those particular
breaches and how. But to actually draw useful lessons from these incidents
that will help improve victims' ability to defend themselves in the future, the
most important question is not: What did the Chinese or Iranian governments do—or might they have done—with the information they accessed?
Rather, the crucial question is: What did the victims and intermediary parties do—or might they have done—to prevent or mitigate that access in
the first place? Dealing with nation-state level espionage might seem like
a more natural burden for the government, rather than individual companies, to bear, but the PLA officer indictment showed that this was not a
problem likely to be solved by the Justice Department. The crucial lessons
of the DigiNotar compromise come from understanding the back-and-forth
between certificate authorities and browsers because that is the dynamic
that will determine how easily similar such compromises can be exploited
in the future. The crucial lessons of the PLA Unit 61398 espionage incidents lie not in blaming China but in understanding the range of different
organizations that Unit 61398 relied on to help perpetrate different components of these breaches and the potential defensive capabilities each of
those third parties possesses.

As with financially motivated incidents, such as the TJX and SCDOR
breaches, the most immediate and obvious place to lay the blame for successful espionage operations is on the direct victims: the companies who
let their data be stolen, like U.S. Steel, Westinghouse, and ATI. In another
parallel with TJX and SCDOR, the inclination when blaming these entities is to focus on the earliest and seemingly simplest of the errors they

made—the poorly encrypted wireless network at a Marshalls store, the lack of two-factor authentication in the South Carolina government, the hapless employees who clicked on phishing emails and attachments at U.S. Steel. Certainly, the moment when those phishing emails arrived in employees' inboxes was an opportunity for defensive intervention, and the more people know about how to identify suspicious emails the more likely they are to be able to cut off the intrusion at that early stage. But to believe espionage can be prevented solely by educating people about phishing is to severely misunderstand the complexity of these incidents and the technical design decisions that enable phishing.

In many ways, the design of email facilitates impersonation and makes it difficult to definitively identify a message's sender. Anyone can send an email message from any email address on the planet and display any sender name they want alongside that address. Some—but not all—of these forged messages can be caught by filters, inbox restrictions, or symbols indicating whether the sender authenticated (i.e., logged into) the address they used. But ultimately the ability to impersonate others is fundamentally built into email itself, and that can only be altered by major email providers and technical application designers. Rethinking how easy it is to send persuasive phishing emails is only one of a variety of different defensive interventions that could be used to interrupt the lifecycle of the PLA Unit 61398 intrusions. These interventions range from the design of email and the treatment of attachments to the registration of domain names and regulation of outbound traffic to changes in international trade policy—and few if any of them are within the sole control of the companies directly targeted for espionage.

As with financially motivated incidents, the most effective means of defending against espionage incidents is cutting off or restricting an absolutely essential, bottleneck stage of the intrusion—for instance, the monetization stages of the TJX and SCDOR breaches. Though phishing emails were a recurring feature of PLA intrusions, they are not actually essential to conducting espionage any more than they were essential for stealing data from the SCDOR—there are numerous other ways of gaining an initial foothold within a protected network, for instance, by guessing user passwords or distributing infected USB drives. The phishing stage of PLA intrusions was a useful one for espionage—but not an *essential* one. If phishing were no longer easy or effective, the intruders would have other means of accomplishing that same goal of downloading malware onto victims' machines.

The essential stages of espionage incidents come later: making outbound connections to C2 servers through which the intruders can find and package useful information and then the exfiltration of that information to servers they control. These are the stages intruders bent on espionage absolutely must carry out in order to achieve their ultimate aims. These are therefore also the intrusion stages that make for the most promising defensive bottlenecks, analogous to the monetization stages of financially motivated incidents. While organizations do have significant control over the outbound connections and flow of traffic from their networks, the use of stolen credentials makes it difficult to distinguish between legitimate and malicious activity, forcing defenders to rely on the volume and sensitivity of outbound traffic to identify espionage. Outbound connections to C2 servers controlled by foreign governments could offer some other clues—for instance, if the connections are made to servers in untrusted locations or on a suspiciously regular, unchanging schedule. But these clues, too, could be obscured by intruders—Unit 61398 officers, whom the investigators ultimately trace back to networks in Shanghai, typically compromised third-party servers and used those servers to communicate with the targets of their espionage indirectly. This suggests yet another set of potential intermediary defenders—the owners and operators of the infected third-party servers that are used as platforms for espionage attacks.

Companies that are the direct targets of espionage efforts usually implement defensive mechanisms aimed at detecting or interrupting the exfiltration of sensitive information from their systems. Third-party defenders, who are not directly targeted by the espionage efforts, may be less able to disrupt the information theft directly, but may, in some cases, have opportunities to go after the perpetrators' infrastructure and profits. For instance, the Mandiant report notes that PLA Unit 61398 has a vast infrastructure supporting its espionage efforts, which includes over a thousand servers, several encryption certificates, hundreds of domain names registered by the intruders, and many more domains owned by compromised third parties. These domain names play a vital role in the group's espionage efforts, operating both as delivery vectors for initial backdoors via phishing emails and as embedded C2 server addresses in those backdoors. The report notes that by using domain names instead of specific IP addresses as the C2 addresses, the intruders "may dynamically decide where to direct C2 directions from a given backdoor" so that "if they lose control of a specific hop point (IP address) they can 'point' the C2 [fully qualified domain name] address to a different IP address and resume their control over victim backdoors."[24] This system is similar in purpose to Bogachev's use of the DGA to ensure that he could easily resume control of the GOZ-infected computers in the event that his C2 servers were shut down, but is somewhat less flexible than the GOZ model because it relies on redirecting hard-coded domain names to new servers rather than generating entirely new domain names each week any of which could serve as a new C2 server address.

The domain names registered by the PLA Unit 61398 could occasionally present opportunities for additional defensive intervention, especially when they were designed to imitate a trusted third party (e.g., microsoft -update-info.com, cnndaily.com, and nytimesnews.net). In September 2011, for instance, Yahoo took issue with one such domain, myyahoonews.com, and filed a complaint against the person who had registered it with registrar GoDaddy.com, using the name zheng youjun. The registrant did not respond to Yahoo's complaint, and the National Arbitration Forum subsequently ruled that the domain be transferred from its current owner to Yahoo following an investigation that showed it was being used as a "phishing web page … in an effort to collect login credentials under false pretenses."[25]

Despite Yahoo's victory, trying to tear down Unit 61398's infrastructure domain name by domain name, or hop point by hop point, could never have been a feasible defensive strategy. It would have required the coordinated attention and action of far too many different actors—not just Yahoo, but all of the hundreds of organizations whose names and websites were being used in misleading ways by the PLA. Moreover, all of these infrastructural resources were easily replaceable at relatively low cost to the PLA. If one—or even a few hundred—domain names were seized from them, they could quickly register another hundred. Similarly, if the compromised intermediary machines that Unit 61398 relied on to route their intrusions through were identified and wiped so that the PLA officers could no longer use them, it would only require the work of hours or days to compromise another set of serviceable intermediary nodes.

In this regard, the opportunities for cooperation and collaboration between different third-party defenders stand in stark contrast to the ones suggested by the TJX and DigiNotar incidents. In those cases, third parties, such as payment processing networks and web browsers, had visibility into the harm being inflicted, and an ability to control some of the most essential, bottleneck stages of attacks, where perpetrators options had drastically narrowed. Moreover, that visibility was concentrated in the hands of a relatively small group of actors with broad global reach (i.e., credit card companies and browser manufacturers) who could conceivably coordinate their defensive efforts. The PLA Unit 61398 strategy relies in part on the diversity and dispersion of potential defenders across their espionage infrastructure. These potential third-party defenders have, in general, less visibility into the espionage efforts than the actual targets and can exercise control over only the most easily replaced resources and stages of those attacks.

Yahoo shouldn't be blamed for the existence of misleading domain names that trade on the company's popular websites, or be required to monitor and file complaints against every such offending domain. But the extent to which the PLA Unit 61398 online espionage infrastructure is embedded in its adversaries' machines and brands makes it difficult to imagine any kind of effective defensive strategy that does not rely, in some fashion, on greater liability being assigned to intermediary actors—perhaps not the ones whose names are traded on, but rather those whose compromised computer systems served as crucial infrastructural stepping stones, or hop points, for Unit 61398. The PLA officers carrying out these espionage efforts knew that it would look suspicious to suddenly start channeling large quantities of data from U.S. companies directly to their own computers in Shanghai, so instead they compromised other machines at U.S.-based organizations, such as universities, that they could route their stolen data through. A government agency or U.S.-based tech company might well be in regular contact with researchers or students at those universities and traffic between the two networks would therefore generate little suspicion if monitored. These compromised intermediary machines—many of which were located on college campuses across the U.S.—were crucial to Unit 61398's success, especially since universities often take a less strict approach to network security than other organizations in order to foster collaboration and provide access to a regular stream of visitors and guests.

The role of the compromised computers at universities and other intermediary organizations raises the question of whether those institutions bear any responsibility for the espionage incidents. The topic of intermediary liability is a sensitive one in the context of Internet policy, where it has been most thoroughly explored in the context of copyright protection. Websites like YouTube and Wikipedia, which primarily feature user-generated content, rely heavily on the intermediary liability protections enshrined in Section 230 of the 1996 Communications Decency Act. These protections guarantee that no online intermediary will be treated as a "publisher" of any copyright infringing content that occurs on their platforms, so long as they do not post that content themselves and review and remove infringing content when alerted to it.

As vitally important as these protections have been to fostering the development of new and innovative online services, the notion of intermediary liability takes on a slightly different cast in discussions of security. While protecting intermediaries from liability claims in the context of user-generated content may be beneficial for users and innovative content models, it is not so clearly advantageous to protect online intermediaries from bearing any liability for harmful outcomes that result from security breaches. Creating an online environment in which companies can reasonably be expected to successfully monitor and control outbound connections and traffic flows requires that they be able to count on those servers they connect to actually being controlled by the people and organizations who officially own and operate them. If those hop points have nothing at stake in protecting their own systems—if they bear no responsibility for the breaches perpetrated using their networks—it seems unlikely that they will go to great lengths to secure themselves, which, in turn, leaves everyone who communicates with them at greater risk.

One alternative to holding intermediaries partially responsible for the role they play in espionage breaches is to focus on mitigating the harm posed by these breaches, rather than the technical pathways through which they are perpetrated. This is akin to focusing on interrupting the monetization of stolen data in financially motivated incidents—its emphasis is on what happens *after* data is stolen, not how to prevent it from being stolen in the first place. But designing defenses to mitigate the harms imposed by cyberespionage, rather than the technical stages of the espionage itself, is tricky, given how many different ways stolen information can be used. The intruders themselves may not even know beforehand exactly what information they will turn up or how they will use it. So the safest strategy in defending against espionage is to assume that the exfiltration of sensitive data is, itself, a form of harm. Interrupting or defending against exfiltration necessitates assigning some blame, and liability, to the intermediary hop points that are so essential for carrying out that exfiltration.

In some cases, particularly when espionage efforts are geared toward the theft of stolen intellectual property, there may be some means of trying to limit any resulting illicit profits through economic restrictions. For instance, in May 2013 a group of U.S. senators introduced the Deter Cyber Theft Act, aimed at fighting espionage efforts by blocking U.S. imports of products that benefitted from stolen intellectual property. This was an attempt to target the monetization stage of the PLA Unit 61398 intrusions, assuming they were perpetrated for the purpose of economic espionage that would ultimately lead to Chinese companies manufacturing products developed using stolen U.S. intellectual property. Just as law enforcement officers targeted the monetization stages of the TJX and Cryptolocker incidents, so, too, the Deter Cyber Theft Act was intended to leverage policymakers' control over financial flows to disincentivize economic espionage by making it less profitable. Rather than going after the PLA officers who conducted the espionage, the bill's authors wanted to target directly the overseas companies who were profiting from it. Just as it didn't matter if Gonzalez stole millions of payment card numbers unless he was able to sell them, perhaps it wouldn't matter if China stole U.S. corporate secrets if there was no way for them to use that information to hurt the American economy. The Deter Cyber Theft Act tried to make defending against economic espionage a matter of protecting the nation's economy, rather than its individual computer systems—the former task, if not necessarily easier, was certainly better suited to the particular powers of Congress. But policy-based measures along these lines are limited by the extent to which foreign companies conducting espionage require the economic support of international customers, and their effectiveness depends entirely on being able to reliably identify the perpetrators of espionage—a problem the Deter Cyber Theft Act sidestepped by delegating that function to the Director of National Intelligence.[26]

Cybersecurity incidents perpetrated for the purpose of espionage are much harder to defend against than those perpetrated for financial gain because there are fewer opportunities to intervene outside the context of the targeted computer systems: once the data is stolen, the harm is done. That cuts short the chain of events leading up to success from the perpetrator's point of view, removing the useful monetization stages that provide so much assistance during law enforcement investigations and cutting out the large, centralized financial actors who have control over and visibility into anomalous financial flows. It also means the defensive opportunities are largely restricted to computer-based technical controls around exfiltration and outbound connections that are only effective if the third parties whom organizations connect to are not themselves compromised. Further complicating this picture is the ambiguity of the harm being imposed by these breaches and the uncertainty around whom they affect and how significant the related costs are. TJX, the South Carolina Department of Revenue, and DigiNotar were all victims of breaches, but they were, in some sense, intermediate victims; the real targets were TJX customers, South Carolina taxpayers, and Iranian Google users. The organizations targeted by Unit 61398, by contrast—like the victims of Cryptolocker—seem to bear most of the ill effects of the espionage efforts themselves, while compromised third-party hop points and impersonated domains serve as intermediate victims. Yet, unlike TJX, SCDOR, and DigiNotar, those third-party hop points and other intermediate victims who enabled Unit 61398's espionage efforts have largely avoided any liability. Part of what makes espionage incidents so difficult to defend against is this reluctance to engage with the question of what responsibility intermediaries play for enabling such breaches and how they might be incentivized to do their part to prevent such compromises from recurring through their infrastructure.

7 "Decades in the Making": The Office of Personnel Management Breach and Political Espionage

On May 27, 2014, the United States Office of Personnel Management (OPM) shut down almost all of its computer systems. During the outage, the agency created brand new user accounts for many of its employees, reset Internet routers, removed software processes running on its machines, and instituted a requirement that administrators use a physical key card in addition to a password to authenticate to their computer accounts. Dubbed the "Big Bang" within the agency, the day was intended to serve as a massive reset of OPM's network, aimed at eliminating the presence of intruders who had been accessing the agency's computers since July 2012 and had recently begun delivering keylogging malware to workstations across the agency. But despite the extensive overhaul of OPM servers and accounts, the Big Bang ultimately failed to root out the malware and backdoor access pathways that those intruders had planted in the OPM network. In the months that followed the system reset, OPM would experience its most extensive and damaging security intrusions yet, culminating in the theft of personal information belonging to more than 20 million current and former federal employees.

The OPM breach unfolded over the course of months and was only discovered with the assistance of several private security firms, highlighting the often fraught interactions between government agencies and private companies, the major obstacles government entities face in trying to upgrade and protect legacy technology, and broader industry concerns about the public sector's ability and willingness to take a leadership role on issues related to cybersecurity. On May 27, 2015, exactly one year after the Big Bang, OPM notified Congress that a major incident had occurred involving the exfiltration of background investigation data.[1] The Big Bang, it turned out, marked the beginning, rather than the end, of OPM's security woes, imbuing the agency with a false sense of security right at the moment when its adversaries were ready to begin their espionage activity in earnest.

The range and variety of data stolen from OPM was staggering not just in its volume, but also its degree of personal detail. OPM is the agency responsible for recruiting and investigating U.S. government civilian employees so it maintains extensive records on civil servants and their security clearances, as well as on applicants for government positions. In the 2015 breach, fingerprint data for 5.2 million people and background investigation information for 21.5 million current and former government employees were stolen, including responses to questions on the lengthy Standard Form 86 (SF-86) used for security clearances. The SF-86 asks individuals not just for their own personal information but also for that of their friends and family members. It includes the types of personal information stolen in other breaches—names, birth dates, Social Security numbers, credit card numbers—but it also covers a variety of other intimate details. During a Committee on Oversight and Government Reform hearing on the breach on June 16, 2015, Massachusetts Representative Stephen Lynch described the SF-86:

> This is a copy of the application. It is online if people want to look at it; it is 127 pages online. And we ask them everything; what kind of underwear they wear, what kind of toothpaste. I mean, it is a deep dive. And that is for a good reason, right? Because we want to know, when people get security clearance, that they are trustworthy. There is information here if you have ever been arrested; your financial information is in here. There is a lot of information in this form.[2]

Most of this specialized information would be of little use to someone trying to commit identity theft or financial fraud, but the OPM breach—like the DigiNotar compromise and the PLA Unit 61398 espionage efforts—was not motivated by financial greed.

Instead, government officials speculated, the OPM breach seemed to suggest that a foreign nation—likely China—was building a massive database of personal information about U.S. government employees. Such a database could aid the Chinese government in identifying undercover agents, blackmailing federal employees, guessing government officers' passwords, and impersonating those employees to perpetrate future insider attacks or phishing campaigns like those used by PLA Unit 61398.[3] Unlike Unit 61398's efforts to compromise U.S.-based companies such as Westinghouse and U.S. Steel, however, the OPM breach appeared to be an example of espionage driven by political rather than economic motivations. This distinction was particularly poignant at the time because the U.S. government was itself fending off accusations of widespread espionage and surveillance activities, following the discovery that U.S. intelligence officers had infiltrated the servers of Huawei, a major Chinese technology company. The incident was revealed in documents leaked by Edward Snowden and raised repeatedly by the Chinese government when the U.S. government attempted to condemn the actions of Unit 61398 through the indictment of PLA officers. In response to criticisms that its condemnation of Chinese espionage was hypocritical, the United States tried to distance itself from what Unit 61398 had done on the grounds that China was conducting economic espionage rather than the more generally accepted practice of political espionage. That made it harder for the U.S. government to blame China for the OPM breach, an act of clearly political espionage, and centered more of the focus on finding someone to blame within the U.S. government for failing to prevent the incident. In the OPM case, as in the case of the indictment charging officers of PLA Unit 61398, the Chinese government denied any wrongdoing or responsibility. China even later claimed to have arrested the individuals responsible for the OPM breach.[4]

In the wake of the OPM breach, Congress held several extended hearings on the incident, unraveling a series of ignored warnings from the inspector general's office about OPM's inadequate security measures. As with all major breaches, the discovery of the OPM incident was followed by a lengthy and bitter struggle over who should bear primary responsibility for the target's security failings. OPM director Katherine Archuleta resigned in July 2015. In February 2016, OPM Chief Information Officer Donna Seymour also resigned, two days before she was scheduled to testify about the breach before a House panel.

But even with the departure of high-level OPM employees, there was relatively little to be done in the wake of the breach to protect the individuals whose information was stolen—there were no credit card numbers to cancel, no way to alter the victims' fingerprints or take back the (often very personal) contents of the background checks that had been performed on employees needing security clearances. OPM offered credit monitoring services to the victims and those services themselves quickly became the source of many fraudulent scams, with several websites and phone calls purporting to provide identity theft monitoring demanding further personal information from the victims. The ineptitude of the post-breach mitigation efforts highlighted the stark differences between financially motivated and espionage-driven breaches. Meanwhile, the government's inability to protect its own data in this incident fueled ongoing tensions between the public and private sectors about the role of government in regulating data security efforts, policymakers' ability to offer guidance and support to private companies, and regulatory agencies' efforts to hold negligent companies responsible for breaches.

Deep Panda and the Attack of the Avengers

The extended timeline of the OPM breach and the numerous ignored warning signs leading up to its execution highlight how profoundly inept OPM's leadership was, despite specific government rules and security procedures. OPM was unable to make timely or sensible decisions about computer security, heed clear signs of threats and suspicious activity, and prioritize data protection measures that might in any way inconvenience users or invite criticism. The compromise of OPM's data occurred in roughly three stages, each of which consisted of several smaller steps on the part of the intruders. The first, "pre-Big Bang" phase lasted from July 2012 through May 27, 2014, during which period the intruders planted their initial backdoors and stole reconnaissance materials about how the OPM networks were structured and operated. During the second "exfiltration" phase, from May 28, 2014, through April 23, 2015, the intruders stole large volumes of personal information from the OPM systems and a Department of the Interior (DoI) data center that was used to store government data. The third and final "containment" phase began on April 24, 2015, when OPM began to quarantine its infected systems and actively attempted to mitigate the breach, and lasted through February 22, 2016, when Seymour resigned, effectively concluding the Congressional investigation.

Computer security had been a major concern at OPM since long before even the earliest stages of this breach commenced. Government agencies regularly audit their information security practices to ensure they are in compliance with the Federal Information Security Management Act (FISMA), which lays out security requirements for protecting government data, such as continuous monitoring of networks, a system security plan, and an inventory of information systems. Michael Esser, the assistant inspector general for audits at OPM, testified before the House of Representatives that FISMA audits had identified a "severe control deficiency that prohibits the organization from protecting its data" at OPM as far back as 2007—a conclusion reiterated in FISMA audits through 2013.[5] OPM's repeated poor performance on FISMA audits and the agency's repeated refusal to take those audits seriously reflect not only how low a priority security was for OPM, but also the broader inclination of agencies across the government to disregard or pay only cursory attention to FISMA.

The FISMA audits of OPM noted, among other failings, that the agency did not have an "accurate centralized inventory of all servers and databases that reside within the network," that many of its servers were never scanned to ensure they had been configured correctly, and that OPM had failed to meet the government's recommendations for implementing multi-factor authentication.[6] Esser noted that some of the security failings were due to structural administrative issues:

> [E]ach OPM program office had primary responsibility for managing its own IT systems. The program office personnel responsible for IT security frequently had no IT security background and were performing this function in addition to another full-time role. The agency had not clearly defined which elements of IT security were the responsibility of the program offices, and which were the responsibility of the [Office of the Chief Information Officer]. As a result of this decentralized governance structure, many security controls went unimplemented and/or remained untested, and OPM routinely failed a variety of FISMA metrics year after year.[7]

Another problem Esser identified was the complete lack of consequences for departments that continued to operate computer systems after failing their FISMA security assessments. He testified that eleven of the forty-seven OPM IT systems did not have a valid security authorization but continued to be used regardless, despite his office's recommendations to shut them down.

In short, OPM had been paying minimal attention to computer security for years by the time HiKit malware (which allowed intruders to command infected machines remotely) began appearing on the agency's servers in July 2012. The following year, in May 2013, Archuleta was appointed OPM director with the express intent of modernizing the agency's computer networks and, in her own words, "develop[ing] the important pillar of cybersecurity within our systems."[8] Archuleta did not come from a security or even a technology background. She had previously served as National Political Director for Barack Obama's 2012 presidential campaign and, prior to that, as a lawyer and chief of staff at the Department of Transportation. So to tackle the technical challenges of updating OPM's infrastructure, Archuleta hired Seymour as the agency's Chief Information Officer in December 2013. A career bureaucrat, Seymour came to OPM from the Department of Defense, where she had served as acting Deputy Assistant Secretary of Defense for the Office of Warrior Care Policy, but, like Archuleta, she had spent part of her career Department of Transportation, where she served as CIO of the Maritime Administration. Seymour's official government biography highlighted the fact that in 2007, while she was at the Maritime Administration, she was named a "Top 100 Chief Information Officer" by the magazine *Computerworld*.

Right around the time of Seymour's hiring, in late 2013, the intruders who had already planted HiKit in OPM's systems began harvesting and exfiltrating login credentials for OPM contractors. In March 2014, the United States Computer Emergency Readiness Team (US-CERT) alerted OPM to the breach of its network, and subsequent investigation revealed that the intruders had accessed security documents, computer system manuals, and IT system architecture information. In June 2015, Seymour testified before Congress that the stolen files in the 2014 breach were "outdated security documents about our systems and some manuals about our systems."[9] After the 2015 breach of personal information, however, OPM IT security contractor, Brendan Saulsbury, told Congress that the information stolen in 2014 would have provided intruders with "more familiarity with how the systems are architected" and might have included "accounts, account names, or machine names, or IP addresses, which are relevant to these critical systems."[10]

From March through May 2014, Seymour and her team "monitored" the intruders on the OPM network—watching their movements, but not actively interrupting any of their activities. But as the intruders became bolder, delivering new malware and keyloggers to systems belonging to OPM and its contractors, Seymour decided a more aggressive approach was warranted. On Tuesday, May 27, following extensive preparations over the three-day Memorial Day weekend, she launched the Big Bang initiative. Saulsbury, who was involved in the pre-Big Bang monitoring efforts, told Congress:

[W]e would sort of observe the attacker every day or, you know, every couple of days get on the network and perform various commands ... They might take some documentation, come back, and then access, you know, somebody else's file share that might be a little bit closer or have more access into the system. ... And then it got to the point where we observed them load a key logger onto a database administrator's workstation, or actually several database administrators' workstations. At that point, the decision was made that they are too close and OPM needs to remove whatever they were aware of at the time.[11]

OPM felt sufficiently confident to do this type of monitoring of malicious activity on their networks for two months without actually taking any actions to remediate or prevent further intrusions. The agency apparently believed it was in control of the situation and was aware of everything that was happening on its systems. Rather bafflingly, as Seymour later indicated during her 2015 testimony, the agency seemed unconcerned about the loss of documentation about its own network's architecture and operations. The reconnaissance for the later 2015 breach happened with OPM watching—and deliberately choosing not to interfere.

OPM clearly felt it had a handle on the situation during the period from March 20, 2014, when US-CERT first alerted them to the intrusion, through the Big Bang event on May 27 of that year. But the intruders did at least two things during the pre-Big Bang monitoring period that OPM was not aware of at the time and that laid the groundwork for the later, larger breach. The first did not actually involve any access to the OPM network, but indicated that the intruders were making infrastructural investments to target OPM. On April 25, 2014, someone registered the domain opmsecurity.org using the name Steve Rogers (alter ego: comic book character Captain America) and the email address tAPRhpALhl@gmx.com. Less than two weeks later, on May 7, while Saulsbury and his colleagues were still watching the intruders "perform various commands" on the network, an intruder logged in to the OPM network remotely, using credentials belonging to an employee who performed background investigations for OPM through the contractor Key-Point Government Solutions. Using the KeyPoint credentials, the intruder installed a malware program called PlugX on OPM's systems, creating a backdoor into the network that would allow for continued access even after the Big Bang reset of accounts and elimination of the original HiKit malware. PlugX allowed the intruders to capture users' keystrokes, modify and copy files, take screenshots and videos of user activity on the compromised machines, as well as log off and restart machines.[12] The PlugX malware also established an encrypted connection—using fraudulent SSL certificates—between the infected machines and the opmsecurity.org domain, so that the OPM hosts would "beacon" back to the domain at regular intervals for instructions.[a]

It is possible that the intruder who installed PlugX was in fact operating independently of the intruder who downloaded HiKit and stole the documentation prior to the Big Bang, which might explain why OPM, in monitoring the HiKit intruder they "knew" about, missed the new threat. The 2014 intruders were later identified as likely belonging to the "Axiom" group, while the 2015 breach was attributed to "Deep Panda," a group that has also been named as the likely perpetrator of the 2015 theft of personal information belonging to more than 78 million people from health insurance company Anthem, Inc. A Congressional investigation later concluded that the Axiom and Deep Panda OPM intrusions were probably linked, based on how quickly the Deep Panda intruders were able to navigate the complicated OPM systems and access personnel records. A report on the investigation published by the House Committee on Oversight and Government Reform concluded that the two groups probably shared a "digital quartermaster." In particular, the report noted, the 2015 attackers' ability to gain access to personnel files and highly sensitive OPM data within just forty-five days of their initial PlugX installation suggests that they "relied on information obtained by the 2014 hackers, who had access to OPM's network for years and were unable to compromise the most sophisticated systems."[13]

The Big Bang left the PlugX malware untouched and in the following weeks, the intruders used the PlugX backdoor to deliver additional malware to systems belonging to OPM and its contractors. By late June, as DHS was issuing a final incident report on the 2014 OPM documentation breach, the Deep Panda intruders had already begun connecting to servers containing background investigation data and compressing it into RAR files (i.e., archive files with the .rar extension) to transfer out of OPM's network.[b] By July

---

a. This beaconing allowed the intruders to regularly communicate with and control the infected OPM machines from the servers they controlled at the opmsecurity .org domain, while the SSL encryption made it more difficult for OPM to detect what information was being sent back and forth between their own network and the intruders' servers.

b. RAR files are a form of archive files that store data in compressed form so that the large volumes of data can be sent more easily. As in the case of the SCDOR

2014, the intruders had begun exfiltrating background investigation data, and, by late 2014, they had managed to access the Department of the Interior data center, where OPM personnel records were stored, and had exfiltrated 4.2 million personnel records as dictated by instructions relayed from the opmsecurity.org domain. In addition to opmsecurity.org, on July 29, 2014, Deep Panda registered another domain, opm-learning.org, under the name Tony Stark (alias Iron Man) and the email address vrzunyjkmf@gmx.com, which was also used for data exfiltration.[14]

These OPM-related domain names—like the misleading domain names registered by PLA Unit 61398—were no doubt intended to look legitimate to anyone monitoring outbound connections from the OPM or DOI servers, but their registration information was easily viewable in publicly available domain registration databases. Had anyone bothered to look up this registration information, it would have served as a warning sign, both because it was obviously not owned by OPM and because using Marvel comic book character names and gmx.com email addresses to register domains was a trademark of breaches perpetrated by Deep Panda. Their infrastructure for other intrusions included domains registered under the names Natasha Romanoff (Black Widow), James Rhodes (War Machine), John Nelson (the visual effects supervisor for the movie "Iron Man"), and Dubai Tycoon (the name of a character in the movie "Iron Man").[15]

Buoyed by the supposed success of the Big Bang operation and their ongoing IT upgrades, OPM does not seem to have noticed any of the connections to these suspicious domains until April 14, 2015, nearly a year after the Big Bang, when OPM contractor Assurance Data noticed a suspicious SSL certificate on OPM's machines while deploying a new web traffic filter tool.[c] Alerted to the domain by Assurance Data, OPM employees looked into opmsecurity.org the next day and deemed the domain "sketchy at best" in their response to Assurance Data after finding the clearly fraudulent registration details. But by then the intruders had already registered a new command-and-control domain—in fact, the final use of opmsecurity

---

breach, the RAR files allowed the intruders to exfiltrate stolen data more efficiently and potentially helped them to evade any attempts by OPM to detect large amounts of outbound data.

c. This was the certificate that allowed the compromised OPM machines to recognize the opmsecurity.org servers as legitimate—and to send and receive encrypted communications with those servers.

.org came on March 9, 2015, more than a month before OPM was made aware of the domain. On March 3, the intruders had registered wdc-news-post.com, which they then used to exfiltrate the stolen fingerprint data later that month. OPM did not notice the new command and control server, but other warning signs, in addition to the suspicious connections to opm-security.org, began to emerge over the course of April 2015. Most notably, IT administrators discovered a suspicious file named macutil.dll that was masquerading as a McAfee dynamic link library—despite the fact that OPM did not use any McAfee anti-virus products.[16]

On April 17, 2015, OPM brought in security firm Cylance to deploy a monitoring tool called CylanceProtect in "alert" mode. The alert mode of CylanceProtect looked for any suspicious files, processes, or malware running on OPM's machines—but did not stop, delete or interrupt that suspicious activity. When Cylance rolled out the service to 2,000 OPM servers, the alert function "lit up like a Christmas tree," said Cylance Director of Incident Response and Forensics Chris Coulter.[17] Among other problems, CylanceProtect detected lingering variants of HiKit, as well as the PlugX malware and several password-protected RAR files containing stolen data. Less than a week after deploying the CylanceProtect alert mode, another security firm, CyTech Services, visited OPM to demonstrate their Forensics and Incident Response (CyFIR) tool and identified more malware running on the OPM networks during the sales pitch demonstration.[18] At that point, OPM decided it was time to stop monitoring the malicious activity and take more active steps to end it.

So, on Friday, April 24, 2015, the agency upgraded its CylanceProtect service to "auto-quarantine mode"—which meant that any agency computer flagged for suspicious activity or possible compromise would be immediately disconnected from the larger OPM network and shut down. That weekend, beginning Saturday at 9am, OPM shut off power to most of its computers. In an email to his colleagues at Cylance on April 24, Coulter said of the shift to quarantine mode: "This is a desperate move, tomorrow is even more desperate by unplugging every device and moving over to new networks. They will blame any issues on the power outage."[19] He also noted that some "mission critical" services would be exempt from the quarantine, including the USA JOBS website and related applications, because "they said if we bring that down senators will come for us."[20] Over the course of its deployment, CylanceProtect scanned over 10,250 devices at OPM and detected almost two thousand pieces of malware.

At the time of Cylance's quarantine operation, OPM still did not have a sense of the scope and size of the breach. But by early May, US-CERT had concluded that the intruders had likely stolen personnel records and personal information. Later that month, OPM's own investigation found that background investigation information had been stolen, forcing it to notify Congress and the Office of the Inspector General of the incident on May 27, 2015. On June 4, 2015, OPM announced the breach of 4.2 million personnel records—the initial exfiltration in late 2014—to the public. The full scope of just how much data had been stolen and how many people had been affected would not be realized until a month later, on July 9, when OPM announced that in fact background investigation data for 21.5 million people had been accessed by the intruders. The next day, Archuleta resigned. Some months later, in September 2015, OPM would make another public announcement, this time confirming that 5.6 million sets of fingerprints had been stolen, rather than the initial estimate of 1.1 million. In February 2016, two days before a scheduled House hearing on the breach, Seymour resigned—and, as a result, the Oversight Committee's final hearing was canceled.

"The Whole of Government Is Responsible"

The hearings that followed the OPM breach were strongly reminiscent of the investigation of the South Carolina Department of Revenue breach in their narrow focus on encryption and two-factor authentication, as well as their frequent invocations of government security standards and the responsibility of other government agencies to determine and enforce appropriate data protection controls. For instance, when Archuleta was questioned by the House Oversight Committee at a hearing on June 16, 2015, she was asked repeatedly by members of the Committee why OPM had failed to encrypt the stolen data. In her responses, she pointed out— correctly—that encryption would have been unlikely to block an intrusion that, like Deep Panda's, relied on the use of stolen credentials. But she also attempted to deflect blame for the decision onto the Department of Homeland Security—the government agency responsible for civilian cybersecurity efforts—implying that it was not, or should not have been, her decision what security standards to implement at OPM. In a tense back and forth with Committee chair Representative Jason Chaffetz, Archuleta blamed everyone and everything from DHS to the age of OPM's IT systems for the lack of encryption:

Chaffetz: Why wasn't this information encrypted?

Archuleta: The encryption is one of the many tools that systems can use. I will look to my colleagues at DHS for their response.

Chaffetz: No, I want to know from you why the information wasn't encrypted. This is personal, sensitive information: birth dates, Social Security numbers, background information, addresses. Why wasn't it encrypted?

…

Archuleta: An adversary possessing proper credentials can often decrypt data. It is not feasible to implement on networks that are too old.[21]

Later during the hearing, when the same question was put to DHS—the agency that Archuleta was eager hold responsible for OPM's security posture—Andy Ozment, the DHS assistant secretary for cybersecurity and communications, reiterated the same point, saying: "If an adversary has the credentials of a user on the network, then they can access data even if it is encrypted, just as the users on the network have to access data, and that did occur in this case, so encryption in this instance would not have protected this data."[22]

As with the SCDOR incident—and so many other security breach postmortems—these after-the-fact accusations of negligence are largely valid criticisms of the victim's security posture, but also largely irrelevant to the breach in question. OPM probably should have been encrypting more of its sensitive data—but it's also true that encryption would have been unlikely to prevent this particular breach since the intruders had access to valid credentials. Similarly, the Oversight Committee's claim that OPM could have "significantly delayed or mitigated" the 2015 breach and "locked out attackers" by implementing two-factor authentication procedures for all employees assumes that the intruders had no way to intercept a second authentication factor, in addition to a password. This claim seems especially misguided in light of the fact that, according to US-CERT's report on the incident, the initial installation of PlugX was carried out using a KeyPoint employee's multi-factor credentials that included both a password and a temporary code provided by a security token. (KeyPoint disputed this conclusion and maintained that "no unaccounted security tokens were used" at the time of the breach.)[23]

Archuleta's appeals to DHS to justify the security mechanisms that were and were not in place at OPM also recalls the back-and-forth between South Carolina's governor and the IRS in the wake of the SCDOR breach, with one government agency accusing another of failing to set appropriate security requirements and standards. In her testimony, Archuleta pointed to DHS as responsible for OPM's decision about whether or not to encrypt data, but that was not the only explanation OPM offered for how its security posture had been shaped—and hindered—by government-issued recommendations. Soon after the agency was made aware of the first breach in March 2014, OPM Director of IT Security Operations Jeff Wagner had recommended that OPM purchase CylanceProtect, one of the tools that was ultimately used to detect and remediate the malware used in the later breach. But OPM failed to carry out this recommendation, instead opting to purchase a less thorough security screening tool, because CylanceProtect had not yet been certified by the Federal Risk and Authorization Management Program (FedRAMP) mandated by the Office of Management and Budget (OMB) for government agencies procuring cloud-based technologies.[24] "In a perfect world, we would have deployed [CylanceProtect] earlier, but because we were trying not to break rules and trying to live within structures ... we didn't deploy it," Wagner told Congress.

Wagner's and Archuleta's attempts to deflect responsibility for OPM's security decisions to DHS and OMB hint at the complexity and confusion around government-issued security recommendations and requirements, but also belie OPM's seeming ambivalence to those recommendations—and security in general—in the years leading up to the breach. OPM, after all, had repeatedly failed to address concerns raised by FISMA audits going back as far as 2007, and was operating nearly a quarter of its IT systems without a valid security authorization from the inspector general. Furthermore, when OPM finally did decide to purchase CylanceProtect on June 30, 2015—more than a year after Wagner initially recommended it—the product had still not been certified as FedRAMP-compliant. In other words, OPM appeared to follow the recommendations of other government branches with regards to computer security only very intermittently and not as part of a broader commitment to "trying not to break rules" or "live within structures."

The agency's top priority prior to the breach appears to have been not letting security audits or updates interfere in any way with their day-to-day operations. When asked by Chaffetz why she didn't shut down the systems without proper security authorizations, Archuleta replied obliquely: "to shut down the system we need to consider all of the responsibilities we have with the use of our systems ... As the director of OPM, I have to take into consideration all of the work that we must do."[25] Even after the full extent of the breach began to come to light, forcing OPM to deploy CylanceProtect and shut down most of its systems, the agency continued to prioritize making sure that some of its services—including the USA JOBS website—were not interrupted over the remediation of its compromised network. That OPM was able to continually ignore the poor FISMA audits and failed security assessments indicates just how much autonomy the agency had to make independent security decisions—and also how little importance it attached to those decisions.

During the Congressional hearings, Georgia Representative Jody Hice asked Seymour if her office imposed any consequences for the operators of the OPM systems who continued to run their computer systems without proper security authorizations from the inspector general. Seymour responded: "The consequences that we have are we report to OMB on a quarterly basis about the status of our security and our network." Hice replied: "That doesn't sound like consequences; that sounds like just reporting that you are required to do anyway."[26] The fundamental failing of OPM's leadership was not in their slowness to implement encryption or two-factor authentication, much less in their diligent adherence to arcane or out-of-date government security standards. Those were merely symptoms of a broader determination on the part of the agency to ignore or minimize any and all warning signs of potential threats and insecure systems for as long as possible, and encourage similar behavior at all levels across the agency by failing to create any incentives for OPM employees or IT administrators to take action when security concerns were flagged by audits or outside contractors.

Even as she deflected blame for security decisions to other government agencies, Archuleta still attempted to frame the detection of the breach as a victory for OPM—and herself—despite the fact that they had ignored several warning signs in the months leading up to the largest exfiltration efforts and chosen to monitor the situation for months rather than taking prompt action to remove the identified threats. Pressed on why she failed to act on all the recommendations put forth during FISMA audits, Archuleta told Chaffetz: "It was as a result of our security systems that we were able to detect this intrusion." She took credit for the Inspector General's determination that OPM's IT security posture exhibited a "significant deficiency" in 2014, a (modest) improvement over its classification of demonstrating "material weakness" in previous years. Archuleta contended that she and Seymour had been making great strides toward securing the OPM systems—they just hadn't had enough time to undo all the damage that had already been done when they arrived at the agency in 2013. "If there is anyone to blame, it is the perpetrators," Archuleta told a Senate appropriations subcommittee.[27] Far from accepting responsibility for the breach, Archuleta was determined to cast blame on anyone else—including her predecessors and other government bodies—and paint herself as not only blameless, but actually the savior of OPM's systems, as in the following exchange with Chaffetz:

> Archuleta: I would note that in the IG's report that he acknowledges the fact that we have taken important steps in reforming our IT systems. Advanced tools take time.
>
> Chaffetz: So what kind of grade would you give yourself? Are you succeeding or failing?
>
> Archuleta: Cybersecurity problems take decades.
>
> Chaffetz: We don't have decades. They don't take decades.
>
> Archuleta: I am sorry, cybersecurity problems are decades in the making. The whole of government is responsible, and it will take all of us to solve the issue and continue to work on them. My leadership with OPM is one that instigated the improvements and changes that recognized the attack.[28]

Oklahoma Representative Steve Russell later mocked Archuleta's claim that without her system upgrades the attack would never have been detected. "That is tantamount to saying if we had not watered our flower beds, we would have never seen the muddy footprints on the open windowsill," he told her.[29]

Remediation of Political Espionage

How intruders will use stolen data depends entirely on their larger motivation—whether they're driven by financial gain, espionage, or a desire to publicly humiliate their victims—but the mitigations and responses undertaken by breached organizations in the aftermath of these incidents are almost identical, regardless of the suspected motivation. At the time of the breach, OPM had no established policy or standards about offering identity theft protection services to individuals whose data was leaked or stolen. Operating under time pressure, OPM ultimately decided to follow the same template that many companies used in the aftermath of data breaches.[30] When the Government Accountability Office (GAO) later reviewed OPM's decision-making process, they found that OPM officials were unable to provide any records concerning how or why they decided on the identity protection services offered to breach victims. OPM officials said that the decisions were not documented because "they were made during a crisis, under intense pressure, and were principally the subject of oral discussions during meetings."[31] The only document OPM was able to turn up was a list of other organizations' responses to past breaches that might have been consulted at the time. So it should come as no surprise that the aftermath of the OPM breach closely resembled the aftermath of the financially motivated data breaches at TJX and the South Carolina Department of Revenue. In the months that followed the public announcement of the OPM breach, the government estimated that the costs of providing identity monitoring and protection services to the victims would total $500 million and require contracting several different firms to provide the necessary amount of coverage.[32] The Government Accountability Office found that the agency ended up spending only $240 million on just two contracts for identity monitoring, one with the Winvale Group and another with Identity Theft Guard Solutions, LLC, and, in doing so, ended up purchasing duplicate protection for roughly 3.6 million people affected by both of its 2015 breaches.[33] But, while the U.S. government offered many of the same identity theft insurance and restoration services provided to victims of financially motivated breaches—including credit monitoring and identity theft insurance—these mitigations were less significant in the wake of a breach that was not designed to commit fraud.

Initially, the government announced it would offer identity protection services through December 2016 to individuals whose personnel records were stolen, and through December 2018 for those whose background investigation records were stolen. In late 2015, President Obama extended the identity protection services for both groups to last ten years, and the 2016 Consolidated Appropriations Act also required that the coverage last at least a decade. But the extension, though it seemed to acknowledge the enduring nature of the stolen data, did little to address concerns about targeting from foreign governments. Moreover, the expanded protections OPM was required to offer after the passage of the Consolidated Appropriations Act were not always very meaningful. For instance, prior to the Act's passage, the agency had offered breach victims up to $1 million each in identity theft insurance coverage, until the Act forced them to increase that limit to $5 million. The identity monitoring firms with whom OPM had contracted raised the limit of each victims' insurance coverage to $5 million, from the initially agreed upon $1 million, without demanding any additional payment from the government, because they knew the allowable claims would be so small that they would never approach even $1 million, much less $5 million. The GAO, assessing OPM's response to the breach, later concluded that "the high dollar amount of the required insurance coverage might give consumers the impression that the insurance coverage is broad when the scope of items covered by identity theft insurance is generally limited to out-of-pocket expenses that are typically modest."[34]

Federal employees and their unions filed two lawsuits against OPM and its contractors following the breach. The American Federation of Government Employees (AFGE) filed a class action suit against OPM, Archuleta, Seymour, and KeyPoint in June 2015, and the National Treasury Employees Union (NTEU) filed another complaint the following month. Both complaints alleged negligence on the part of OPM, with the AFGE suit stating that the agency "willfully, intentionally and with flagrant disregard refused to take steps to implement" security safeguards.[35] The NTEU complaint was filed after Archuleta's resignation and therefore named her successor, Beth Cobert, citing the director's "reckless indifference to her obligation to protect the personal information of current and former federal employees."[36] But, as in the case of the SCDOR breach victims, the AFGE and NTEU plaintiffs faced considerable difficulties in trying to establish standing to sue in cases where they could not link the breach to clear financial losses.[37] OPM took advantage of this in their August 2016 motion to dismiss the class action suits, arguing that "mere allegations of identity theft, untethered to this particular cyber intrusion, cannot establish the requisite harm necessary to obtain money damages or injunctive relief" and that the instances of financial fraud cited by the plaintiffs were not "fairly traceable" to the OPM breach in particular.[38]

Ultimately, the real value of the stolen background investigations and personnel files to a foreign government was unlikely to be financial—foreign officials were probably not going to open up bank accounts or claim tax returns for federal employees. But financial harms were what OPM provided protections against simply because those were the typical protections to provide in the wake of a breach. The OPM breach highlights the limitations of existing mitigations for espionage breaches, and the extent to which they mirror the same steps taken in the aftermath of financial breaches, despite the very different motivations of the perpetrators involved. Making stolen information less valuable to foreign governments as a political tool is much more difficult than making stolen information less valuable to fraudsters, and requires much more extreme and onerous steps, such as the U.S. decision to pull spies from China and CIA operatives out of the U.S. Embassy in Beijing for fear their covers might have been blown by information stolen during the breach.[39]

Effective remediation to contain the harm caused by data breaches depends on the victims being able to control the value and spread of data even after it has been exfiltrated and is no longer in their sole possession. In political espionage cases like the OPM breach, where access to the stolen data is itself the end goal, there is very little that can be done by way of remediation after that data is exfiltrated. This is more often true of espionage incidents than financially motivated breaches, where there are often monetization stages of an attack that can be interrupted even after data is stolen. But the OPM breach is more extreme in this regard than the DigiNotar compromise where the certificate security compromise was a means to reading other people's email, or even the PLA Unit 61398 breaches where the stolen data was a means to manipulate trade disputes and manufacture products using proprietary intellectual property. Each of those incidents had later stages that defenders could hope to interfere with, whether by using browser security mechanisms to identify fraudulent certificates, or legislation and economic policies to penalize companies suspected of intellectual property theft. In the case of the OPM breach, however, exfiltration of the agency's information essentially was the final stage of the breach—making it appropriate, and indeed, necessary, to focus on defenses that allowed the breach to progress to that point. Following the data exfiltration from OPM, the perpetrators did not have to rely on any subsequent financial gain or transmission of their stolen information to a wider audience—so at that point, the only potential further remediation required making personnel changes that would render the stolen data inaccurate and obsolete.

The purely political espionage motivation behind the OPM breach—as opposed to the economic drivers for the data thefts perpetrated by PLA Unit 61398—was notable not just because it changed the available options for after-the-fact remediation, but also because the U.S. government had implicitly endorsed political espionage when it filed the indictment against PLA Unit 61398 officers in 2014. At the time, the United States faced international criticism for accusing a foreign government of espionage activities that, to many, closely resembled the United States' own spying operations. The Department of Justice maintained that there was an important distinction between political espionage, conducted for the purposes of national security, and economic espionage, conducted for the purposes of commercial benefit and private sector enrichment.[40] This distinction is not always clear-cut, especially in countries with major state-owned businesses, but the United States government clung to it in the aftermath of the PLA Unit 61398 espionage efforts. So the OPM breach espionage, which appeared to be purely political in nature, was in many ways more difficult for the United States to respond to than the private sector breaches by PLA Unit 61398. This was not just because the OPM breach revealed far more data affecting millions more people, but also because it was a type of espionage that the U.S. had, itself, seemingly endorsed just a year earlier—without any apparent ability to defend itself against such efforts.

The OPM breach gave rise to a series of conflicts between different government agencies, between government employees and their employer, and between government agencies and their private industry contractors, all of which called into question government agencies' ability and willingness to take a leadership role on issues related to cybersecurity. OPM's eagerness to cast blame on KeyPoint for the initial intrusion—as well as Archuleta's claim that it was she, rather than Cylance or CyTech, who was responsible for the breach's detection—did little to foster strong cooperation between the public and private stakeholders involved in the incident. Many firms were already skeptical of the expertise and technical skills of policymakers in this area, a bias that the OPM breach not only confirmed, but also worsened, by demonstrating how, beyond just a lack of technical expertise, policymakers had additionally not attempted to set much of an example for incident reporting, analysis, transparency, and consumer protection in the aftermath of major breaches. As a very public and embarrassing security failing, the OPM breach and its fallout cemented the challenges policymakers faced in trying to influence industry stakeholders or impose clearer liability regimes. Meanwhile, the bitter infighting and race to assign blame among government actors in the wake of the OPM breach paralleled similar fights among private stakeholders involved in other breaches, reinforcing the notion that placing blame and assigning responsibility to someone else—even within the government itself—is always everyone's primary focus in the aftermath of a security incident, regardless of what is at stake and who the victim is.

The espionage incidents involving DigiNotar, PLA Unit 61398, and OPM highlight both important similarities and key differences between trying to defend against spying versus financial crimes. From a strictly technical perspective, there is no clear difference between the kinds of vulnerabilities and techniques that enable intruders to access protected computer systems for espionage and financial fraud. Phishing emails, malware, and stolen credentials recur across incidents motivated by both financial gain and espionage. On the one hand, this is good news for defenders—security controls targeting these technical stages common to all types of security incidents can have far-reaching impacts, providing protection against more than just one type of crime. But these technical stages, though they recur over and over again, are also often the least essential, most easily replaceable steps for intruders when it comes to carrying out their ultimate goals. The essential, bottleneck stages of security breaches, the ones that intruders absolutely must carry out in order to be successful, usually occur toward the end of an incident's lifecycle, when the perpetrators are ready to execute their end goal, whether that is monetization or access to secret information or something else entirely. And when it comes to mitigating those final stages, there are simply many more bottleneck opportunities for interrupting financially motivated cyber crimes, especially those that rely on centralized financial intermediaries, than there are for defending against the exfiltration of stolen data from compromised computer systems for espionage purposes.

Financially motivated breaches like the ones directed at TJX and SCDOR have only just begun at the moment when stolen data is retrieved from a breached organizations' systems. That data still has to be successfully sold

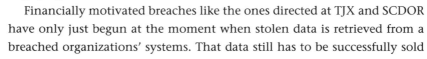

and used, and the money from those sales has to be transmitted back to the perpetrators before their work is done. Not so for espionage incidents like the breach of OPM and the PLA Unit 61398 efforts—in such cases, the last real opportunity for defensive intervention comes at the moment of data exfiltration, so there are fewer bottleneck stages for defenders to try to cut off. After exfiltration, the targeted governments can file indictments, change the terms of international trade, relocate overseas spies, and offer identity protection services—but to a large extent the harm has already been done.

The Cryptolocker and DigiNotar cases are both interesting examples of deviations from that pattern in ways that make them, respectively, harder and easier to mitigate than other incidents perpetrated for similar reasons. By relying on cryptocurrency payments and selling data directly back to its original owners, Cryptolocker eliminated centralized financial intermediaries and black market forums that law enforcement routinely relied on to help police financial cyber crimes. Because of this, Cryptolocker (and ransomware, more generally) proved impervious to many of the traditional models of dealing with financially motivated cyber crimes for the same reason that espionage incidents are typically difficult to mitigate—the harm is inflicted essentially at the moment that a ransomware program manages to infect a computer. There are few later-stage monetization steps that criminals have to clear beyond that, offering correspondingly fewer opportunities for defensive intervention. By contrast, the DigiNotar compromise in some ways resembled a traditional financial cyber crime in that the generation of rogue certificates was only the first step in a larger espionage scheme that required several more stages before the perpetrators could actually access the contents of Iranian users' Google accounts. These additional stages—the DNS cache poisoning and redirection of users to fraudulent Google webpages signed by the rogue certificates—involved some powerful centralized parties, such as the DNS operators and browser manufacturers, and provided several additional opportunities for defensive intervention beyond the technical compromise of DigiNotar's own network. As with the financially motivated TJX breach, it was exactly those later stages that led to the compromise eventually being detected and addressed.

The lessons of both financially motivated and espionage cybersecurity incidents echo each other in this regard. They indicate that there are more opportunities to mitigate incidents that require more than just the technical compromise of a computer system or exfiltration of stolen data. The greatest opportunities for defensive intervention are when the perpetrators, in order to be successful in their ultimate aims, have to act on that illicit access or stolen data in some way, whether by selling it, using it to perpetrate fraud, or for surveillance. Regardless of whether those actions are aimed at financial profit or espionage, the bottleneck attack stages that afford defenders a strategic advantage over attackers often occur when perpetrators' attempts to carry out those final stages of an incident, following an initial technical compromise, can be monitored, mitigated, or controlled by a relatively small number of powerful, centralized stakeholders. This is more often the case with financially motivated incidents than espionage-driven ones, but there are exceptions. The least successful espionage efforts, like DigiNotar, resemble financially motivated cybercrimes in that they involve a set of powerful intermediary stakeholders, while the most successful financial cybercrimes, like Cryptolocker, eliminate intermediaries as much as possible and, in doing so, mirror the model of many espionage incidents.

III   Lessons from Online Acts of Public Humiliation

8   Operation Stophaus: The Spamhaus Denial-of-Service Attacks

Many cybercrimes are motivated by money, others by economic or political espionage missions, and all of these can be damaging and embarrassing for the victims in different ways. But perhaps the most flagrant and vituperative cybersecurity incidents are those perpetrated with the express purpose of publicly humiliating the victims. Attackers who are out to gain something, be it money or valuable information, have some stake in keeping their actions relatively under wraps—and their victims relatively solvent—at least until they get what they want. But if the perpetrators of a breach are just out to publicly shame their victim and wreak as much havoc as possible, then they have less to lose from exposure or attention, since that is often exactly what they most want. Furthermore, there are relatively few opportunities to interrupt them both because there may not necessarily be stolen money or information flowing back to the perpetrators in such cases, and because what they want is often malleable, since their mission can be adapted to whatever access or information they can get their hands on. Sometimes, they're not even trying to obtain any proprietary information or access—just making use of resources that are publicly available online. That was the case in March 2013, when the Dutch hosting company CyberBunker decided to exact its revenge on the Spamhaus Project, a nonprofit organization that compiles and distributes lists of DNS servers, IP addresses, and domains known to be used by spammers so that Internet service providers can block them. Spamhaus also maintains a ranking of the "World's Worst Spammers," complete with photographs and biographical information, as well as a Register of Known Spam Operations (ROKSO) database, intended to help other organizations identify and block spammers.

CyberBunker bills itself as an "anything goes" type of service provider, advertising its willingness to host any and all content and websites except those featuring child pornography and terrorism-related material. This sort of lenient approach to hosting illegal or suspect content for customers is also sometimes referred to as "bulletproof hosting." Because of its comparatively lax standards for customers, CyberBunker attracts a large number of websites and customers who engage in the kinds of business that other service providers might be less willing to put up with—people who send large volumes of online spam, for instance, or provide pirated movies and music, or distribute malware. For instance, The Pirate Bay, a peer-to-peer file sharing service notorious for its copyright-infringing content, was a CyberBunker customer until a court in Hamburg ordered CyberBunker to terminate their connection in 2010.[1] The injunction against providing online access to The Pirate Bay was not CyberBunker's only run-in with the law—in 2002, when a fire broke out in the bunker in the Netherlands where CyberBunker was based at the time, police discovered an MDMA lab operating in the building. Outspoken CyberBunker spokesman Sven Olaf Kamphuis later dismissed the incident, explaining, "That was a Chinese triad gang renting a room."[2]

CyberBunker's embrace of questionable customers and their associated shady online businesses made it a natural target for Spamhaus, an organization devoted to fighting spam and cybercrime by helping companies figure out whose traffic they should block from reaching their customers. Founded in 1998, Spamhaus maintains several popular blacklists that are used widely by service providers, companies, and governments all over the world to help block spam and other malicious online activity. Because its core business is blocking not individual spammers but the servers, service providers, and IP addresses they use, Spamhaus, by design, targets not just criminals and spammers but the online infrastructure they rely on to deliver traffic to their victims. In fact, the term "spamhaus" is intended to refer not to the spammers themselves, but rather to the service providers and online hosts who house them and provide them with the connectivity and resources they need to send spam—service providers like CyberBunker. So, in March 2013, presumably after witnessing an influx of bad behavior from CyberBunker's customers, Spamhaus blacklisted the company. This meant that all of the thousands of organizations that relied on Spamhaus's blacklists stopped accepting emails and other online traffic from many

CyberBunker customers. The blacklisting essentially cut off CyberBunker's servers from much of the Internet, rendering their service largely worthless to their customers.

Then, on March 18, 2013, Spamhaus began experiencing an unusually large volume of traffic—around 10Gbps—to their website. The traffic saturated the organization's Internet connection, taking their site offline. The next day, Spamhaus hired security firm Cloudflare to help mitigate the massive distributed denial-of-service (DDoS) attacks they were facing. A DDoS attack involves using a bot comprised of many infected machines, often distributed across the entire world, to bombard a victim with so much online traffic that they cannot keep their systems up and running. The Spamhaus attacks were apparently motivated neither by espionage nor financial theft but instead intended as retaliation against the organization for blacklisting CyberBunker. It was part of a revenge operation dubbed Stophaus that involved representatives from CyberBunker, as well as other companies that had been blacklisted by Spamhaus. A denial-of-service attack is, by design, very different from a data breach, so the lines of defense implemented by Spamhaus and Cloudflare in this case operated very differently from those used to mitigate espionage and fraud efforts, since there were no data exfiltration or financial theft stages to interrupt—indeed there was no access to sensitive information or proprietary systems at all. Instead, defensive efforts had to be pushed up to the very earliest stages of the incident because there were no later stages to fall back on—the damage to Spamhaus was done almost in the same instant that communication with their public-facing web servers was initiated.

Not all public humiliation incidents are denial-of-service attacks—tampering or deleting data and defacement or redirection of a website might also be driven by similar motives. Moreover, not all denial-of-service attacks are intended solely to wreak havoc—occasionally they are used for financial gain as a means of extorting money from victims. Still, denial-of-service attacks offer a useful model for thinking about how to defend against attacks that essentially begin and end with harm—rather than building to it through a series of spread out intermediate steps. Because the victims themselves have so little ability to defend against these types of incidents, DDoS attacks put particular pressure on Internet service providers (ISPs) to assume more defensive responsibilities. Like other third-party defenders who do not directly bear the costs of security incidents, however, it is not clear that

ISPs have any incentive to assume responsibility for defending against these types of attacks. This lack of motivation on the part of the defenders best equipped to address these threats adds to the challenge of defending against security incidents that are intended only to humiliate, inconvenience, or disrupt targets rather than to extract their money or sensitive information. Not only are there fewer steps involved in accomplishing this kind of harm, and therefore fewer opportunities for defensive intervention, there are also fewer intermediaries who can help.

"Finally Pay Back"

One of the reasons that tracing the full timeline of cybersecurity incidents is often challenging is that frequently neither the victims nor the perpetrators want to reveal much about what happened. The victims worry that providing too much information about an incident could invite lawsuits and negative press coverage and maybe even offer other potential adversaries hints about what kinds of tactics can be used against them. The perpetrators, meanwhile, worry about criminal charges and not being able to reuse their same attack strategies if they announce to everyone what those strategies are. In general, incidents motivated by a desire to publicly humiliate the victims tend to garner more publicity than many other kinds of security incidents since attracting attention is often part of the point—the perpetrators want people to know what they have done as part of shaming the victim. Still, the 2013 DDoS attacks directed at Spamhaus offer an unusual degree of transparency on both sides, thanks to a series of blog posts written by Cloudflare outlining the defensive strategy, as well as extensive Skype and IRC chat transcripts of conversations among the Stophaus co-conspirators, from March 17 through March 25, 2013, giving insight into the attackers' perspectives and aims. The chat transcripts were released more than three years after the attacks by security blogger Brian Krebs, who presumably received them from someone in the chat (anyone could join the conversation with the IRC channel name: "stophaus" and the group password: "fucklinford"—a reference to Spamhaus's founder Steve Linford).[3] Putting together Cloudflare's account of defending against the attacks with the real-time conversations among the attackers offers a window into the tools at the disposal of both sides and the week-long back and forth between defense and offense, as both groups tried to adapt to each other's tactics and outlast the other.

The chat logs begin on March 17, 2013, when a group of disgruntled Spamhaus critics congregated in a chat room to consider options for taking down Spamhaus once and for all. The participants included, among others, Kamphuis of CyberBunker (under the username "HRH Prinz Sven Olaf von CyberBunker-Kamphuis MP"), Andrew Jacob Stephens (username: eDataKing), a spamware seller who had been listed in the Spamhaus ROKSO (Register of Known Spam Operations), Sean Nolan McDonagh (username: Narko), a British teenager who later pleaded guilty to coordinating the attacks, and Yuri Bogdanov (username: Yuri), the owner of a Russian hosting company used by many spammers, and a former member of the Russian Business Network cybercrime organization. Over the course of the chat, the participants laid out a litany of reasons they wanted to exact revenge on Spamhaus, most of them related to Spamhaus blocking their services at some point by adding them to the widely used Spamhaus Block List (SBL), or pressuring the companies that provided Internet service and server space to their companies to drop them as customers or risk being added to the SBL themselves. One chat member, Alex Optik, who hosted a Russian "bulletproof hosting" company—i.e., a hosting company with no rules or restrictions on what type of content its customers could post—explained his hatred for Spamhaus:

Alex Optik:	man from slovakia
Alex Optik:	was providing to me servers too
Alex Optik:	for spamhaus
Alex Optik:	nearby 3–4 mounthes [sic]
Alex Optik:	but spamhaus pressed him filtering important subnets
Alex Optik:	and he had to stop working with me
Alex Optik:	but he is good man
Alex Optik:	made a refund to me
Alex Optik:	for unused time[4]

Pressuring companies that provide server space, domain names, and connectivity to spammers to drop them as customers is, of course, exactly what Spamhaus aims to do by compiling its block lists. If Slovakian servers are being used to spew spam, then Spamhaus can add the addresses of those servers to its block lists, and when their owner finds that some of his traffic has been blocked and goes to Spamhaus to ask them to unblock him, they will tell him he first has to get rid of the customers who are sending spam (in this case, Optik). It's a model for policing the Internet that is based on holding every company responsible for what their customers do, regardless of whether or not they themselves are directly responsible for the behavior that got them blocked. Given how hard it is to definitively identify—much less prosecute—spammers online, it's an approach that makes a lot of economic sense: trying to cut spammers off from infrastructure and resources by forcing the companies that sell Internet service, web hosting, and domain names to drop them as customers. On the other hand, holding companies responsible for the actions of their customers and users can cause a lot of headaches for those companies since it often means that many of their customers are blocked due to the misbehavior of just one person or a handful of people. The outcry from other, legitimate customers is what Spamhaus relies on to pressure those companies to take the steps needed to remove themselves from the block list.[a]

But what to Spamhaus and its supporters seemed like a logical way to leverage the design of the Internet, forcing infrastructural intermediaries to police the behavior of their customers and cut off spammers' resources, looked to Kamphuis and his co-conspirators like bullying and censorship. Stephens also used the chat to discuss his grievances with Spamhaus, particularly a time they blocked a registrar[b] that had sold Stephens a new domain name, causing the registrar to suspend the domain:

> eDataKing: SPamhaus attacked Moniker for hosting my sites …
>
> eDataKing: The most damage they ever did was when they got one registrar to suspend the domain and then they allowed me to transfer it out to another registrar (applying the 90 [day] wait from ICANN) and then attacking the new registrar to cause a 90 day loss of site.
>
> eDataKing: By the time the 90 days was up the site has lost its momentum …
>
> eDataKing: Finally pay back[5]

Shutting—or slowing—down the domains of spammers is another example of exactly what Spamhaus aims to do, but that doesn't make it any

---

a. Registrars are companies that sell domain names to individuals and companies.

b. A DNS resolver is another name for a DNS server that responds to queries about the IP addresses for certain domain names. This process of translating a domain name into an IP address is sometimes referred to as "resolving a domain name."

less objectionable to spammers. One of the most striking things about the Spamhaus attackers, in fact, is how deeply they believed they were in the right and that Spamhaus was the real villain, censoring the Internet and coercing companies into blocking anyone they deemed troublesome. There was surprisingly little awareness among the conspirators that their support of illegal activities was in any way a justification for Spamhaus's actions. Consider this exchange between McDonagh and Stephens:

> narko: i think spamhaus wrote to my pamyent [sic] processor
>
> narko: has it happened before?
>
> narko: an IP address started to browse my site. assigned to 2Checkout Inc. now my merchant account is put into a review status....
>
> eDataKing: what have you done illegal on 2checkout?
>
> eDataKing: anything?
>
> narko: no
>
> narko: well
>
> narko: I sell hosting for illegal sites[6]

In spite of—or perhaps because of—their shady lines of work, the conspirators were surprisingly ambivalent about the possibility that what they were doing in attacking Spamhaus was illegal and might lead to encounters with law enforcement. They chatted, half-serious, half-joking, about moving to Cambodia, Moldova, Belarus, Ukraine, or Russia to evade the police, debating the relative merits of different countries and which ones do—and do not—extradite to the United States (Romania was vetoed on those grounds). At various moments during the attacks they posted to social media channels about the attacks using their real names but then occasionally panicked when other users posted screenshots showing their involvement. At the same time, they were quick to dismiss the capabilities of law enforcement based on past experiences. McDonagh told his co-conspirators that "UK police are useless" because when he hosted phishing sites that were reported to the authorities they did nothing.[7] At least one early participant in the chat seemed to take seriously from the outset the possibility that the planned attacks might have repercussions for the perpetrators. Marcel Edler, of the German hosting company Optimate-Server, chose not to become involved in Operation Stophaus, writing in the chat on the evening of March 17:

> ok guys. yes, i sold some ip space and servers for you guys in past. and had some big problems with spamhaus, but all of them is solved now. i dont like spamhaus, yes, but with german law i cannot help you and will quit this channel here. i am

at skype with my real name and you know my website. when anyone is from fbi or police i will get big trouble. so i hope you understand me, that i cannot work with you on that project:)[8]

Less than an hour later, Kamphuis chimed in: "sooo.. time to kill spamhaus lol" and the group launched its first barrage of traffic at Spamhaus. As packets began to bombard the Spamhaus servers, the attackers viewed the whole operation as a richly deserved act of retribution. "As much as they are proud of themselves when someone else loses their connectivity it is quite a grand show to see it happen to them for sure," Stephens said in the chat with satisfaction.

Reflection Attack

Spamhaus first contacted Cloudflare on March 18, and the attacks quickly escalated the next day, after Spamhs hired Cloudflare to help them combat the flood of online traffic swamping its servers. On March 19, soon after Cloudflare got involved, Kamphuis observed "fuck they're back up."[9] Indeed, Cloudflare used its twenty-three data centers to absorb and filter the DDoS traffic by redirecting all of the online traffic intended for Spamhaus's servers to one of its own data centers and then passing on to Spamhaus only the traffic that appeared to be legitimate.[10] This required being able to distinguish between the malicious DDoS traffic and legitimate requests to Spamhaus's servers, a distinction that is not always clear when dealing with denial-of-service attacks routed through a large number of compromised machines. However, the techniques for perpetrating the largest such attacks are usually the ones that make it easiest to detect and filter malicious traffic.

There are multiple ways to launch a DDoS attack and flood a target's servers with traffic. Perhaps the most common strategy is to use a botnet—a network of many compromised machines that can be controlled by whoever infected them—and simply instruct all the infected machines that comprise the bot to bombard a particular website or server with traffic by continually trying to connect to that server. In these cases, it can be very difficult to distinguish between the malicious and legitimate traffic until it is possible to identify which machines have been compromised, for instance, by observing which ones are making unusually large numbers of requests. DDoS attacks that take this approach can reach a significant scale, but they are limited in size by how large and powerful the perpetrators' botnet is. These types of DDoS attacks can therefore be expensive to launch, requiring perpetrators to rent out extremely large botnets if they wish to incapacitate powerful targets with substantial bandwidth for incoming traffic.

The Stophaus conspirators did use bots to bolster their attacks on Spamhaus, recruiting friends and acquaintances to direct traffic and bot-power at Spamhaus's servers. McDonagh, for instance, told the group at one point "I have a friend with a small botnet. I asked him to contribute … my friend is in saudi arabia. he has bots in arab regions. will provide some diversity to the attack. … if you know anyone with botnet - ask them to help too."[11] The geographic diversity of botnets is valuable because it makes it harder for the defenders—in this case, Cloudflare—to profile the attack traffic and differentiate it from the legitimate traffic trying to reach Spamhaus. If all of the malicious traffic is coming from one group of machines, or one specific region, that makes it easier to filter and block. If, on the other hand, it's coming from machines all over the world operated by different botmasters, that makes the filtering trickier.

But merely harnessing the processing power of the bots operated by their friends and having all of the infected machines in those bots directly bombard Spamhaus's servers with connection requests would not have enabled the Stophaus conspirators to launch an attack as massive and crippling as they wanted. So, instead of using their bots to directly bombard Spamhaus with connection requests, the conspirators used what is called a DNS reflection attack, a variation on the traditional DDoS attack. The DNS, or Domain Name System, is the same infrastructure that had to be compromised to make use of the rogue DigiNotar certificates—it's the Internet's address book, the set of servers that help machines translate URLs like www.spamhaus.org into numeric IP addresses like 192.42.118.104. In order to make that translation, a computer trying to connect to a specific website or server will send a query to a DNS server, asking it for more information about the particular URL or web address. The DNS server will look up the information for that address, called a DNS record, and then send it back to the machine that asked for it. A DNS reflection attack takes advantage of the traffic that DNS servers send directly to machines to help them complete connections online by supplying them with DNS records.

To exploit these DNS records, the Stophaus conspirators used their bots to issue queries to DNS servers asking for the records associated with certain sites. These queries appeared to be from Spamhaus machines asking for information about web addresses. The queries weren't actually coming from Spamhaus—they were coming from the machines in the bots that Stophaus controlled—but the conspirators forged their originating IP addresses to look like the requests were actually sent by Spamhaus's servers. Only some DNS resolvers are susceptible to this type of trickery—called "open" DNS resolvers, they respond to queries from any machine at all, regardless of who its owner is. Other DNS resolvers will only respond to queries from machines on their own network that they can associate with particular users making it impossible to do the kind of impersonation that the Stophaus conspirators relied on. Unfortunately for Spamhaus, at the time of the attack in 2013, there were some 21.7 million open DNS resolvers operating online, providing the attackers with ample opportunities for manufacturing DNS reflection traffic.[12]

From an attacker's perspective, there are two important benefits of DNS reflection-based DDoS attacks over the simpler approach of using infected machines to directly bombard a target like Spamhaus. The first is that the source of the attacks—i.e., which machines, specifically, are launching them—is trickier for the victims to pin down. Since the bombardment of unwanted packets directed at the victim is coming from open DNS resolvers rather than individual compromised machines, the victim—and law enforcement—has no easy way to identify which machines are infected and need to be cleaned, or how to trace the attackers back through the computers that comprise their bot. The Stophaus crew was particularly conscious of this after Cloudflare got involved in defending against the attack. At one point in the chat, Russian web host Vitalii Boiko (alias Cali) warns McDonagh that Cloudflare may be able to trace the attacks back to him:

Cali: but you know that they can find the source of the attack also?
narko: with DNS reflection?
Cali: ah it is DNS reflection:D
narko: yes[13]

The other advantage of a DNS reflection attack was that it allowed McDonagh to direct considerably more traffic at Spamhaus than would have been possible just using the bots he had at his disposal. The infected machines that made up those bots could each only send a certain amount of traffic, so McDonagh amplified that traffic by having the bots request very large DNS records, called zone files, which contain lots of information about a domain beyond just its IP address. At McDonagh's command, the infected machines would send repeated requests for zone files to open DNS resolvers and forge the source IP addresses of these requests so they looked like they came from Spamhaus. Each of these requests, or queries, was relatively small, about 36 bytes, so the infected machines could send lots of them. But the DNS servers' responses containing the requested zone files with lots of detailed information about a given domain were much larger, around 3,000 bytes, or nearly 100 times the size of the initial query. And the DNS resolvers sent these 3-kilobyte files to Spamhaus, not to the actual machines that generated the queries, because of the spoofed source IP addresses. Using these methods, the attackers were able to generate up to about 90Gbps of traffic directed at Spamhaus—much more than they would have been able to create using only the compromised machines, without the DNS amplification factor of 100.[14] Cloudflare CEO Matthew Prince explained: "Unlike traditional botnets which could only generate limited traffic because of the modest Internet connections and home PCs they typically run on, these open resolvers are typically running on big servers with fat pipes. They are like bazookas."[15]

Playing Defense

Despite the record-setting levels of traffic that Stophaus managed to direct at Spamhaus, Cloudflare was largely able to mitigate the DDoS and keep Spamhaus's servers up and running. McDonagh was astonished; "i don't understand this," he wrote in the group chat on March 19, "how can cloudflare take 100gbps … and latency is not even increased by 1ms[?]" Relying on DNS reflection traffic for a DDoS attack changes the defensive landscape—and not just because of the potential size of the attack. In a more traditional DDoS attack (that does not make use of DNS reflection traffic), there are relatively few defensive options. The target can filter traffic it receives (or hire someone else like Cloudflare to do it for them) and try to identify malicious packets by detecting high-volume senders or suspicious patterns. Alternatively, the owners of the compromised machines sending that malicious traffic may notice (or be informed of) the large volume of outbound traffic and patch their systems. Moving earlier up the attack chain, it may be possible to go after the actors renting out botnets, but much of the defensive responsibility falls on the targets and occasionally on the machines directly bombarding them with traffic.

By introducing DNS resolvers as an intermediary for sending that traffic, attackers can greatly increase the volume of such attacks, but they also create a new defensive opportunity for the DNS operators who run these resolvers. These operators can restrict which queries their DNS resolvers respond to, so that queries from unknown or unauthorized machines are ignored and the resolvers are no longer open. DNS operators can also "rate limit" their resolvers, rather than closing them completely to the public, so that they only respond to a set number of queries in a certain time period and therefore cannot be used to generate as much traffic directed at a single server. Following the Spamhaus attacks, the Open Resolver Project publicly released a list of millions of open resolvers online in hopes of pressuring their operators to shut them down or further restrict them, highlighting the potential power of this group of intermediaries.

Besides introducing a new class of defensive intermediaries in the form of the DNS operators, DDoS amplification attacks also make it easier for targets and companies like Cloudflare to distinguish between malicious and non-malicious traffic. In standard DDoS attacks, both types of traffic may look very similar, like people trying to connect to a particular website or server. But in DNS amplification attacks the malicious traffic is likely to be of a very specific type (large DNS records) that can be recognized and dropped without affecting legitimate users. Another type of attack traffic involved in the DDoS attack directed at Spamhaus was generated by an ACK reflection attack, in which the compromised machines initiated TCP sessions[c] ostensibly from a Spamhaus IP address and the receiving servers therefore responded to Spamhaus with an ACK (acknowledgment) connection, acknowledging receipt of the session initiation. This type of DDoS does not have the amplification effect afforded by DNS reflection but still helps with identifying malicious traffic, since targets can simply drop all unmatched ACKs that they know they did not request. Both DNS amplification and ACK reflection attacks rely on the ability of senders to spoof the originating IP address of any traffic they send. If the attackers couldn't make it look like the DNS queries and TCP session initiation requests had come from Spamhaus, then these methods would be of no use. So another possible defensive approach is to target this spoofing of sender IP addresses

---

c. TCP, or Transmission Control Protocol, is a protocol for establishing a network connection between two computers so that they can communicate with each other.

by ingress filtering, or forcing routers to check source IP addresses of packets they receive.

Strangely, when Cloudflare went public with a blog post detailing how the attacks had been perpetrated—in particular the ACK and DNS reflection traffic—the attackers were upset that their techniques had been revealed. On March 20, McDonagh wrote to the group chat, with no apparent irony:

narko: they wrote about my ACK reflection
narko: ...
narko: they need to not write information like this
narko: they're just going to give people the information to do more attacks[16]

McDonagh was so certain that he is in the right in perpetrating this attack that he appears to have been utterly unaware of the irony of his worrying about other people perpetrating exactly the type of attack he was engaged in launching against Spamhaus.

Leveraging their capacity to collect and filter enormous volumes of traffic, Cloudflare helped Spamhaus mitigate the attacks for two days until the DDoS attacks appeared to cease on March 21. On March 22, the attacks resumed—but they were no longer directed at Spamhaus. Instead, the attackers shifted their focus to the service providers and interconnection facilities that Cloudflare used to connect to the Internet. This change in strategy to try to knock Cloudflare offline pushed the defensive responsibilities upstream, forcing Cloudflare's bandwidth providers to filter traffic and, reportedly, causing some collateral congestion for other users so that people began noticing Internet performance problems more broadly.[17]

There are two basic models for defending against DDoS attacks. The first is to target the early stages of an attack by preventing the perpetrators from generating large volumes of traffic. This might mean trying to break up botnets, disinfect compromised machines, or rate limit how much traffic an individual machine, or group of machines, can send to a particular destination. The second type of defense, aimed at a later stage of DDoS attacks when traffic is directed at a particular target, aims to prevent those large volumes of traffic from reaching, or incapacitating, their targets. This was the role Cloudflare played in the attacks on Spamhaus by absorbing the malicious traffic and filtering it before it reached Spamhaus's servers. It's a model built on the idea that protecting themselves against certain types of online harm is something victims don't always have the visibility or resources to do themselves and must therefore rely on intermediaries, like Cloudflare, to do by inserting their infrastructure in between the attackers and their targets. Even without deliberately redirecting incoming traffic through a company like Cloudflare, there are already intermediaries between DDoS attackers and their victims—namely, the service providers who carry online traffic across the Internet.

Service providers are equipped with greater visibility into online traffic patterns than any other group of intermediaries, since they can track where that traffic is coming from and going to across millions of machines. This gives them a unique ability to identify malicious traffic and botnets when they see large groups of machines all being contacted by the same command and control servers at regular intervals, or all bombarding the same target with large volumes of traffic. Service providers also have the power to decide whether that traffic should be dropped or delivered to its intended recipients. Furthermore, the major "Tier 1" service providers, which carry the bulk of online traffic, are relatively concentrated in a handful of large companies, making them significantly easier to regulate than, for instance, the thousands of dispersed DNS operators or millions of owners of compromised machines. While DNS operators and the owners of compromised machines can in theory assist with defending against DDoS attacks, they have little visibility into when it is necessary, and even less incentive to bother.

Because of service providers' unique defensive capabilities and relative market concentration, some governments have targeted them as the intermediaries best equipped to defend against denial-of-service attacks—and bots more generally. In both the United States and Australia, regulators have helped develop voluntary codes of conduct for service providers recommending measures that could help mitigate bots by taking advantage of service providers' unparalleled visibility into malicious traffic patterns and ability to deliver—or not deliver—packets to their intended destination. Like other third-party defenders who do not directly bear the costs of security incidents, however, service providers do not necessarily have strong incentives to assume these voluntary defensive responsibilities.

In the Spamhaus case, law enforcement also ended up playing a defensive role—Kamphuis and McDonagh were both later arrested—but this is often a tricky line of defense for a class of attack that rarely leaves a clear money trail or beneficiary. Successful law enforcement intervention was possible in the Spamhaus case partly because CyberBunker was so outspoken in assuming responsibility for the attacks. Kamphuis posted on Facebook and Twitter about the attacks while they were happening, and publicly acknowledged in an interview with the *New York Times* that CyberBunker was using the DDoS attacks to punish Spamhaus for "abusing their influence."[18]

McDonagh—who was a minor when he launched the attacks—pleaded guilty and was sentenced to only 240 hours of community service on the grounds that he suffered from severe mental illness.[19] Kamphuis, who was arrested in Spain in April 2013 and later extradited to the Netherlands, was sentenced to 240 days in jail in November 2016, but had already spent 55 days in jail after being extradited and the remaining 185 days of his sentence were suspended by the judge. Linford later expressed disappointment in the light sentence in an email to Krebs, writing:

> We had hoped for a longer jail sentence to send the message that organising and conducting DDoS attacks is a crime not acceptable to law courts or society, however the ease with which Kamphuis was arrested and extradited, and the two months already served in jail will hopefully have delivered the message to him that there is no escape from the law should he attempt any attacks in the future.[20]

"Custard's Last Stand"

The DDoS attacks were the centerpiece, and undoubtedly the most effective and eye-catching component, of Operation Stophaus, but Kamphuis and his co-conspirators intended to do more than just temporarily incapacitate Spamhaus, they wanted to put it out of business for good. On March 20, when Cloudflare appeared to be managing fine handling the attack traffic, the conspirators tried to find a way to get Spamhaus kicked off Cloudflare's service. One Chinese counterfeiter in the chat suggested: "let me find some customers who using cloudflare, and sent a complaints to cloudflare 'cloudflare's netowrking is too slow these days, even can not access our sites'. we have about 200 customers using cloudflare's service. cloudflare will fell overwhelming force." Stephens concurred: "no one thing is what will work ... this campaign as a whole will end them though."[21] The campaign as a whole involved not just the DDoS and an attempt to turn Cloudflare's other customers against Spamhaus, but also a series of attempts to undermine Spamhaus's online infrastructure and promote the attackers' own anti-Spamhaus agenda as publicly as possible. For instance, on March 18, as

the attacks were beginning, McDonagh filed a report with the WHOIS database, which is maintained by the Internet Corporation for Assigned Names
and Numbers (ICANN) to track who owns different domain names online.[d]
McDonagh's complaint alleged that the entry for spamhaus.org was invalid
because the people listed as contacts for the domain were "fake names,"
and emails and phone calls to the listed contact addresses and numbers did
not go through. They didn't go through, of course, because the organization was under attack and its networks were down.

In reporting that the organization had filed incorrect information in
WHOIS, McDonagh was hoping to get the spamhaus.org domain suspended
by ICANN. When that failed, the attackers tried to displace spamhaus.org
as the top-ranked Google search result for people who searched for "spamhaus." They wanted their own site, stophaus.com, on which they listed their
many grievances with Spamhaus, to come up first instead so they started
"tagging" their site with keywords related to Spamhaus. A Lithuanian bulletproof hosting provider involved in the chat asked: "do you mind if we
put spamhaus metatags on stophaus? so we can come up first on google
soon:D"—and Kamphuis enthusiastically agreed.[22] The same Lithuanian
provider later tried (and failed) to reset the Google Apps administrative
password for spamhaus.org in an attempt to take over the organization's
email accounts, which were administered through Google.[23]

While the Stophaus conspirators struggled to extend their efforts beyond
the DDoS attack to cause more lasting damage to Spamhaus by undermining its partnership with Cloudflare, its domain, its search rankings, and its
email accounts, Spamhaus launched a similar—and much more successful—
offensive directed at the group's own website, stophaus.com. On March 20,
McDonagh received notification from his service provider that Spamhaus
had blocked them because of his website and he would have to sever all
ties with stophaus.org or they would disconnect his service. When he pro-
tested, the provider responded:

> Unfortunately our hands are tied. Spamhaus tell us that you are harbouring a
> known ROKSO spammer, we're not happy to be associated with this as it affects
> other clients whom have no control on the situation. As such I'm afraid you will
> need to move this client from our network within the next 24hrs or we will have

d. The WHOIS database is publicly available online and contains names and contact
information for the owners of all registered domain names (except for individuals
who pay an additional fee in order to withhold their information from being listed).

to interrupt service. Please update us when this client no longer utilises *any* part of our network so we can get back in touch with Spamhaus.[24]

To the Stophaus conspirators, this was just further proof of Spamhaus's unwarranted power and ability to censor sites it didn't like online. McDonagh complained:

narko: they treat it like it's a request from law enforcement

narko: not some moron on a boat

eDataKing: right

eDataKing: and this is the reason we fight …[25]

Then, on March 21, the domain for stophaus.com was suspended by the registrar that McDonagh had purchased it from, called AHnames. Kamphuis was furious and began lashing out at AHnames on Facebook, threatening them: "if you're not with us, you're against us. turn it back on or we turn YOU OFF … take your pick … 80gbit/s up your ass, orrrr … turning the domain back on."[26] Within the chat, Kamphuis instructed McDonagh to target AHnames with a brief attack so they would know the threats were serious:

HRH Prinz Sven Olaf von CyberBunker-Kamphuis MP: send them a few packets so they know

HRH Prinz Sven Olaf von CyberBunker-Kamphuis MP: narko: ddos on that ahnames for like 1 minute …

HRH Prinz Sven Olaf von CyberBunker-Kamphuis MP: we;re not gonna change the god damn domain name

HRH Prinz Sven Olaf von CyberBunker-Kamphuis MP: we're gonna make them turn it back on

HRH Prinz Sven Olaf von CyberBunker-Kamphuis MP: simple as that.[27]

Stephens was more sanguine about Spamhaus's attempts to blacklist its own attackers. He took these efforts as a sign of the company's desperation, optimistically predicting on March 21, "this is very likely to be their version of Custard's Last Stand [sic]."[28]

The Stophaus conspirators tried to target Spamhaus on several different fronts, combining one of the most massive DDoS attacks ever witnessed at the time with a barrage of other efforts intended to make the organization lose its customers, web domain, and partnership with Cloudflare. Because the attack was so large and had such far-reaching consequences, even for Internet users who weren't trying to access Spamhaus, and because

Spamhaus later gave Cloudflare permission to publicly discuss the details of the attack, the incident had a significant impact on the defensive landscape for DDoS attacks. It drew attention to the threats posed by open DNS resolvers and the inability of many targets of denial-of-service attacks to defend against such incidents on their own, as well as the corresponding need for intervention from third parties like Cloudflare to absorb and filter large volumes of traffic. The incident, and others like it, also fueled ongoing debates around defining the defensive roles and responsibilities of Internet service providers, the intermediaries best positioned and equipped to help mitigate denial-of-service attacks—and bots more generally—given their unique visibility into traffic patterns and ability to identify malicious traffic.

Operation Stophaus was a reminder, too, of how the different motivations of attackers can change their tactics, as well as determine the opportunities for defensive intervention. The Stophaus conspirators, out for revenge, exhibited none of the subtlety or inconspicuousness of intruders looking to steal money or secrets, who would typically try to lie low and maintain their illicit access to the victims' computers for as long as possible. Instead, publicity was part of the Stophaus conspirators' goal—to take their revenge on Spamhaus, they needed everyone to know that they were the ones responsible for bringing the organization down. This aspect of the attack not only made the perpetrators easier for authorities to track down and arrest, it also opened them up to counterattacks like having their domain name suspended and their service provider dropping them as customers. These interventions did not stop the DDoS attacks—Cloudflare's filtering was responsible for mitigating the flood of traffic—but they did make the DDoS attacks less satisfying and less worthwhile for the conspirators. Taking away Stophaus's ability to promote its anti-Spamhaus message was the equivalent, in some sense, of taking away Gonzalez's ability to profit off his stolen credit card numbers, or removing China's ability to act on the economic information it stole from U.S. companies. After all, the DDoS attack itself was never the point, the point was proving to the world that Spamhaus was—in the words of Kamphuis' Stophaus manifesto, posted on stophaus .com—"an offshore criminal network of tax circumventing self declared internet terrorists pretending to be 'spam' fighters."[29] To have their own Stophaus website declared as spam by Spamhaus—and then to have their service provider and domain registrar unquestioningly accept that designation and suspend their service—only reinforced how completely Operation

Stophaus had failed to degrade Spamhaus's influence and legitimacy with other online stakeholders. It was that influence, even more than the technical mitigations undertaken by Cloudflare, that enabled Spamhaus to so completely triumph over its attackers in the face of a crushing onslaught of malicious traffic. To generate that traffic, Stophaus took advantage of the underlying architecture of the Internet itself. That reliance on infrastructural components of the Internet's addressing system, especially open DNS resolvers, gave rise to questions about who, besides the Stophaus conspirators, was to blame for allowing the attack to happen in the first place. The owners of the infected machines used to comprise the Stophaus botnets, the operators of the open DNS resolvers that bombarded Spamhaus with enormous zone files in response to forged requests, and the Internet service providers who carried and delivered that traffic all played a role in enabling Operation Stophaus. But since they had not been attacked themselves—had indeed felt none of the ill-effects of the Stophaus DDoS—they had no strong incentives to try to make it more difficult for people to launch similar attacks in the future.

9 "An Epic Nightmare": The Sony Breach and Ex-Post Mitigation

At first glance, the computer virus at Sony Pictures Entertainment (SPE) appeared both amateurish—and confusing. When employees arrived at the studio's Los Angeles headquarters the morning of November, 24, 2014, their computer desktops displayed a picture of a glowing red skeleton overlaid with an ambiguous, ungrammatical message: "Warning: We've already warned you, and this is just a beginning. We continue till our request be met. We've obtained all your internal data including your secrets and top secrets. If you don't obey us, we'll release data shown below to the world."[1] There was no demand for money included in the threat—no demand for anything, in fact, just the reference to an unspecified "request." It didn't seem like a threat that needed to be taken too seriously, but the computers still weren't working; so the IT staff shut down the company's internal network and Sony Pictures CEO Michael Lynton and co-chairman Amy Pascal called in the security firm FireEye. Earlier that year, FireEye had acquired Mandiant—the company that investigated the South Carolina Department of Revenue breach and PLA Unit 61398 espionage efforts—so the investigation of the Sony breach commenced in much the same way those other incidents unfolded. But it quickly became apparent to the team of investigators, led by Mandiant-CEO-turned-FireEye-CEO Kevin Mandia, that this was a breach unlike any other they had encountered before. In early December, Mandia reported to Lynton:

> The scope of this attack differs from any we have responded to in the past, as its purpose was to both destroy property and release confidential information to the public. The bottom line is that this was an unparalleled and well planned crime, carried out by an organized group, for which neither SPE nor other companies could have been fully prepared.[2]

What made the Sony incident unique—and, in its way, terrifying and unparalleled—was not any particular technical tool or method that the intruders had used to access the SPE networks, nor was it the vast quantity of data they had accessed, including unreleased movies, scripts, emails, digital certificates, employee databases, payroll information, and health insurance records. In the weeks that followed the November 24 compromise, as that stolen data began to be distributed to journalists and posted online, it became clear that what really set this breach apart from others that Mandia and his team had investigated was the motivation and mentality of its perpetrators. Whoever had compromised the SPE network was not looking to steal money or conduct any familiar form of secretive espionage. Rather, they were looking to cause chaos—to publicly shame and torment SPE and its employees before as wide a global audience as possible by any means available, ranging from releasing high-level executives' embarrassing email exchanges and salary data, to posting employee Social Security numbers and financial information, to disseminating as-yet-unreleased movies and scripts. There was a certain irony in watching these secrets unfold in such spectacular fashion around a company whose primary purpose was public entertainment. The fact that this breach was an entertainment industry story—that it involved movie stars and big-budget drama of every variety— was a large part of what made it such an enticing and exciting story for journalists and their readers.

Breaches perpetrated for the purposes of financial gain or espionage can cause plenty of damage, but they tend to follow certain expected and explicable templates that make it easier to understand—and anticipate—what an attacker will do with the access and data they have acquired and why. But, like Operation Stophaus, the 2014 Sony Pictures breach did not follow any of those expected templates—it was motivated purely by malice, perpetrated by people who had no agenda for personal gain, and therefore no interest in keeping their actions secret and no concerns about restricting their activity, and the resulting damage, to any particular mission. It was the lack of any rational motivation or clear self-interest driving this very public, free-wheeling, no-holds-barred assault on Sony Pictures and its thousands of employees that made this breach different right from the start. Two other developments contributed to making the incident even more unusual and unprecedented. The first was the very public involvement of the U.S. government in an incident directed at a private company. On December 19, the FBI announced it had determined that the government of North Korea was responsible for the breach, and President Barack Obama vowed that the United States would "respond proportionally."[3] It was only the second time—after the charges brought against the members of PLA Unit 61398—that the U.S. government had publicly accused a foreign government of compromising an American company's computer systems, and the first time that the federal government had ever appeared to promise any sort of in-kind respond or retaliation on behalf of a private company. Companies and government agencies had been talking for years about public-private partnerships for cybersecurity, but the president promising a response to what was essentially a corporate compromise indicated that the inter-mingling of public and private cybersecurity incidents and priorities had reached new heights.

This response from the U.S. government was surprising and so, too, was the response from SPE itself. Far from accepting the conventional wisdom that there was little they could do once the data had been stolen, the studio used both legal and technical means to go after many of the online and media intermediaries distributing their stolen data. These—largely unsuccessful—attempts by SPE to extend the commonly understood limits of ex-post mitigation by targeting distribution intermediaries was the second development that made this incident so remarkable and significant. Though the studio's efforts seemed to have relatively little impact on how widely the stolen information was shared and reported on, their attempts to rein in the distribution of their leaked data offered a template of sorts for companies and policymakers interested in making it easier for victims of similar breaches to recover financially and to punish those who participated in their public humiliation. SPE's actions also made clear just what was at stake for anyone who took up that template and how stark the trade-offs would be, especially with regard to free speech and free press protections, if policymakers tried to make it easier for victims to control information flows and publication through legal means as a way of trying to mitigate the impacts of similar breaches.

The Guardians of Peace

Regardless of the perpetrators' ultimate motives, the early stages of many computer security breaches—from the South Carolina Department of Revenue breach to the GameOver ZeuS Cryptolocker infections to the PLA Unit 61398 espionage efforts—look remarkably similar, and the Sony breach was no exception. It began with phishing emails sent to Sony Pictures employees that included web links or attachments containing special "wiper" malware. The malware program included in these emails, called igfxtrayex. exe, was designed to look like a legitimate Microsoft Windows service when installed.[4] In fact, there is a valid Windows program called igfxtray (stored in a file named igfxtray.exe) that is used to provide users with an easy way to modify the graphics settings on their computers. When a Sony employee downloaded the igfxtrayex.exe file from a phishing email, the malware infected that employee's computer and immediately created a network fileshare connection, allowing it to communicate with all the other machines on the same local network operated by Sony Pictures.[5] That communication was essential for the perpetrators to spread their malware across the entire Sony Pictures network to all of the computers at the company's headquarters; otherwise they could only have compromised the machines owned by people who fell for their phishing messages.

If Sony Pictures had made it more difficult for the computers on its internal network to communicate with each other then the studio might have been better able to control the scale and scope of the intrusion. For instance, the studio might have tried to segment their network in a manner similar to DigiNotar's system of DMZs and more secure network portions, so that a compromise of one computer connected to it could not be easily spread to all of the others—of course, even that system ultimately failed DigiNotar. Besides opportunities for network segmentation, the phishing messages themselves provided an early opportunity to stem the breach, had those messages been filtered by Sony's email programs or ignored by the employees who received them. However, training thousands of employees to reliably recognize suspicious emails was—and still is—likely to be a losing battle, especially if any individual failure could lead to the compromise of the entire company's network. Trying to isolate and quarantine infected machines by making it more difficult for them to spread malware to other computers might have been a more effective strategy for containing the damage and interfering with the early stages of the breach. As it was, the studio was only able to isolate roughly half of its machines from the malware, and the igfxtrayex wiper successfully deleted everything stored on 3,262 of the company's 6,797 personal computers and 837 of its 1,555 servers.[6]

From the moment of its execution, the igfxtrayex wiper malware was focused on spreading itself. First, it would try to copy itself onto other computers on the network over the shared connection it had created. Then, it would create another four copies of itself and cut off the infected machine's email access by shutting down the Microsoft Exchange Information Store service.[7] The malware then attempted to connect to a set of command-and-control servers whose IP addresses were hardcoded into the wiper and were presumably controlled by the perpetrators. One of the hardcoded IP addresses was traced back to a Virtual Private Network server in Italy operated by a service called HideMyAss that helped users protect their anonymity online through VPNs. Another command-and-control IP address was traced back to a Polish import-export company, and a third to a university in Thailand.[8] As in the case of the command-and-control servers used to control the GameOver ZeuS bot, these were almost certainly not servers that the perpetrators themselves directly owned—rather, they were probably compromised or rented machines that were being used as intermediaries to control the igfxtrayex wiper without leading investigators directly back to the intruders. Finally, the wiper accessed and deleted the entire contents of the infected machine's hard drive and then rebooted the machine, completely wiped of all its data, to display the red skeleton and warning message that Sony Pictures employees discovered the morning of November 24.[9]

That morning, as FireEye and Sony were attempting to regain control of their network, it looked like the destruction of Sony Pictures' data was the primary goal of the breach. But five days later, while the studio was still struggling to get their computers back up and running, it became apparent that there was an even earlier stage of the attack, one that must have taken place before the SPE data was wiped but could no longer be reliably traced because so much of the relevant evidence had been deleted by the wiper malware. On the morning of November 29, 2014, several journalists began receiving emails from a group that had dubbed itself the Guardians of Peace, or G.O.P. The emails included several links to the website Pastebin, a site that lets users paste and store text anonymously. The G.O.P provided the chosen journalists with a password—diespe123—that they could use to access the Pastebin links, which turned out to grant access to twenty-six folders containing all manner of internal data stolen from Sony Pictures, including employee salary information, Social Security numbers, and performance reviews.[10] As reporters began publishing stories about the data, detailing pay discrepancies and internal disputes at Sony Pictures, the studio realized that at some point before their systems had been wiped, their data must have been copied and exfiltrated by the intruders. Far from losing all their data in the incident, the studio's information was now more easily available than ever—to anyone with an Internet connection.

One of the unresolved mysteries of the Sony breach is how, exactly, the intruders managed to steal such a vast quantity of data without attracting any attention or raising any flags within Sony's IT team. The Guardians of Peace claimed to have taken just under 100 terabytes of data, but thanks to the destruction of the wiper malware it was difficult to reconstruct exactly when or how that had happened. The mystery surrounding the mechanics of the earlier stages of the breach led to a number of competing theories, including a vocal minority who argued that in order to exfiltrate such a large quantity of data and exploit the studio's network so thoroughly and knowledgeably, the intruders must have had inside help from Sony Pictures employees.[11] Mandia and many others dismissed these claims as unsupported by evidence, and Mandia later indicated he believed the intruders had exfiltrated the stolen data a little bit at a time over an extended period in order to evade detection.[12] Since media companies routinely transfer large files, like movies, Sony Pictures probably had a relatively high threshold—if, indeed, it had any threshold—for the volume of data leaving their network that would trigger an alert or investigation.[13]

Despite the holes in the early stages of the Sony Pictures breach timeline, it is clear that the studio had at least three crucial opportunities to intervene and interrupt the intrusion prior to November 24. The first would have been to flag the copying and exfiltration of the data that was stolen by monitoring large volumes of outgoing data, anomalous recipients of outbound data streams, regular patterns in outbound data (e.g., files of a certain size and format being sent to a particular destination every day or every hour), or even suspicious-seeming staging of data for exfiltration (e.g., files being compressed and bundled into a series of archives of a certain size that could then be transferred). As with espionage-motivated breaches like the PLA Unit 61398 missions and the OPM breach, exfiltrating Sony's data turned out to be central to the intruders' mission of publicly humiliating the company. They had to find a way to carry out this stage of the intrusion or give up on their goal of embarrassing the studio on a global stage. At the very least, defending against high-volume exfiltration would

have mitigated the impacts of the breach—even if it wouldn't have necessarily prevented the wiper from erasing the data.

The phishing messages bearing the wiper malware presented another possible point of interruption for SPE—the studio might have identified these messages as fraudulent and filtered them out of employees' inboxes. Alternatively, had the employees who received them successfully identified them as fraudulent and avoided the enclosed links and attachments, that, too, might have prevented at least the deletion stage of the breach. But besides the significant challenges of actually preventing any phishing emails from being received or opened, this was not an absolutely essential, or bottleneck, stage of the breach from the intruders' perspective. There are other ways of delivering malware to a victim's system besides phishing (for instance, the DigiNotar breach exploited a software vulnerability in a public-facing web server). Finally, there was an opportunity for Sony to segment its network more aggressively so that an infection of one—or even a few—machines could not be so easily spread to so many others at the company. Segmentation could have helped contain the damage caused by the wiper (and possibly also the exfiltration, by limiting what data the intruders could access based on their initial points of compromise), though it would still have offered few guarantees. DigiNotar's network, for instance, was elaborately segmented into multiple different zones with more than one hundred firewall rules separating them and dictating how they communicated with each other, all to no avail.

Undoubtedly, the Sony Pictures breach was a carefully planned intrusion carried out over a relatively extended period of time using some particularly nasty malware. But in terms of overall technical sophistication, it followed, to a large extent, the same basic template as many previous incidents: phishing emails followed by the delivery and spreading of malware across an internal network and, finally, large-scale data exfiltration. The wiper malware was new, but closely related to similar types of malware that had been used in earlier breaches, researchers later found, and it made use of commercially available software drivers to overwrite data on the SPE hard drives without administrator privileges. In other words, it was an effective but not incredibly novel or advanced piece of code. Similarly, the steps Sony could have taken to prevent, or at least mitigate, the impacts of the breach were pretty standard security practices—outbound traffic monitoring, phishing filtering and education, network segmentation—none of them impossibly cumbersome or excessive measures. When Mandia called the breach an "unparalleled and well planned crime, carried out by an organized group, for which neither SPE nor other companies could have been fully prepared," he was almost certainly not referring to the technical sophistication of the incident. Indeed, the previous sentence of his email to Lynton makes clear that what sets the breach apart from others, in his opinion, is not *how* it was carried out but *why*, the fact that "its purpose was to both destroy property and release confidential information to the public." A later analysis of the incident led by security firm Novetta echoed this point in a report that concluded the group responsible for the Sony Pictures breach had "executed numerous successful attacks due in large part to their organization and determination, more so than due to any highly sophisticated malware."[14]

What made the Sony Pictures breach unique and significant—and difficult to predict or prepare for—was not the igfxtrayex wiper, or any of the other technical components of the intrusion, but instead the vindictive, wide-ranging destructive impulses of its perpetrators. Sony, however, had a vested interest in portraying the intrusion as technically sophisticated, otherwise the major technology company looked like it had carelessly failed to implement expected lines of defense for its network—and not for the first time. Sony, the parent company of SPE, had a long history of computer security breaches, and it quickly became apparent, in the aftermath of the 2014 incident, that the lesson it had taken away from those previous episodes was not to beef up its security, but instead to paint the breach as the cybercrime of the century and its perpetrators as brilliant, cutting-edge, relentless criminals. It turned out Sony would receive some assistance in this mission from an unexpected source—the United States government.

A Very Public Accusation

Less than a month after the Guardians of Peace made their presence in the Sony Pictures network known by wiping hundreds of the studio's computers, the FBI announced that it had determined that the North Korean government was responsible for the incident. According to the FBI, the attribution was based on similarities between the wiper malware and code used by North Korea to attack South Korean banks and media companies in 2013. Additionally, several of the command-and-control IP addresses that the wiper software was programmed to contact were known to be associated with North Korean infrastructure.[15] The FBI stressed that their determination was made only "in part" based on this evidence, implying that there was other (presumably classified) evidence that further supported their assertion. Still, many people were skeptical of how circumstantial the FBI's evidence appeared to be, and North Korea—to no one's surprise—vehemently denied any involvement.[16]

The 2016 analysis by Novetta of the wiper malware provided a clearer picture of the similarities between the igfxtrayex code and other malware that had previously been linked to North Korea. Analysts found that the code used to infiltrate the SPE network relied on the same, relatively obscure, encryption scheme called Caracachs that was used in malware that targeted U.S. and South Korean government agencies, military networks, and companies in 2011 and 2013. Furthermore, the same key—"abc defghijklmnopqrstuvwxyz012345\0\0\0\0\0"—was used to initialize the Caracachs encryption algorithms across many of these malware programs, including the SPE wiper.[17] Besides the use of similar cryptographic keys and encryption schemes, the analysts also found a common pattern in how the Sony intruders had masked their communication with command-and-control servers. After infecting their victims' computers, the wiper malware would disguise its communications with the command-and-control servers to look like TLS, the standard Transport Layer Security encryption protocol commonly used for web browsing, even though the malware program was actually using a different type of encryption. This helped the intruders evade network-monitoring tools looking for anomalous outbound traffic because it made the communications between infected machines and the intruders' C2 servers look like normal web connections to popular websites. The malware authors let the wiper choose either www.amazon.com or www.google.com, at random, and then pretend it was communicating with the selected site when it was instead talking to a command-and-control server operated by the intruders.[18] The Novetta analysts traced this technique in the SPE wiper code to previous pieces of malware used against U.S. and South Korean targets. They also found that the SPE wiper's overzealous deletion process figured in many of those other malware programs as well. The process involved first overwriting files with randomly generated garbage data, and then renaming the files with more randomly generated text, and, finally, deleting the renamed, overwritten files.[19]

Despite these similarities, Novetta stopped short of attributing the SPE breach—and the other incidents perpetrated with similar malware—to the North Korean government, choosing instead to make the more modest assertion that the incident had been perpetrated by an organization they dubbed the "Lazarus Group," which had carried out several other attacks on U.S. and South Korean targets using similar tools and techniques. Novetta even pointed out in its report that the IP addresses and command-and-control servers the FBI had previously traced back to North Korea were not necessarily damning evidence. The Novetta report noted: "While the infrastructure used in the SPE attack overlaps with infrastructure attributed to malicious cyber activity linked to North Korea, previously malicious IP addresses are not necessarily still used by the same attackers." These IP addresses—the ones that had been traced back to VPN providers, businesses, and universities in Italy, Poland, and Thailand—were, in fact, "almost all public proxies used by a variety of malware operators in the past," the analysts concluded.[20]

But while Novetta was reluctant to place blame squarely on North Korea, the FBI had no such hesitations. The agency's statement left little room for uncertainty or doubt, despite their having had only four weeks to investigate the incident and never before having made such a public and unequivocal accusation against a foreign government for a computer crime directed at a private company. Something about this incident, the FBI indicated in its statement, was different—and required a sterner response. "Though the FBI has seen a wide variety and increasing number of cyber intrusions, the destructive nature of this attack, coupled with its coercive nature, sets it apart," the agency said, adding that, "North Korea's actions were intended to inflict significant harm on a U.S. business and suppress the right of American citizens to express themselves."[21]

The FBI's decision to publicly denounce the North Korean government over the SPE breach was surprising, but the real shock came a few days later, on December 22, 2014, when North Korea suddenly lost its access to the Internet in an apparent distributed denial-of-service attack on the country's limited number of routers.[22] The incident followed closely on President Obama's promise that the United States would "respond proportionally" to the SPE breach and subsequent fear-mongering by the intruders, including threats of violence that were never realized. Although the United States government did not admit to taking North Korea offline, neither did it deny responsibility for the incident. A State Department spokesperson told reporters: "We aren't going to discuss, you know, publicly operational details about the possible response options ... as we implement our responses, some will be seen, some may not be seen."[23]

For the United States to respond in any way to a cybersecurity breach directed at a private company with something other than an indictment or routine law enforcement proceedings was unprecedented and, to many, alarming. The U.S. government's intention appeared to be deterrence in sending a clear signal that anyone who came after a U.S. company would face the significant technical capabilities of the federal government by way of retribution. But by responding—or even just threatening to respond—in kind to a computer security incident directed at a private company, the United States took a significant step toward blurring the line between the protection of industry and government networks. Through their response to the SPE breach, the U.S. government not only opened the door for private companies to turn to them to avenge attacks, they also gave license to other governments to involve themselves in industry disputes and leverage their cyber arsenals on behalf of businesses within their borders. By entering the fray to retaliate on Sony's behalf, the United States appeared ready to eliminate—or at the very least obscure—the distinctions between attacks on private companies and government institutions. To some extent, those distinctions were already eroding, given how much Internet infrastructure is operated by industry and how many systems critical for national security and stability are run by private companies. But for the government to lash out over a breach directed at a movie studio, rather than, for instance, a power plant, or a hospital, suggested that the government considered it their job not just to protect the nation's critical infrastructure, but also the reputation and digital resources of every major company within its borders.

"A Strong and Merciless Countermeasure"

For Sony, the FBI's statement that North Korea was responsible for the breach was a godsend. It was a clear confirmation of Mandia's earlier assessment that no company could possibly have prepared for such a breach or defended themselves against such a well-resourced, sophisticated adversary as the North Korean government. (Incidentally, that assessment from Fire-Eye was so exactly the message that Sony wanted to convey about the breach that Lynton forwarded Mandia's email to all SPE employees.) Sony—like many firms in the aftermath of a breach—was understandably eager to clarify that what had happened was not their fault, that no one could have been better prepared for the breach or could have known to expect it. There were, however, warning signs in the months leading up to the breach, which, coupled with the company's history of computer breaches, might have led the studio to strengthen its defenses, or at the very least prepare a contingency plan.

From the earliest stages of developing Seth Rogen and Evan Goldberg's planned movie about North Korea, the studio had been trying to decide exactly how far they could go with the comedy about the CIA-orchestrated assassination of Korean dictator Kim Jong Un. The studio was less concerned with upsetting North Korea than it was with offending the Chinese government and alienating a major international audience for the film. Pascal went along with the creators' desire to set the movie in North Korea and call the central character Kim Jong Un, rather than shifting it to a fictional country or ruler, though the studio did soften the title from "Kill Kim Jong Un" to the more innocuous "The Interview."[24] Rogen and Goldberg were also warned by a consultant they hired to change their banking and email passwords and to monitor their online accounts in preparation for likely retaliation from North Korea.[25]

Then, in June 2014, when the first trailer for the film was released, the North Korean Central News Agency issued a statement calling it "undisguised terrorism and a war action," and threatening "a strong and merciless countermeasure" if the movie was released.[26] The threats were sufficiently worrisome to prompt Lynton to consult with international relations experts at the Rand Corporation and the State Department. Bruce Bennett, a North Korea expert at Rand, wrote to Lynton in June: "As soon as they do find out about it, they will likely explore Sony's computer systems to see if Sony is ready to deal with North Korean criticism." Bennett had also consulted with the State Department's special envoy for human rights in North Korea, Robert King, who deemed the threats "typical North Korean bullying, likely without follow-up."[27] Ironically, given how aggressively they would involve themselves later on, in the summer of 2014, the U.S. government appeared eager to distance itself from the skirmish. One Sony executive who spoke in

June with Daniel Russell, the assistant secretary of state for East Asian and Pacific affairs, was told that "the North Koreans were going to do whatever they were going to do with or without the film" and "this was not an area the U.S. government would get involved in."[28]

Within Sony, the strongest pushback came from Sony CEO Kazuo Hirai, who told Pascal the movie needed to be toned down—particularly the actual depiction of the assassination in the final dramatic scene in which a "tank shell strikes Kim's helicopter and kills him in a slow-motion, head-popping, flesh-dripping ball of fire."[29] Hirai and Lynton both wanted the scene cut entirely, but Rogen insisted that the scene was "awesome" and the movie was "supposed to be controversial." They ultimately compromised by reducing Kim's "flaming hair by 50%," eliminating "three out of four of the face embers," and changing "the color of the head chunks to try to make them less gross."[30] Other concessions on the part of the studio included altering the images of Kim family members who were shown in the film and writing a statement that described the movie as "fictionalized comedy that is not in any way related to current events."[31]

Sony took the possibility that North Korea might retaliate in some fashion—possibly electronic—seriously enough to talk to government officials and consultants about the threat, and even to alter some of the carnage in the film. That they did not also ramp up their digital security is surprising, not least because the company had suffered a major breach just three years earlier, in 2011, when its popular PlayStation Network was compromised, exposing information about 77 million Sony customers. That breach—which PlayStation chief Tim Schaaff would later describe in Congressional testimony as "highly sophisticated" and "unprecedented in its size and scope"—ultimately cost the company $171 million. The costs of the 2014 breach were, in many ways, trickier to calculate. There was, presumably, some loss of revenue to the studio, but it is hard to say how much. Some movies and scripts had been leaked online by the G.O.P., but there was no way of knowing how that had impacted their box office performance. The Christmas release of "The Interview" was canceled at many theaters, following threats by the Guardians of Peace in a December 16 email that said:

> Soon all the world will see what an awful movie Sony Pictures Entertainment has made.
>
> The world will be full of fear. Remember the 11th of September 2001.

> We recommend you to keep yourself distant from the places at that time. (If
> your house is nearby, you'd better leave.)[32]

These threats may have motivated some of the active involvement of the U.S. government, and appeared sufficiently credible to Sony Pictures to warrant pulling the movie. But "The Interview" was released online, and shown in several independent theaters, earning more than $40 million in online sales and $12 million in theaters. The online sales, at least, seemed to suggest that even in the age of massive and humiliating data breaches there might still be no such thing as bad publicity. Meanwhile, the biggest embarrassments—and highest costs—of the breach, both for the studio and the individual employees who worked there, came from the wealth of emails, and personal information, including Social Security numbers and salary data, stolen from the studio's systems.

A group of Sony Pictures employees filed a class action suit against the studio to try to recoup some of their losses. "An epic nightmare, much better suited to a cinematic thriller than to real life, has been unfolding in slow motion for thousands of current and former employees of SPE," they wrote in the suit, arguing that the breach was only possible because "SPE failed to maintain reasonable and adequate security measures to protect the employees' information from access and disclosure."[33] The plaintiffs described no fewer than ten types of injury that had been imposed on them as a result of the breach, ranging from the compromise and publication of their personal information, to the out-of-pocket costs required for them to detect and recover from identity theft, the time and productivity they lost trying to protect themselves against identity theft, the possibility of tax fraud, and the "future costs in terms of time, effort, and money that will be expended to prevent and repair the impact of the data breach."[34] Sony was responsible for these losses, the plaintiffs argued, because of its lax computer security. Specifically, they noted:

> (1) SPE failed to implement security measures designed to prevent this attack
> even though there have been similar cyber-attacks of SPE and its sister companies;
> (2) SPE failed to employ security protocols to detect the breach and removal of
> nearly 100 terabytes of data from its computer networks; and (3) SPE failed to
> maintain basic security measures such as access controls and requiring passwords
> with appropriate levels of complexity and encryption, measures that would have
> ensured that data would be harder to access or steal and, in the event data were
> accessed or stolen, it would be unreadable and thus cause less damage to SPE
> employees and their families.[35]

This line of reasoning was exactly why Sony was so invested in the idea that the breach had been perpetrated by the North Korean government, a determined and sophisticated adversary with ample resources that would have been able to penetrate any amount of technical protection. The company quickly filed a motion to have the lawsuit dismissed, responding to the plaintiffs' complaint by stating that SPE "in every respect denies liability, denies that it acted negligently or otherwise violated any law, and denies that plaintiffs are entitled to relief."[36]

Judge R. Gary Klausner agreed to dismiss many—but not all—of the plaintiffs' allegations. Along the same lines as the dismissal of the SCDOR complaint and the Supreme Court's ruling in the *Clapper* surveillance case, Klausner determined that the plaintiffs' concerns about potential "future harms" that had not yet occurred, as well as their claims about losing time to dealing with the breach's fallout and losing the "value" of their personal information, could not support a claim for negligence because such harms were too hazy and speculative. Klausner was more sympathetic, however, to the money the plaintiffs had spent on credit monitoring, password management, freezing and unfreezing their credit, and obtaining credit reports. Those costs were voluntarily assumed by the plaintiffs to help defend themselves in the aftermath of the breach, not costs directly imposed on them as a consequence of the breach. This was exactly the sort of cost that the Supreme Court had dismissed in the *Clapper* case as an attempt by the plaintiffs to "manufacture standing by choosing to make expenditures based on hypothetical future harm."[37] But Klausner was more sympathetic than the Supreme Court to the idea that voluntary prophylactic costs of this nature might still be sufficient grounds for a negligence claim. Klausner referenced the precedent set in a 1993 case brought against Firestone Tire & Rubber Company for allowing toxic waste from a tire manufacturing plant in northern California to seep into groundwater. In that case, Klausner pointed out, the California Supreme Court held that Firestone was responsible for paying for the costs of prophylactic monitoring of the water chemical levels because "the need for future monitoring is a reasonably certain consequence of the defendant's breach of duty, and ... the monitoring is reasonable and necessary."[38] Accordingly, Klausner argued, it might make sense to hold Sony liable for some of the monitoring and preventative protection measures taken by the people affected by the breach.

After Klausner denied the motion to dismiss the suit, Sony settled the case for roughly $15 million in April 2016 and agreed to provide the plaintiffs with identity protection services through the end of 2017, as well as a $2 million fund that could be used to reimburse the plaintiffs for preventive measures they took to protect themselves from identity theft in the aftermath of the breach.[39] The settlement was, in some ways, a victory for the plaintiffs—who had managed to elicit protections often extended only to customers whose information was breached—but also a reminder of how narrowly courts viewed the harm inflicted by computer breaches only in terms of direct financial losses. Klausner's partial dismissal of the plaintiffs' allegations largely aligned with previous failed lawsuits trying to hold companies responsible for non-monetary losses associated with data breaches. It reinforced the idea that, even in cases like SPE's where much of the damage done by a breach did not necessarily take the form of financial fraud, financial losses were the only costs a court was likely to take seriously.

The settlement's focus on monetary losses also highlighted the fact that, even though the Guardians of Peace had clearly not perpetrated their breach with the intention of profiting financially (otherwise they would hardly have published the stolen information online for anyone to access), their crime had enabled many second-order crimes, by providing thousands of people's personal information and Social Security numbers to anyone who wanted to exploit them. Because the case was settled before going to trial, Klausner's theory that Sony might be financially liable for its employees' voluntary prophylactic measures was never tested in court, though it left open a possible avenue for trying to extract damages from breached firms in the future. But the personal, professional, and reputational damage that had been done to the people whose embarrassing emails had been leaked or whose in-progress negotiations had been revealed carried no weight in court. And yet, browsing through the slew of articles that came out of the SPE leaks—stories about snide insults exchanged among coworkers, executives' attempts to get their children into high-profile universities, entertainment industry salaries—it is abundantly clear that data breaches can inflict multiple different types of harm, and that financial loss was only one of the ways the SPE breach hurt the people and firms involved.[40]

The dynamics between Sony Pictures and its employees in the aftermath of the breach have important implications for understanding how hard it is to protect all of the different parties affected by a public humiliation-motivated incident. For instance, one way to protect the corporate victims of such incidents might be to limit their financial liability so that it is harder for individuals to sue them, making breaches less likely to take a major financial toll on their resources and therefore less satisfying for perpetrators to undertake as a means of revenge. But limiting the losses imposed on a victim like Sony Pictures in this fashion, even if it did deter some would-be attackers, would also effectively increase the losses imposed on its individual employees, forcing a trade-off between who, of the different types of victims, deserves the greatest protection for which types of harm.

"No Choice but to Hold You Responsible"

Focusing on the financial harms inflicted on SPE employees in the class action suit had the benefit of implicating a fairly clear-cut set of mitigations that SPE could offer as part of the settlement, such as credit monitoring, identity theft insurance, and reimbursements for credit freezes. But while such mechanisms might help mitigate financial harm to SPE employees by flagging and restricting money flows to and from the perpetrators, the studio itself had no analogous strategy to turn to for containing the humiliating flood of its most sensitive information appearing online. In the absence of a clear template for how to do ex-post mitigation for such a far-reaching and public-facing breach, Sony attempted to fight back against its attackers in two ways. The first was technical. When SPE's data began to appear online, the studio reportedly initiated a series of denial-of-service attacks directed at the sites that were hosting its stolen data and even went so far as to plant fake torrent files online. They hoped to misdirect users trying to find the stolen films and data to the fake files, so that people who believed they were downloading the stolen information instead spent hours downloading empty files.[41] Whether or not the studio successfully managed to trick any users into downloading their planted, empty files instead of the actual stolen information, they were clearly unsuccessful in stemming the spread of the stolen information through media sources, which reported widely on the leaked data.

The studio also attempted a less technical set of legal efforts intended to try to stop their stolen information from spreading. These included filing takedown notices under the Digital Millennium Copyright Act (DMCA) to try to make websites remove postings of the studio's copyrighted material, such as scripts and movies, as well as sending letters to news organizations demanding that they delete the stolen data and cease to report on its content. In the letters, sent out in December 2014 to media outlets by high-power lawyer David Boies on SPE's behalf, the studio threatened legal action if the recipients continued to publish the details of the breached information. "SPE does not consent to your possession, review, copying, dissemination, publication, uploading, downloading, or making any use of the Stolen Information," the letter stated, ordering the recipient to destroy any of Sony's data in its possession. "If you do not comply with this request, and the Stolen Information is used or disseminated by you in any manner, SPE will have no choice but to hold you responsible for any damage or loss arising from such use or dissemination by you," the letter further threatened—a bold, if largely futile attempt on Sony's part to find a new entity (or entities) on which to shift blame and liability for the breach.[42]

Most press outlets appear to have ignored Boies's letter, and there was ultimately little SPE could do to stop the further distribution of information after it had left the confines of its own computer systems. Mitigating public humiliation by controlling information flows is much harder than mitigating financial losses by controlling money flows, especially in a country with strong legal protections for freedom of speech and freedom of the press. However, the idea that the journalists covering the breach were at least partially at fault in spreading the stolen information as the perpetrators so clearly wanted them to do was not limited to Sony and its lawyers. Screenwriter Aaron Sorkin, some of whose emails were released in the breach, wrote an op-ed piece for the *New York Times* in December 2014, arguing that the contents of the leaks were not "newsworthy" and that "every news outlet that did the bidding of the Guardians of Peace is morally treasonous and spectacularly dishonorable."[43] Sorkin's language, and in particular his reference to treason, raises the question of whether the spread of stolen information that does not meet certain standards of "newsworthiness" could—perhaps in other countries, under other policy regimes—be more heavily restricted in an attempt to mitigate the harm imposed by this type of breach. Clearly, any such approach would come at the cost of protections for journalistic freedom, making them an unlikely fit for the United States—but not necessarily out of the question for countries that place greater restrictions on speech and the press. Restricting what people can publish is of little value if all of the stolen data is still easily available online to anyone who wants to look for it. Similarly, making that data harder to find online is of little use if it is being constantly written about in the press. Therefore, limiting the accessibility of breached data and limiting its dissemination through the press and third-party websites—the two strategies attempted by Sony through legal and technical means—go hand in hand. Achieving one serves little purpose if the other is unsuccessful, and in Sony's case it is not clear that either strategy met with much success.

For making a lasting impression on millions of people, there were few breaches that could touch the SPE incident in terms of sheer excitement and salacious details. As the class action plaintiffs pointed out, the breach featured a plot worthy of a blockbuster movie, and, further, it gave rise to dozens of engrossing news stories—from details of the pay discrepancies between male and female actors in Hollywood, to the inner-workings of a studio executive's efforts to get his daughter into an Ivy League college, to the snide remarks by celebrities about their coworkers. But beyond its value as a rich source of Hollywood gossip, the Sony breach was notable for two reasons: first, the involvement of the U.S. government on behalf of a private company and the government's forceful response and assertions about the origins of the attack; and, second, Sony's aggressive if unsuccessful efforts to prevent the spread of the breached information online and in the media. The studio sought to mitigate damage both by seeding the Internet with virtual machines in hopes of luring would-be viewers of the stolen content to the planted downloads, and by trying to persuade journalists and media outlets not to report on the leaked data. This active effort to prevent the spread of stolen information suggested a possible avenue for attempting ex-post mitigation efforts that might apply even to cybersecurity incidents motivated by political retribution and a desire to publicly humiliate the victims. But many considered it politically and legally objectionable to target media reports about the stolen information, even if it was a means of broadening the landscape of potential defenses and relevant intermediaries. The hostilities that arose between Sony and its employees in the aftermath of the breach, as well as the tensions between Sony and media outlets reporting on the breach, highlighted the complex layers of victims, the different types of harm each of them suffered, and the lack of clarity around who was responsible for mitigating those harms. That these different stakeholders turned on each other in the aftermath of the breach was only to be expected, given their complicated relationships to each other and the incident itself. Meanwhile, the unprecedented convergence of public and private interests in claiming the attack was a sophisticated effort sponsored by a foreign government suggested just how intertwined government and industry cybersecurity interests had become, not just when it came to critical cyber infrastructure, but even when the stakes were as low as a silly movie.

10 An Imperfect Affair: Ashley Madison and the Economics of Embarrassment

The Sony Pictures breach provided a window into the private correspondence and behind-the-scenes gossip of Hollywood celebrities, but the 2015 breach of the website Ashley Madison, a dating site aimed at people interested in pursuing extramarital affairs, offered something that was arguably even more tantalizing: a chance to gawk at the private lives of neighbors and co-workers. In the summer of 2015, a group calling itself the "Impact Team" published information stolen from Ashley Madison's Toronto-based parent company, Avid Life Media (ALM), including the names, photos, profile information, email addresses, credit card numbers, and billing addresses of many of the site's 37 million users. As with the Spamhaus and Sony Pictures incidents, the perpetrators of the ALM breach made no attempt to hide the fact that they were out to publicly shame the company, in this case apparently because of its poor security. In a long manifesto published alongside the stolen data, the Impact Team claimed that the breach had been motivated largely by ALM's misrepresentation of its own data security practices. In particular, the Impact Team called out the "full delete" option offered to Ashley Madison customers to erase their information from the site for a fee of $19 as a "complete lie," writing: "Users almost always pay with credit card; their purchase details are not removed as promised, and include real name and address, which is of course the most important information the users want removed."[1]

Rather confusingly for a group's ostensible concerns about the defrauding and privacy of Ashley Madison users, the Impact Team's decision to release the information it stole harmed those customers much more than ALM's weak security did. The perpetrators' overall plan to punish ALM for its dishonesty seemed to rely on a flawed understanding of how easily

Ashley Madison users could hold the company liable for the breach. In a message to ALM prior to the release of the stolen data, the Impact Team demanded that the company shut down two of its sites, Ashley Madison (AM) and Established Men (EM), a site for wealthy men who wanted to date younger women. They wrote:

> Shutting down AM and EM will cost you, but non-compliance will cost you more: We will release all customer records, profiles with all the customers' secret sexual fantasies, nude pictures, and conversations and matching credit card transactions, real names and addresses, and employee documents and emails. Avid Life Media will be liable for fraud and extreme harm to millions of users.[2]

In the aftermath of the breach, several of the site's users did, indeed, bring a class action lawsuit against ALM, but it was ultimately settled in July 2017 for just over $11 million, or less than ten percent of the $115.5 million in revenue that Ashley Madison brought in during 2014.[3] The Ashley Madison breach, like the Sony Pictures breach before it, highlighted just how easily attempts to publicly shame companies through data breaches could devolve into little more than large-scale public shaming of thousands of individuals to whom the targeted company ultimately paid only token compensation for direct financial losses.

The costs associated with breaches like those perpetrated against Ashley Madison and Sony Pictures are nearly impossible to calculate in any meaningful way because they ultimately weigh most heavily on so many dispersed victims living out their own personal, small-scale tragedies. In the wake of the Ashley Madison breach, the Canadian police investigated at least two suicides that were reportedly linked to the stolen information. Many Ashley Madison users received extortion demands from people threatening to send their friends, families, and employers the leaked information about them unless they made Bitcoin payments of roughly $230 each.[4] And yet, the Impact Team seemed determined to reinforce that it was ALM they were targeting, not the company's customers. "Find yourself in here?" the perpetrators wrote to users listed in the stolen Ashley Madison data they published. "It was ALM that failed you and lied to you. Prosecute them and claim damages. Then move on with your life. Learn your lesson and make amends. Embarrassing now, but you'll get over it."[5] The Impact Team's expectation that the affected users would "get over it" was, at least in some cases, deeply misguided, but so too was their idea that Ashley Madison customers would exact revenge on ALM for them in the form of successful lawsuits. The Impact Team's call to action directed at Ashley Madison customers echoed the goal articulated by members of Operation Stophaus of getting Cloudflare and Spamhaus customers to turn on those companies and withdraw their business due to outages and performance issues caused by their denial-of-service attack. And yet, while they certainly succeeded in making a visible, public splash, these incidents, both of which were ostensibly motivated by dreams of shutting down a hated company by driving away its customer base, ended up doing little to impact the victims' businesses.

Spamhaus's customers, including Internet service providers and hosting providers, rallied to the organization's defense and took steps to bring Stophaus's infrastructure offline rather than deserting the anti-spam group when it was attacked. Similarly, although Ashley Madison served a far less important function than Spamhaus, instead of driving away the site's users, the Impact Team's breach—like the Sony Pictures breach—seemed to serve primarily as a catalyst for a number of third-party crimes, many of them financially motivated, and almost all of them directed not at Ashley Madison or ALM but at the individual users whose data had been leaked. Perhaps leaking stolen information that could serve as a platform, or starting point, for numerous other crimes was part of the Sony Pictures and ALM perpetrators' intentions and contributed to their larger aim of wreaking havoc and driving up liability costs for the targeted companies. However, even though both of these breaches created significant negative publicity and reputational damage for Sony Pictures and Ashley Madison, the third-party financial crimes that the stolen data enabled—the identity theft or credit card fraud or extortion attempts directed at individual employees and customers—were never likely to result in any legal settlements that would translate to significant financial damages for companies of their size. The very public nature of breaches motivated by a desire to humiliate the victims often works against their usefulness as platforms for large-scale financial fraud. Since the victims are alerted to the theft and publication of their information at the same time that would-be profiteering criminals are, they can take steps to protect their financial accounts.

To some extent, the Impact Team was successful in turning ALM customers on the company—there was, after all, a class action suit, and a multi-million dollar settlement, as well as a $1.7 million settlement to end an investigation by the Federal Trade Commission and the state attorneys general. But that could hardly be seen as a major victory for the perpetrators since the settlement sums were a relatively small price to pay for a company of ALM's size. Moreover, the various victims of computer security incidents almost always end up turning on each other and trying to take advantage of the ambiguous liability rules to extract as much as possible from each other in the aftermath of a breach, regardless of how it occurred or why it was perpetrated. The Impact Team's reliance on those liability mechanisms to put ALM out of business and exact crippling damages for "fraud and extreme harm" seems to have been based on a fundamental misunderstanding of how these sorts of disputes typically play out in the aftermath of computer security incidents.

There were some significant embarrassments in store for ALM in the wake of the breach, most notably the discoveries that many of the female users on Ashley Madison were fictitious bots, and that the paid delete service was largely a sham—but those revelations appeared to have a negligible, or, at any rate, short-lived impact on the company's business. In May 2017, the site's new parent company Ruby Life announced that its user base had grown to 52.7 million people (though it declined to say how many of those users were active), indicating an average sign-up rate of more than 750,000 people per month since the 2015 breach. Ruby Life's vice president of communications Paul Keable implicitly credited the breach with the site's subsequent remarkable growth, saying: "In the summer of 2015 we experienced unprecedented media coverage of our business."[6] If Keable is right about the drivers of the site's business then the Impact Team's actions massively backfired when it came to hurting Ashley Madison by driving away customers. In echoes of the online sales success of "The Interview," the news of the Ashley Madison breach appeared to provide surprisingly good publicity for the company.

"Kind of Untouchable"

Ashley Madison was a tough victim to feel sorry for, and not just—or even primarily—because their stated mission was to encourage infidelity and their site slogan was "Life is short. Have an affair." The company had touted the security and privacy of its services so often and hyperbolically in the years leading up to the breach that it was hard not to feel that they should have done more to protect their users' data, or, at the very least, delete it when they said they would. In particular, then-ALM CEO Noel Biderman, who resigned shortly after the breach, had made much of the site's security in admittedly vague but strongly reassuring terms. "We have done a really great job of making sure our data is kept secret," he told one magazine in an interview just months before the breach.[7] In another interview, he alluded to custom-tailored Ashley Madison technology that helped keep customers' data private, saying: "The perfect affair is not just meeting someone, it's not being discovered. So we really had to build the technology to help create the discretion. Unlike other websites you encounter, we're closed."[8] He made repeated references to the ability of his company's technology to provide users with the elusive "perfect affair," saying of user activity on the site that "every step is looked at as how do we keep this private between you and this other person? How do we keep your photos under lock and key?"[9]

Of course, Biderman's threat model for who might try to steal users' data was not geared toward intruders like the Impact Team. Rather, he seemed more concerned with snooping spouses and the power of his technology to prevent them from spying on their cheating husbands and wives, telling a reporter for the *Calgary Herald* in January 2015:

> It's not lipstick on our collars anymore getting us caught, it's digital lipstick. Voice mails you leave behind, text messages you leave behind—so I focus on that. The technology I've built: the photo masquerading, the anonymous billing, even the way my messaging works—the password protection—even to the Nth degree.[10]

From a technical perspective, it's hard to know what any of this boasting actually meant in terms of the site's security. Indeed, the password protection "to the Nth degree" and the digital photos kept "under lock and key" on a "closed" website sound, in retrospect, like exactly the kinds of meaningless security nonsense that someone with no technical understanding would come up with if he were just making things up to reassure customers. The site itself displayed no fewer than three security-specific icons, one of which designated the site as the winner of a (fictitious) "Trusted Security Award" alongside a graphic of a gold medal.[11]

Beyond trumpeting the site's security in general, Biderman also spent considerable time promoting, in similarly hyperbolic and hand-wavy terms, the extra secure "ghost delete" (also called "full delete" or "paid delete") feature that allowed users to remove all of their data from the site for a fee of $19, and generated $1.7 million in revenue for ALM in 2014.[12] Biderman said the service would "make it like you were a ghost[,] like you were never here" because it "allows you to recall every message or photo that you have ever shared, and we even blow it off our own servers, which, by the way, sit in a remote location, kind of untouchable."[13] Here, again, were more hints that he had no idea what he was talking about when it came to security—the reference to "blowing" data "off" a server as if that process involved some kind of physical explosion and the misplaced pride in the geographic remoteness of the company's physical servers as if that somehow made them more difficult to compromise because would-be hackers would first have to hunt them down.

Biderman's pre-breach statements about Ashley Madison's security were significant not just because they hinted at the company's general cluelessness when it came to security, but also because they would help provide the basis for customers and the Federal Trade Commission (FTC) to hold the company accountable after the breach occurred. Under Section 5 of the Federal Trade Commission Act, the FTC's purview for investigating and penalizing companies covers "unfair and deceptive" business practices, and the agency has at times struggled to figure out how exactly poor data protection practices fit into these designations and where to draw the line between fair and unfair security. But by overpromising on their security—and lying outright about the paid delete function—Ashley Madison made it much easier for FTC investigators, as well as its customers, to allege deception and fraud, both of which are more clearly within the FTC's remit to police "unfair and deceptive" business practices than failing to protect customers' personal data. Beyond Biderman's boasts, advertisements for the site that claimed it was "secure," "anonymous," and "risk free," were cited in the FTC's complaint as evidence of the company's deception, as was the site's privacy policy, which stated "we use industry standard practices and technologies including but not limited to 'firewalls,' encrypted transmission via SSL (Secure Socket Layer) and strong data encryption."[14]

While touting its "untouchable" servers, Ashley Madison's network was, in fact, regularly compromised during the months leading up to the Impact Team breach. Beginning in November 2014, investigators found evidence that intruders were able to log in to the company's Virtual Private Network (VPN) to remotely access the company's servers using shared credentials stored in documents on the ALM Google Drive. On two occasions, in May and June 2015, intruders used these stolen credentials to log in to one of the site's payment processors—but the company did not notice any anomalous activity until July 12, 2015, when a large file was transferred from one of its databases to another.[15] That same day, the Impact Team's first warning message appeared on the screens of employee computers at the ALM offices in Canada, accompanied by the AC/DC rock song "Thunderstruck." In the message, the intruders threatened to release a huge cache of stolen data unless the company shut down its Ashley Madison and Established Men websites.

The company hired the security firm Cycura to investigate, but did not make any public statement about the incident until a week later, after the Impact Team made its first online public leaks on July 19, releasing information about just two of the site's customers, a man from Mississauga, Canada, and another from Brockton, Massachusetts.[16] The next day, ALM issued a press release about the breach and went to the Toronto police for help with their internal investigation. One month later, on August 18, 2015, the Impact Team made its first major release of the stolen data in a Pastebin post containing 9.7 gigabytes of user profile and payment information. Included in the stolen information was data about several customers who had previously purchased the Ashley Madison paid delete service and been assured that their user profiles had been "blown off" the ALM servers in exchange for the $19 fee. Later releases by the Impact Team, on August 20 and 23, contained lists of user accounts organized by employer and state, as well as users' sign-up dates, the amount they had spent on Ashley Madison services, the IP addresses they used to access the site, and 19 gigabytes of internal company emails and source code for the Ashley Madison website.

The source code leaks were hardly the most salacious bits of leaked data, but they gave outside security researchers the opportunity to vet the company's software security more thoroughly in the wake of the breach. One London-based security consultant, Gabor Szathmari, found that the site's coders had hardcoded several passwords and other credentials into the site's source code.[17] This meant that passwords and login credentials for Amazon Web Services and digital certificate private keys had all been typed directly into the website's source code in plaintext, making it easy for anyone who got access to that code to also access the company's other accounts and authenticate to other parts of its network so they could find and exfiltrate additional data more easily. Furthermore, hardcoding credentials in source code would have made it more difficult for the company to update or change those credentials, since any such changes would have required editing the site's source code. And, as Szathmari pointed out, many of the hardcoded passwords found in the source code were also relatively short—between five and eight characters long—and could easily have been guessed using a dictionary attack.

The vulnerabilities that enabled the Impact Team to access ALM's network and move laterally across it to access so much user and company information were largely due to carelessness—poorly chosen passwords, credentials stored in shared Google documents and embedded in website source code, few audits, and minimal monitoring of network activity. There was no evidence of the custom-designed privacy-protecting technologies Biderman had boasted of building, nor does there seem to have been much attention given to the potential for breaches and data theft—a surprising oversight in light of how often the company harped on its security and the responses to a leaked internal memo about ALM executives' top priorities. In the internal self-assessment memo, Biderman, as well as ALM Chief Technology Officer Trevor Sykes and vice president for operations Kevin MacCall, all cited the importance of security. One of the questions in the self-assessment was: "In what area would you hate to see something go wrong?" To this query, Biderman responded: "Data exfiltration, confidentiality of the data." Sykes said: "I would hate to see our systems hacked and/or the leak of personal information." And MacCall commented: "There's a lack of security awareness across the organization."[18] But whatever awareness or concern there may have been on the part of the company's management about the potential for a breach, very little of that translated into ALM's technical operations and decisions, almost all of which seemed to favor convenience and speed over security, undermining to a large extent the measures that ALM did have in place to protect its users' data.

"Password Protection—Even to the Nth Degree"

Much of the data stolen from Ashley Madison was released in plaintext, suggesting it had been stored unencrypted on the company's servers, but—to the company's credit—the passwords belonging to its users had, in fact, been encrypted using an algorithm called bcrypt. The bcrypt algorithm was strong enough so that password-cracking tools would not have been able to decrypt the user passwords for a period of centuries running on modern computers. For the millions of users whose names, emails, and addresses had been revealed, it was most likely a small comfort, but still, it at least lent some credence to Biderman's claims about password protection and security. And while the victims may not have cared much by then whether their Ashley Madison profiles were compromised, the encryption probably helped protect any accounts they may have had on other sites that shared the same passwords.

Then, in September 2015, a group of recreational password crackers studying the Ashley Madison site source code discovered something unusual about the way the site encrypted user passwords. In the same database as the bcrypt-encrypted passwords, millions of those passwords had also been hashed using a different algorithm called MD5. MD5 essentially translates a password into a number—called a hash—that can be used to quickly check an attempted login without storing the password in plaintext. So when a user entered their password into the Ashley Madison site, the site would hash whatever text they entered using MD5 and then compare the result to the hash number they had stored for that user to see if the password was correct. MD5 does the same thing bcrypt does—turn a password into a number that's not the password itself—but in a much simpler manner that requires much less computation to undo than bcrypt.

If ALM had hashed all of the bcrypt-encrypted passwords with MD5 that wouldn't have mattered—anyone who cracked the MD5 hashes would still have been left with a relatively useless encrypted password. But for many of the stored passwords, ALM didn't apply MD5 to the encrypted passwords. Instead, the company first encrypted a plaintext password with bcrypt; then they combined the plaintext password with the associated username, inserting two colons between the username and password; changed all the letters to lowercase; and then hashed the entire combined, lowercase phrase containing both username and password with MD5. Those MD5 hashes were then stored in the same database as the encrypted passwords, possibly to allow users to login without having to enter their passwords every time.[a]

a. For instance, for someone with the username "User" and the password "SecReT" both would be converted to lowercase and then concatenated with two colons separating the username and password. The combined string of "user::secret" would then be hashed using MD5 and could then be cracked to determine that the user's password was some version of the word "secret"—that could be determined from testing each possible combination of capital letters in the word to find one that matched the bcrypt-encrypted version of the user's password, which was also stored in the site's database.

More than 15 million user passwords were stored in both forms—encrypted with bcrypt and hashed with MD5—and most of those in the latter format could be guessed quite easily by generating passwords, adding them on to the username, with two colons, and then taking the MD5 hash to see if it matched the entry stored in ALM's database. Because MD5 hashing, unlike bcrypt encryption, is so fast, it was possible to test billions of guesses per second this way, and guessing passwords in this manner allowed the hobbyist crackers to figure out more than 11.2 million of the leaked passwords within only a month of the data's release.[19]

What made the aftermath of the Ashley Madison breach so unusual and so bitter, besides the sensitive nature and personal consequences of the stolen information, was not ALM's security, or lack thereof, but rather that ALM had so boastfully exaggerated its extraordinary security measures beforehand. In subsequent complaints filed about the incident, both Ashley Madison customers and the FTC emphasized the ways in which the company had aggressively overpromised—and outright lied—to users repeatedly about how well protected their data was and how much control they had over it. In both cases, their strategy was precisely that prescribed by the Impact Team: accuse ALM of lying to their customers about their site's security and paid delete service in order to shift liability for the consequences of the breach onto the company. It was a strategy that made sense since there is a much clearer legal way, particularly for the FTC, to punish companies for engaging in "deceptive" business practices than there is to punish them for failing to protect customer data from being stolen. This is especially true when the harm inflicted by that theft is largely emotional, psychological, and personal, rather than financial, and therefore offers fewer opportunities for legal remedies. At the same time, it was a case that highlighted, yet again, the ambiguity surrounding what a company's obligations are when it comes to securing customer data, particularly if the company doesn't make false promises about the quality of their security.

If ALM was at fault primarily because they had overpromised and underdelivered when it came to security, then what did that mean for companies that never promised their customers any kind of security? Could they be breached with impunity and then insist that they had never deceived anyone by pretending to have good security? Or was there some baseline level of security that firms owed their customers by default, in the name of "fairness"? At the time of the Ashley Madison breach, the FTC was fighting out precisely that question with Wyndham, the hotel chain that suffered three breaches in a span of two years but contended it had done nothing deceptive or unfair in failing to protect its customers' data. When it came to investigating ALM, the FTC stuck to more familiar and certain ground for the agency, arguing that the company had deceived its customers, not just with an ineffective paid delete service, but also by creating profiles for fake female users that tricked customers into believing they were meeting women on the site, causing them to spend more money on the credits used for sending messages to other profiles.

The Engager Profiles

When the Impact Team first released the Ashley Madison accounts data, it cautioned in the message that accompanied the posting: "Keep in mind the site is a scam with thousands of fake female profiles." They referenced a lawsuit filed in 2012 by a former ALM employee, Doriana Silva, who alleged that the company had her create up to one thousand fake profiles for women on Ashley Madison, causing her to develop a repetitive strain injury in her wrist. The stolen information about millions of Ashley Madison users provided an opportunity for reporters to investigate that suit's claim that the site was "riddled with fake profiles for women that encourage men to spend more money subscribing to the site."[20] (In order to initiate conversations with other users, customers had to purchase credits through the site.)

Annalee Newitz, writing for *Gizmodo* in August 2015, identified 70,572 accounts created by Ashley Madison to engage other users—70,529 of those "engager profiles" were female, and many were linked to @ashleymadison .com email addresses or accessed the site from IP addresses associated with the ALM offices.[21] Since these bots kept detailed logs of how often they contacted other users, and whom they contacted, Newitz was able to figure out that 20 million of the site's 31 million male users had received messages from the engagers, as well as the list of messages they were programmed to send. Their initial messages were mostly variations on the theme of "hi" and "hey there," but further into a conversation, they were given longer snippets of dialogue, including: "Hmmmm, when I was younger I used to sleep with my friend's boyfriends. I guess old habits die hard although I could never sleep with their husbands." And: "I'm sexy, discreet, and always up for kinky chat. Would also meet up in person if we get to know each other and think there might be a good connection. Does this sound intriguing?"[22]

Although the creation of automated engager accounts was unrelated to issues of data security, Ashley Madison customers and the FTC seized on the evidence provided by the stolen information to pursue charges that ALM had deceived its customers into spending money on conversations with bots. The FTC pointed out in its complaint that when new users joined the site they were greeted with a welcome message that promised "we have thousands of women in your city who are in the exact same situation as you and looking to have a discreet affair," and that the site used photos of existing members who had not been active in recent years to create these fake accounts. Because users had no way of knowing whether or not the women messaging them on the site were real or fake, unless they could tell from the quality of the bots' pre-programmed conversation snippets, many of the real users "were induced to upgrade to full memberships so that they could send emails and engage in online real-time chats with these fake profiles," the FTC concluded.[23]

The same complaint was leveled by several Ashley Madison customers in a series of lawsuits filed in 2015 and later consolidated into a single class action suit. David Yagel of Colorado, for instance, said in the suit that he spent at least $850 on credits for the site "to send messages as a result of Defendants' female profiles, which were in fact fraudulent 'bots' created by Defendants, rather than actual users of the website." Paul Jack of North Carolina reported a similar experience while spending roughly $1500 on Ashley Madison credits.[24] Despite the fact that ALM mentioned automated "Angel" accounts used for marketing research in its terms of service agreement, the FTC accused them of falsely implying that messages received by members were from actual women, and the plaintiffs in the class action suit alleged they would never have signed up for the site, or purchased credits, had they known that so many of the women they met on it would be fictitious. In this case, as with the paid delete function, it was not so much what ALM did that got them in legal trouble—it's not illegal to build chat bots, or even to charge people to chat with them—but how they had misrepresented it to their customers.

Damages

Misrepresentation, then, was the crux of the class action suit brought against ALM, as well as the FTC investigation—not just that the site had failed to protect its customers' data, but that it had egregiously misled customers about the steps it had taken (or claimed to have taken) related to data security, deletion, and the creation of fake accounts. But while the company's deceptions might have offered the clearest legal recourse, the real harms at the root of Ashley Madison's customers' grievances were much more personal and emotional than money wasted on a futile paid delete service, or on credits to chat with fictitious bot-women. The class action complaint states: "[T]he fact that this information has been made public has caused and will continue to cause irreparable harm, including public humiliation, ridicule, divorce, extortion, loss of employment, and increased substantial risk of identity theft and other types of fraud, among other catastrophic personal and professional harm."[25] The intensely personal nature of the consequences of the breach for many Ashley Madison customers led to them demanding impossibly high damages in their initial lawsuits. In just the first month following the breach, the lawsuits filed against ALM claimed, in total, more than $1 billion in damages.[26]

But these were exactly the types of harm that lawsuits had proven least effective at compensating victims for in the wake of data breaches. Most of the types of harm alleged by Ashley Madison's customers had no clear-cut physical or financial toll for which ALM could be held liable. Looked at in a certain light, the victims could even be said to have brought many of the personal consequences of the breach on themselves, simply by signing up for the website—though Ashley Madison undoubtedly played a crucial role in outing their activities through its poor security practices and empty promises of total deletion. Even the potential consequences that did have a clear financial cost, such as identity theft and extortion, were mostly examples of the kinds of speculative, future harm that courts had been skeptical of in prior cases. So it was no great surprise that the ultimate settlement for the U.S. class action lawsuit, agreed to in July 2017, came to just over $11 million. Individuals affected by the breach were permitted to claim up to $3,500 of that money each to cover documented losses stemming from the breach.[27] Meanwhile, the FTC, which had initially sought a penalty of $17.5 million for the company's misrepresentation of its user accounts, paid delete service, and inadequate security measures, ultimately agreed in November 2016 to a $1.6 million settlement.

In addition to the financial penalty, the company agreed as part of its settlement with the FTC to implement a "comprehensive data-security program," and permit assessments of that program by a third-party auditor.[28] What, exactly, this new security program would look like was left up to the company itself, which offered few hints about how it planned to revamp its security measures in the wake of the breach. In fact, beyond pursuing legal settlements, the only clear public efforts ALM made to try to contain the impacts of the breach were legal, not technical, and drawn directly from the Sony Pictures playbook. In August 2015, ALM took advantage of the takedown notice regimes implemented by many websites to comply with the Digital Millennium Copyright Act (DMCA) and used these systems to report posts that discussed or showed screenshots of their stolen data as copyright violations. "Avid owns all intellectual property in the data, which has been stolen from our data centre, and disclosed in this unauthorized and unlawful manner," the company wrote in one complaint, filed with Twitter over a reporter's posts of internal spreadsheets, on which all financial information had been redacted prior to posting.[29]

The DMCA was a blunt instrument for this purpose—it stipulates that websites that post user content must take down any infringing content on their sites shortly after they are made aware of it; otherwise the site itself can be held liable for infringing material that other people post to it. In practice, many sites have notice-and-takedown reporting tools for users to flag potentially infringing content, in order to claim this legal immunity for infringement. Internal company spreadsheets or email excerpts are hardly the types of content the DMCA was designed to protect. Per the Constitution, copyright laws are intended to "promote the progress of science and useful arts, by securing for limited times to authors and inventors the exclusive right to their respective writings and discoveries"—and it's hard to see how protecting Ashley Madison's internal files could conceivably promote science or any useful art. Still, some sites simply remove all such flagged posts rather than go to the trouble of determining which ones actually constitute infringement. ALM's complaints—like Sony Pictures' efforts—succeeded in getting a few tweets blocked, but did little to stem the spread of news of the breach overall. The company's largely—though not entirely—unsuccessful attempt to twist a copyright law into serving as a tool for preventing people from discussing the company's publicly available stolen data was yet another reminder of how few options are available for ex-post mitigation when it comes to containing the damage of breaches motivated by a desire to publicly shame victims, and how closely some of those options resemble censorship.

For ALM, the costs incurred by the 2015 breach were not trivial. By some estimates, between legal fees, settlements, and new security investments, the incident cost the company more than one-quarter of its annual revenue—but neither did the breach put ALM out of business, as the Impact Team seems to have hoped it would.[30] And ALM went to great lengths to ensure that the legal proceedings would be every bit as costly and personally distressing to the individual plaintiffs as they were to the company itself, successfully persuading a judge that any plaintiffs who joined the case should be compelled to use their real names rather than hiding behind pseudonyms. Anonymous John Does had filed most of the early suits against ALM, but after many of those suits were consolidated into a single class action case in Missouri, Judge John Ross ruled in April 2016 that plaintiffs who wished to proceed with the suit would have to provide their real names. The plaintiffs argued that revealing their names could "expose them to the threat of personal humiliation as well as extortion," but ALM countered that its customers' "sexual preferences and habits do not constitute information of the utmost intimacy so as to require anonymity."[31]

In his ruling, Ross at first appears to sympathize with the plaintiffs' wish to remain anonymous, writing that the "possible injury to Plaintiffs rises above the level of mere embarrassment or harm to reputation"—and conceding that perhaps the "injury litigated against would be incurred as a result of the disclosure of the plaintiff's identity." In other words, by bringing a public lawsuit against ALM with their real names attached to it, the Ashley Madison customers suing the company might only serve to worsen the humiliation and consequences of the data breach that had caused them to bring the suit in the first place. But ultimately, Ross decided, those considerations were outweighed by the fact that this was a class action "where a plaintiff seeks to represent a class of consumers who have a personal stake in the case and a heightened interest in knowing who purports to represent their interests in the litigation."[32] For a group whose information had already been published all over the Internet, it was, at once, a small additional humiliation and a significant reminder that their names and reputations would forever be tied to this one incident and website.

Because the plaintiffs in the class action suit were, in part, trying to allege that ALM had been negligent in its failure to protect their personal data, they emphasized that the company's security practices were "in violation of accepted industry practices and FTC guidelines." The complaint stated that Ashley Madison failed to meet the Payment Card Industry Data Security Standards (PCI DSS)—the same industry-set standards that the payment card companies sued TJX for failing to meet after its own breach, a decade earlier. Were that indeed the case, it would have been a matter for ALM to settle with the credit card companies and banks with whom it had agreed to adhere to PCI DSS, not with its customers, with whom it had no such agreement. But this breach, unlike the financially motivated TJX breach, apparently resulted in too little financial fraud for the payment industry to get involved. The class action complaint also invoked ALM's failure to meet the—entirely voluntary—Department of Homeland Security's Fair Information Practice Principles, or FIPPs, which provide organizations with broad recommendations for protecting information, such as offering users choice about how to control their data, and ensuring that data's integrity and security. It is not surprising that, in alleging negligence, the plaintiffs tried to establish a set of "accepted industry practices" based on the PCI DSS and DHS FIPPs that ALM failed to implement. But their complaint often goes too far in trying to justify the importance and effectiveness of these types of standards. For instance, the plaintiffs allege that "[h]ad Defendants complied with the PCI DSS and other basic industry standards governing data security, the Ashley Madison data breach could not have occurred."[33] This is an especially strange assertion to make given that PCI DSS standards pertain only to the protection of payment data and would have done little to stop the theft of the many other types of data stolen from ALM's network.

Adultery aside, what's most startling, and perhaps most depressing, about the Ashley Madison complaint is how closely it resembles the lawsuits filed in the aftermath of incidents such as the TJX breach, the SCDOR breach, and the OPM breach, which were perpetrated for very different reasons and had very different consequences. Since there was no clear legal pathway for trying to redress the very particular and personal damage that the victims of the Ashley Madison breach suffered, they had to try to turn their case into one centered on monetary losses and PCI DSS compliance, even though the financial component was, for many of them, only a tiny piece of the harm caused by this incident. The Ashley Madison breach pitted a company against its customers and attempted to put price tags on the highly subjective impacts of non-financially motivated breaches that take their toll primarily in broken marriages, public humiliation, and other personal tragedies with no obvious dollar equivalent. There is no clear legal path to dividing, settling, and assigning blame for these types of costs, and so, instead, the victims were forced to resort to the familiar legal templates carved out by payment card breaches, as if every data breach were just like any other, and all data equivalent in its sensitivity and capacity to cause harm that was, above all else, financial in nature.

The Spamhaus, Sony Pictures, and Ashley Madison incidents do not align neatly with as coherent a unifying motivation as financial profit or espionage. In all three cases, the perpetrators were driven by some desire to exact revenge on the company in question through some form of large-scale public-facing humiliation, but that revenge and humiliation manifested in very different ways. The Stophaus team wanted to shut down Spamhaus's operations and drive away their customers; the Sony Pictures intruders wanted to prevent the release of a movie and humiliate everyone who was in any way involved or associated with it; and the Ashley Madison breach was ostensibly intended to shed light on the site's inadequate security practices and mobilize users against ALM and its overblown security promises. What these incidents have in common—and the reason they are grouped together in this section—is that their perpetrators gained very little from them in terms of money or secrets, while their victims' losses were, similarly, profoundly intangible and often quite personal. Both of these features have important implications for defense, mitigation, and remediation. The fact that the perpetrators had no later stage plans to monetize or act on the information they stole meant that, even more than in espionage cases, there were very few opportunities for intervention once a target's technical lines of defense had failed. For the individual victims whose information was released it also meant that the traditional tools that helped insulate people from the costs of data breaches—laws requiring credit card companies to cover fraudulent charges, for instance, or credit freezes, or identity monitoring services—were largely useless.

This was true to a lesser extent for espionage incidents, including the Digi-Notar compromise, the PLA Unit 61398 campaign, and the OPM breach. But in those cases the damage inflicted on individuals seemed, for the most part, to be less personal and less immediate—or at the very least, less public. Moreover, state-engineered espionage efforts seemed like something for other governments to address—as the U.S. government indeed tried to do in a variety of different ways ranging from trade restrictions to indictments to personnel reassignments. Similarly, the risks posed by espionage, whether economic, political, or both, seemed aimed at entire countries, rather than at particular individuals. Even in the case of the DigiNotar compromise, which may have directly affected the lives of individuals in Iran, there are no clear examples of people who had their personal and professional lives decimated in the same way that some victims of the Sony Pictures and Ashley Madison breaches did. And yet, even when there were clear-cut examples of the serious, long-term harm that a data breach like Sony Pictures or Ashley Madison had caused, there was still no meaningful legal path to remedying that harm or holding the responsible parties accountable.

Breaches intended to wreak general havoc and humiliate a particular targeted party are not necessarily worse or even more damaging than espionage incidents, or financial crimes. But they are harder to defend against at every level, from the targeted organizations on down to the individuals involved, because they inflict harms so intangible, so specific to individuals, and so difficult to quantify that they are all but unrecognizable for the purposes of existing legal and policy remedies. Operation Stophaus provides an interesting counterpoint to this problem, given its relative lack of success in inflicting any long-term harm on either Spamhaus or anyone else affiliated with the company. The Spamhaus incident suggests that with sufficient cooperation from the infrastructural stakeholders across the Internet, and in the absence of harm directed at individual people, it may in fact be possible to effectively mitigate security threats perpetrated for no purpose beyond a desire for revenge. The relatively rapid and effective response to the Stophaus DDoS attacks has implications that extend to espionage and financially motivated incidents as well. It highlights not just how important it is to have an array of online stakeholders coordinating defensive efforts, but also how much more complicated the harms inflicted by cybersecurity incidents become when they extend to individuals, not just organizations. Incidents that impose not just financial costs on their victims, but also take personal, psychological, and professional tolls, often cannot be meaningfully addressed through existing legal pathways, leaving victims with token settlements and little recourse. Incidents intended to humiliate their targets, rather than simply rob them, impose an additional burden on victims even beyond the harm directly inflicted by the breach itself—the burden of trying to make others recognize and acknowledge that harm and how much it has cost them, despite the fact that no one stood to benefit.

IV Who Should Safeguard Our Data?
Distributing Responsibility and Liability

11 "Email the Way It Should Be": The Role of Application Designers and Software Developers

Defensive lessons derived from past cybersecurity incidents are sometimes criticized for only helping people protect themselves against yesterday's attack methods instead of the innovative, never-before-seen, cutting-edge attacks likely to be leveled at them in the future. This is a valid concern, to some extent—focusing too much on the technical mechanisms used to compromise computer systems in the past could potentially blind a defender to other, newer techniques—but it's often overstated, especially when it comes to less technical lines of defense that revolve around economic, policy, and legal changes. Cybersecurity incidents, and the modes of compromise employed by their perpetrators, evolve less rapidly than this argument implies. None of the security incidents presented in the previous chapters are identical, but many share some common stages and techniques, including phishing, theft of authentication credentials, use of bots, and exfiltration of large compressed files. And in the immediate aftermath of many breaches—almost regardless of how or why they were perpetrated—people routinely fault targeted organizations for failing to implement the same two technical controls: multi-factor authentication and encryption. That same criticism has been leveled at the South Carolina Department of Revenue, the Office of Personnel Management, Sony Pictures, and Ashley Madison— all of whom suffered very different breaches, at the hands of very different intruders motivated by very different goals, across a span of several years. Intruders can and do come up with entirely novel means of compromising the computers they target, but more often they rely on at least some of the same techniques that have worked so well for others before them.

More importantly, the technical mechanics of breaches are far from the most significant or critical causes of cybersecurity incidents and their resulting harms. The most important lesson that emerges from revisiting major cybersecurity incidents of the past decade is not that everyone would be secure if they would only use multi-factor authentication and encryption—quite the opposite, in fact. To believe that the success of a breach hinges on one or two specific technical decisions made by an individual or an organization is fundamentally to misunderstand the complicated and cooperative work of defending computer networks and systems. The history of computer security breaches demonstrates over and over again that there are a variety of different stakeholders involved in defending computer systems, each of whom has an important defensive role to play and each of whom is far more likely to devote significant time and energy to shifting that defensive responsibility onto someone else than to shouldering it themselves.

Making progress on defending computer systems therefore requires a clearer picture of who is responsible for doing what, a clearer set of incentives for all of the stakeholders involved to assume the defensive roles they are best suited to, and penalties and legal consequences for those who fail to do so. The final section of this book considers the defensive responsibilities that can best be undertaken—or, in some cases, only be undertaken—by three groups of stakeholders: application designers, organizations, and policymakers. These categories are by no means exhaustive. There are several other stakeholder groups and subgroups, such as individual users, Internet service providers, and online payment processors, who can exercise vital defensive capabilities when it comes to mitigating and preventing computer intrusions. But these three broad distinctions provide a useful starting point for trying to envision what it might mean to design a defensive ecosystem that plays to the particular strengths and unique capabilities of the many different people, companies, and groups who interact and overlap online.

Security practitioners often talk about how there is no single silver bullet for computer security—no one security tool or control to solve all problems and neutralize all threats. A corollary to that maxim, perhaps, is that there is no single bulletproof defender who can, unilaterally, prevent all compromises and detect every breach. Having visibility into and control over the different stages of computer-based threats requires the skillsets and capabilities of a wide range of different defenders, from individual users, to service providers, content providers, system administrators, payment processors, software developers, and even policymakers. In a world of increasingly networked computers, a breach of one organization's computer systems often occurs only after several different stakeholders—not just the organization whose data was stolen—have missed opportunities to interrupt the intrusion or put in place stronger defenses. The interconnectedness and interdependence among these different stakeholders and their computer systems contributes to the difficulty of sorting out who should be responsible for protecting those systems and means that, ultimately, there is always someone else for any individual stakeholder to blame for a breach besides themselves.

The failure to foster better defensive cooperation and coordination among those stakeholders—or even to recognize the importance of broadening the defensive landscape beyond individual breached organizations—is the dominant recurring theme of the major cybersecurity incidents of the past decade. It's the story of the payment networks, banks, and retailers turning on each other in the aftermath of the TJX breach, the story of the SCDOR handing off blame for its breach to the IRS who in turn passed the buck to NIST, the story of Internet service providers looking the other way while Bogachev built up his GameOver ZeuS bot, and cryptocurrency exchanges around the world blithely cashing out the Bitcoin payments made by the victims of Cryptolocker. It's the story, too, of browser manufacturers and certificate authorities scrambling to figure out how to trust each other but also place checks on that trust in the aftermath of the DigiNotar compromise; the story of the PLA Unit 61398 compromising computers on U.S. college campuses in order to infiltrate U.S. companies; the story of OPM ignoring security audit after security audit only to blame their breach on third-party contractors and overly restrictive OMB-issued guidelines. And it's also the story of Spamhaus partnering with Cloudflare and rallying its network of online service providers to overcome the Stophaus DDoS attacks; the story of Sony Pictures failing to notice when its data was being stolen and deleted and then going after the journalists who reported on that stolen data; and the story of Ashley Madison users turning on a company that had so often boasted of its incredible security and whose breach had cost them so much, only to learn that in order to pursue any attempts to hold the company responsible for their loss of privacy they would have to submit to yet another embarrassing, public ordeal by revealing their own names. In many of these incidents, the central conflict between the victims and the perpetrators was quickly overshadowed by the conflicts and in-fighting that emerged between the various victims and other stakeholders. There are many ways that individuals, organizations, and governments can strengthen computer security, from using stronger encryption algorithms to passing new legislation, and this book is not intended to be a comprehensive catalog of them. In particular, there is a vast array of technical tools and techniques that are not covered here. Instead, this section focuses on solutions that can enable greater collaboration and cooperation between different stakeholders who can help defend against and mitigate future cybersecurity incidents, as well as ways to clarify the respective roles and responsibilities of those stakeholders and incentivize them to assume defensive postures that may be as much about protecting others as they are about protecting themselves.

Application Design as Defense

Long before a company like TJX or Sony Pictures, or a government agency like SCDOR or OPM, makes any decisions about how to secure its data and networks, a host of design decisions are made about the software programs, technical protocols, and online services they rely on, and what types of behavior those applications will and won't permit. These decisions by application designers and software developers have tremendous security consequences, even beyond developers' traditional security roles of finding and fixing technical bugs and code vulnerabilities. Bugs and vulnerabilities allow intruders to do things using an application that the application designers did not intend users to be able to do. But equally important are the deliberate decisions those designers make about what constitutes legitimate behavior—the behaviors that developers do intend for users to be able to exhibit—in the context of their particular applications. Those limitations are important because one of the hardest elements of defending computer systems is recognizing that something unusual, or illicit, is happening in the context of that system. And while those distinctions between allowable and illegitimate activity in the context of an application often manifest as technical controls, they stem from what are essentially policy decisions made by application designers about what people should and should not be allowed to do using their applications—in much the same way that regulators make decisions enshrined in law, rather than code, about what people, and companies, should and should not be allowed to do with computers.

The individual technical stages that comprise the early stages of cyber-security incidents are often indistinguishable from the normal, everyday, legitimate uses of computers. For instance, these stages may involve the perpetrators doing things like connecting to servers and wireless networks, sending and receiving email messages, logging into accounts, sending and receiving files, and downloading and executing software. Gonzalez and his co-conspirators initiated the TJX breach by joining the Marshalls wireless network. The perpetrator of the DigiNotar compromise started out by connecting to the company's public web servers. PLA Unit 61398 officers commenced their espionage efforts by sending emails to U.S. companies. The Stophaus group launched their DDoS attack by directing DNS queries at Spamhaus. All of these are activities that might be perfectly reasonable to allow, that are in fact entirely permissible when some people do them—but not when other people do them. And yet, one of the most basic and fundamental assumptions underlying any attempt to defend computer systems is that malicious and legitimate uses of these systems are—at some point, in some way—different and therefore possible to profile or identify using various security controls and network monitoring techniques. There has to be some indicator of malicious activity that defenders can look for or block or monitor, some way of distinguishing the good guys from the bad guys even when they're doing almost identical things. The hardest stages of threats to defend against are the ones that most closely resemble legitimate use by legitimate users.

In the aftermath of these breaches, there is often disagreement about who was responsible for noticing early indicators of maliciousness, or best poised to constrain attackers' ability to masquerade as legitimate. For instance, in the case of the South Carolina Department of Revenue breach, at what point should someone have noticed the intruder? When the phishing emails first arrived? When the phished credentials were used for remote access? When large amounts of data were packaged in archive files? When those files were exfiltrated from the SCDOR network? Each of those stages was, for a while at least, indistinguishable to the agency from the activity of legitimate SCDOR users on the Department's computer systems, who were receiving emails, logging in remotely, or accessing and moving data. That was partly a failure on the part of the SCDOR to do more aggressive monitoring—but it was also partly a failure on the part of the people who designed their software and systems who could have made it easier for the

Department to distinguish between legitimate and malicious activity. The SCDOR employees who opened phishing emails bear some responsibility for failing to notice that those messages were not from their purported senders, but so, too, do the people who designed email to make it possible for anyone to send an email message from any email address. That's not a bug in email; it's a deliberate design decision—one that makes life a little easier for phishers and a little harder for every individual and organization that uses email.

Organizations have considerable control and autonomy when it comes to protecting their networks, but they are also constrained in many ways by the applications they use, including email, web content management programs, and messaging services. Those constraints are most apparent in the distinctions that application designers—and their applications—make between malicious and legitimate activity and how difficult it is for users to disguise the former as the latter. Application designers' decisions about what types of behavior to allow and disallow for users often lay the groundwork for how intruders will attempt to infiltrate a protected system, by disguising their initial steps as legitimate activity within the permitted bounds of a particular application. Those boundaries put in place by application designers help dictate how attackers initiate intrusions, how organizations using their applications monitor and define malicious behavior, and they have even been invoked by courts as the grounds for determining what is—and is not—considered illegal hacking.

The first person convicted of illegal computer hacking under the U.S. Computer Fraud and Abuse Act (CFAA) was Robert Morris, then a graduate student in computer science at Cornell, who in 1988 released a computer worm that replicated itself by exploiting software vulnerabilities, including bugs in an email program and a directory service. Since no one else had ever been convicted under the CFAA of accessing a computer without authorization, and since the text of the law itself offers no definitions of either "access" or "authorization," there was some uncertainty about whether Morris's behavior clearly fit that description. His lawyers, naturally enough, argued that it did not—because he was a Cornell student, they argued, he was authorized to use the Cornell computers, as well as the computers at MIT where he first released the worm, since they were connected to Cornell's via the Internet (the ruling, incidentally, was the first court

[handwritten margin note: & cf Orin Kerr article about CFAA vagueness- e.g. how terms of use breach can constitute violation]

decision in the United States to refer to "the Internet"). But the final ruling on the Morris case, issued by the Second Circuit Court of Appeals in 1991, determined that authorization to access computers did not derive from the university that owned and operated them, but rather from the application designers who had programmed their software. Judge Jon Newman wrote in the ruling:

> Morris did not use either of those features [the email and directory applications] in any way related to their intended function. He did not send or read mail nor discover information about other users; instead he found holes in both programs that permitted him a special and unauthorized access route into other computers.[1]

In other words, what made Morris's worm unauthorized—and therefore illegal—in Newman's view was not that Morris didn't have permission to release it from the people who owned and operated the computers he used, but rather that he didn't have permission from the people who designed the email and directory programs to use their applications in the way he did. By exploiting bugs in the email and directory programs to propagate his worm, Morris used those programs in a way other than their designers presumably intended them to be used, and, in doing so, broke the law. This is a remarkable amount of power to give application designers—to say that people who use their code for anything other than its "intended function" have illegally accessed a computer without authorization essentially means that application designers get to decide what is legal and what is illegal to do with computers based on how they intend users to use their programs. The designers themselves had created the bugs that Morris exploited, but that was not their fault, according to the court's interpretation, because they had not meant for anyone to use their programs the way Morris did.

Yet, if the application designers have the power to determine what constitutes acceptable and even legal use of their programs, they are rarely held responsible when those decisions lead to bad outcomes. In fact, the CFAA—the very same law that Newman interpreted as giving application designers the power to decide how people are authorized to use computer code—explicitly forbids suing anyone for "negligent design or manufacture of computer hardware, computer software, or firmware." This immunity for the hardware and software industries is often blamed for enabling coders and companies to put out buggy or vulnerable code without fear of legal consequences, but its implications go beyond just absolving developers for making coding mistakes. After all, application designers' role in defending computer systems is more than just catching errors, and the framework put in place in the CFAA to shield them from charges of negligence in some sense also distances and shields them from the consequences of the design decisions they make about what constitutes legitimate user behavior.

Increasing Work and Sending Signals

The crucial contribution of application designers to protecting computer systems is making it as difficult as possible for intruders to masquerade as legitimate users. There are two general ways application designers can do this: one is to make it harder for all users to do things that could be used for malicious purposes—like sending attachments and links via email; and the other is to offer clues to legitimate users, administrators, or other potential defenders, to help them detect potential malicious activity. Both of these models of defense require the application designer to be able to distinguish between what types of capabilities, in the context of a particular application, are most likely to be linked to something illicit or malicious. Assuming that those capabilities also have some legitimate purposes—as, indeed, emailed attachments and website links do—it may not make sense for the designer to ban them outright. Instead, a designer might choose to increase the amount of work required of users for them to be able to exercise those capabilities, making it a slower or more resource intensive process for attackers, by forcing them to acquire some additional credentials or reputation. Examples of this include payment processing sites like PayPal that limit users' access to funds until after they have had their accounts for a certain period of time, or review sites like Yelp that demote or hide reviews published by brand new accounts. Both of these restrictions make it a little harder for a user to make off with funds from a fraudulent transaction or write an unwarranted disparaging review of a competitor. The malicious acts are still possible, but they require a bit more work—e.g., a few weeks invested in building the reputation of an online account or writing other reviews. Ideally, forcing users to earn the right to exercise these capabilities can contribute directly to the signaling process, if the work needed to acquire potentially malicious capabilities itself serves as a signal to legitimate users.

Both PayPal and Yelp are examples of applications in which users have credentials—a login username and password, that is—through which their capabilities can be restricted and adjusted according to their actions. Often, however, cybersecurity incidents are initiated using applications that enable online interaction between strangers and therefore require no vetted credentials. The TJX breach, SCDOR breach, DigiNotar compromise, Unit 61398 espionage, and the OPM breach, all involved intruders who leveraged email and websites that required no authentication to steal credentials that then enabled further compromises. For an application like email, that is not operated by a single, centralized entity, and that regularly facilitates online communication between people who do not know each other, defenders are especially dependent on the clues afforded them by application designers to distinguish between malicious and legitimate interactions.

The central challenge of application defense is identifying specific capabilities of particular applications that indicate or lend themselves to malicious behavior. The narrower an application's intended function is, the easier it tends to be to distinguish between malicious and legitimate use, because legitimate activity takes on a very specific and repeated form. Indeed, the value in focusing defensive interventions at the application layer is precisely applications' specificity of function and use that makes it easier to pinpoint malicious indicators and ascribe intention to early access capabilities. More general pieces of software, such as operating systems or web browsers, are more difficult to defend because they offer less specific templates of what allowable behavior should look like.

If the strength of application defenses lies in designers' ability to tailor definitions of malicious and legitimate activity to individual application functions, their weakness stems from the wide range of applications used by individual people and machines. Restricting or blocking off one capability in any individual application does not prevent intruders from using other capabilities (or applications) to achieve the same ultimate goal—so application designers can, at best, hope to defend against malicious capabilities acquired through only one of many substitutable channels. In this regard, defense at the application layer closely corresponds to the proposed model in which attackers have the advantage over defenders because the latter group has to protect everything while the former only has to find one vulnerable point of entry. Many applications help users distinguish between who is a legitimate user and who is a malicious one based on whether a user has a known, trusted set of credentials—this avoids the problem of figuring out whether the user's *activity* looks particularly malicious by simply trusting that the user is not malicious, based on their credentials. However, a few applications intentionally facilitate interaction with unknown users, or users who do not possess vetted credentials. Since these applications, which are accessible to unknown users, are often the starting point for acquiring credentials that grant further access, they offer an interesting set of challenges for defenders—decidedly different from those faced by designers of authentication-based applications.

Application-Layer Security for Email and Web Browsers

The espionage incidents Mandiant investigated in 2013 all began with an email message (or several) sent to employees at the target organizations. It's the same way that the SCDOR breach began and the Cryptolocker ransomware spread to new victims. Thanks to its ubiquity and flexibility, email figures in a variety of security incidents, spanning different classes of harm, from espionage to financial fraud. And, because anyone can send an email to anyone else, it is often used in early stages of these incidents since it requires no prior capabilities or access. For malicious actors who have not managed to illicitly procure credentials, email offers opportunities to do just that—as well as to encourage recipients to initiate financial transfers or download malware. Many of the security challenges associated with email stem from the fact that, as an application, email was designed to allow anyone to send messages from any "from" address, regardless of whether they possess credentials for that address or its domain. This makes impersonation and, by extension, phishing very easy to accomplish in the context of email. While several solutions have been proposed over the years—many of them involving some version of digital signatures to verify that emails were actually sent from the person they claim to be from—few have caught on with any significant number of email users.

In 2008, PayPal became concerned about the large volumes of phishing emails being sent to its users, so its owner eBay made an agreement with Yahoo and Google that it would send only digitally signed emails, and the two email providers, in turn, agreed to discard any messages sent from the

PayPal (or eBay) domain that were not signed or had invalid signatures. In a blog post announcing the agreement, Gmail Spam Czar Brad Taylor wrote:

> Now any email that claims to come from "paypal.com" or "ebay.com" (and their international versions) is authenticated by Gmail and—here comes the important part—rejected if it fails to verify as actually coming from PayPal or eBay. That's right: you won't even see the phishing message in your spam folder. Gmail just won't accept it at all. Conversely, if you get a message in Gmail where the "From" says "@paypal.com" or "@ebay.com," then you'll know it actually came from PayPal or eBay. It's email the way it should be.[2]

This notion of "email the way it should be" hints at the crucial challenge of trying to delineate malicious and legitimate application-specific behaviors, or defining the shoulds and should-nots of email use: users should be able to receive emails from PayPal, but should not receive such emails from senders who don't have any affiliation with the company. They should be able to open links and attachments they want to view, but should not be able to open ones designed to steal their credentials or encrypt their files. They should be able to correspond with strangers and receive bulk emails, but should not be able to correspond with users who are known to be malicious or receive their bulk emails. These restrictions are implemented through technical tools, but fundamentally they are social decisions about what sorts of communications should be permitted online between people who may not know each other.

Email defenses correspond to a range of these restrictions, not just those designed to combat impersonation. These include blacklists of known spammer IP addresses, domains, and open proxies (like those maintained by Spamhaus), visual indicators of attachment file types (of the sort manipulated by the PLA espionage efforts, in which executable files were disguised as PDFs), or filters that reject emails on the basis of particularly suspicious text or content. None of the potentially malicious behaviors that these techniques are designed to defend against—impersonation, sending email through open proxies, sending executable attachments—are inherently malicious. All of them may serve useful and legitimate purposes in certain circumstances, making it that much harder to draw clear-cut distinctions between what users should and shouldn't be able to do, and what types of behavior should and shouldn't be flagged as suspicious. This ambiguity and overlap between legitimate and malicious uses of applications makes it possible for intruders to disguise their initial access attempts, via email or other applications, as legitimate. It also means that the most effective and feasible means of defense through application design is often not banning certain capabilities outright (e.g., preventing all users from sending email attachments), but instead increasing how much work attackers must do to execute these capabilities, by honing in on the subtle discrepancies between potentially malicious and legitimate activity.

Web browsers, like email, often facilitate interactions between users and unknown actors, who own and operate websites. Also, like email, these capabilities are often used to impersonate trusted actors, obtain credentials or financial information, and install malicious programs, but are not necessarily tied to a particular class of harm. In the case of both applications, the potential for maliciousness increases with capabilities that allow for impersonation, downloads, and requests to users to input or provide information. Existing browser security mechanisms address certain components of these capabilities, for instance, by notifying users when they connect to sites with invalid certificates, blocking sites with known malicious certificates, or blocking JavaScript. But the variety of different ways malicious actors can use these capabilities, individually and in combination, to achieve the same goals—such as stealing credentials, or sending outbound traffic from targeted machines—makes it difficult to pinpoint any single capability that is common to all malicious uses of browsers. The relationship between email and web browsers is particularly messy, since email is often used to send links to websites, while browsers are increasingly used to access email. The interplay between the two applications adds to the challenges of defending them individually. In the SCDOR breach, for instance, a phishing email was used to access credentials that could then be used to login to the Department's servers remotely through a separate remote access application. From a defensive standpoint, the number of steps and different applications involved in such a compromise can be both advantageous, in that it offers lots of opportunities for intervention, and also problematic, in that it complicates the question of who (or which application) is responsible for identifying and preventing which components of the intrusion.

Two defensive strategies follow from this dilemma. One is to limit the allowed interaction between different applications—the extent to which capabilities in one can be used in the context of another—for instance, by restricting the circumstances under which links to websites can be sent via email. This sandboxing approach narrows the broader range of malicious capabilities presented by other applications that a designer must worry about. An alternative is for application designers and operators to actively broaden their scope by creating their own versions of multiple, related applications and using their increased control of and visibility into the interaction among those applications to reinforce security mechanisms across all of them. For example, the fraudulent certificates stolen in the DigiNotar breach and used to access Gmail accounts were largely ineffective for users who used both Google's email service and its browser, because the approved credentials for the company's email site had been pinned to its browser. Had both of those applications not been operated by the same entity, it would have been much more difficult to identify the use of fraudulent certificates. On the other hand, Google's approach also introduces a new means of compromising the company's websites, by going after the pinned certificate information in their Chrome browser, rather than forging certificates as the DigiNotar intruder did.

Thinking through security design for web browsers and email requires defining certain very narrow parameters under which people and organizations with no pre-existing relationships should interact via computer systems and excluding any forms of interaction that have clear potential to be harmful or serve malicious ends. From a defensive perspective, this means making malicious actors work harder to be able to achieve those forms of interaction. That work can come from many different types of restrictions, ranging from only restricting the capabilities of known malicious actors—by blacklisting their IP addresses, certificates, or other specific identity indicators—to restricting the capabilities of all unknown actors (for instance, by blocking JavaScript or attachments by default for all websites or emails). However, all of these defenses have limitations, especially when it comes to fending off adversaries with considerable resources. For example, blacklists would probably have done little to hinder PLA Unit 61398, which, according to Mandiant's report, was using at least thirteen X.509 encryption certificates, forty families of malware, and more than three thousand domain names, IP addresses, and hashes of malware. Blacklists may help defenders identify reuse of those resources, but the volume of indicators also suggests how easily the PLA can afford to replace them with new ones. There are also several ways email services and web browsers can, and do, signal users about the possibility of impersonation, providing icons, warning messages, and other indications of suspicious activity within a browser or email client. Often, however, these signals go unnoticed or unheeded by users.[3]

These are all essentially technical controls, but, crucially, they are technical controls designed to provide a defensive function that organizations and users often cannot take on themselves. While organizations can maintain credentials for their employees and monitor what goes on inside their own networks, they may have much less visibility into the origins of incoming email messages or websites. Organizations can set restrictions about what sites their employees are able to visit, or what types of attachments they can open, but, ultimately, they rely heavily on application designers to help them figure out which indicators to use in distinguishing between legitimate and malicious activity when they encounter an email message or a website that could have been authored by anyone. Limiting what intruders can do without credentials through email and web browsers places greater pressure on those intruders to acquire trusted credentials. Once an intruder has acquired credentials, distinguishing between malicious and legitimate use of those capabilities becomes much trickier because the credentials themselves typically serve as the crucial indicator of legitimacy.

Monitoring Anomalous User Behavior

Efforts aimed at distinguishing between legitimate and illegitimate credentialed users are largely predicated on the idea that much application use is habitual—that users routinely go to the same sites, communicate with the same people and in fairly regular volumes, transfer money to the same places (and in fairly regular volumes), use the same devices and IP addresses—and deviations from those habits may therefore serve as indicators of malicious activity. Such defenses are most effective for applications that encourage standard use patterns, and the role of application designers lies in understanding what particular regular routines users are likely to develop in the context of their applications that might be difficult for attackers to replicate. Often, these fall into the categories of volume-based habits (e.g., number of emails sent per day), interaction identity-based habits (e.g., popular contacts or frequently visited websites), user identity-based habits (e.g., typing speed or eye movement patterns), or hardware and network-based habits (e.g., MAC addresses or IP addresses).

But there are not always clear changes in users' behavior after their credentials are compromised. For instance, a group of researchers at Google analyzed the behavior of manual hijackings of Google accounts using stolen credentials and found that these incidents are difficult to defend against in part because what manual hijackers do when interacting with Google's services is not very different from what normal users do. Normal users also search their inboxes and read emails, set up email filters, and change their password and their recovery options.[4] In other words, in this context, malicious activity looks too much like legitimate activity to be reliably identified or defended against. The researchers' analysis also suggests a slightly different approach to identifying malicious use of authenticated capabilities— looking for identifiable habits of attackers, rather than legitimate users. For instance, the Google analysis found that account hijackers were likely to search for certain terms in their victims' email (e.g., wire transfer, bank, investment, password, username), connect from IP addresses in certain countries (China, Ivory Coast, Malaysia, Nigeria, and South Africa), and send messages to, on average, 630 percent more recipients per day than the legitimate users of those accounts. On the other hand, the researchers also describe active efforts on the part of the hijackers to "blend in" with legitimate activity, noting particularly that: "on average, the hijackers attempted to access only 9.6 distinct accounts from each IP, which makes their activity extremely difficult to distinguish from organic traffic."[5] The number of outgoing emails from hijacked accounts was also only 25 percent higher, on average, than the number of legitimate messages sent from the account the day before the hijacking, though each message was typically sent to many more recipients, accounting for the 630 percent increase in distinct recipients. This suggests the extent to which perpetrators' motives dictate the constraints of their intrusion and the elements of their malicious activity that may be more or less easily disguised. IP addresses, for instance, can be easily altered to avoid suspicion, as can the volume of outbound emails, but hijackers must still reach a large number of recipients for attempts at email-based phishing or financial scams to be successful.

Attempts like these by hijackers to disguise their activity to more closely resemble that of legitimate users make sense in the context of a defensive strategy that is dependent on distinguishing between malicious and legitimate behavior. This is part of what makes the role of application designers so important in thinking about defense—they have significant control over how effectively intruders will be able to disguise their actions to resemble legitimate ones. Additionally, they play an important role in flagging suspicious behavior for legitimate users, especially after credentials are stolen. While intruders use email or websites primarily to catch victims' attention in some fashion or deliver malware, once they've successfully stolen credentials their behavior often shifts to emphasize greater discretion, and they put more effort into covering their tracks so as to prolong the value of the stolen credentials. This makes signaling a more valuable form of defense through mechanisms such as highlighting when those credentials were used and from what IP address, what they were used for, and whether they are being used simultaneously in multiple instances. Signaling users about potential malicious activity shifts some of the burden of distinguishing between malicious and legitimate activity onto users and system operators, relieving application designers of the need to be able to characterize maliciousness and legitimacy in general terms that apply to everyone. Users and organizations may not always welcome that burden, but by putting the appropriate tools in place to provide these signals, application designers can help guide other stakeholders' thinking about what they should be monitoring and which indicators will be most relevant for them. By setting these parameters for legitimate behavior and offering these signals to users, application designers can manifest, through the technical architecture of their applications, a set of deeply important decisions about what defenders should be on the lookout for, and how they should think about what malicious activity might look like in the context of their own systems.

Beyond catching bugs and vulnerabilities in their code, the security goals of an application designer ultimately fall into three primary categories. First, to send such clear, prominent, and understandable signals to users about suspicious activity in the context of their applications that the users themselves can be held accountable for ignoring or failing to notice those signals. Second, to draw sharp enough distinctions between legitimate and potentially malicious uses of their applications that intruders have to expend significant effort to engage in the latter, and cannot do so without triggering notice from monitoring users or organizations. And, finally, to put in place restrictions that might limit any intruder's ability to leverage a compromise of the application to cause harm—for instance, by encrypting stored information or regularly deleting data. Each of these goals presents significant challenges in the context of applications in which legitimate activity is not easily distinguishable from malicious uses. Still, the crucial advantage of embedding these defenses at the application layer, through decisions made by application designers, is that it allows for these distinctions to be tailored to specific applications and their particular uses, rather than trying to make them across the board for an entire computer system, as organizations are often forced to do.

12 Reasonable Security: The Role of Organizations in Protecting Their Data and Networks

While application designers play an important role in shaping how easily malicious actors can acquire different access capabilities, security incidents are most often closely associated with—and blamed on—the individual institutions whose systems are breached rather than the particular applications through which their adversaries gained access. This notion that organizations that store data are responsible for its protection is a natural extension of private law liability principles, in which the owner of property is seen as the locus of control. The assumption implicit in the ways these incidents are most often discussed and labeled—the TJX breach, the Sony leaks, the OPM breach—is that the organization that operated the compromised machines and owned the stolen data failed in its responsibilities to protect those assets. Critics and litigants point to the failures: TJX could have provided stronger encryption for its wireless networks; the South Carolina Department of Revenue could have used two-factor authentication; DigiNotar could have segmented its network more effectively; Sony could have noticed the massive quantities of data leaving its network; OPM could have encrypted its personnel files. These are all valid criticisms, and the fact that other stakeholders, including application designers and policymakers, had the ability to defend against certain elements of these incidents does not absolve the targeted organizations from taking steps to protect their computer systems and data. It can be difficult, though, to define their responsibility in concrete terms.

After a breach occurs, it's common to point out exactly where organizations went wrong with their security: members of Congress took OPM administrators to task for failing to use encryption; state legislators in South Carolina criticized the Department of Revenue for failing to use multi-factor authentication; and the credit card companies crucified TJX for using out-dated encryption on its wireless network. But these criticisms, offered in hindsight, often do not grapple with the question of whether these missing controls would, in fact, have been likely to prevent the breach altogether, or would instead have posed a mere inconvenience that the perpetrators could have circumvented relatively easily. This is the crucial question for defending computer systems: Which security controls create the greatest obstacle for intruders by restricting the stages of an attack that cannot be easily replaced or rerouted through another attack vector? Stronger wireless encryption would be of relatively little value to TJX if the credentials that Gonzalez and his co-conspirators wanted to steal could have been acquired just as easily through phishing or dictionary attacks. Similarly, encrypting the OPM files would have served little purpose if the intruders who stole them also had access to the decryption keys or credentials needed to view the information in plaintext. It is not enough just to list the security controls that an organization might have had in place when considering its culpability. It is also essential to evaluate how effective those controls would have been at preventing the breach in question and whether the breached entity could reasonably have been expected to select and implement them out of the sea of available security mechanisms.

While there is no shortage of available security products, services, and standards documents to purchase or consult, the sheer quantity of tools and recommendations can itself be an obstacle to organizations trying to figure out how they should spend a limited security budget. For instance, the catalog of Security and Privacy Controls for Federal Information Systems and Organizations, provided in the National Institute of Standards and Technology Special Publication 800–53 and often referenced by private companies as well as government agencies, is more than four hundred pages long and lists nearly three hundred different security controls. That excess of security advice and services, coupled with a lack of reliable, empirical data on which controls and techniques are most effective at preventing intrusions, leads to a security environment in which companies are expected to adhere to an amorphous set of "best practices" that are almost never explicitly codified until after a breach occurs. Then, in the aftermath of breaches of customer data in the United States, the Federal Trade Commission is often responsible for determining whether a company provided "reasonable" protections for that data. In the case of the 2013 breach of the retailer Target, for instance, the FTC did not file a complaint, deeming the company to have taken adequate steps to protect its customers' data, even though it was ultimately breached. By contrast, TJX and Ashley Madison both faced FTC complaints for failing to meet their data protection responsibilities. And yet, as the FTC complaints themselves illustrate, it is not entirely straightforward to articulate what, precisely, those responsibilities are, or how a company can be certain it has fulfilled them.

Indeed, the FTC deliberately does not define what, exactly, constitutes a reasonable set of security measures for a company. Instead, private coalitions, such as the Payment Card Industry Security Standards Council, set standards for certain industry sectors, and the FTC points to an assortment of these various guidelines and standards documents (including NIST Special Publication 800–53), thereby sidestepping the question of which specific measures companies must have in place in order to avoid punitive action from the government. The FTC has good reasons for not defining a clear set of baseline security requirements for companies—the crucial security measures may depend on an organization's particular function, as well as its infrastructure and data assets. Furthermore, the recommended set of controls changes over time as threats evolve, presenting a challenge for keeping such a list up-to-date. But the vague nature of the security guidance and recommendations given by the government adds to the uncertainty that institutions face when forced to make concrete decisions about how to define the scope of their responsibility for protecting computer systems and what tools to use for that purpose.

Headlines and news stories about breaches like TJX, the South Carolina Department of Revenue, DigiNotar, OPM, and Sony serve as cautionary tales for other companies and agencies hoping to avoid a similar fate. But the broader messages of these incidents are mixed for outside observers when it comes to figuring out just how much more seriously they should be taking their computer security and what, in concrete terms, it even means to take computer security seriously. With the exception of DigiNotar, none of these companies ended up going out of business because they failed to protect their computer systems. This suggests that a large-scale breach may be the kind of problem money can solve. On the other hand, many of those organizations saw directors and chief executives felled by the ensuing controversies and reckoning, indicating that even if a firm is likely to weather the storm, its senior leadership might not be so lucky. All of which points to the obvious but relatively unhelpful conclusion that an organization should take seriously the question of how best to defend its networks, but spend no more on security than they would have to spend to recover from a major breach. And what should they spend that security budget on? Here, history is again a somewhat inconsistent guide for organizations trying to learn from their less fortunate, or capable, peers. The immediate technical moral of the TJX breach would seem to be to invest in stronger encryption for wireless networks. The South Carolina Department of Revenue incident points to the importance of multi-factor authentication and encryption of stored data. The Cryptolocker ransomware model suggests sandboxing foreign programs so they can't immediately interact with the rest of a computer's contents. The DigiNotar compromise implicates overly complicated firewall rules and regular software updates. The PLA Unit 61398 espionage efforts would seem to recommend stronger email filters and more phishing training. The OPM breach would suggest more malware detection. The Spamhaus denial-of-service attacks point to the need for a greater reliance on third parties who can absorb and filter malicious traffic, and an end to open DNS resolvers. The Sony breach suggests the need for better network segmentation and tighter restrictions on outbound data. And the Ashley Madison breach points to the need for stronger encryption and regular data deletion. None of these are necessarily bad technical micro-lessons for other organizations to draw from these stories, but neither do they clearly provide a coherent set of measures that add up to a "reasonable" amount of security for companies.

Part of the challenge for organizations safeguarding computer systems and data is that the technical measures available to them are often significantly constrained and influenced by the security decisions made by other stakeholders, including both the design decisions of application developers and the policy decisions made by governments. The initial stages of many of these breaches are typically governed by access through websites and emails, granting an early foothold to outsiders that can then be used to procure credentials or other sensitive information. The design of those applications is largely out of the hands of the organizations using them, though they can sometimes take steps to tailor their use within the confines of their own network. At the same time, mitigating the final stages of these incidents, after the perpetrators have successfully procured an organization's data or compromised its networks and are trying to use that access

to profit financially, or conduct espionage, or publicly humiliate their victims, is also largely beyond the control of the breached organization. At
that point, it is often up to policymakers and law enforcement officials to
decide on any retaliatory measures or impose restrictions on how the perpetrators will be able to exploit their illicitly gained information or access.
So, organizations protecting their systems and data occupy an in-between
set of defensive functions, targeted primarily at the intermediate stages of
computer security incidents. Their system administrators have less control over the distinctions between legitimate and malicious activity baked
into the applications they use than do developers, and less ability to trace
and regulate illicit money flows than government agencies. But they do
have important defensive roles that center on restricting credential theft
and outbound information flows, covering some of the holes left by other
groups' defensive capabilities.

Tailoring Application Capabilities

Companies and government agencies often use software applications they
did not design themselves, making them reliant on the decisions of application designers, but they do control some decisions about how to monitor
and implement those applications. Just because an organization decides to
use email—as, indeed, most do—does not mean it has no control over how,
exactly, it will filter and safeguard against threats like phishing. The defensive
roles of application designers are focused on making it easier to distinguish
between legitimate and malicious activity in the context of their applications, but they can also allow some leeway to users and organizations to tailor
those distinctions to their own particular circumstances and threat models.
For instance, an organization might decide to add a special warning label to
any emails sent from outside domains so that employees are not fooled into
believing such messages were sent by colleagues. Alternatively, organizations
could restrict email attachments to permit only certain types of files, or files
that had been cleared by administrators, or files that had first been tested for
any malicious behavior in a quarantined computing environment. Similarly,
an organization can restrict which websites people on its network can visit,
or how easily they can download programs and files from online.

These sorts of restrictions are not feasible, or sensible, for every organization. Their different decisions depend on what they do, and what their

employees and customers need to be able to do in the course of their normal business. More generally, the distinction between legitimate and malicious capabilities varies according to context—for instance, some organizations may require regular communication with outside, unknown entities, while others may view that capability as a threat and wish to instead limit communication to authenticated users within their own network. Similarly, other types of online activity may be viewed as more or less suspicious depending on the setting. For instance, periods of unusually high-volume email may be routine at places that send large-scale legitimate mailings, and new and unknown devices or IP addresses may not trigger any strong suspicion for organizations whose employees travel frequently, or who provide network access to a large number of visiting guests. Just as application designers can tailor these distinctions to the particular function of their application, so, too, can organizations further tailor them to suit their particular circumstances and preferences. Part of defending against abuse of online applications as an organization involves building on the analysis of potentially malicious and legitimate capabilities done by application designers. An organization with a clear sense of what kind of activity it expects to witness from legitimate employees and users can ideally refine the distinctions and indicators decided on by application designers and determine the extent to which they actually mirror the organization's own particular threat model and mission.

Where there is a mismatch between the types of malicious capabilities and signals selected by application designers, organizations may either choose not to implement a given application or tailor it to their needs, depending on the extent to which designers have made it customizable. These customizations may apply at either the individual or institutional level—for instance, many browsers allow users to choose whether or not to enable JavaScript, or manage the default list of trusted SSL certificates. Application designers may find it useful to allow users and organizations to define some of the distinctions between legitimate and malicious activity for themselves. However, enabling this kind of flexibility can give rise to additional risks by creating pathways for adversaries to enable malicious capabilities or remove useful signals under the guise of tailoring an application to fit legitimate needs. If it's possible for someone with the right credentials to alter or remove safeguards and alerts, then intruders may take advantage of those capabilities. This tension between allowing users to define their own security parameters and enabling intruders to change those parameters, or remove defensive signals is a tricky one for application designers and organizations. It suggests there may be some advantages to a one-size-fits-all, unalterable approach to security—even though every application and every organization is different and faces slightly different threats—if only because it removes an intruder's ability to alter that approach for nefarious purposes.

Many defenses pose questions about how organizations wish to interact with outsiders, or people without trusted credentials. Sony Pictures knew it needed to be able to send and receive large video files, for instance, but it's less clear why that would have needed to be the case for the South Carolina Department of Revenue or OPM. DigiNotar needed a public-facing website that outside potential customers could view, but did Marshalls stores need a wireless network that outside devices could connect to? The desired level of interaction with the outside world helps dictate which applications a company or government agency should use, as well as customization of those applications' security settings. This essentially means assessing what capabilities an organization is comfortable granting to people whom it has never encountered in person or subjected to personnel screening or training procedures. Many, if not most, organizations would probably choose to severely restrict the circumstances under which these interactions with unknown users may take place—but the precise nature of those restrictions may vary depending on whether an organization's mission is to produce movies, audit tax returns, store personnel files, issue digital certificates, or facilitate extramarital affairs.

Organizations, like application designers, also play a vital role in defending user credentials from theft and misuse. Tailoring application restrictions and protecting authentication credentials are intended, respectively, to restrict any potentially malicious capabilities to credentialed users and to restrict any access to trusted credentials to only that group of users, or employees. This central defensive ambition is dictated primarily by what institutional actors can control. Application designers can dictate what capabilities are afforded by the applications they design under what conditions, so their defensive function centers on distinguishing between malicious and legitimate capabilities. Organizations have greater control over physical security—including access to machines on protected premises, personnel screening, and credential issuing procedures. Therefore, their defensive role centers on

"how "who

using that to reinforce computer security by trying to force adversaries to tackle physical security measures—by stealing employees' phones or physical devices, for instance—and personnel screening processes in order to achieve desired computer capabilities.

Multi-factor Authentication and Encryption

The crucial ex-ante defensive role of organizations lies in protecting the authentication credentials that restrict who can access potentially malicious capabilities. For organizations that link credentials to users' real identities (e.g., employers, governments, schools), this includes ensuring that credentials are issued to the correct people, and for all organizations, it means trying to issue credentials that cannot be easily stolen, guessed, or imitated. This form of defense is about trying to tie credentials to a particular user in a way that makes them difficult to replicate or extract without physical access to that person. Authentication also presents a relatively rare opportunity for defenders to implement multiple, overlapping lines of defense in the context of a computer system through multi-factor authentication. This means that an adversary wishing to take advantage of any of those capabilities must compromise all of the protected credentials—and in the uncertain environment of computer systems, where intruders are often able to replace one access path with another and thereby simply bypass well protected applications and devices, that is an unusual and valuable feature. This does not that mean multi-factor authentication systems cannot be compromised. Mechanisms for compromising two-factor authentication schemes, which rely on both a password known to the user and a one-time code or notification transmitted by phone or other physical token, include compromising each of the victim's credentials individually, and tricking victims into entering all of the credentials into forged or compromised authentication interfaces.

FBI Special Agent Elliott Peterson describes one such scheme, as implemented using the GameOver ZeuS bot:

> GOZ ... is sufficiently advanced that its operators can harvest both static and variable information in real time from the victims. Specifically, after the initiation of a man-in-the-middle attack, the GOZ operators will be queried by the bank for the variable portion of the victim's two factor initiation. The GOZ operators pass this query on to the victim in the form of a fictitious web injection. While

the victim thinks that the information is being sent to the bank, it is instead sent directly to the GOZ operators. After stealing victims' personal information, the defendants use the stolen credentials to log into victims' bank accounts and to initiate fraudulent electronic funds transfers from the victims' banks.[1]

This approach calls into question the independence of multiple authentication credentials: if the credentials are all entered into a single interface, then it may not actually be necessary for adversaries to independently compromise each credential individually. This implies that one key component of protecting credentials is actually the protection of the authentication interface, not just the stored credentials themselves—that means increasing the work required to impersonate or compromise that interface, and providing signals that help users verify the legitimacy of the interface demanding their credentials.

Defending authentication credentials is complicated because, while the credentials themselves may be essential to intruders in some cases, there are a number of replaceable methods for obtaining them—and only some of those methods can be effectively controlled by the organization issuing the credentials. Those organizations can, generally, control how easily credentials can be guessed, through the implementation of complexity requirements and internal attempts at guessing, as well as limits on how often users can enter incorrect guesses. But guessing is easier to protect against than imitation and interception because it provides signals of the attacker's work within the context of the protected system—that is, the very act of repeatedly guessing, or entering an incorrect credential, signals potentially malicious behavior. The work required to intercept or imitate an authentication credential does not necessarily provide any such signal to the authenticating organization, even if the work involved is considerable. For example, there was presumably a lot of work that went into decrypting the PIN numbers in the TJX breach perpetrated by Gonzalez, and also into crafting the targeted phishing emails sent by PLA Unit 61398 officers—but all of that work was invisible to TJX and the targets of the PLA's espionage efforts because it wasn't happening inside their networks. The behaviors that enable credential interception and imitation—as opposed to those that enable guessing—may not be behaviors that the issuing organizations are easily able to restrict or even detect.

Multi-factor authentication is useful, in part, because it provides organizations with additional signals of suspicious activity, even before an intruder has successfully authenticated using stolen credentials. The successful entry of one credential can be used to signal to the person to whom it was issued that authentication has been initiated using their credentials—for instance, if a user receives a one-time passcode via text message, that message functions both as a credential and a signal that someone is attempting to login to their account. Similarly, if additional authentication credentials are delivered via email or other applications, the receipt of those messages can serve as a signal in the event of attempted credential theft.

Stolen credentials featured prominently in the TJX, South Carolina Department of Revenue, DigiNotar, PLA Unit 61398, OPM, and Sony incidents, but in all of those cases, only the SCDOR was especially singled out in the aftermath for failing to implement multi-factor authentication. This was perhaps because credential theft was the very first stage of that incident and also because the costs of a two-factor authentication system seemed so low to many SCDOR critics. Recall state senator Kevin Bryant's assertion at hearings on the incident that, "We wouldn't be here had somebody made that decision to use the multifactor authentication."[2] It is certainly true that multi-factor authentication can make it more difficult for intruders to steal credentials. It is also true, as the GOZ interception tactic illustrates, that multi-factor authentication by no means makes it impossible for intruders to steal credentials. So the crucial question is not whether SCDOR could necessarily have prevented its breach by using multi-factor authentication, but rather whether it needed to be using multi-factor authentication in order to provide South Carolina's taxpayers with reasonable security for their data—and whether multi-factor authentication would, on its own, have been sufficient to meet that reasonableness standard.

Along with multi-factor authentication, encryption is probably the security control that breached companies are most frequently lambasted for failing to use, or for using incorrectly. As with multi-factor authentication, many firms would likely be more secure if they employed strong encryption to protect their data—but it would serve as no guarantee that intruders would be unable to access that data in plaintext. Many companies need their employees and customers to be able to access and transmit sensitive information constantly in the course of conducting their normal business. That information can still be encrypted when it is stored on servers and sent over networks, but there needs to be some—relatively cheap, fast—means of decrypting it, usually by providing a set of trusted credentials. So, far from being a replacement for other types of security, the strength of an institution's encryption scheme is often highly dependent on the strength of its authentication system and credential protection. The reason Bryant cites the lack of multi-factor authentication as being responsible for the SCDOR breach, rather than the agency's lack of encryption, is probably because, once the intruders had stolen employee credentials, they might well have been able to decrypt filing information using those credentials, even if the data had been encrypted. In just this manner, the PLA Unit 61398 officers who infiltrated U.S. companies used stolen credentials to decrypt sensitive information stored in those companies' networks. One further challenge of relying on widespread encryption is that it can serve at cross-purposes with defenses intended to help monitor what is going on inside a particular organization's network. For instance, encryption might hinder attempts to monitor and restrict outbound traffic by making it more difficult for targeted firms to recognize attempts to exfiltrate sensitive information—and easier for adversaries to disguise such attempts, as happened in the DigiNotar incident when the intruder used HTTPS encryption to hide his communications with the DigiNotar network.

Network Segmentation and Data Exfiltration

The central problem with focusing attention on one particular element of an organization's missing security in the aftermath of a breach—inadequately protecting credentials, for instance, or failing to filter phishing emails, or encrypting wireless networks poorly, or not encrypting sensitive data at all—is that none of these is absolutely essential to an intruder. There are ways of compromising computer systems without stealing credentials (as in the case of Cryptolocker), or without sending phishing emails (see DigiNotar and TJX), or without relying on organizations' failure to encrypt data (see TJX and Ashley Madison). These techniques are merely a means to some larger end for the intruder, whether that's stealing money or conducting espionage or taking revenge on the victim. From that perspective, these early technical stages of breaches are often interchangeable to their perpetrators. This framing—and, by extension, these stages of intrusions—lends itself to the traditional view of attackers having the advantage over defenders because the former group only has to find one way to compromise a system while the defenders have to block all possible attack pathways. But while capabilities such as sending phishing emails or connecting to unpro-tected wireless networks are not absolutely necessary for inflicting any par-ticular type of harm, some computer capabilities are, in fact, essential.

For instance, attackers' ability to send outbound traffic, or exfiltrate data, from compromised accounts and machines is a necessary prerequisite for stealing data. Often, so is the ability to traverse a target's networks by exploiting a toehold in one part of an organization's networks to access other portions of its computer systems. This was a crucial component of the TJX, SCDOR, DigiNotar, OPM, and Sony Pictures breaches: not being confined to a particular compromised device or user account, but instead being able to move laterally within each organization's networks to search for the information or resources of greatest interest to the intruders.

The TJX and SCDOR breaches depended on the intruders being able to exfiltrate large volumes of payment card information from company serv-ers; the PLA Unit 61398 espionage efforts and Sony Pictures breaches were similarly focused on retrieving sensitive information from the targeted systems; and the Spamhaus denial-of-service attacks and Cryptolocker dis-semination required control of a bot, or the ability to send outbound traffic from thousands of machines. Financial fraud, espionage, and digital service disruption attacks all generally share this dependency on the capability to send outbound traffic from protected machines. (Denial-of-service attacks could conceivably be perpetrated by an adversary who actually owned and operated thousands of computers, instead of using a bot comprised of other people's machines, but in practice this is rare—and it would drive up the cost of initiating such an attack considerably.) In some cases, this is a capa-bility that application designers may be able to restrict—for instance, by flagging unusually high volumes of outgoing messages—but in many cases it may be more effectively restricted by monitoring network connections and traffic rather than individual applications, implying a strong defen-sive role for the organizations that operate these networks. Similarly, those organizations are responsible for segmenting their networks so that a com-promise of one account, application, or device does not easily grant intrud-ers access to everything else stored in their computer systems. The risk of such segmentation efforts is that, especially for large organizations, they can become so complicated and extensive that it is difficult to confirm that they actually work as intended, as was the case with DigiNotar's sprawling set of firewall rules.

Organizations have several tactics at their disposal to help distinguish between malicious and legitimate outbound activity, including monitoring the volume of traffic, its destination, and the repetition (or regular patterns) and timing with which it is sent. Restricting the volume of data that can be sent, or the ease with which it can be sent to unknown recipients, may increase the work required of adversaries to exfiltrate information. This can also be achieved by requiring extra layers of independent approval (or credentials) to send outbound traffic from a protected network—particularly in large volumes or to new recipients—separate from the credentials and restrictions placed on other capabilities.

Restrictions placed on outbound traffic may also force attackers to do extra work that can, in itself, serve as an additional set of signals to organizations. For instance, if organizations use firewalls to restrict outbound connections to only certain servers, or allow outbound data to be sent in limited volumes, then activity that involves moving or copying information to those servers and compressing it or sending it at a steady, gradual rate may indicate malicious exfiltration. Forcing attackers to stage information in this manner before it can be successfully sent to an outside destination may provide organizations with useful signals of intended exfiltration even before it actually occurs. Viewed in this light, the role of defenses like firewalls is not just to prevent some forms of infiltration and exfiltration, but also to channel those behaviors through specific and identifiable paths that can then be monitored for signals of malicious activity.

Outbound traffic can directly harm organizations that have failed to restrict it, as in the cases of Sony Pictures and SCDOR, but it can also harm other organizations that trust the compromised institution. Espionage incidents, for instance, often rely on exfiltrating sensitive information through an organization that is trusted by the victim but has less stringent outbound traffic restrictions than the targeted institution itself. The perpetrators can then send the stolen data on from those third-party hop points to their own servers, which might otherwise trigger suspicion due to their location or ownership. PLA Unit 61398, for example, used computers at American universities as intermediaries for data exfiltration from targeted U.S. companies. In defending against unintended outbound traffic, organizations therefore protect not just themselves but also others from breaches. This makes outbound data flow restrictions all the more important—but also, potentially, diminishes the direct incentives that some institutions may have to implement such defenses.

Limitations of Individual Organizations

There are many steps that companies and government agencies can take to protect their computer systems and sensitive data, but they can't do it alone. That's no excuse for negligence along the lines of Wyndham's decision to reject all security measures wholesale; but it is a reason to consider carefully the scope of what an organization reasonably can—and cannot— control when it comes to their computer security and where their incentives lie. Companies can exercise control over what information they store, and how they store it. They can monitor and restrict what information leaves their networks, and which programs are permitted to be installed on their systems. They can make rules about how many and what types of credentials are required to authenticate to their computer systems, and how easy it is for access to one component of those systems to be leveraged to access every other component and piece of information stored within. Configuring and managing all of those controls is difficult and important work, and it's largely something that firms have to figure out for themselves. That is true not just because there are so many different sets of guidelines and so little clear-cut concrete guidance from policymakers about what is required, but also because the appropriate settings and levels of security depend significantly on the particular features and functions of any individual entity and what it needs to be able to use its computer systems for.

Accepting the wisdom of tailoring computer security to different workplaces—and applications and users—and the wisdom of not imposing a rigid, one-size-fits-all set of security requirements on everyone makes it that much harder to answer the question of when a breach should be blamed on the targeted organization, and when it should be blamed exclusively on the perpetrator. Of course, breached firms argue that their misfortunes are always the fault of the perpetrators—in fact, Wyndham made exactly this point in its failed attempt to challenge the FTC's authority to deem their poor security an unfair business practice. Wyndham contended that a company "does not treat its customers in an 'unfair' manner when the business itself is victimized by criminals."[3] But, especially in an online context where relatively few perpetrators are likely to be both reliably identified and under the jurisdiction of the governments that may wish to charge them for their actions, simply casting blame on the perpetrators is not an effective strategy. In large part, that is why breached organizations instead turn their attention to blaming other stakeholders. It is why, in the aftermath of the TJX breach, the bitterest legal fights and largest financial settlements had less to do with Gonzalez and his co-conspirators than they did with the battles between TJX and the credit card companies and banks. It's why the South Carolina Department of Revenue was eager to throw NIST and the IRS under the bus when it came time to explain their security posture; and why Google publicly called out DigiNotar for being responsible for the compromise of Iranian Google accounts; and why OPM administrators blamed their predecessors, as well as third-party contractors, for the poor state of information security within the agency. What's striking about these disputes is not that organizations in hot water would try to blame someone else for their problems; what's striking is that often, when it comes to computer security, those organizations have a point. Yes, mistakes were made by the breached parties, and security controls were missing—but there were also other potential defenders who could have stepped in to detect or stop certain stages of those breaches, even, in some cases, intermediaries who would have been better poised and equipped to tackle those stages than the breached organization itself. It may seem unfair to consider assigning some responsibility to those parties, and it's certainly not something existing liability regimes have encouraged. But sometimes these intermediaries have visibility into and control over more essential stages of cybersecurity incidents than the breached organizations do. In those cases, the question of who it is "fair" to blame for an incident may be less important, at least in terms of strengthening security for the future, than the question of who could most effectively prevent such an incident from recurring by cutting off perpetrators at a bottleneck stage of their attack.

For instance, compromised accounts and devices at intermediary hop-point organizations were used to run the GOZ bot and distribute Cryptolocker, and to route information stolen by PLA Unit 61398 back to China. The fraudulent or misleading domains used to connect to OPM servers and steal data were purchased through web registrars. The open DNS resolvers used to bombard Spamhaus and Cloudflare with massive volumes of traffic were owned and operated by other organizations, and that traffic was delivered by Internet service providers. Regardless of whether they had any

idea what their infrastructure and resources were being used for, all of those intermediary organizations had opportunities to intervene and protect the victims, and they largely failed to do so. They might well feel that there is no reason why they should be held responsible for the actions or mistakes of others, and for the most part existing legal and policy frameworks have supported that logic. In the various legal battles and settlements that followed in the wake of these incidents, none of these intermediaries bore any of the costs of the breaches, providing little incentive for other organizations to take defensive measures that would protect their own devices and networks from being used as platforms to launch future intrusions.[4] Instead, fights about liability have centered almost exclusively on trying to shift greater responsibility and costs onto the breached organizations themselves. But there are defensive roles that intermediary organizations can play that the breached ones simply cannot assume themselves. So, whether or not it seems fair, or even reasonable, to assign some responsibility to those third parties for security incidents, or to provide incentives for them to help protect others, it is essential for trying to cut off attackers at critical, bottleneck stages of their intrusions.

Breached organizations are often, and sometimes rightly, castigated for their poor security, but it is important to understand both what measures they could take that would have the greatest impact and also the constraints and limitations they face when protecting their own computer systems. Managing encryption, augmenting authentication credentials, effective network segmentation, and carefully monitoring outbound traffic are all important defensive functions of organizations, whether companies or government agencies; the latter two controls, especially, can help cut off essential pathways for intruders attempting to carry out their ultimate aims. But since many of those ultimate aims play out beyond the context of an individual organization's computer systems—in financial transactions or development of new products using stolen intellectual property or widespread publication of embarrassing information, for instance—there are many later stages of these incidents that these organizations are not well-situated to detect or mitigate. Even when it comes to detecting suspicious widespread traffic patterns, individual organizations' ability to identify anomalous patterns, large-scale financial fraud, or malicious command-and-control servers is often inferior to the wider lens of payment networks, who process huge volumes of transactions, or Internet service providers, who monitor much larger swaths of traffic. Meanwhile, security protocols for email and websites—the applications that perpetrators used to initiate access to the systems of DigiNotar, the PLA Unit 61398 espionage victims, OPM, Spamhaus, and Sony—are similarly beyond the control of individual organizations, though administrators can sometimes take steps to tailor those applications' use within their own networks. In order for all of these different stakeholders to play their respective roles in the defensive landscape, disputes over liability in the aftermath of security incidents ultimately need to become more complicated and involve more diverse stakeholders. For that to happen, however, there need to be clearer guidelines governing who is responsible for defending against which stages of cybersecurity incidents, so that both targeted organizations and all the other intermediaries surrounding and interacting with them online have some understanding of what is expected of them and how they fit into the larger security ecosystem.

13 "Happy Talk About Good Ideas": The Role of Policymakers in Defending Computer Systems

The overarching lesson of the past decade is that learning from past security incidents entails defining liability regimes that clarify the defensive roles and responsibilities of all the different actors involved—and this is fundamentally a task for courts and policymakers. Computer security is by no means purely a policy problem. Application designers wield significant defensive power in determining how much work adversaries must do to attain certain capabilities. Organizations and their system administrators can tailor and augment those lines of defense by trying to make authentication credentials harder to steal, and by restricting inbound and outbound network traffic. But these groups, and others, are limited in their ability to enact defenses that protect against the final stages of certain types of attacks, the stages that often extend beyond the context of their particular applications and networks, and involve the perpetrators getting what they are ultimately after, whether that's money, secrets, or revenge. Policymakers and law enforcement actors are better suited to some elements of mitigating the impacts of computer security incidents, particularly those related to addressing harm caused by third parties and curtailing criminals' ability to profit off their activity. Policymakers are particularly well poised to undertake these defensive roles because, unlike application designers and organizations, they are able to restrict and target not just the behavior of attackers but also that of defenders, and all the stakeholders with the potential to play a defensive role.

Policy has struggled to keep up with a field that's advancing rapidly and cybersecurity policy is still at a fairly nascent stage in the United States and other countries. Most current policies focus fairly narrowly on the notification responsibilities owed to victims of data breaches, rather than on the responsibilities of anyone at any level to proactively defend against such breaches. Policy efforts that predate the TJX breach, such as the Digital Millennium Copyright Act and the Computer Fraud and Abuse Act, have largely failed to keep pace with the technical advances and geographic spread of attackers. Still, many governments have been fairly tentative when it comes to enacting cybersecurity policies, unsure of the most effective or appropriate actions to take in a space largely dominated by private firms and choosing to rely heavily on voluntary programs and codes of conduct rather than more stringent requirements or laws. Many policymakers acknowledge that industry should play a leading role in securing private computer systems, but still argue for the importance of government intervention. The tension at the heart of these policy debates is how to let private firms take the lead when it comes to securing the information and computer networks that they own and operate, while still ensuring that governments provide them with the support and motivation to implement adequate security measures.

Several governments are in the process of thinking through how to regulate these issues and have announced plans to implement new cybersecurity policies in the coming years. These policy efforts include: regulations in China to ensure that data collected from Chinese citizens and companies is stored domestically; laws in the European Union to improve incident reporting, users' control over their personal data, and security standards for critical infrastructure; and proposals in the United States to increase penalties for breached companies and bolster the security of voting systems. At present, however, governments have relatively few models to work from or countries to point to as exemplars of how governments can successfully supplement private sector efforts to strengthen cybersecurity. The major security breaches of the past decade should play a prominent role in shaping these policy decisions. Only by thinking clearly about the battles to assign responsibility that follow these incidents, and the coordination challenges of the different intermediary stakeholders involved, can policymakers hope to shape policies that prepare and incentivize private and public institutions to defend against future breaches and their social, financial, and political consequences.

Policies Aimed at Attackers

Cybersecurity policies can either target attackers—the criminals or malicious actors responsible for perpetrating breaches—or the ecosystem of interconnected defenders, organizations and individuals with the ability to help prevent those attackers from achieving their ultimate aims. Laws like the CFAA in the United States, or the Computer Misuse Act in the United Kingdom, are examples of policies that target attackers: they criminalize certain activities (e.g., unauthorized access to computers), enabling law enforcement authorities to prosecute and punish offenders directly. Policies that directly target attackers tend to focus primarily on criminalizing access, leading to considerable controversy and disagreement around what constitutes "unauthorized access" or "access in excess of authorization" in the context of a computer system. The CFAA, for instance, gives the following definition of the latter activity: "to access a computer with authorization and to use such access to obtain or alter information in the computer that the accesser is not entitled so to obtain or alter," implying a fairly broad set of capabilities—centered on data exfiltration and editing—that could be considered access. Even though accessing computers is typically just one step in a larger breach, policies designed to directly target and punish malicious actors focus on the initial, access-oriented stages of attacks, rather than the ultimate harm, such as financial fraud or espionage, since those harms are often already covered by existing laws. In many cases, this makes sense to avoid redundant policymaking, but it also contributes to the emphasis placed on the earliest, technical stages of attacks in breach postmortems as well as the challenges of trying to figure out how to classify and punish types of harm that don't always fit neatly into existing statutes.

Denial-of-service attacks present a particular challenge for policies that target attackers because this type of attack typically harms a particular victim, such as Spamhaus, not through illicit or unauthorized access to that victim's computers, but rather through unauthorized access to many other people's computers. At least two people allegedly involved in orchestrating the attacks on Spamhaus have since been arrested and charged under the Computer Misuse Act. However, it is unclear whether their crime was in flooding Spamhaus's web servers (harmful, but not unauthorized since the web servers were indeed designed to receive queries from external machines) or using compromised hosts to do so (accessing those hosts to send outbound traffic was unauthorized, but not directly harmful to the hosts themselves). Similarly, in 2013, when thirteen people associated with Anonymous were indicted in the United States under the CFAA for launching a series of distributed denial-of-service attacks directed at the copyright industry, the indictment charged that the individuals had conspired to "intentionally cause damage, and attempt to cause damage, without authorization, to a protected computer … causing loss to victims resulting from the course of conduct affecting protected computers aggregating at least $5,000 in value."[1] But the targeted servers belonging to the organizations that actually incurred those losses had not been accessed in a clearly unauthorized manner—they were intended to receive outside queries—and the computers that had been used without authorization, to bombard the targeted servers, incurred no such financial losses. Attempts to use policy to punish attackers for denial-of-service incidents sometimes conflate the technical access to intermediary machines required to carry out an attack and the ultimate harm directed at a slightly different set of victims.

While arresting and punishing attackers directly is an important role— and one that governments are undoubtedly uniquely suited to—there are several reasons policymakers may wish to extend their reach beyond criminal-focused regulations to influence defenders. The challenges of attribution and international investigation make it difficult to identify and prosecute responsible parties in many cybercrime cases. For instance, the perpetrators of the South Carolina Department of Revenue, DigiNotar, and Ashley Madison breaches have never been reliably identified. Meanwhile, PLA Unit 61398 officers responsible for cyberespionage efforts, as well as Evgeniy Bogachev, the man responsible for GameOver ZeuS and Cryptolocker, have all been identified by the U.S. government, but remain out of the reach of its judicial system so long as they reside overseas in countries that refuse to arrest them. Ultimately, given these limitations on catching and prosecuting criminals, a government that wants to prevent or mitigate threats must look to policies that govern intermediary actors and the security measures they have in place. Perhaps the strongest incentive for governments to develop security policies that target intermediaries and defenders is simply that those actors are identifiable and, to some extent, cooperative and governable within a national context. A government cannot reach every attacker who targets its citizens, but it can—to varying degrees—attempt to reach and regulate every company that carries traffic, stores data, and provides services within its borders.

National policies can still play an important role in punishing international bad actors. In fact, recent policy efforts in the United States have focused on trying to cut off money flows to criminals outside the country's borders. The Deter Cyber Theft Act, introduced in the U.S. Senate in June 2014, for instance, proposed to block imports of products manufactured overseas by companies that the U.S. government found to have benefited from cyber espionage. Measures in the controversial U.S. Stop Online Piracy Act (SOPA), introduced in the House of Representatives in 2011 but never passed, were similarly designed to cut off income sources for perpetrators of online crimes. Since SOPA targeted infringing intermediary websites, rather than imports, however, it took a slightly different approach than the Deter Cyber Theft Act. Its provisions would have prevented online advertising and payment companies from conducting business with infringing websites, required U.S. service providers to block access to those sites, and forbidden search engines from linking to them. SOPA, and its Senate counterpart, the PROTECT IP (PIPA) bill, had the same broad goals as the Deter Cyber Theft Act: rendering cybercrime less profitable, foiling criminals by cutting off their financial flows, and mitigating the economic harm inflicted on U.S. industry by international actors. But the means by which SOPA and PIPA proposed to accomplish these goals required extensive involvement of Internet intermediaries—the advertising companies, payment processors, service providers, and search engines who would have carried out the policy measures in accordance with court orders. The measures proposed in the Deter Cyber Theft Act targeted physical imports rather than online content and were therefore more direct, requiring the involvement of fewer intermediaries. Notably, none of these bills were passed into law. Indeed, SOPA and PIPA met with almost unprecedented public backlash from many major websites and tech firms who rallied users in January 2012 to protest both bills as they appeared to be nearing passage.[2] Unsurprisingly, those companies were unenthusiastic about the idea that they might be forced to assume greater responsibility for policing online misbehavior—and face greater penalties for failing to do so. There were other reasons people objected to SOPA and PIPA—the bills took a broad view of what constituted a foreign infringing site, and therefore might well have been susceptible to misuse by people or firms looking for a way to block websites, even in the absence of egregious infringement activity. The outcry over SOPA and PIPA reinforced just how aggressively stakeholders were willing to fight to ensure they would not have to shoulder any additional responsibility for stopping online crime.

SOPA and PIPA, as well as the Deter Cyber Theft Act, are all early examples of failed attempts at crafting policies that take advantage of the power online intermediaries have to mitigate harm and stymie cybercriminals. They offer flawed but thought-provoking templates for how governments can attempt to mitigate financial harms through manipulation of both international trade and domestic markets and intermediaries. They also represent Congress's attempts to think creatively about how to wield policy within the confines of their national jurisdiction, by regulating only U.S.-based companies, while still trying to have a significant international impact on cybercriminals located outside the country.

The strengthening of international cooperation around law enforcement efforts and the development of global norms governing cyber threats are both clearly crucial for the future landscape of computer security policy. National efforts on their own are unlikely to provide sufficient protection or consistency for firms and individuals operating in a global context. Furthering these international efforts should be a central focus of every government looking to engage with computer security issues. Long term, the most promising policy outcomes for computer security may derive from strong, detailed, and comprehensive international partnerships. But this seems like a distant goal at a moment when the United States, Russia, and China—three of the most powerful and technically sophisticated governments in the world—seem incapable of agreeing on anything related to cybersecurity, and are instead actively antagonizing each other online, through election meddling, filing criminal charges against military officers and government informants, and blatantly disregarding the others' charges and calls for extradition. Especially in the aftermath of the 2016 U.S. presidential election, during which U.S. intelligence officials said the Russian government stole and leaked information to influence the results, strong international cooperation and partnerships on cybersecurity policy and cybercrime enforcement do not seem imminent. As nations struggle to find common ground on these issues and even, in some cases, indicate their mistrust of each other's motives and activities, the short-term future of cybersecurity policy, at least, seems destined to involve national governments taking more unilateral action and implementing policies within their own borders aimed at defenders and intermediary stakeholders. The United States is in a uniquely powerful position to put in place national regulations with far-reaching international consequences, since so many of the largest online intermediaries are based in the U.S., and so much of the information and money targeted by cybercriminals also comes from U.S. users and organizations.

Defender-Oriented Policy Levers

Policymakers can impose three types of requirements on defenders: ex-ante safety regulation, ex-post liability, and information reporting or disclosure.[3] Preemptive defensive controls, or ex-ante safety measures, include: encrypting sensitive data, implementing a firewall, mandating password length and complexity, and organizing security efforts according to a set process. Liability regimes, by contrast, focus on security outcomes, or the responsibility of a defender to make some baseline efforts to prevent certain types of damage—e.g., host infection, data theft, financial fraud—but leave the specific means by which those outcomes will be avoided to the discretion of the defenders by never specifying what those ex-ante baseline efforts should look like. Finally, reporting responsibilities—which have been the focus of many existing and proposed security policies to date— deal with what security-related information defenders must reveal and to whom. Though they tend to be handled under separate policies, all of these types of security responsibilities are interrelated. Preemptive measures are only useful insofar as they help defenders achieve positive outcomes; outcomes can only be measured by means of robust reporting; and reported information is only relevant if it can be used to inform the actions defenders should take and assess the associated outcomes.

Each of these categories of responsibilities—focused on controls, outcomes, and reporting—may be applied to defenders with different degrees of pressure. Policymakers may choose to present any of these responsibilities as mandatory, incentivized, or voluntary for defenders. These three levels of pressure correspond to different broad categories of policy: rules, which recommend or prohibit certain behaviors; inducements, which seek to encourage those behaviors through pressure or rewards; and information, which aims to influence behavior solely through the provision of knowledge about breaches, security controls, and potential threats. With the exception of the breach reporting laws enacted in most states in the United States, cybersecurity policies that target defenders have tended toward the voluntary end of this spectrum, with several governments providing suggested guidelines for security controls (including the NIST 800–53 catalog), educational materials for organizations and end users, and voluntary codes of conduct for industry actors, but relatively few concrete incentives or rules around these issues. Instead, regulators have largely deferred to industry to take the lead on trying to develop security guidelines and best practices for the private sector, encouraging companies to do so at the risk of otherwise incurring more burdensome regulation. In June 2014, Tom Wheeler, who was then the Chairman of the Federal Communications Commission, spoke at the American Enterprise Institute (AEI) outlining his agency's approach to dealing with cybersecurity threats in the communications sector. He said:

> We believe there is a new regulatory paradigm where the Commission relies on industry and the market first while preserving other options if that approach is unsuccessful.... we have agreed that industry-based solutions are the right approach. The question is: will this approach work? We are not Pollyannas. We will implement this approach and measure results. It is those results that will tell us what, if any, next steps must be taken.[4]

Wheeler's remarks outline a wait-and-see approach to cybersecurity regulation in which a regulator declines to set clear rules telling companies what they should do to protect their computer systems, but instead uses the potential threat of such rules to urge industry actors to self-regulate. The challenge for regulators taking this approach lies in measuring how effective that self-regulation has been. Wheeler himself calls out the importance of measuring the results of industry efforts several times in his June 2014 speech, at one point telling the audience: "In business school, I learned, 'If you can measure it, you can manage it.'"[5] But computer security is not an easy or straightforward thing to measure—to assess how secure a computer system is, should one measure how many times intruders are able to access it, or how much damage those intrusions do in dollars, or how many controls are in place to protect it, or how many vulnerabilities can be found in those defenses during testing? And how does one factor into those metrics the fact that not all intrusions and vulnerabilities are equally serious, not all security controls are equally useful, and not all intrusions are associated with clear dollar costs?

Wheeler's wait-and-see approach relied on the government's being able to assess how well industry was doing at defending itself, without regulatory intervention—but ultimately he was completely dependent on companies measuring their own progress and reporting back their self-selected metrics to the government. For instance, one of the policy initiatives Wheeler discussed during his talk was the voluntary Anti-Bot Code of Conduct for Internet service providers (or ABCs for ISPs), developed by the FCC's

Communications Security, Reliability and Interoperability Council (CSRIC). The Anti-Bot Code provided a series of recommendations to ISPs on how to mitigate bots, like GameOver ZeuS, using their ability to track suspicious-looking traffic patterns online and identify, or even quarantine, customers whose computers appeared to be infected. The Code was developed in partnership with several industry representatives who sat on the CSRIC and it gave all ISPs not just the freedom to decide whether or not they wanted to implement the entirely voluntary recommendations, but also to decide whether or not they wanted to reveal which recommendations, if any, they had adopted. In other words, not only were the bot mitigation measures optional, the FCC didn't even know whether any ISPs were using them. How, then, could the agency hope to measure or independently assess the impact of those self-imposed measures? It was an approach that seemed at odds with Wheeler's own demand, as articulated in his talk at AEI, for cybersecurity efforts that were "more demonstrably effective than blindly trusting the market." He added: "the bottom line is that this new paradigm can't be happy talk about good ideas—it has to work in the real world."[6]

The month following Wheeler's speech at AEI, the FCC issued a request for comments on the voluntary recommendations for ISPs. The request asked service providers and others to comment on questions including: What progress have stakeholders made in implementing the recommendations? What significant success stories or breakthroughs have been achieved in implementing the recommendations? What are stakeholders' views and/or plans for full implementation of the recommendations? How effective are the recommendations at mitigating cyber risk when they have been implemented? The FCC was trying to determine whether anyone had adopted (or planned to adopt) the recommended, voluntary security practices and, if so, what impact those measures had—questions the FCC had no answers to because the Anti-Bot Code made no concrete demands on any defenders to implement specific measures, or even to disclose which measures they adopted. Perhaps the most comprehensive response to the FCC's call for comments came from the Messaging, Malware and Mobile Anti-Abuse Working Group (M3AAWG), a nonprofit consortium made up primarily of representatives from various ISPs and network operators.

M3AAWG asked its members to volunteer information about how many infected hosts they had identified on their networks and found that, of the ISPs who volunteered information, in 2012 and 2013 the number of infected hosts ranged from 0.67 percent to 1.31 percent, and roughly 98.7 percent of the end users who owned those hosts were notified of the possible infection.[7] Beyond providing a rough estimate of how many end users were notified of infected hosts, the comments provided little by way of assessing how many ISPs had adopted the ABCs or whether it had had any noticeable impact on the growth of bots. The FCC took no further steps—not to gather more data, to set benchmarks for progress, or to implement more stringent rules. The problem of determining whether their market-driven approach was working and deciding whether ISP self-regulation was effective appeared to be intractable for the agency. Wheeler's plan for the FCC to help develop a robust set of security metrics to assess progress would turn out to be no more than "happy talk" about a good idea.

This inability to measure the impact of different security measures and tactics has stymied many policymakers, not just the FCC, in their efforts to set clear and effective cybersecurity policies. It's similar to the problem that the FTC ran into when Wyndham challenged its authority to deem the hotel group's security practices unreasonable because the agency had never specified what constituted a reasonable baseline level of security. In a motion denying Wyndham's request to dismiss the suit, Judge Esther Salas noted that "the FTC does not plead the particularized data-security rules or regulations that Hotels and Resorts' procedures allegedly failed to comply with"—but maintained that "this cannot preclude the FTC's enforcement action."[8] For the FTC, a crucial part of defining security liability regimes is being able to distinguish between breaches where defenders were negligent in their responsibility to provide "reasonable" security to their customers and other incidents where defenders were just unlucky in facing adversaries skilled enough to overcome the expected level of standard defenses. This standards-based approach speaks to the interplay between the different types of policy measures—ex-post liability is determined in part by ex-ante precautions, which comes back to the question, best addressed through reporting policies, of which of those precautions are actually important and effective. The FTC does not specify what security practices companies must have in place to avoid liability in part because they do not know which controls are most effective—they have no way to measure that—and also in part because the effectiveness of different controls can change over time, as the threat landscape shifts and new vulnerabilities and attack techniques emerge.

This sense that security guidelines need to be regularly reassessed and updated is an important reason why both the FCC and the FTC, as well as many other government agencies, have been reluctant to enshrine any specific set of ex-ante protective requirements in regulations and have preferred to leave those decisions to industry where, the assumption is, people can make changes to their security posture and adapt to new threats more quickly and easily.

Both uncertainty around what the most effective measures are and a reluctance to issue inflexible legislation around these issues have led policymakers to explore other options. In particular, governments dissatisfied with the success of purely voluntary regimes have focused significant attention on the role of incentives in driving cybersecurity policy, discussing options that range from tax incentives and liability limitations to government funding and technical assistance. The area where industry stakeholders enjoy the least flexibility in terms of ex-ante precautions is in the security requirements for services and systems sold to the government itself. For instance, OPM cited the U.S. Government's FedRAMP certification process as the reason it did not implement CylanceProtect sooner to defend its computer systems. Certifications like FedRAMP, which label products sufficiently secure for government use, provide an example of a rules-based approach, rather than the FTC's standards-based approach centered on what others are doing, and can serve as a strong incentive for companies to alter their security practices in order to be able to sell to government agencies. Another model for how governments have tried to incentivize specific security actions is the UK Cyber Essentials Scheme, in which businesses can be awarded cybersecurity "badges" by the government for implementing a set list of security controls. This labeling scheme certifies that badge recipients have implemented five types of security controls—boundary firewalls, Internet gateways, secure configuration, user access control, and malware protection. Still, there are relatively few government cybersecurity policies with formal incentives built into them. Instead, the primary incentive for adoption of voluntary security practices has been the avoidance of further regulation threatened by policymakers like Wheeler.

Applying mandatory, or even incentivized, security measures to broad classes of diffuse stakeholders presents considerable enforcement problems—a government cannot easily enforce a policy requiring every Internet user or organization within its borders to adopt a standard set of security practices.

Moreover, such a policy would ignore the unique risks, processes, and preferences of each of those organizations and users, and would also require constant updating to keep up with new threats. So, many governments haven't laid out security standards, choosing instead to defer to private industry's expertise. Therefore, specific security controls are often implemented through voluntary policies or private contracts, as in the case of the Payment Card Industry data security standards that individual merchants agree to in order to process payment card transactions. Voluntary adoption and private agreements of this nature sometimes have the advantage of being more quickly updated than government policies, but allowing the payment card industry to dictate the security responsibilities of other stakeholders has drawbacks as well. After all, the payment networks who dictated the liability shift for microchip-enabled cards, themselves serve as a crucial line of defense in the aftermath of many financially motivated breaches, given their unique ability to detect and mitigate fraud. So it's not clear that allowing them to dictate who is responsible for what—and offloading liability onto other stakeholders who have less sophisticated fraud detection abilities—is in the best interests of consumers. Balancing the responsibilities of different stakeholders is difficult when one party, or group, has the unilateral authority to decide when another should be held liable.

Different levels of pressure may be better suited to certain types of security responsibilities. Ex-ante defensive measures, which evolve rapidly with threats and can be relatively specific to particular defenders, may not be well suited to rules or inducements. Ex-post liability for bad outcomes, on the other hand, requires forms of policy that exert more pressure on defenders, along the lines of the FTC enforcement efforts and class action lawsuits brought against TJX, the SCDOR, Ashley Madison, and others. But these attempts to define liability regimes hinge on some understanding of the ex-ante defensive measures that organizations are supposed to have in place in order to determine whether they should be held liable for a security incident. This leaves policymakers and courts stuck in a difficult cycle of trying over and over again to define who should be held liable for a security incident without specifying what, exactly, an organization must do in order not to be held liable. This interplay between ex-ante and ex-post security policies contributes to the uncertainty and tentativeness with which policymakers have typically approached cybersecurity issues. They want to leave ambiguous the question of what technical controls organizations should be using, both because that list may change over time and because they have no good way of measuring which controls are most effective, so those ex-ante measures are only proposed as voluntary policies in most sectors. But that ambiguity, in turn, feeds a high degree of uncertainty surrounding the ex-post liability regimes these same organizations face in the aftermath of an incident, making it especially difficult to hold third-party intermediaries liable when they had no well-defined security responsibilities at the outset. The only area of cybersecurity policy where U.S.-based firms routinely face mandatory regulation is breach reporting, perhaps because few companies would want to admit to a security breach in the absence of a legal requirement.

Different stakeholders have particular perspectives and sets of capabilities that can be leveraged to protect not just themselves, but also their customers, co-workers, and even complete strangers. The value of a policy such as the CSRIC's Anti-Bot Code of Conduct lies largely in its ability to recognize the particular, unique roles an individual type of stakeholder—in this case, ISPs—can play, and ensuring that those actors implement defensive measures to protect not just themselves but also others. Just as security controls for applications need to be tailored to the application's function, and security controls for organizations need to be tailored to firms' missions and computer uses, so, too, cybersecurity policies must be tailored to the specific of capabilities and roles of the intermediaries they affect. Policies should ideally be targeted at the class, or classes, of stakeholders best situated to have the ultimate desired defensive impact. In some cases, it may not be immediately clear either which sector, or which individual actors within a given sector, are in that position—this excess of intermediaries, stemming from the interconnected nature of the Internet, makes it even more important that policymakers clarify the roles and responsibilities of all involved. While no defender can be said to be "responsible" for security breaches in the same manner that perpetrators are, some may routinely forego commonly accepted security measures and practices, thereby enabling intruders. Stakeholders who could serve a defensive role may even profit from security breaches, for instance, by marketing themselves as hosts with few scruples and a shady clientele—as many of the infrastructure providers who comprised the Stophaus group did. Other stakeholders may not be defensive weak links, but instead offer convenient chokepoints for cutting off certain types of threats in an efficient manner at their crucial bottleneck stages.

Policymaking in this space should reflect the complex interactions between the wide variety of stakeholders involved in defending against these threats and the limitations of any individual group's reach and capabilities in that context. There is no exhaustive list or uniform categorization of those groups, especially given that the appropriate categories and granularity may vary from policy to policy. Several examples of different, potentially policy-relevant classes of stakeholders who could serve as defensive chokepoints for certain bottleneck stages of intrusions are described in table 13.1. This list is not meant to be exhaustive, but rather to highlight the capabilities and defensive potential of many of the recurring stakeholders involved in the cases discussed in the previous chapters.

The ultimate aim of policymakers is to mitigate the harm caused by security incidents, and it may therefore be useful to frame some policies in terms of the desired outcomes, rather than the specific security controls and techniques intended to achieve those outcomes. For instance, a policymaker concerned about the problem of botnets is not worried about the existence of bots but rather the potential of those bots to be used to inflict economic harm by means of financial fraud, denial-of-service attacks, or other avenues. That policymaker's ultimate goal is probably not to reduce rates of malware infection, or even to reduce the size and number or active bots, but rather to reduce the amount of economic damage that is inflicted with those bots. Crafting policies around anti-malware protections and anti-bot practices for service providers are ways of trying to move closer to that goal; but such strategies are not the only—or even necessarily the most effective—means of doing so. An alternative strategy might center on cutting off payments to the operators of bots, thereby preventing the economic profit even while the technical threat (the bot) remains active. For instance, a policy that made it more difficult, or even illegal, for people to purchase or use cryptocurrencies, could serve as a means of making it harder for victims to pay criminals when infected with ransomware like Cryptolocker thereby demonetizing that model of cybercrime. This economic perspective is also partly the rationale behind policies like the Deter Cyber Theft Act, which focus on thwarting perpetrators' ultimate aims (profit) rather than trying to go after the technical means by which they steal intellectual property.

Table 13.1

Different classes of defenders and the scope of their control within the security ecosystem

Class of defender	Risks within their scope of detection & control	Number and size of entities	Ability to be regulated
Hardware manufacturers	Device supply chain counterfeit	Group of established private actors, primarily for-profit firms	Subject to domestic commerce and import/export regulations
Software developers	Exploitable coding errors	Numerous entities, ranging in size from large companies to individuals	Difficult to regulate, both domestically and internationally, due to number of developers and ease with which code crosses national borders
Service providers	Malicious traffic	Relatively few major companies within an individual country	Fairly straightforward to regulate, especially since many major service providers are already subject to existing telecom regulatory regimes
Content providers and hosts	Malicious content	Large number of disparate entities, ranging from major firms to individuals	Difficult to regulate both due to sheer number and diffuse nature of entities
DNS operators	Fraudulent records	Many thousands of DNS servers are operated across the world, mainly by organizations	Difficult to regulate because of how many DNS operators there are and how loosely they are tracked
Merchants and payment processors	Fraudulent transactions	Large number of merchants, ranging from large firms to individuals; fewer payment processors	Policymakers may find it difficult to regulate merchants directly, but can more easily regulate credit card associations—which can, in turn, influence merchants through private contracts
System administrators	Compromised machines, breaches of sensitive data	Very numerous with immense range in size and scale of systems	Difficult to regulate as a group, but can be subdivided and regulated according to those who possess certain types of data, operate at a certain threshold size, perform certain functions, etc.

Not all intruders have financial motives, but where they do, policymakers can wield considerable control over financial flows. Focusing in this manner on the ultimate threat of harm posed by a security compromise, rather than the technical details that enabled it, may in some cases guide policymakers toward more targeted and creative solutions. On the other hand, a policy like the Deter Cyber Theft Act would rely so heavily on the government being able to reliably detect and attribute cybercrimes before the perpetrators could extract their profits that it's not clear how feasible or effective such a solution would be.

Policies aimed at security outcomes need not be exclusively focused on an attacker's end goal. Rather, they may center on the end goals of the defensive stakeholders to which they apply. Policymakers may try to specify either how those stakeholders should address threats (i.e., which security controls should be implemented) or instead what they should aim to achieve when tackling those threats (i.e., which outcomes to strive for). A policy for hardware manufacturers might therefore give specific guidelines for combating supply chain counterfeit or instead detail metrics for assessing the extent of such counterfeit and benchmarks for driving down those cases, leaving it to the affected firms' discretion how they want to meet those benchmarks. Similarly, policies aimed at end users might specify actions (e.g., installing security updates) or designate outcomes that those users are responsible for avoiding, such as the participation of their machines in bots.

Holding stakeholders responsible for the security outcomes that result from their actions, rather than the specific actions they must take, allows them more freedom in designing their own security strategies and tailoring those strategies to their business and needs. In some cases, where defenders have limited security resources and expertise, they may not want that freedom. Instead, they may prefer to have a set of clear and concrete security controls laid out for them and be held accountable only for whether they have implemented those, regardless of whatever else may go wrong. In other instances, however, especially for stakeholders with significant resources and expertise in this area, it may be preferable to allow industry actors who encounter these threats directly to craft their own, customized set of security measures. This approach has the advantage of enabling rapid updating and development of security controls while also keeping policies more focused on the attackers' end goals rather than individual defensive maneuvers. Security outcomes are significantly more static than actions.

While the specific, technical means by which threats propagate are constantly evolving, the ultimate aims—and even the intermediate aims—of malicious actors have remained fairly consistent over time. Financial gain, political and economic espionage, and system disruption or degradation continue to motivate cybercriminals, and these actors continue to use a fairly stable set of tools, including malware, botnets, and denial-of-service attacks, to achieve those aims. The primary drawback to designing policies around outcomes rather than actions is that the former are often challenging to measure or verify, as Wheeler quickly discovered. Accordingly, there has been relatively little policymaking focused on these outcomes, as it is nearly impossible to implement an effective outcomes-based regime in the absence of comprehensive reporting responsibilities that go far beyond the current status quo for security reporting.

Security Reporting Policies

Policies that govern ex-ante defensive measures and ex-post liability regimes should be shaped by the information the stakeholders responsible for those controls or outcomes report in order to ensure compliance and measure progress. Conveniently, reporting requirements represent the area of security policy where regulators have been most active. However, depending on their purpose, these reporting policies can vary greatly with regard to what information stakeholders are expected to report, and to whom. These policies can have several different goals, including protecting people whose information has been breached, helping others to defend against threats that have been previously experienced or identified, and contributing to a better understanding of the types of threats observed and the effectiveness of various countermeasures. Each of these three goals has very different implications for security reporting regimes, as described in table 13.2, and may pose different challenges for both defenders and regulators.

The oldest and most common template for computer security reporting policies is the data security breach notification law, an early example of which was enacted in California in 2002. That law, SB 1386, requires everyone who conducts business in California to notify "any resident of California whose unencrypted personal information was, or is reasonably believed to have been, acquired by an unauthorized person." Since then, most other states in the U.S. have adopted similar laws requiring that data breaches of personal information be disclosed, shortly following their discovery. These breach notification laws are distinct from another set of reporting policies, often referred to as cybersecurity information sharing policies, which are aimed not at the notification of users affected by security breaches but rather at the other entities that may need to defend themselves against similar threats. For instance, the Cybersecurity Information Sharing Act (CISA), passed by Congress in 2015, focuses on shielding companies from being held liable for sharing threat information that may aid others' defense efforts. Unlike state breach notification laws, CISA does not actually mandate any reporting or information sharing on the part of firms. Instead, it serves to eliminate potential legal obstacles. There are several industry and government organizations and consortiums that also facilitate information sharing for the purposes of real-time threat mitigation and help spread the word about emerging threats. For instance, a set of Information Sharing and Analysis Centers (ISACs) perform this function, with varying degrees of success, for several specific industry sectors, including the automotive, financial services, communications, healthcare, and electricity sectors, among others. ISACs are typically nonprofit organizations that collect information from their member companies on a voluntary basis—so the success and effectiveness of each individual ISAC is generally dependent on the level of participation from, and access to, the firms in its respective industry sector. Moreover, most threat intelligence data collected by ISACs is not made publicly available in order to protect members, so its utility is limited to other members. This secrecy can help encourage greater sharing, but at the same time it restricts how widely threat intelligence can be aggregated and dispersed. The ISACs are not the only existing institutions for facilitating real-time threat intelligence sharing and incident response. Computer Emergency Readiness Teams (CERTs), as well as Computer Security Incident Response Teams (CSIRTs), also operate all over the world, and are often run or coordinated by government agencies. These organizations, many of which collaborate through the Forum of Incident Response and Security Teams, typically collect and publish information on computer vulnerabilities and threats, and also help victims respond to security problems they are facing. As the success of many CERTs, CSIRTs, and ISACs indicates, facilitating the sharing of threat information for real-time response and mitigation purposes is not purely a job for policymakers—though governments have often played a role

Table 13.2

Different purposes of security incident reporting endeavors

Purpose of Reporting	Examples	What is reported?	When is it reported?	To whom is it reported?
Consumer protection	Data breach notification laws (California SB 1386)	Who was affected by a data breach and what personal information was revealed	Shortly after a breach is detected	Affected parties (i.e., those whose information was accessed)
Real-time threat mitigation	Information sharing laws (CISA, CISPA)	Signature and detection information, countermeasures	Immediately following detection	Other parties in a position to mitigate the identified threat
Analysis of root causes and countermeasure impact	Industry reports (Microsoft SIR, Verizon DBIR)	Type of threat, why it was successful, what defenses were in place, what damage it caused	Following a (potentially lengthy) internal investigation	A party in a position to aggregate other incident reports

in setting up CERTs and tend to have a particular interest in the question of when such information can be shared between private companies and government agencies.

Beyond reporting breaches and sharing threat intelligence, there is another important role of reporting responsibilities that is less commonly promoted by policymakers, but gets directly at questions of how they can do a better job of clarifying ex-ante defense and ex-post mitigation policies: data collection for the purpose of measuring the types of threats defenders face and the effectiveness of different strategies at defending against those threats. Reporting policies trying to achieve this goal would not help individuals or companies protect themselves against current threats and risks in the short term, but would instead focus on what can be learned from threat trends and defensive strategies over time and across a large number of incidents and actors.

Policymakers have different roles to play in promoting each of these three goals of security reporting policies. All three may be challenging for private actors to address adequately in the absence of government intervention, but for different reasons. For instance, industry actors may be reluctant or unwilling to notify customers of security breaches for fear of damaging their reputations or incurring legal action. Policymakers who want to ensure that individuals are aware of any breaches of their personal information and the consequent risks can overcome these obstacles by mandating notification procedures—voluntary, and even incentivized, policies are unlikely to be widely effective given the potential drawbacks of notifying the breached parties. Real-time threat information sharing between defenders may be hindered by some of the same fears, particularly concerns about litigation and liability that arise from sharing sensitive information or publicizing security breaches, as well as logistical and competitive considerations. Logistically, private actors may not always have easy avenues for spreading threat information to all of the other defenders who could benefit from it. Furthermore, given that some of these defenders are competitors, firms may not want to share that information with everyone else who could use it. The varied security resources and expertise of industry actors also mean that a small number of firms, those with the largest investments in security, are likely to glean most of the threat information, and their smaller peers are likely to have relatively little novel intelligence to offer in exchange. This inequity creates a heavily imbalanced information sharing ecosystem in which the defenders who have the most valuable information to share have little incentive to do so with those who would potentially have the most to gain from receiving it.

Policymakers wishing to encourage information sharing between defenders to combat real-time threats have several options to try to lessen these barriers. One possible role for policy is to absolve the sharers of liability for providing that information to others—but this runs counter to trying to clarify or strengthen different stakeholders' sense of their security responsibilities. Another possible role of policy could be to create channels for government organizations to provide industry with real-time threat intelligence. CISA includes versions of both of these measures in efforts to facilitate both more private-to-private sharing and government-industry sharing. Coordinating information sharing efforts through a centralized government authority is another potential function of policy and may help address the logistic and competitive barriers to sharing. But a government-centric model, of the sort adopted by the European Union, also presents drawbacks. In particular, information sharing done for the purpose of real-time threat mitigation requires very rapid turnaround that may be hindered by the insertion of a government body between private defenders.

In terms of the third potential function of security reporting—collecting data on threat trends and countermeasure efficacy—government actors can help industry actors overcome a similar set of obstacles related to the challenges of collective action. While such data would potentially be valuable to nearly all defenders, individually, many firms are reluctant to champion such an effort in the absence of participation by their peers. No company wants to be the first to release that data about the threats they see and the impact of their countermeasures, for fear of drawing attention to their security incidents. Furthermore, no company stands to gain anything by unilaterally releasing such information—since they benefit only by what they learn from others and the creation of a broader data set beyond what they already know internally. Mandating that companies report information on all of their breaches could even be counterproductive, causing defenders to stop actively monitoring for such incidents for fear of having to report them.

These three distinct potential goals of security reporting policies rely on very different types of information, and this can put them at odds with each other. Breach notification generally involves reporting what information was breached and who was affected by that breach. This often translates into the sorts of media attention that firms most want to avoid—focused on the magnitude of breaches and the number of breached records—and that may discourage them from engaging in further sharing. Threat information sharing, by contrast, revolves around sharing specific threat signature information, or the ways that other defenders can identify current threats and remediate them. Reporting intended to contribute to longer term data on threats and countermeasures would require yet a different set of information, including a detailed description of the root causes of security incidents and the defensive measures that were (and were not) in place when they occurred. This information, collected from a wide range of firms over time, could enable analysis of both the broader engineering design decisions that might combat the most common threats and the effectiveness of different existing countermeasures against these threats. There may be legitimate reasons to share each of these types of information with different actors at certain points, but, where possible, restricting the fields of necessary data may help encourage participation from defenders. For instance, not requiring firms to report data about the magnitude of breaches may help assuage their concerns about the reputational damage that may be incurred by releasing that information. However, this strategy also has drawbacks and comes in direct conflict with many data breach notification laws, which specifically require breached organizations to report how many records were compromised or the number of individuals affected.

Cyber Insurance

The insights gleaned from compiling security incident data across different firms could help individual organizations make better investment and design decisions for security. They could also help drive the development of a more robust insurance market for these risks that standardizes and alleviates some of that individual responsibility. Insurers encounter many of the same challenges as individual firms when it comes to determining which defensive measures should be required of their customers and how to evaluate those customers' current defensive postures. An incident data repository could contribute to insurers' ability to make these determinations, besides offering greater insight into the frequency of common threats and the damages associated with them. Representatives of the insurance industry have themselves suggested that such a repository would be useful to their efforts.[9]

At a series of roundtables and workshops in 2012 and 2013, coordinated by the Department of Homeland Security's (DHS) National Protection and Programs Directorate, insurance providers who were beginning to offer policies that covered cybersecurity incidents discussed how policymakers could help encourage the emerging market. The need for a security incident data repository was a major theme of these discussions, with insurers citing such data collection efforts as crucial to their efforts to model and quantify cyber risk for the purposes of underwriting insurance policies. A July 2014 DHS summary report on the meetings noted:

> Most of the participants identified the Federal government as being in a unique position to compile cyber incident data across sectors. In particular, they noted that it could help facilitate the sharing of anonymized information between the vendor and insurance industry communities regarding the top cyber risks that organizations face.[10]

It's striking that the insurers—who were trying to establish a market solution for cyber risk—were asking for help from policymakers. In order for their firms to be able to characterize computer-based risks and insure against them, in the same manner as health risks or car crashes or natural disasters, the insurance brokers first wanted some assistance from the government to help them better understand these risks. To price insurance policies, their understanding had to go well beyond just the data gleaned from companies reporting breaches of personal information under state reporting laws. For one thing, those laws only applied to incidents involving the theft of customer personal information and many cybersecurity incidents, such as the Spamhaus DDoS attacks or the Cryptolocker ransomware, do not involve customer data being stolen. Furthermore, the information that breached firms are required to report under state breach notification laws typically does not include all of the things an insurer would want to know about an incident, such as how much it cost the firm, or what the root cause of the incident was, or what defenses were and were not in place when it occurred.

Assembling the "missing data" on the frequency and financial impacts of cybersecurity incidents was not the only obstacle that insurers faced in trying to establish a robust market for cyber insurance. They, like the FTC, had been stymied by the challenges of trying to define a list of safeguards that their customers would be required to implement in order to be covered by their policies. Just as insurers place conditions on other types of policies—a fire insurance policy might only be valid if there are smoke detectors installed in the buildings it covers, for instance—so, too, when writing policies to cover customers' cyber risks, insurers needed to be able to audit the overall effectiveness of those customers' security postures. The audits were supposed to help insurers figure out whether their potential customers were using good security controls or had effective monitoring systems, and also identify what additional measures, if any, the insurer might require to be put in place prior to offering coverage. But in order to do those assessments, insurers needed better guidance, and better data, on which controls actually worked to prevent or detect incidents. Their existing "checklist" method of asking firms whether they had certain safeguards and processes in place was not working, as several insurers said at the DHS meetings. Additionally, the various security recommendations and frameworks provided by the government were not sufficiently clear or specific to suit the insurance industry's purposes.

Insurers cited in particular the NIST Framework for Improving Critical Infrastructure Cybersecurity as an example of a set of government security guidelines too ambiguous to use for evaluating firms' security. According to the DHS report, insurers argued:

> [V]oluntary use of the Framework must be accompanied by specific, ongoing actions that apply its principles to a specific company's specific business processes. Absent this individualized application—and measurement of results— so-called "use" of the Framework loses much of its implied meaning for both insurance and other risk management purposes.[11]

This condemnation of the value of a major government cybersecurity initiative suggested just how useless many stakeholders in industry had found these government recommendations to be for actually trying to measure or quantify cyber risk and the impact of individual security controls. When it came to strengthening and assessing insurance customers' security, the insurers asked for two things from the U.S. government, besides better data: a "ubiquitously recognized 'Smokey the Bear' equivalent for cyber risk that could be used in public education campaigns" and a "rating or symbol that publicizes the cybersecurity level of organizations."[12] The former, insurers believed, would raise overall cybersecurity awareness among industry actors, while the latter would help insurers decide who to cover without needing to immediately build up their own in-depth security audit processes. Eventually, insurers believed, they would have collected enough data from their own customers to be able to analyze for themselves which computer safeguards did and did not help, and to model the frequency and costs of cybersecurity incidents. However, while the market was still relatively new, and included only a small number of customers, insurers wanted help from the government in order to grow this emerging market without going bankrupt.

The threat of losing money on cyber insurance loomed large for insurers, not just because they were unsure how costly or how frequent cyber incidents were and did not know which safeguards to require of their customers, but also because of how interconnected they feared cyber risks could be. Insurance markets operate on the assumption that insurers will not have to pay out claims to all of their customers simultaneously. To ensure this is the case, insurers seek a diverse pool of customers with very different demographic and geographic risk profiles. For instance, if there were an earthquake in California that required paying out claims to many customers there, an insurer could cover those costs with the premiums paid by customers located in other places who were not affected. But, when it comes to cyber risk, it's tricky to know how to diversify that risk across different types of customers. One piece of malware targeting a popular operating system or other software program could potentially affect computers all over the world, in all different industry sectors, and all at once. Since cyber risks spread rapidly across networks, insurers suspected they could see massive cascading effects in the event of a major incident, and end up being forced to pay out claims to many customers simultaneously. This was yet another reason for them to move cautiously when it came to pricing and selling these policies—and another reason they wanted help from the government collecting the data they needed to profile the interconnectedness of cyber risks and model the associated costs accurately. Insurance is fundamentally an industry solution to handling risk—it's typically up to firms and individuals to purchase insurance policies, and up to insurers to design and price policies. And yet, for the cyber insurance industry to move forward and meet the anticipated demand for coverage, the insurance firms first wanted help from policymakers.

The risk characterization and defense assessment enabled by aggregated security incident data could be used in more ways than just building

actuarial models. It could also help pave the way for clearer liability standards surrounding security breaches, something that insurers could further
help clarify through their policies covering these incidents. A clearer determination of what types of incidents an organization might reasonably be
expected to defend against, as well as what measures should be taken to
provide that level of protection, may help define what incidents an organization should and should not be liable for failing to prevent. These determinations are likely to evolve and be strongly influenced by the requirements
imposed by insurers. In the absence of reliable data about incidents and
defenses, however, there is a real risk that these ongoing liability disputes
and lawsuits will continue to fail to yield concrete guidance for stakeholders about their responsibilities and leave insurers floundering as they try to
figure out how to understand and model cyber risks.

14 Conclusion: "It Will Take All of Us"

In the aftermath of major computer security incidents that involve the theft of millions of people's personal information it is hard to feel much sympathy for the breached organizations. Why pity TJX, or the South Carolina Department of Revenue, or OPM, or DigiNotar, or Ashley Madison when it was their own carelessness that allowed for millions of other people's credit cards or fingerprint records or email accounts to be compromised? When the leaders of those organizations begin pointing fingers and trying to show why other stakeholders are really the ones responsible for letting this happen, they look like they're desperately attempting to dodge blame and save their own jobs—and often they are. And yet, buried in even the most contemptible and cowardly of these blame game exercises, there is a profoundly true message: protecting data and computer systems in an online, networked world is not the work of any individual company or government agency, it is the work of many interconnected, interdependent stakeholders whose decisions influence each other's security and constrain each other's options. Consider, for instance, the plea of former OPM director Katherine Archuleta for her role in the OPM breach to be understood in the larger context of her predecessors, colleagues, and the labyrinthine bureaucracy of the federal government. Pressed by Representative Chaffetz, at a hearing on the breach, to assign herself a "grade" for the work she had done and assess whether she was "succeeding or failing" at securing the OPM computer systems, Archuleta responded:

> [C]ybersecurity problems are decades in the making. The whole of government is responsible, and it will take all of us to solve the issue and continue to work on them. My leadership with OPM is one that instigated the improvements and changes that recognized the attack.[1]

Archuleta's defense is both pitiful and poignant. Pitiful because she is so determined to paint herself as the agency's savior, as the person who discovered the breach but played no role in enabling it—and so completely unwilling to assume any blame for running an organization that, time and again, including during her tenure, ignored clear warnings about the poor state of its information security infrastructure. But she's also right.

Cybersecurity problems of the kind OPM faced *are* decades in the making. The OPM institutional technology culture was one of ignoring security warnings and continuing to run insecure systems, relying on out-of-date tools and software, giving login access to a range of third-party contractors, storing sensitive files indefinitely, and employing slow, bureaucratic procurement processes. But it was not an institutional culture entirely of Archuleta's own making. The OPM breach reflected not just her own misguided leadership of OPM; it also reflected the decisions made by her predecessors at the agency, and other agencies all over the government; decisions made by private companies manufacturing the software OPM relied on; decisions made by firms selling domain names and server space to the perpetrators of the breach; and decisions made by organizations that carried the massive volume of traffic exfiltrated from OPM's servers to external machines. On some level, the entire U.S. government *was* responsible for the OPM breach, though Archuleta was exactly the wrong person to be trying to point that out when she herself was so clearly culpable as well. She's even right that "it will take all of us"—government and industry actors and individual end users alike—to make progress toward solving the threats posed by insecure computer systems; though, again, it's hard to imagine a worse courier for that particular message.

One unfortunate feature of computer security incidents is that the people and companies who trumpet the importance of shared blame—and shared responsibility—in the aftermath of major breaches usually have very little credibility. No one listens to them because they are so clearly motivated by self-interest and self-preservation, so blatantly attempting to dodge blame for their own egregious mistakes. Wyndham, for instance, made a valid point when it argued that the FTC had not clarified what defensive measures companies needed to have in place to provide their customers with "reasonable" security for their personal information. But the court had no patience for this argument precisely because Wyndham hadn't even done the bare minimum, regardless of how that bare minimum was or was not defined. Wyndham was every bit as guilty of blatantly disregarding data security practices as Archuleta. However, as with Archuleta's appeal to Congress, there is a kernel of truth underlying Wyndham's desperate attempts to absolve itself of blame. Yes, Wyndham (and Archuleta) made a series of appallingly terrible, obviously stupid, outrageously careless decisions about computer security; and, yes, they could have done a (much) better job of protecting the data they were entrusted with—but they also could have used some better outside support. The same could be said of the South Carolina Department of Revenue, looking to the IRS for guidance on how to protect tax filings, and of Cloudflare for pointing the finger at operators of open DNS resolvers for enabling the denial-of-service attacks directed at Spamhaus. We're only one tiny piece of a much larger network, Wyndham and Archuleta and so many other breach victims seem to be saying in the aftermath of their own disgrace—please don't leave us out here on our own.

Intermediary Liability and Security

One of the most cherished and deeply enshrined principles of Internet policy in the United States, particularly when it comes to dealing with copyright infringement and free speech issues, is the idea that online intermediaries are not responsible for the content that other people post or provide through their platforms. Articulated in Section 230 of the Communications Decency Act, and further refined in the safe harbor provisions of the Digital Millennium Copyright Act, this principle of intermediary liability is often hailed as the reason that websites built on user-generated content, such as YouTube and Wikipedia, are able to exist at all, without the threat of crippling copyright infringement or defamation lawsuits hanging over them. Section 230 established a distinction between publishers, or companies who vet the content they post and therefore are liable for it, and platforms, or companies that merely serve as neutral forums for anyone to post anything they want without preemptive screening. This distinction between platforms and publishers and the legal protections afforded to the former group are important for online companies because, on the Internet, everyone is reliant on many layers of intermediaries. These include: Internet service providers, who carry traffic between servers; hosting providers, who rent out server space; registrars, who sell and manage domain names; software developers, who design applications like web browsers and email clients that users rely on to access online information; hardware manufacturers, who build the physical devices that users rely on to access those applications; search engines, who organize and prioritize information users are looking for; and ad networks, that distribute and serve online advertisements to external websites. The underlying principle of intermediary liability protection is essentially that each of these actors is only responsible for its own behavior online and not that of anyone else who is using its service. More specifically, as articulated in Section 230: "No provider or user of an interactive computer service shall be treated as the publisher or speaker of any information provided by another information content provider." On the Internet, in other words, most intermediaries, who are not deliberately picking and choosing what they want to publish in the manner of newspapers or magazines, qualify as platforms rather than publishers and therefore bear no responsibility for what the people who use them choose to say or do through their services.

These legal protections insulate many Internet companies from having to worry about copyright infringement or police illegal speech on their platforms, and that has helped many of those firms flourish and grow. But as the principle of intermediary liability has seeped into the security realm, it has proved much more problematic as a means of protecting third-party intermediaries from bearing any of the blame associated with crimes committed by other people using their platforms. When it comes to security, the network of intermediaries and stakeholders involved can be understood very broadly—going beyond strictly technical interactions and interdependencies. Firms rely on policymakers to help them figure out which security controls they should be using, they rely on the people and organizations they regularly communicate with to keep their accounts and servers secure, they rely on their employees not to respond to phishing emails or be careless with their login credentials, and they often rely on third-party contractors and vendors to provide them with, among other things, security monitoring, data storage, and analysis services. Additionally, firms that are working to protect their own data and systems can themselves become intermediaries, or platforms, for attacks on other targets, if their user accounts and servers are compromised and used as hop points for staging intrusions directed at other institutions.

On the Internet, everyone is an intermediary—or, at the very least, has the potential to serve as one in an attack directed at someone else. In the context of a policy landscape built largely around limiting intermediary liability, there is very little understanding of how these different stakeholders ought to share responsibility for a breach, in its aftermath. There is always someone else for each intermediary to point to as partly responsible, and to try to shift liability onto, rather than focusing on strengthening security themselves, as in the case of the payment networks, banks, and retailers, fighting over who will cover the costs of payment card fraud. The intermediary liability protections for online speech codified in Section 230 are not the only examples of policymakers working to roll back liability in this area. Many cybersecurity information sharing policy proposals, including the CISA law, include measures that absolve companies of liability in the hopes of enabling more sharing about online threats that will allow for better real-time remediation and long-term data collection.

One of the rationales for protecting companies from being held responsible for the security information they reveal under a statute like CISA is that there is no way to learn about these threats and the larger security landscape, no way to measure which security controls actually work and which ones don't, unless the firms who are fending off attacks and experimenting with security controls feel comfortable revealing their successes and failures. Recall how the FCC wrestled with the problem of trying to measure whether its Anti-Bot Code of Conduct had had any impact at all— by asking the service providers themselves to tell the agency whether they had seen any signs of progress. Encouraging firms to report more about the types of threats they witness, and what controls, policies, or practices, if any, help mitigate them, is crucial for trying to measure what works and what doesn't; and promising that those firms can't be sued for what they report is one way of trying to make that happen. In other words, rolling back the potential liability of intermediaries and Internet companies in the short term may be partly intended to help figure out exactly what security practices and controls work best against current threats, and who should be implementing them for maximal impact. This approach could ultimately yield improved, empirical guidance on defenses and also help shape how insurance companies can better model cyber risks and audit customers for cyber insurance. Long-term, such policies may actually help to formalize liability regimes and insurance markets more effectively, using empirical evidence, in the future. But for that to work, the protections from liability and rewards for reporting information voluntarily will have to be short-term incentives designed to help build a more definitive structure in which those same guarantees won't hold. The risk is that instead of translating into more clearly defined security responsibilities and liability regimes in the future, these legal protections for online intermediaries sharing security information may well turn out to be permanent, especially once firms have grown accustomed to them.

As more organizations outsource their data storage and management to large cloud-based providers, the issues of intermediary liability as they relate to security incidents become more complicated because security responsibilities end up split among multiple different firms. The private contracts cloud service customers sign with those large providers may help clarify some of those divisions of responsibility. But, as is often the case when private actors get to dictate liability regimes themselves, those con-tracts will probably be designed to prioritize protecting the interests of their authors—typically the cloud service providers—above the security of stored data. Given the current landscape of uncertain liability, it makes sense that most intermediaries are trying to avoid shouldering any responsibil-ity for security—even in areas in which they might be able to make a big difference—for fear that they will then become the de facto responsible parties. It would be expecting a lot for firms to voluntarily assume those responsibilities without a push from policymakers or courts; and yet, so far, those policies have operated largely on a voluntary basis (as in the case of the FCC's Anti-Bot Code of Conduct), or avoided defining any clear-cut responsibilities (as in the ruling against Wyndham in its challenge to the FTC). Policymakers and courts have been reluctant, it seems, to go too far down the path of trying to sort out who, among the many possible inter-mediaries, should be specifically responsible for doing what.

One reason these disputes over liability are messy, and often confusing, is that not only are there many different types of intermediaries when it comes to online security, but several of them are largely invisible to the general public, as well as to policymakers. This was an important element of the DigiNotar compromise—the challenge of conveying to the people whose email accounts had been compromised what, exactly, a certificate authority was, and why the potential compromise of thousands of Iranian Google accounts was the fault of a Dutch CA, not Google. In that particular case, DigiNotar clearly bore the brunt of the consequences for the compromise when it went out of business—but rather than clarify the division of security responsibilities between certificate authorities and browser manufacturers, the DigiNotar incident instead marked the beginning of an ongoing back-and-forth between the two groups of stakeholders trying to force each other to assume greater responsibility for users' security online. The major browser vendors have considerable power to influence CAs' behavior by threatening to remove them from their list of trusted root CAs. But the CAs have an odd kind of power of their own: most online users don't really understand who they are or what they do. That means browser manufacturers' ultimate power—refusing to load the websites with certificates issued by CAs they deem to be disreputable—has the potential to backfire, if users blame the browser, not the CA, for not being able to reach a certain website. This is related to the strategy of the Stophaus group that launched the denial-of-service attack directed at Spamhaus in hopes that any resulting slow down or disruption from the attack would drive away Spamhaus's customers, even though the attack was the direct result of Spamhaus doing its job and blacklisting malicious online actors. Providing users with stronger security protections would, ideally, reward a company with more customers—not fewer. But if those customers don't understand what they're being protected from or why, that principle may not necessarily hold true, complicating companies' decisions about how best to approach security from a business standpoint.

The liability issues surrounding security incidents are further complicated by the ways many computer security breaches primarily affect customers and users who played no role in securing the data in the first place, and the extent to which those breaches often involve multiple intermediary parties. But they are also spurred in part by the challenges associated with catching and prosecuting the perpetrators of these attacks. The attribution challenges posed by computer networks do not make computer incidents impossible to defend against, but they do put greater pressure on non-law enforcement stakeholders to provide protections—and they often mean those stakeholders are left with no one to blame but each other when things go wrong. There are rare exceptions, where people are more willing to view breached organizations as victims and focus blame and repercussions on the perpetrators. This is most often the case when news of an incident is coupled with an immediate and forceful accusation about who was behind it—as happened with the report on PLA Unit 61398 and the Sony breach. In the absence of a clear enemy to hold responsible, users and policymakers end up focusing blame on the breached organizations, and those organizations, in turn, devote their time and energy to trying to shift defensive responsibilities onto each other. Everyone involved in this process is prone to rapidly losing sight of how limited each stakeholder's individual window into security incidents really is, and how blindly those stakeholders are often forced to make decisions and exercise control without knowing exactly what they are defending against or how it can best be prevented.

Who Can Do What?

The incidents described in the first three sections of this book are organized around three common, sometimes overlapping motives—financial gain, political and economic espionage, and public humiliation of the victims. Tracing these incidents from their unassuming technical beginnings to their sweeping, sometimes devastating ends highlights how many different stages, and how many different intermediaries, are involved in any individual breach and how significantly the perpetrators' ultimate aims shape the landscape of possible defenses and defenders. This perspective, focused on the perpetrators' end goals, diverges from many attempts to classify security intrusions by their earlier, technical stages, such as phishing, software vulnerabilities, or stolen credentials. Those technical means of access cut across incidents perpetrated for every reason, from financial fraud to espionage to vengeance, and, while the controls and defensive techniques aimed at preventing intrusions at these early stages are important, they are only one element of a larger defensive landscape. Looking at security from the perspective of restricting those early technical stages of intrusions means classifying attacks according to the behaviors and activities that attackers exploit in the context of computer systems, even if those behaviors are not, themselves, directly harmful. It means restricting those capabilities so that adversaries have to do more work to acquire them, and legitimate users have more signals to indicate when those early stages of an intrusion are being attempted. This approach defines computer security incidents not by how they end but rather by how they begin and attackers not by what they want to achieve but by how they achieve it. This is a fundamentally general notion of defense—one that offers defenders a vague charge to prevent the unwanted and unknown even if they are unsure where those unwanted and unknown activities may be leading. Most importantly, these various technical maneuvers are often interchangeable to perpetrators, so defending against one will not necessarily prevent attackers from being able to find another path to their ultimate goal.

Looking at security incidents from the other end, however, from the perspective of what the perpetrators are aiming to accomplish, can offer a more specific picture of what defenders are trying to protect against by organizing attacks according to their ultimate goal, rather than their particular implementation. Instead of trying to restrict the unknown or unexpected, mitigations that focus on blocking perpetrators from meeting their end goals focus directly on what those intruders ultimately want and how to prevent them from achieving that result. These end goals often occur beyond the context of a targeted computer system, in forms that include large-scale financial fraud, sale of products designed using stolen intellectual property, targeting of undercover spies, or broadcasting stolen information, and therefore, by necessity, defending against these stages of attacks requires the intervention of stakeholders beyond just the breached firm or agency. These final attack stages are often ones perpetrators cannot easily replace, if blocked—they are the whole point of the breach, not merely a means to an end like a phishing email or a stolen password.

These two framings help reconcile some of the conflicting general wisdom around computer defense, particularly the tension around whether attackers or defenders have the advantage in the context of computer systems. This is the tension between the "Wild West" model, in which the attackers supposedly have every advantage, and the "kill chain" model, in which defenders have the advantage because they only need to stop one stage of an incident. The former model corresponds closely to trying to defend against all the possible early, technical intrusion stages when defenders have to find and protect every possible access pathway to be effective, and attackers only need to find one open avenue of attack because these pathways are so easily replaceable, or substituted for each other. The kill chain model, by contrast, speaks to the framing that focuses on attacker end goals, or the final stages of an attack that are so absolutely essential to the perpetrator's success that if they can be interrupted the entire incident is effectively thwarted.

Assessing where defenders may have some advantages over attackers also requires understanding which defenders may be most advantageously poised to interrupt certain types of attacks. The three classes of defenders discussed in the previous chapters—application designers, organizations, and policymakers—are able to intervene at very different stages of security breaches. Application designers can contribute primarily to defense efforts aimed at early stages of intrusions by distinguishing between malicious and legitimate capabilities and placing more cumbersome restrictions on the former. Organizations are well poised to address intermediate stages of incidents that occur within the bounds of their own computer systems, particularly through careful monitoring and restriction of outbound network traffic. Policymakers have a more limited ability than organizations to restrict information flows to attackers, but can do much more to cut off illicit money flows and interrupt financially motivated security incidents, as well as collect the needed information to understand how these incidents occur and who is best poised to interrupt them and prevent perpetrators from achieving their ultimate goals.

When we talk about (and report on, and litigate) security incidents, our inclination is too often to latch on to the earliest or most easily understood point of access—the phishing email, the software vulnerability, the unprotected wireless network—and harp on the defense that seems like it would have made all the difference at that one particular stage—two-factor authentication, or software patches, or WPA encryption. But that perspective oversimplifies the much more complicated narrative of the gradual, escalating capabilities acquired by perpetrators, as well the more limited and challenging environment that individual defenders operate in, constrained both by the extent to which they can see and control access attempts and by their ability to witness and mitigate the ultimate harms that the perpetrators wish to inflict. The optimistic takeaway from security breaches like those discussed in this book is that there are lots of opportunities for defending against computer security incidents and lots of stakeholders who can help contribute to those efforts. The more pessimistic interpretation is that each of those stakeholders can, on its own, have only a relatively small impact by implementing defensive measures—forcing only a slight readjustment of attackers' plans, rather than a dramatic increase in the work and resources required of the perpetrator. Many of those stakeholders are understandably reticent to play an active role in security or assume any responsibility voluntarily—while policymakers are often equally reluctant to interfere in a space they believe private industry is better equipped to handle itself.

Policymakers are not wrong to believe that many (though not all) companies possess more technical expertise and familiarity with online threats than regulators do, but they are wrong to assume that this technical sophistication is the only thing needed—or, indeed, the most important thing needed—to resolve computer security risks. The mistakes made by TJX, SCDOR, DigiNotar, OPM, Sony, and others, were not primarily due to a lack of available technical tools or resources; they were due to an unclear understanding of their responsibilities when it came to protecting computer systems, a lack of well defined liability regimes indicating just how much they stood to lose in the event of a major compromise, and a vast network of other stakeholders who they thought would, at the very least, share in those losses. Policymakers who embrace a wait-and-see regulatory approach because they are counting on industry to take the lead on addressing cybersecurity challenges risk confusing the technical know-how of the private sector with the much less technical judicial and political skills required to sort out liability issues and collective action problems, and to coordinate disparate, diffuse groups of intermediaries. It is the professed hope of many policymakers that cybersecurity, at least for non-government computer systems, will be handled by industry. Wheeler articulated that philosophy when he described letting industry move first, with policymakers sitting back to assess how they're doing and, perhaps, taking vague, undefined steps later on, if insufficient progress is made. But that model gets the order of who should act when precisely backward. For cybersecurity threats to be effectively addressed by industry, and for the risks and losses associated with computer systems to be handled by companies and insurers in a way that takes full advantage of each stakeholder's particular security capabilities and scope of control, policymakers first need to step in and help sort out which stakeholders should be responsible for doing what and how policy-based incentives and penalties can be used to achieve that end. Otherwise, those determinations will be made by the industry stakeholders themselves, with the largest and most powerful of them, like the payment

liability - first

networks and service providers, shifting responsibility onto the rest, even though those large and powerful firms are often the ones best poised to exercise the most far-reaching and effective lines of defense.

It is precisely these dynamics and negotiations among different stakeholders that have been the greatest hindrance to identifying defensive bottlenecks, leveraging the capabilities of different intermediary stakeholders, and strengthening cybersecurity in the early 21st century. These conflicts have shaped the security ecosystem's disregard for the crucial lessons of past incidents and dismissal of these breaches as nothing more than the result of poor technical decisions on the part of people like Archuleta about which security controls to purchase and implement.

So much changes about cybersecurity incidents from month to month and from year to year, but so much also stays the same: what the perpetrators are after, which applications they primarily use to initiate access, and what infrastructural components and configurations they rely on to carry out their ultimate goals. It is these recurring patterns that are most helpful in trying to identify the bottleneck stages of incident lifecycles. They indicate which elements of cybersecurity incidents remain static across time because perpetrators are so dependent on them and have so few alternatives. Locating these bottlenecks helps, in turn, to identify which stakeholders may be able to cut off or mitigate these particular attack stages. Characterizing the set of stakeholders who are best poised to contribute to overall defensive efforts and the potential roles each can play in this manner sets the stage for making policies that leverage and combine these different capabilities effectively. The variety of different intermediaries and competing interests involved in cybersecurity incidents has largely served to undermine cybersecurity efforts and progress. But that diversity of stakeholders and their combined reach and influence should be an asset when it comes to security. Recognizing the full defensive potential those stakeholders can wield together, however, will require policies focused on building relationships between those intermediaries in ways that actually take advantage of the complexity and interconnectedness of the online ecosystem to strengthen Internet security.

Notes

Chapter 1

1. Ross Anderson, "Why Information Security Is Hard—an Economic Perspective," in Seventeenth Annual Computer Security Applications Conference, 2001, 358–365, https://doi.org/10.1109/ACSAC.2001.991552.

2. Eric M. Hutchins, Michael J. Cloppert, and Rohan M. Amin, "Intelligence-Driven Computer Network Defense Informed by Analysis of Adversary Campaigns and Intrusion Kill Chains," *Leading Issues in Information Warfare & Security Research* 1 (January 2011).

3. Kirill Levchenko et al., "Click Trajectories: End-to-End Analysis of the Spam Value Chain," in *Proceedings of the 2011 IEEE Symposium on Security and Privacy, SP '11* (Washington, DC: IEEE Computer Society, 2011), 431–446, https://doi.org/10.1109 /SP.2011.24.

4. Levchenko et al., "Click Trajectories."

5. Levchenko et al., "Click Trajectories."

6. Gabriella Coleman, *Hacker, Hoaxer, Whistleblower, Spy: The Many Faces of Anonymous*, 1st ed. (London: Verso, 2014).

7. Ross Anderson et al., "Measuring the Cost of Cybercrime," in *The Economics of Information Security and Privacy* (Berlin: Springer, 2013), 265–300.

8. Anderson et al., "Measuring the Cost of Cybercrime."

9. Sasha Romanosky, Rahul Telang, and Alessandro Acquisti, "Do Data Breach Disclosure Laws Reduce Identity Theft?," *Journal of Policy Analysis and Management* 30, no. 2 (March 1, 2011): 256–286, https://doi.org/10.1002/pam.20567.

10. Romanosky, Telang, and Acquisti, "Do Data Breach Disclosure Laws Reduce Identity Theft?"

11. Sasha Romanosky and Alessandro Acquisti, "Privacy Costs and Personal Data Protection: Economic and Legal Perspectives," *Berkeley Technology Law Journal* 24 (December 12, 2009).

12. Daniel Solove and Danielle Citron, "Risk and Anxiety: A Theory of Data Breach Harms," Texas Law Review 96 (2017), https://papers.ssrn.com/abstract=2885638.

13. Ronald J. Deibert, *Black Code: Inside the Battle for Cyberspace* (Plattsburgh, NY: Signal, 2013).

14. Thomas Rid, *Cyber War Will Not Take Place*, 1st ed. (Oxford: Oxford University Press, 2013).

15. Martin C. Libicki, *Conquest in Cyberspace: National Security and Information Warfare*, 1st ed. (New York: Cambridge University Press, 2007).

16. Brandon Valeriano and Ryan C. Maness, *Cyber War versus Cyber Realities: Cyber Conflict in the International System*, 1st ed. (Oxford: Oxford University Press, 2015).

17. Scott J. Shackelford, Managing Cyber Attacks in International Law, Business, and Relations: In *Search of Cyber Peace*, rev. ed. (Cambridge: Cambridge University Press, 2014).

18. Sal Stolfo, David Evans, and Steven M. Bellovin, "Measuring Security," *IEEE Security & Privacy*, 2011.

Chapter 2

1. Brad Stone, "Global Trail of an Online Crime Ring," *New York Times*, August 11, 2008, sec. Technology, https://www.nytimes.com/2008/08/12/technology/12theft.html.

2. Joseph Pereira, "How Credit-Card Data Went Out Wireless Door," *Wall Street Journal*, May 4, 2007, http://www.wsj.com/articles/SB117824446226991797.

3. George Ou, "TJX's Failure to Secure Wi-Fi Could Cost $1B," *ZDNet*, May 7, 2007, http://www.zdnet.com/article/tjxs-failure-to-secure-wi-fi-could-cost-1b.

4. Eric Bangeman, "Blame for Record-Breaking Credit Card Data Theft Laid at the Feet of WEP," *Ars Technica*, May 6, 2007, https://arstechnica.com/information-technology/2007/05/blame-for-record-breaking-credit-card-data-theft-laid-at-the-feet-of-wep.

5. Scott R. Fluhrer, Itsik Mantin, and Adi Shamir, "Weaknesses in the Key Scheduling Algorithm of RC4," in *Revised Papers from the 8th Annual International Workshop on Selected Areas in Cryptography, SAC '01* (London: Springer-Verlag, 2001), 1–24, http://dl.acm.org/citation.cfm?id=646557.694759.

6. Nancy Gertner, *United States v. Watt*, 707 F. Supp. 2d 149 (United States District Court, D. Massachusetts 2010).

7. Carmen Ortiz, *United States v. Gonzalez*, Government's Sentencing Memorandum, No. 1:08-cr-10223-PBS (United States District Court, D. Massachusetts. March 18, 2010).

8. Ortiz, *United States v. Gonzalez*.

9. Ortiz, *United States v. Gonzalez*.

10. James Verini, "The Great Cyberheist," *New York Times*, November 10, 2010, https://www.nytimes.com/2010/11/14/magazine/14Hacker-t.html.

11. Ortiz, *United States v. Gonzalez*.

12. Verini, "The Great Cyberheist."

13. Ortiz, *United States v. Gonzalez*.

14. Ortiz, *United States v. Gonzalez*.

15. Verini, "The Great Cyberheist."

16. Verini, "The Great Cyberheist."

17. Verini, "The Great Cyberheist."

18. TJX Companies Inc., "Form 10-K" (SEC Filing, March 28, 2007).

19. In the Matter of The TJX Companies, Inc., A Corporation, No. C-072–3055 (Federal Trade Commission 2008).

20. Ortiz, *United States v. Gonzalez*.

21. Julie Saville and Nancy Loomis, "Why Wait for EMV to Solve Your Fraud Problems? One-Time Use Card Numbers Can Reduce Debit Fraud Now," First Data White Paper, (December 2010), https://www.firstdata.com/downloads/thought-leadership /one-time-card-star-cert-wp.pdf.

22. Saville and Loomis, "Why Wait for EMV to Solve Your Fraud Problems?"

23. Josephine Wolff, "Why Is the U.S. Determined to Have the Least-Secure Credit Cards in the World?," *The Atlantic*, March 10, 2016, https://www.theatlantic.com /business/archive/2016/03/us-determined-to-have-the-least-secure-credit-cards-in -the-world/473199.

24. Wolff, "Why Is the U.S. Determined to Have the Least-Secure Credit Cards in the World?"

25. Wolff, "Why Is the U.S. Determined to Have the Least-Secure Credit Cards in the World?"

26. Robin Sidel, "Home Depot Files Antitrust Lawsuit Against Visa, MasterCard," *Wall Street Journal*, June 15, 2016, http://www.wsj.com/articles/home-depot-u-s -credit-card-firms-slow-to-upgrade-security-1466000734.

27. Frank Lowrey, *The Home Depot Inc. v. Visa Inc., Mastercard Inc.*, No. 1:16-cv-01947-MHC (District Court Northern District of Georgia June 13, 2016).

Chapter 3

1. Hal Berghel, "The SCDOR Hack: Great Security Theater in Five Stages," *Computer* 46, no. 3 (March 2013): 97–99, https://doi.org/10.1109/MC.2013.117.

2. Marshall Heilman and Christopher Glyer, "South Carolina Department of Revenue: Public Incident Response Report" (Mandiant, November 20, 2012), https://oag .ca.gov/system/files/Mandiant%20Report_0.pdf.

3. Andrew Shain, "S.C. Tax Data Hacked: What's Known Three Weeks Later," *The Beaufort Gazette*, November 17, 2012, http://www.islandpacket.com/news/local /community/beaufort-news/article33488127.html.

4. Andrew Shain, "S.C. Hack Victims to Get Lifetime ID Theft Resolution Aid," *The State*, October 30, 2012.

5. Shain, "S.C. Tax Data Hacked."

6. Shain, "S.C. Tax Data Hacked."

7. Tim Smith, "State Sending Some Tax Refunds by Mail," *Greenville Online*, March 2, 2015, http://www.greenvilleonline.com/story/news/politics/2015/03/02/state-sending -tax-refunds-mail-deter-fraud/24275417.

8. Smith, "State Sending Some Tax Refunds by Mail."

9. Tim Smith, "Experts: Link Possible between 2012 Hacking, Tax Fraud," *Greenville Online*, March 8, 2015, http://www.greenvilleonline.com/story/news/politics/2015 /03/08/experts-link-possible-hacking-tax-fraud/24499699.

10. Brian Krebs, "The Rise in State Tax Refund Fraud," *Krebs on Security* (blog), February 17, 2015, https://krebsonsecurity.com/2015/02/the-rise-in-state-tax-refund-fraud.

11. Tim Smith, "Four Years Later, Case Still Open in DOR Data Breach," *Greenville Online*, August 12, 2016, http://www.greenvilleonline.com/story/news/crime/2016 /08/12/four-years-later-case-still-open-dor-data-breach/88453548.

12. Andrew Shain, "Security Contractor Didn't Detect Hacker from SCDOR Website," *The State*, November 14, 2012, http://www.goupstate.com/news/20121114/security -contractor-didnt-detect-hacker-from-scdor-website.

13. John Hawkins, *Phillip Morgan v. South Carolina Department of Revenue*, No. 2012-CP-40-7331 (County of Richland, Court of Common Pleas for the Fifth Judicial Circuit November 5, 2012).

14. Matt Long, "Department of Revenue Chief: No Security Officer for Nearly a Year before Breach," *South Carolina Radio Network*, November 28, 2012, https://www.southcarolinaradionetwork.com/2012/11/28/department-of-revenue-chief-no-security-officer-for-nearly-a-year-before-breach.

15. Long, "Department of Revenue Chief."

16. James Rosen, "S.C. Gov. Nikki Haley Takes Blame for State's Data Breach," *McClatchy DC*, November 28, 2012, http://www.mcclatchydc.com/news/politics-government/article24740893.html.

17. Rosen, "S.C. Gov. Nikki Haley Takes Blame."

18. Michael Isikoff, "One Email Exposes Millions of People to Data Theft in South Carolina Cyberattack," *NBC News*, November 20, 2012, http://investigations.nbcnews.com/_news/2012/11/20/15313720-one-email-exposes-millions-of-people-to-data-theft-in-south-carolina-cyberattack.

19. Isikoff, "One Email Exposes Millions of People to Data Theft."

20. Long, "Department of Revenue Chief."

21. Matthew Goldstein, Nicole Perlroth, and Michael Corkery, "Neglected Server Provided Entry for JPMorgan Hackers," *The New York Times*, December 22, 2014, https://dealbook.nytimes.com/2014/12/22/entry-point-of-jpmorgan-data-breach-is-identified/.

22. Brian Fung, "Apple's Basically Blaming Hack Victims for Not Securing Their Own iCloud Accounts," *Washington Post*, September 2, 2014, https://www.washingtonpost.com/news/the-switch/wp/2014/09/02/apples-basically-blaming-hack-victims-for-not-securing-their-own-icloud-accounts.

23. Daniel J. Solove and Woodrow Hartzog, "The FTC and the New Common Law of Privacy," *Columbia Law Review* 114, no. 4 (2014): 583–676.

24. Thomas Ambro, Federal Trade Commission v. Wyndham Worldwide Corporation, No. 14-3514 (United States Court of Appeals for the Third Circuit August 24, 2015).

25. Jess Kamen, "Haley Writes IRS on Data Protection; IRS Responds," *Politico*, November 21, 2012, http://politi.co/YRB0fq.

26. Jada F. Smith, "Cyberattack Exposes I.R.S. Tax Returns," *New York Times*, May 26, 2015, https://www.nytimes.com/2015/05/27/business/breach-exposes-irs-tax-returns.html.

27. Charles Riley, "Insurance Giant Anthem Hit by Massive Data Breach," *CNN*, February 6, 2015, http://money.cnn.com/2015/02/04/technology/anthem-insurance-hack-data-security/index.html.

28. Andy Greenberg, "Hack Brief: Health Insurer Excellus Says Attackers Breached 10M Records," *Wired*, September 10, 2015, https://www.wired.com/2015/09/hack -brief-health-insurance-firm-excellus-says-attackers-breached-10m-records.

29. Caroline Humer and Jim Finkle, "Your Medical Record Is Worth More to Hackers than Your Credit Card," *Reuters*, September 24, 2014, https://www.reuters.com /article/us-cybersecurity-hospitals/your-medical-record-is-worth-more-to-hackers -than-your-credit-card-idUSKCN0HJ21I20140924.

30. Andrea Peterson, "The Security That IRS Provided Tax-Fraud Victims Just Got Hacked," *Washington Post*, March 3, 2016, sec. The Switch, https://www .washingtonpost.com/news/the-switch/wp/2016/03/03/the-security-the-irs-provided -tax-fraud-victims-just-got-hacked.

31. Smith, "Experts: Link Possible between 2012 Hacking, Tax Fraud."

32. John J. Tharp, Jr., *Amber J. Strautins v. Trustwave Holdings, Inc.*, No. 1:12-cv-09115 (District Court for the Northern District of Illinois Eastern Division March 12, 2014).

33. *Clapper v. Amnesty International USA*, 638 F. 3d 118 (U.S. Supreme Court 2013).

34. *Clapper v. Amnesty International USA*, 638 F. 3d.

Chapter 4

1. Michael Schwirtz and Joseph Goldstein, "Russian Espionage Piggybacks on a Cybercriminal's Hacking," *New York Times*, March 12, 2017, https://www.nytimes .com/2017/03/12/world/europe/russia-hacker-evgeniy-bogachev.html.

2. Elliott Peterson, "Declaration in Support of Application for an Emergency Temporary Restraining Order and Order to Show Cause Re Preliminary Injunction." (United States District Court for the Western District of Pennsylvania, May 27, 2014).

3. Peterson, "Declaration in Support of Application for an Emergency Temporary Restraining Order and Order to Show Cause Re Preliminary Injunction."

4. Schwirtz and Goldstein, "Russian Espionage Piggybacks on a Cybercriminal's Hacking."

5. Schwirtz and Goldstein, "Russian Espionage Piggybacks on a Cybercriminal's Hacking."

6. Peterson, "Declaration in Support of Application for an Emergency Temporary Restraining Order and Order to Show Cause Re Preliminary Injunction."

7. Peterson, "Declaration in Support of Application for an Emergency Temporary Restraining Order and Order to Show Cause Re Preliminary Injunction."

8. James K. Craig, *U.S. v. Evgeniy Bogachev*, No. 2:14-cr-00127-UNA (District Court for the Western District of Pennsylvania May 30, 2014).

9. Peterson, "Declaration in Support of Application for an Emergency Temporary Restraining Order and Order to Show Cause Re Preliminary Injunction."

10. Peterson, "Declaration in Support of Application for an Emergency Temporary Restraining Order and Order to Show Cause Re Preliminary Injunction."

11. Peterson, "Declaration in Support of Application for an Emergency Temporary Restraining Order and Order to Show Cause Re Preliminary Injunction."

12. Peterson, "Declaration in Support of Application for an Emergency Temporary Restraining Order and Order to Show Cause Re Preliminary Injunction."

13. Craig, *U.S. v. Evgeniy Bogachev*.

14. Craig, *U.S. v. Evgeniy Bogachev*.

15. Craig, *U.S. v. Evgeniy Bogachev*.

16. "GameOver Zeus Botnet Disrupted. Collaborative Effort Among International Partners," FBI statement, June 2, 2014, https://www.fbi.gov/news/stories/gameover -zeus-botnet-disrupted.

17. "Department of Justice Provides Update on GameOver Zeus and Cryptolocker Disruption," FBI statement, July 11, 2014, https://www.fbi.gov/news/pressrel/press -releases/department-of-justice-provides-update-on-gameover-zeus-and-cryptolocker -disruption.

18. "Verizon 2016 Data Breach Investigations Report" (Verizon, April 2016), http:// www.verizonenterprise.com/verizon-insights-lab/dbir/2016.

19. Josephine Wolff, "Ransomware and the New Economics of Cybercrime," *The Atlantic*, June 7, 2016, https://www.theatlantic.com/business/archive/2016/06 /ransomware-new-economics-cybercrime/485888.

20. Herb Weisbaum, "CryptoLocker Crooks Launch New 'Customer Service' Web- site for Victims," *NBC Today*, November 14, 2013, https://www.today.com/money /cryptolocker-crooks-launch-new-customer-service-website-victims-2D11586019.

21. Wolff, "Ransomware and the New Economics of Cybercrime."

22. Arjun Kharpal, "WannaCry Ransomware Hackers Have Only Made $50,000 Worth of Bitcoin," *CNBC*, May 15, 2017, https://www.cnbc.com/2017/05/15/wannacry -ransomware-hackers-have-only-made-50000-worth-of-bitcoin.html.

23. Thomas P. Bossert, "It's Official: North Korea Is Behind WannaCry," *Wall Street Journal*, December 19, 2017, sec. Opinion, https://www.wsj.com/articles/its-official -north-korea-is-behind-wannacry-1513642537.

24. Devlin Barrett, "Paying Ransoms to Hackers Stirs Debate," *Wall Street Journal*, November 9, 2015, https://www.wsj.com/articles/paying-ransoms-to-hackers-stirs -debate-1447106376.

25. Wolff, "Ransomware and the New Economics of Cybercrime."

Chapter 5

1. Hans Hoogstraaten et al., "Black Tulip: Report of the Investigation into the Digi-Notar Certificate Authority Breach" (Fox-IT BV, August 13, 2012).

2. Hoogstraaten et al., "Black Tulip."

3. VASCO Data Security International, Inc., "Form 8-K" (Securities and Exchange Commission filing, September 2, 2011).

4. Rick Andrews, phone interview, September 6, 2016.

5. Josephine Wolff, "How a 2011 Hack You've Never Heard of Changed the Internet's Infrastructure," *Slate*, December 21, 2016, http://www.slate.com/articles/technology /future_tense/2016/12/how_the_2011_hack_of_diginotar_changed_the_internet_s_ infrastructure.html.

6. Wolff, "How a 2011 Hack You've Never Heard of Changed the Internet's Infrastructure."

7. Daniel Kahn Gillmor, phone interview, September 6, 2016.

8. Kathleen Wilson, "Revoking Trust in One CNNIC Intermediate Certificate," Mozilla Security Blog, March 23, 2015, https://blog.mozilla.org/security/2015/03/23 /revoking-trust-in-one-cnnic-intermediate-certificate.

9. Richard Chirgwin, "Apple Chops Woeful WoSign HTTPS Certs from IOS, MacOS," *The Register*, October 3, 2016, https://www.theregister.co.uk/2016/10/03 /apple_wosign_certificates.

10. Kathleen Wilson, "Distrusting New WoSign and StartCom Certificates," Mozilla Security Blog, October 24, 2016, https://blog.mozilla.org/security/2016/10 /24/distrusting-new-wosign-and-startcom-certificates.

11. Andrew Whalley, "Distrusting WoSign and StartCom Certificates," Google Security Blog, October 31, 2016, https://security.googleblog.com/2016/10/distrusting -wosign-and-startcom.html.

12. Ryan Sleevi, "Intent to Deprecate and Remove: Trust in Existing Symantec-Issued Certificates," Chromium Forum (blog), March 23, 2017, https://groups.google .com/a/chromium.org/d/msg/blink-dev/eUAKwjihhBs/rpxMXjZHCQAJ.

13. Sleevi, "Intent to Deprecate and Remove."

14. Roxane Divol, "A Message to Our CA Customers," Symantec Official Blog, March 26, 2017, https://www.symantec.com/connect/blogs/message-our-ca-customers.

15. Adrienne Porter Felt et al., "Improving SSL Warnings: Comprehension and Adherence," in *Proceedings of the 33rd Annual ACM Conference on Human Factors in Computing Systems, CHI '15* (New York, NY, USA: ACM, 2015), 2893–2902, https://doi.org/10.1145/2702123.2702442.

16. Gillmor, interview.

Chapter 6

1. David J. Hickton, *U.S. v. Wang Dong, Sun Kailiang, Wen Xinyu, Huang Zhenyu, and Gui Chunhui*, No. 14-118 (District Court for the Western District of Pennsylvania May 1, 2014).

2. Hickton, *U.S. v. Wang Dong, Sun Kailiang, Wen Xinyu, Huang Zhenyu, and Gui Chunhui*.

3. David Talbot, "Cyber Espionage Nightmare," *MIT Technology Review*, June 10, 2015, https://www.technologyreview.com/s/538201/cyber-espionage-nightmare.

4. "APT1: Exposing One of China's Cyber Espionage Units" (Mandiant, February 19, 2013), 1.

5. "APT1: Exposing One of China's Cyber Espionage Units," 1.

6. "APT1: Exposing One of China's Cyber Espionage Units," 1.

7. Hickton, *U.S. v. Wang Dong, Sun Kailiang, Wen Xinyu, Huang Zhenyu, and Gui Chunhui*.

8. "APT1: Exposing One of China's Cyber Espionage Units," 1.

9. "APT1: Exposing One of China's Cyber Espionage Units," 1.

10. "APT1: Exposing One of China's Cyber Espionage Units," 1.

11. Hickton, *U.S. v. Wang Dong, Sun Kailiang, Wen Xinyu, Huang Zhenyu, and Gui Chunhui*.

12. Hickton, *U.S. v. Wang Dong, Sun Kailiang, Wen Xinyu, Huang Zhenyu, and Gui Chunhui*.

13. Hickton, *U.S. v. Wang Dong, Sun Kailiang, Wen Xinyu, Huang Zhenyu, and Gui Chunhui*.

14. "APT1: Exposing One of China's Cyber Espionage Units," 1.

15. "APT1: Exposing One of China's Cyber Espionage Units," 1.

16. "APT1: Exposing One of China's Cyber Espionage Units," 1.

17. "APT1: Exposing One of China's Cyber Espionage Units," 1.

18. Hickton, *U.S. v. Wang Dong, Sun Kailiang, Wen Xinyu, Huang Zhenyu, and Gui Chunhui*.

19. Hickton, *U.S. v. Wang Dong, Sun Kailiang, Wen Xinyu, Huang Zhenyu, and Gui Chunhui*.

20. Hickton, *U.S. v. Wang Dong, Sun Kailiang, Wen Xinyu, Huang Zhenyu, and Gui Chunhui*.

21. Hickton, *U.S. v. Wang Dong, Sun Kailiang, Wen Xinyu, Huang Zhenyu, and Gui Chunhui*.

22. Qin Gang, "China Reacts Strongly to U.S. Announcement of Indictment Against Chinese Personnel," Statement of the Chinese Foreign Ministry, May 20, 2014, http://www.fmprc.gov.cn/mfa_eng/xwfw_665399/s2510_665401/2535_665405/t1157520.shtml.

23. Gang, "China Reacts Strongly to U.S. Announcement."

24. "APT1: Exposing One of China's Cyber Espionage Units," 1.

25. Tyrus R. Atkinson, Jr., *"Yahoo! Inc v. Zheng Youjun*, Claim Number: FA1109001409001" (National Arbitration Forum Decision, October 31, 2011), http://www.adrforum.com/domaindecisions/1409001.htm.

26. Carl Levin, Deter Cyber Theft Act, Pub. L. No. S. 884 (2013), https://www.govtrack.us/congress/bills/113/s884/text.

Chapter 7

1. Jason Chaffetz, Mark Meadows, and Will Hurd, "The OPM Data Breach: How the Government Jeopardized Our National Security for More than a Generation" (Committee on Oversight and Government Reform, U.S. House of Representatives, 114th Congress, September 7, 2016).

2. "OPM: Data Breach," House of Representatives Committee on Oversight and Government Reform (2015).

3. Kevin Liptak, Theodore Schleifer, and Jim Sciutto, "China Might Be Building Vast Database of Federal Worker Info, Experts Say," *CNN*, June 6, 2015, http://www.cnn.com/2015/06/04/politics/federal-agency-hacked-personnel-management.

4. Ellen Nakashima, "Chinese Government Has Arrested Hackers It Says Breached OPM Database," *Washington Post*, December 2, 2015, https://www.washingtonpost.com/world/national-security/chinese-government-has-arrested-hackers

-suspected-of-breaching-opm-database/2015/12/02/0295b918-990c-11e5-8917
-653b65c809eb_story.html?utm_term=.7fab0d5921ec.

5. Michael R. Esser, "OPM: Data Breach," § Committee on Oversight and Government Reform (2015).

6. Esser, "OPM: Data Breach."

7. Esser, "OPM: Data Breach."

8. Katherine Archuleta, "OPM: Data Breach," § Committee on Oversight and Government Reform (2015).

9. Chaffetz, Meadows, and Hurd, "The OPM Data Breach: How the Government Jeopardized Our National Security for More than a Generation."

10. Chaffetz, Meadows, and Hurd, "The OPM Data Breach."

11. Chaffetz, Meadows, and Hurd, "The OPM Data Breach."

12. Chaffetz, Meadows, and Hurd, "The OPM Data Breach."

13. Chaffetz, Meadows, and Hurd, "The OPM Data Breach."

14. Chaffetz, Meadows, and Hurd, "The OPM Data Breach."

15. Chaffetz, Meadows, and Hurd, "The OPM Data Breach."

16. Chaffetz, Meadows, and Hurd, "The OPM Data Breach."

17. Chaffetz, Meadows, and Hurd, "The OPM Data Breach."

18. Chaffetz, Meadows, and Hurd, "The OPM Data Breach."

19. Chaffetz, Meadows, and Hurd, "The OPM Data Breach."

20. Chaffetz, Meadows, and Hurd, "The OPM Data Breach."

21. "OPM: Data Breach," House of Representatives Committee on Oversight and Government Reform (2015).

22. "OPM: Data Breach," House of Representatives Committee on Oversight and Government Reform (2015).

23. Chaffetz, Meadows, and Hurd, "The OPM Data Breach."

24. Chaffetz, Meadows, and Hurd, "The OPM Data Breach."

25. "OPM: Data Breach," House of Representatives Committee on Oversight and Government Reform (2015).

26. "OPM: Data Breach," House of Representatives Committee on Oversight and Government Reform (2015).

27. Gary E. Mason, *American Federation of Government Employees, AFL-CIO vs. OPM*, No. 1:15-cv-01015 (District Court for the District of Columbia June 29, 2015).

28. "OPM: Data Breach," House of Representatives Committee on Oversight and Government Reform (2015).

29. "OPM: Data Breach," House of Representatives Committee on Oversight and Government Reform (2015).

30. "Identity Theft Services: Services Offer Some Benefits but Are Limited in Preventing Fraud" (United States Government Accountability Office, March 2017), https://www.gao.gov/assets/690/683842.pdf.

31. "Identity Theft Services: Services Offer Some Benefits but Are Limited in Preventing Fraud."

32. Kaveh Waddell, "Feds Expect to Spend at Least $500 Million on the Next Five Years of Data Breaches," *The Atlantic*, August 13, 2015, https://www.theatlantic.com/politics/archive/2015/08/feds-expect-to-spend-at-least-500-million-on-the-next-five-years-of-data-breaches/458358/.

33. "Identity Theft Services: Services Offer Some Benefits but Are Limited in Preventing Fraud."

34. "Identity Theft Services: Services Offer Some Benefits but Are Limited in Preventing Fraud."

35. Mason, *American Federation of Government Employees, AFL-CIO vs. OPM*.

36. Paras Shah, *NTEU v. Cobert*, No. 1:15-mc-01394-ABJ (District Court for the District of Columbia June 3, 2016).

37. Katie Williams, "Lawsuits against Government over Hack Are Adding Up," *The Hill*, August 17, 2015, http://thehill.com/policy/cybersecurity/251326-lawsuits-against-government-over-hack-are-adding-up.

38. Kat Sieniuc, "OPM Calls for Dismissal of Government Workers' Data Breach Suit," *Law360* (blog), August 4, 2016, https://www.law360.com/articles/824965/opm-calls-for-dismissal-of-gov-t-workers-data-breach-suit.

39. Ellen Nakashima and Adam Goldman, "CIA Pulled Officers from Beijing after Breach of Federal Personnel Records," *Washington Post*, September 29, 2015, https://www.washingtonpost.com/world/national-security/cia-pulled-officers-from-beijing-after-breach-of-federal-personnel-records/2015/09/29/1f78943c-66d1-11e5-9ef3-fde182507eac_story.html.

40. David E. Sanger, "With Spy Charges, U.S. Draws a Line That Few Others Recognize," *New York Times*, May 19, 2014, https://www.nytimes.com/2014/05/20/us/us-treads-fine-line-in-fighting-chinese-espionage.html.

Chapter 8

1. Motion Picture Association, "CyberBunker Prohibited From Providing Internet Access to The Pirate Bay" (MPA press statement, May 13, 2010).

2. Sam Clements, "The Shady Geeks Hiding in Bunkers Trying to Nuke the Internet," *Vice*, April 17, 2013, https://www.vice.com/en_uk/article/mvw8x8/shady-server-hosters-are-hiding-in-nuclear-bunkers.

3. Brian Krebs, "Inside 'The Attack That Almost Broke the Internet,'" Krebs on Security (blog), August 26, 2016, https://krebsonsecurity.com/2016/08/inside-the-attack-that-almost-broke-the-Internet/#more-35925.

4. "Stophaus Chat Transcripts: March 2013" (Krebs on Security (blog), August 26, 2016), http://krebsonsecurity.com/wp-content/uploads/2016/08/Spamhaus-2013-DDoS-chat-log1.txt.

5. "Stophaus Chat Transcripts: March 2013."

6. "Stophaus Chat Transcripts: March 2013."

7. "Stophaus Chat Transcripts: March 2013."

8. "Stophaus Chat Transcripts: March 2013."

9. "Stophaus Chat Transcripts: March 2013."

10. Matthew Prince, "The DDoS That Almost Broke the Internet," Cloudflare Blog, March 27, 2013, https://blog.cloudflare.com/the-ddos-that-almost-broke-the-Internet.

11. "Stophaus Chat Transcripts: March 2013."

12. Prince, "The DDoS That Almost Broke the Internet."

13. "Stophaus Chat Transcripts: March 2013."

14. Matthew Prince, "The DDoS That Knocked Spamhaus Offline (And How We Mitigated It)," Cloudflare Blog, March 20, 2013, https://blog.cloudflare.com/the-ddos-that-knocked-spamhaus-offline-and-ho/.

15. Prince, "The DDoS That Knocked Spamhaus Offline."

16. "Stophaus Chat Transcripts: March 2013."

17. Prince, "The DDoS That Almost Broke the Internet."

18. John Markoff and Nicole Perlroth, "Online Dispute Becomes Internet-Snarling Attack," *New York Times*, March 26, 2013, http://www.nytimes.com/2013/03/27/technology/internet/online-dispute-becomes-internet-snarling-attack.html.

19. Gordon Corera, "UK Teenager Sentenced over 'Biggest' Web Attack," *BBC*, July 10, 2015, http://www.bbc.com/news/technology-33480257.

20. Brian Krebs, "Adobe Fined $1M in Multistate Suit Over 2013 Breach; No Jail for Spamhaus Attacker," Krebs on Security (blog), November 17, 2016, https://krebson-security.com/2016/11/adobe-fined-1m-in-multistate-suit-over-2013-breach-no-jail-for-spamhaus-attacker/.

21. "Stophaus Chat Transcripts: March 2013."

22. "Stophaus Chat Transcripts: March 2013."

23. "Stophaus Chat Transcripts: March 2013."

24. "Stophaus Chat Transcripts: March 2013."

25. "Stophaus Chat Transcripts: March 2013."

26. "Stophaus Chat Transcripts: March 2013."

27. "Stophaus Chat Transcripts: March 2013."

28. "Stophaus Chat Transcripts: March 2013."

29. "Stophaus Chat Transcripts: March 2013."

Chapter 9

1. *Lynn Lincoln Sarko, Michael Corona, Christina Mathis, et al. vs. Sony Pictures Entertainment*, No. 2:14-CV-09600-RGK-SH (District Court, Central District of California March 2, 2015).

2. Rebecca Keegan, "Sony Hack 'Unprecedented, Damaging and Unique' Cyber Security Firm Says," *Los Angeles Times*, December 6, 2014, http://www.latimes.com/entertainment/envelope/cotown/la-et-ct-sony-hack-20141206-story.html.

3. Federal Bureau of Investigation, "Update on Sony Investigation" (FBI statement, December 19, 2014), https://www.fbi.gov/news/pressrel/press-releases/update-on-sony-investigation.

4. Sean Gallagher, "Inside the 'Wiper' Malware That Brought Sony Pictures to Its Knees," *Ars Technica*, December 3, 2014, https://arstechnica.com/information-technology/2014/12/inside-the-wiper-malware-that-brought-sony-pictures-to-its-knees/.

5. Gallagher, "Inside the 'Wiper' Malware That Brought Sony Pictures to Its Knees."

6. Peter Elkind, "Sony Pictures: Inside the Hack of the Century," *Fortune*, June 25, 2015, http://fortune.com/sony-hack-part-1/.

7. Gallagher, "Inside the 'Wiper' Malware That Brought Sony Pictures to Its Knees."

8. Gallagher, "Inside the 'Wiper' Malware That Brought Sony Pictures to Its Knees."

9. Gallagher, "Inside the 'Wiper' Malware That Brought Sony Pictures to Its Knees."

10. Mark Seal, "An Exclusive Look at Sony's Hacking Saga," *Vanity Fair*, March 2015, http://www.vanityfair.com/hollywood/2015/02/sony-hacking-seth-rogen-evan -goldberg.

11. Noah Rayman, "New Research Blames Insiders, Not North Korea, for Sony Hack," *Time*, December 30, 2014, http://time.com/3649394/sony-hack-inside-job -north-korea/.

12. Elkind, "Sony Pictures: Inside the Hack of the Century."

13. Elkind, "Sony Pictures: Inside the Hack of the Century."

14. Novetta Threat Research Group, "Operation Blockbuster: Unraveling the Long Thread of the Sony Attack" (Novetta, November 24, 2016), https://www .operationblockbuster.com/wp-content/uploads/2016/02/Operation-Blockbuster -Report.pdf.

15. Federal Bureau of Investigation, "Update on Sony Investigation."

16. Bruce Schneier, "Did North Korea Really Attack Sony?," *The Atlantic*, December 22, 2014, https://www.theatlantic.com/international/archive/2014/12/did-north-korea -really-attack-sony/383973/.

17. Novetta Threat Research Group, "Operation Blockbuster: Unraveling the Long Thread of the Sony Attack."

18. Novetta Threat Research Group, "Operation Blockbuster."

19. Novetta Threat Research Group, "Operation Blockbuster."

20. Novetta Threat Research Group, "Operation Blockbuster."

21. Federal Bureau of Investigation, "Update on Sony Investigation."

22. Nicole Perlroth and David E. Sanger, "North Korea Loses Its Link to the Internet," *New York Times*, December 22, 2014, https://www.nytimes.com/2014/12/23/world /asia/attack-is-suspected-as-north-korean-Internet-collapses.html.

23. Perlroth and Sanger, "North Korea Loses Its Link to the Internet."

24. Seal, "An Exclusive Look at Sony's Hacking Saga."

25. Elkind, "Sony Pictures: Inside the Hack of the Century."

26. Justin Moyer, "Why North Korea Has Every Reason to Be Upset about Sony's 'The Interview,'" *Washington Post*, December 16, 2014, https://www.washingtonpost .com/news/morning-mix/wp/2014/12/16/why-north-korea-has-every-reason-to-be -upset-about-the-interview.

27. Elias Groll, "Internal Emails Show Sony Struggling to Comprehend North Korea Threat," *Foreign Policy*, April 16, 2015, http://foreignpolicy.com/2015/04/16/internal -_emails_show_sony_struggling_to_comprehend_north_korea_threat.

28. Groll, "Internal Emails Show Sony Struggling to Comprehend North Korea Threat.".

29. Elkind, "Sony Pictures: Inside the Hack of the Century."

30. Elkind, "Sony Pictures: Inside the Hack of the Century."

31. Elkind, "Sony Pictures: Inside the Hack of the Century."

32. Elkind, "Sony Pictures: Inside the Hack of the Century."

33. *Lynn Lincoln Sarko, Michael Corona, Christina Mathis, et al. vs. Sony Pictures Entertainment*, No. 2:14-CV-09600-RGK-SH (District Court, Central District of California March 2, 2015).

34. *Sarko, et al. vs. Sony Pictures Entertainment.*

35. *Sarko, et al. vs. Sony Pictures Entertainment.*

36. William F. Lee, Michael Corona, Christina Mathis, et al. vs. Sony Pictures Entertainment, No. 2:14-cv-09600-RGK-E (District Court, Central District of California June 29, 2015).

37. *Clapper v. Amnesty International USA*, 638 F. 3d 118 (U.S. Supreme Court 2013).

38. *R. Gary Klausner, Michael Corona, Christina Mathis, et al. vs. Sony Pictures Entertainment*, No. 2:14-CV-09600-RGK-SH (District Court, Central District of California June 15, 2015).

39. *Klausner, et al. vs. Sony Pictures Entertainment.*

40. Daniel Solove and Danielle Citron, "Risk and Anxiety: A Theory of Data Breach Harms," *Texas Law Review* 96 (2017), in press, https://papers.ssrn.com/abstract=2885638.

41. Dawn Chmielewski and Arik Hesseldahl, "Sony Pictures Tries to Disrupt Downloads of Its Stolen Files," *Re/Code*, December 10, 2014, https://www.recode.net/2014/12/10/11633708/sony-pictures-tries-to-disrupt-downloads-of-its-stolen-files.

42. David Boies, "RE: Your Possession of Privileged and/or Confidential Information Stolen From Sony Pictures Entertainment," December 14, 2014, http://www.hollywoodreporter.com/sites/default/files/custom/Sony%20Letter.pdf.

43. Aaron Sorkin, "The Sony Hack and the Yellow Press," *New York Times*, December 14, 2014, https://www.nytimes.com/2014/12/15/opinion/aaron-sorkin-journalists-shouldnt-help-the-sony-hackers.html.

Chapter 10

1. Brian Krebs, "Online Cheating Site Ashley Madison Hacked," Krebs on Security (blog), July 19, 2015, https://krebsonsecurity.com/2015/07/online-cheating-site-ashleymadison-hacked.

2. Krebs, "Online Cheating Site Ashley Madison Hacked."

3. Julian Hammond, *John Doe v. Avid Life Media Inc.*, No. 2:15-cv-06405-PSG-AJW (District Court Central District of California Western Division August 21, 2015).

4. Katie Rogers, "After Ashley Madison Hack, Police in Toronto Detail a Global Fallout," *New York Times*, August 25, 2015, https://www.nytimes.com/2015/08/25/technology/after-ashley-madison-hack-police-in-toronto-detail-a-global-fallout.html.

5. Josephine Mason and Alastair Sharp, "Hacker's Ashley Madison Data Dump Threatens Marriages, Reputations," *Reuters*, August 18, 2015, http://www.reuters.com/article/us-ashleymadison-cybersecurity-idUSKCN0QN2BN20150819.

6. Richard Morgan, "Ashley Madison Is Back—and Claims Surprising User Numbers," *New York Post*, May 21, 2017, http://nypost.com/2017/05/21/ashley-madison-is-back-and-claims-surprising-user-numbers.

7. John J. Driscoll, Amended Consolidated Class Action Complaint in RE: Ashley Madison Customer Data Security Breach Litigation, No. 4:15MD2669 JAR (District Court Eastern District of Missouri Eastern Division June 24, 2016).

8. Driscoll, Amended Consolidated Class Action Complaint.

9. Driscoll, Amended Consolidated Class Action Complaint.

10. Stephen Hunt, "AshleyMadison.Com Founder Noel Biderman Says Vice Comes Naturally," *Calgary Herald*, January 26, 2015, http://calgaryherald.com/entertainment/local-arts/ashleymadison-com-founder- noel-biderman-says-vice-comes-naturally.

11. Shameka L. Walker, *Federal Trade Commission v. Ruby Corp.* Complaint for Permanent Injunction and Other Equitable Relief, No. 1:16-cv-02438 (District Court for the District of Columbia December 14, 2016).

12. Joseph Bernstein, "Ashley Madison's $19 'Full Delete' Option Made The Company Millions," *Buzzfeed*, August 19, 2015, https://www.buzzfeed.com/josephbernstein/leaked-documents-suggest-ashley-madison-made-millions-promis.

13. Driscoll, Amended Consolidated Class Action Complaint in RE: Ashley Madison Customer Data Security Breach Litigation.

14. Walker, *Federal Trade Commission v. Ruby Corp.*

15. Walker, *Federal Trade Commission v. Ruby Corp.*

16. Jim Armstrong, "Brockton Man Is First Ashley Madison User Exposed By Hackers," CBS Boston, July 21, 2015, http://boston.cbslocal.com/2015/07/21/brockton-man-is-first-ashley-madison-user-exposed-by-hackers.

17. Gabor Szathmari, "Credentials in the Ashley Madison Sources," Rainbow & Unicorn (blog), September 7, 2015, https://blog.gaborszathmari.me/2015/09/07/credentials-in-the-ashley-madison-sources/.

18. Steve Ragan, "Ashley Madison Self-Assessments Highlight Security Fears and Failures," *CSO Online*, August 19, 2015, http://www.csoonline.com/article/2973575 /business-continuity/ashley-madison-self-assessments-highlight-security-fears-and -failures.html.

19. Dan Goodin, "Once Seen as Bulletproof, 11 Million+ Ashley Madison Passwords Already Cracked," *Ars Technica*, September 10, 2015, https://arstechnica .com/information-technology/2015/09/once-seen-as-bulletproof-11-million -ashley-madison-passwords-already-cracked/.

20. Driscoll, Amended Consolidated Class Action Complaint in RE: Ashley Madison Customer Data Security Breach Litigation.

21. Annalee Newitz, "Ashley Madison Code Shows More Women, and More Bots," Gizmodo (blog), August 31, 2015, http://gizmodo.com/ashley-madison-code-shows -more-women-and-more-bots-1727613924.

22. Newitz, "Ashley Madison Code Shows More Women."

23. Walker, *Federal Trade Commission v. Ruby Corp.*

24. Driscoll, Amended Consolidated Class Action Complaint in RE: Ashley Madison Customer Data Security Breach Litigation.

25. Driscoll, Amended Consolidated Class Action Complaint.

26. Alex Johnson, "Ashley Madison Faces Multiple Suits Seeking More Than a Half-Billion Dollars," *NBC News*, August 26, 2015, http://www.nbcnews.com/news/us-news /ashley-madison-faces-multiple-suits-seeking-more-half-billion-dollars-n415281.

27. Jonathan Stempel, "Ashley Madison Parent in $11.2 Million Settlement over Data Breach," *Reuters*, July 14, 2017, http://www.reuters.com/article/us - ashleymadison-settlement-idUSKBN19Z2F0.

28. Shameka L. Walker, FTC v. Ruby Corp. Stipulated Order for Permanent Injunction and Other Equitable Relief, No. 1:16-cv-02438 (December 14, 2016).

29. Joseph Cox, "Ashley Madison Sent Me a DMCA Request for Tweeting 2 Cells of a Spreadsheet," *Vice*, August 19, 2015, https://motherboard.vice.com/en_us /article/xywbd4/ashley-madison-sent-me-a-dmca-request-for-tweeting-two-cells-of-a -spreadsheet.

30. Stempel, "Ashley Madison Parent in $11.2 Million Settlement over Data Breach."

31. John A. Ross, Memorandum and Order in RE: Ashley Madison Customer Data Security Breach Litigation, No. MDL No. 2669 (District Court Eastern District of Missouri Eastern Division April 6, 2016).

32. Ross, Memorandum and Order in RE: Ashley Madison Customer Data Security Breach Litigation.

33. Driscoll, Amended Consolidated Class Action Complaint in RE: Ashley Madison Customer Data Security Breach Litigation.

Chapter 11

1. Jon O. Newman, *U.S. v. Morris*, 928 F.2d 504 (Court of Appeals for the Second Circuit 1991).

2. Brad Taylor, "Fighting Phishing with eBay and PayPal," Official Gmail Blog, July 8, 2008, http://gmailblog.blogspot.com/2008/07/fighting-phishing-with-ebay -and-paypal.html.

3. Serge Egelman, Lorrie Faith Cranor, and Jason Hong, "You've Been Warned: An Empirical Study of the Effectiveness of Web Browser Phishing Warnings," in *Proceedings of the SIGCHI Conference on Human Factors in Computing Systems, CHI '08* (New York: ACM, 2008), 1065–1074, https://doi.org/10.1145/1357054.1357219.

4. Elie Bursztein, et al., "Handcrafted Fraud and Extortion: Manual Account Hijacking in the Wild," in *Proceedings of the 2014 Conference on Internet Measurement Conference, IMC '14* (New York: ACM, 2014), 347–358, https://doi.org/10.1145/2663716 .2663749.

5. Bursztein, et al., "Handcrafted Fraud and Extortion."

Chapter 12

1. Elliott Peterson, "Declaration in Support of Application for an Emergency Temporary Restraining Order and Order to Show Cause Re Preliminary Injunction." (United States District Court for the Western District of Pennsylvania, May 27, 2014).

2. Matt Long, "Department of Revenue Chief: No Security Officer for Nearly a Year before Breach," *South Carolina Radio Network*, November 28, 2012, https:// www.southcarolinaradionetwork.com/2012/11/28/department-of-revenue-chief-no -security-officer-for-nearly-a-year-before-breach/.de.

3. Thomas Ambro, *Federal Trade Commission v. Wyndham Worldwide Corporation*, No. 14–3514 (United States Court of Appeals for the Third Circuit August 24, 2015).

4. David D. Clark and Susan Landau, "The Problem Isn't Attribution: It's Multi-Stage Attacks," in *Proceedings of the Re-Architecting the Internet Workshop, ReARCH '10* (New York: ACM, 2010), 11:1–11:6, doi:10.1145/1921233.1921247.

Chapter 13

1. Jay V. Prabhu, *Indictment in U.S. v. Dennis Owen Collins et al.*, No. 1:13-cr-383 (District Court for the Eastern District of Virginia 2013).

2. Jonathan Weisman, "After an Online Firestorm, Congress Shelves Antipiracy Bills," *New York Times*, January 20, 2012, sec. Technology, https://www.nytimes.com/2012/01/21/technology/senate-postpones-piracy-vote.html.

3. Sasha Romanosky and Alessandro Acquisti, "Privacy Costs and Personal Data Protection: Economic and Legal Perspectives," *Berkeley Technology Law Journal* 24 (December 12, 2009).

4. Tom Wheeler, "Remarks of FCC Chairman Tom Wheeler" (American Enterprise Institute, June 12, 2014), http://www.fcc.gov/document/chairman-wheeler-american-enterprise-institute-washington-dc.

5. Wheeler, "Remarks of FCC Chairman Tom Wheeler."

6. Wheeler, "Remarks of FCC Chairman Tom Wheeler."

7. Messaging, Malware and Mobile Anti-Abuse Working Group, "Comments on Implementation of CSRIC III Cybersecurity Best Practices," September 26, 2014, https://www.m3aawg.org/sites/default/files/document/m3aawg_fcc_crsic_iii_cyber-security_2014-09.pdf.

8. Esther Salas, FTC v. Wyndham Order Denying Wyndham Hotels and Resorts LLC's Motion to Dismiss, No. 13-cv-01887-ES-JAD (District Court for the District of New Jersey April 7, 2014).

9. "Insurance Industry Working Session Readout Report: Insurance for Cyber-Related Critical Infrastructure Loss: Key Issues" (National Protection and Programs Directorate, Department of Homeland Security, July 2014), https://www.dhs.gov/sites/default/files/publications/July%202014%20Insurance%20Industry%20Working%20Session_1.pdf.

10. "Insurance Industry Working Session Readout Report: Insurance for Cyber-Related Critical Infrastructure Loss: Key Issues."

11. "Insurance Industry Working Session Readout Report: Insurance for Cyber-Related Critical Infrastructure Loss: Key Issues."

12. "Insurance Industry Working Session Readout Report: Insurance for Cyber-Related Critical Infrastructure Loss: Key Issues."

Chapter 14

1. "OPM: Data Breach," House of Representatives Committee on Oversight and Government Reform (2015).

Bibliography

Ambro, Thomas. *Federal Trade Commission v. Wyndham Worldwide Corporation*, No. 14-3514 (United States Court of Appeals for the Third Circuit August 24, 2015).

Anderson, Ross. "Why Information Security Is Hard—an Economic Perspective." In *Seventeenth Annual Computer Security Applications Conference*, 358–65, 2001. https://doi.org/10.1109/ACSAC.2001.991552.

Anderson, Ross, Chris Barton, Rainer Böhme, Richard Clayton, Michel J. G. van Eeten, Michael Levi, Tyler Moore, and Stefan Savage. "Measuring the Cost of Cybercrime." In *The Economics of Information Security and Privacy*, 265–300. Berlin: Springer, 2013. https://doi.org/10.1007/978-3-642-39498-0_12.

Andrews, Rick. Phone interview, September 6, 2016.

"APT1: Exposing One of China's Cyber Espionage Units." Mandiant, February 19, 2013.

Archuleta, Katherine. "OPM: Data Breach." Committee on Oversight and Government Reform, 2015.

Armstrong, Jim. "Brockton Man Is First Ashley Madison User Exposed By Hackers." *CBS Boston*, July 21, 2015. http://boston.cbslocal.com/2015/07/21/brockton-man-is-first-ashley-madison-user-exposed-by-hackers.

Atkinson, Jr. Tyrus R. "Yahoo! Inc v. Zheng Youjun, Claim Number: FA1109001409001." National Arbitration Forum Decision, October 31, 2011. http://www.adrforum.com/domaindecisions/1409001.htm.

Bangeman, Eric. "Blame for Record-Breaking Credit Card Data Theft Laid at the Feet of WEP." *Ars Technica*, May 6, 2007. https://arstechnica.com/information-technology/2007/05/blame-for-record-breaking-credit-card-data-theft-laid-at-the-feet-of-wep.

Barrett, Devlin. "Paying Ransoms to Hackers Stirs Debate." *Wall Street Journal*, November 9, 2015. https://www.wsj.com/articles/paying-ransoms-to-hackers-stirs-debate-1447106376.

Berghel, Hal. "The SCDOR Hack: Great Security Theater in Five Stages." *Computer* 46 (3) (March 2013): 97–99. https://doi.org/10.1109/MC.2013.117.

Bernstein, Joseph. "Ashley Madison's $19 'Full Delete' Option Made the Company Millions." *Buzzfeed*, August 19, 2015. https://www.buzzfeed.com/josephbernstein /leaked-documents-suggest-ashley-madison-made-millions-promis.

Boies, David. "RE: Your Possession of Privileged and/or Confidential Information Stolen From Sony Pictures Entertainment," December 14, 2014. http://www .hollywoodreporter.com/sites/default/files/custom/Sony%20Letter.pdf.

Bossert, Thomas P. "It's Official: North Korea Is Behind WannaCry." *Wall Street Journal*, December 19, 2017, sec. Opinion. https://www.wsj.com/articles/its-official -north-korea-is-behind-wannacry-1513642537.

Braman, Sandra. *Change of State: Information, Policy, and Power.* Cambridge, MA: MIT Press, 2006.

Bursztein, Elie, Borbala Benko, Daniel Margolis, Tadek Pietraszek, Andy Archer, Allan Aquino, Andreas Pitsillidis, and Stefan Savage. "Handcrafted Fraud and Extortion: Manual Account Hijacking in the Wild." In *Proceedings of the 2014 Conference on Internet Measurement Conference, IMC '14*, 347–358. New York, NY: ACM, 2014. https://doi.org/10.1145/2663716.2663749.

Chaffetz, Jason, Mark Meadows, and Will Hurd. "The OPM Data Breach: How the Government Jeopardized Our National Security for More than a Generation." Committee on Oversight and Government Reform, U.S. House of Representatives, 114th Congress, September 7, 2016.

Chirgwin, Richard. "Apple Chops Woeful WoSign HTTPS Certs from IOS, MacOS." *The Register*, October 3, 2016. https://www.theregister.co.uk/2016/10/03 /apple_wosign_certificates.

Chmielewski, Dawn, and Arik Hesseldahl. "Sony Pictures Tries to Disrupt Downloads of Its Stolen Files." *Re/Code*, December 10, 2014. https://www.recode.net/2014 /12/10/11633708/sony-pictures-tries-to-disrupt-downloads-of-its-stolen-files.

Clapper v. Amnesty International USA, 638 F. 3d 118 (U.S. Supreme Court 2013).

Clark, David D., and Susan Landau. "The Problem Isn't Attribution: It's Multi-Stage Attacks." In *Proceedings of the Re-Architecting the Internet Workshop, ReARCH '10*, 11:1–11:6. New York: ACM, 2010. https://doi.org/10.1145/1921233.1921247.

Clements, Sam. "The Shady Geeks Hiding in Bunkers Trying to Nuke the Internet." *Vice*, April 17, 2013. https://www.vice.com/en_uk/article/mvw8x8/shady-server -hosters-are-hiding-in-nuclear-bunkers.

Coleman, Gabriella. *Hacker, Hoaxer, Whistleblower, Spy: The Many Faces of Anonymous.* 1st ed. London, New York: Verso, 2014.

Corera, Gordon. "UK Teenager Sentenced over 'Biggest' Web Attack." *BBC*, July 10, 2015. http://www.bbc.com/news/technology-33480257.

Cox, Joseph. "Ashley Madison Sent Me a DMCA Request for Tweeting 2 Cells of a Spreadsheet." *Vice*, August 19, 2015. https://motherboard.vice.com/en_us /article/xywbd4/ashley-madison-sent-me-a-dmca-request-for-tweeting-two-cells-of-a -spreadsheet.

Craig, James K. *U.S. v. Evgeniy Bogachev*, No. 2:14-cr-00127-UNA (District Court for the Western District of Pennsylvania May 30, 2014).

Deibert, Ronald J. *Black Code: Inside the Battle for Cyberspace*. Plattsburgh, NY: Signal, 2013.

"Department of Justice Provides Update on GameOver Zeus and Cryptolocker Disruption." FBI statement, July 11, 2014. https://www.fbi.gov/news/pressrel/press -releases/department-of-justice-provides-update-on-gameover-zeus-and-cryptolocker -disruption.

Divol, Roxane. "A Message to Our CA Customers." Symantec Official Blog, March 26, 2017. https://www.symantec.com/connect/blogs/message-our-ca-customers.

Driscoll, John J. Amended Consolidated Class Action Complaint in RE: Ashley Madison Customer Data Security Breach Litigation, No. 4:15MD2669 JAR (District Court Eastern District of Missouri Eastern Division June 24, 2016).

Egelman, Serge, Lorrie Faith Cranor, and Jason Hong. "You've Been Warned: An Empirical Study of the Effectiveness of Web Browser Phishing Warnings." In *Proceedings of the SIGCHI Conference on Human Factors in Computing Systems, CHI '08*, 1065–1074. New York: ACM, 2008. https://doi.org/10.1145/1357054.1357219.

Elkind, Peter. "Sony Pictures: Inside the Hack of the Century." *Fortune*, June 25, 2015. http://fortune.com/sony-hack-part-1.

Esser, Michael R. "OPM: Data Breach." Committee on Oversight and Government Reform, 2015.

Federal Bureau of Investigation. "Update on Sony Investigation." FBI statement, December 19, 2014. https://www.fbi.gov/news/pressrel/press-releases/update-on -sony-investigation.

Felt, Adrienne Porter, Alex Ainslie, Robert W. Reeder, Sunny Consolvo, Somas Thyagaraja, Alan Bettes, Helen Harris, and Jeff Grimes. Improving SSL Warnings: Comprehension and Adherence. In *Proceedings of the 33rd Annual ACM Conference on Human Factors in Computing Systems, CHI '15, 2893–2902*. New York: ACM, 2015. https://doi.org/10.1145/2702123.2702442.

Fluhrer, Scott R., Itsik Mantin, and Adi Shamir. "Weaknesses in the Key Scheduling Algorithm of RC4." In *Revised Papers from the 8th Annual International Workshop on*

Selected Areas in Cryptography, SAC '01, 1–24. London: Springer-Verlag, 2001. http://dl.acm.org/citation.cfm?id=646557.694759.

Fung, Brian. "Apple's Basically Blaming Hack Victims for Not Securing Their Own iCloud Accounts." *Washington Post*, September 2, 2014. https://www.washingtonpost.com/news/the-switch/wp/2014/09/02/apples-basically-blaming-hack-victims-for-not-securing-their-own-icloud-accounts.

Gallagher, Sean. "Inside the 'Wiper' Malware That Brought Sony Pictures to Its Knees." *Ars Technica*, December 3, 2014. https://arstechnica.com/information-technology/2014/12/inside-the-wiper-malware-that-brought-sony-pictures-to-its-knees.

"GameOver Zeus Botnet Disrupted. Collaborative Effort Among International Partners." FBI statement, June 2, 2014. https://www.fbi.gov/news/stories/gameover-zeus-botnet-disrupted.

Gang, Qin. "China Reacts Strongly to U.S. Announcement of Indictment Against Chinese Personnel." Statement of the Chinese Foreign Ministry, May 20, 2014. http://www.fmprc.gov.cn/mfa_eng/xwfw_665399/s2510_665401/2535_665405/t1157520.shtml.

Gertner, Nancy. *United States v. Watt*, 707 F. Supp. 2d 149 (United States District Court, D. Massachusetts 2010).

Gillmor, Daniel Kahn. Phone interview, September 6, 2016.

Goldstein, Matthew, Nicole Perlroth, and Michael Corkery. "Neglected Server Provided Entry for JPMorgan Hackers." *New York Times*, December 22, 2014. https://dealbook.nytimes.com/2014/12/22/entry-point-of-jpmorgan-data-breach-is-identified.

Goodin, Dan. "Once Seen as Bulletproof, 11 Million+ Ashley Madison Passwords Already Cracked." *Ars Technica*, September 10, 2015. https://arstechnica.com/information-technology/2015/09/once-seen-as-bulletproof-11-million-ashley-madison-passwords-already-cracked.

Goodin, Dan. "Top 100 List Shows Ashley Madison Passwords Are Just as Weak as All the Rest." *Ars Technica*, September 11, 2015. https://arstechnica.com/information-technology/2015/09/new-stats-show-ashley-madison-passwords-are-just-as-weak-as-all-the-rest.

Greenberg, Andy. "Hack Brief: Health Insurer Excellus Says Attackers Breached 10M Records." *Wired*, September 10, 2015. https://www.wired.com/2015/09/hack-brief-health-insurance-firm-excellus-says-attackers-breached-10m-records.

Groll, Elias. "Internal Emails Show Sony Struggling to Comprehend North Korea Threat." *Foreign Policy*, April 16, 2015. http://foreignpolicy.com/2015/04/16/internal-_emails_show_sony_struggling_to_comprehend_north_korea_threat.

Hammond, Julian. *John Doe v. Avid Life Media Inc.*, No. 2:15-cv-06405-PSG-AJW (District Court Central District of California Western Division August 21, 2015).

Hawkins, John, *Phillip Morgan v. South Carolina Department of Revenue*, No. 2012-CP-40-7331 (County of Richland, Court of Common Pleas for the Fifth Judicial Circuit November 5, 2012).

Heilman, Marshall, and Christopher Glyer. "South Carolina Department of Revenue: Public Incident Response Report." Mandiant, November 20, 2012. https://oag.ca.gov /system/files/Mandiant%20Report_0.pdf.

Hickton, David J. *U.S. v. Wang Dong, Sun Kailiang, Wen Xinyu, Huang Zhenyu, and Gui Chunhui*, No. 14-118 (District Court for the Western District of Pennsylvania May 1, 2014).

Hoogstraaten, Hans, Ronald Prins, Daniël Niggebrugge, Danny Heppener, Frank Groenewegen, Janna Wettinck, Kevin Strooy, et al. "Black Tulip: Report of the Investigation into the DigiNotar Certificate Authority Breach." Fox-IT BV, August 13, 2012.

Humer, Caroline, and Jim Finkle. "Your Medical Record Is Worth More to Hackers than Your Credit Card." *Reuters*, September 24, 2014. https://www.reuters.com /article/us-cybersecurity-hospitals/your-medical-record-is-worth-more-to-hackers -than-your-credit-card-idUSKCN0HJ21I20140924.

Hunt, Stephen. "AshleyMadison.Com Founder Noel Biderman Says Vice Comes Naturally." *Calgary Herald*, January 26, 2015. http://calgaryherald.com/entertainment/ local-arts/ashleymadison-com-founder-noel-biderman-says-vice-comes-naturally.

Hutchins, Eric M., Michael J. Cloppert, and Rohan M. Amin. "Intelligence-Driven Computer Network Defense Informed by Analysis of Adversary Campaigns and Intrusion Kill Chains." Paper presented at the 6th Annual International Conference on Information Warfare & Security Research, Washington, DC, January 2011.

"Identity Theft Services: Services Offer Some Benefits but Are Limited in Preventing Fraud." United States Government Accountability Office, March 2017. https://www .gao.gov/assets/690/683842.pdf.

In the Matter of The TJX Companies, Inc. A Corporation, No. C-072–3055. Federal Trade Commission, 2008.

"Insurance Industry Working Session Readout Report: Insurance for Cyber-Related Critical Infrastructure Loss: Key Issues." National Protection and Programs Directorate, Department of Homeland Security, July 2014. https://www.dhs.gov /sites/default/files/publications/July%202014%20Insurance%20Industry%20 Working%20Session_1.pdf.

Isikoff, Michael. "One Email Exposes Millions of People to Data Theft in South Carolina Cyberattack." *NBC News*, November 20, 2012. http://investigations.nbcnews

.com/_news/2012/11/20/15313720-one-email-exposes-millions-of-people-to-data
-theft-in-south-carolina-cyberattack.

Johnson, Alex. "Ashley Madison Faces Multiple Suits Seeking More Than a Half-
Billion Dollars." *NBC News*, August 26, 2015. http://www.nbcnews.com/news
/us-news/ashley-madison-faces-multiple-suits-seeking-more-half-billion-dollars
-n415281.

Kamen, Jess. "Haley Writes IRS on Data Protection; IRS Responds." *Politico*, November 21, 2012. http://politi.co/YRB0fq.

Keegan, Rebecca. "Sony Hack 'Unprecedented, Damaging and Unique' Cyber Security Firm Says." *Los Angeles Times*, December 6, 2014. http://www.latimes.com
/entertainment/envelope/cotown/la-et-ct-sony-hack-20141206-story.html.

Kharpal, Arjun. "WannaCry Ransomware Hackers Have Only Made $50,000 Worth
of Bitcoin." *CNBC*, May 15, 2017. https://www.cnbc.com/2017/05/15/wannacry
-ransomware-hackers-have-only-made-50000-worth-of-bitcoin.html.

Klausner, R. Gary, Michael Corona, Christina Mathis, et al. vs. Sony Pictures Entertainment, No. 2:14-CV-09600-RGK-SH (District Court, Central District of California
June 15, 2015).

Krebs, Brian. "Adobe Fined $1M in Multistate Suit Over 2013 Breach; No Jail for
Spamhaus Attacker." Krebs on Security (blog), November 17, 2016. https://krebson
security.com/2016/11/adobe-fined-1m-in-multistate-suit-over-2013-breach-no-jail
-for-spamhaus-attacker.

Krebs, Brian. "Inside 'The Attack That Almost Broke the Internet.'" Krebs on Security
(blog), August 26, 2016. https://krebsonsecurity.com/2016/08/inside-the-attack-that
-almost-broke-the-internet/#more-35925.

Krebs, Brian. "Online Cheating Site Ashley Madison Hacked." Krebs on Security
(blog), July 19, 2015. https://krebsonsecurity.com/2015/07/online-cheating-site
-ashleymadison-hacked/.

Krebs, Brian. "The Rise in State Tax Refund Fraud." Krebs on Security (blog), February 17, 2015. https://krebsonsecurity.com/2015/02/the-rise-in-state-tax-refund-fraud/.

Lee, William F., Michael Corona, Christina Mathis, et al. vs. Sony Pictures Entertainment, No. 2:14-cv-09600-RGK-E (District Court, Central District of California June 29,
2015).

Levchenko, Kirill, Andreas Pitsillidis, Neha Chachra, Brandon Enright, Márk Félegy-
házi, Chris Grier, Tristan Halvorson, et al. "Click Trajectories: End-to-End Analysis
of the Spam Value Chain." In *Proceedings of the 2011 IEEE Symposium on Security and
Privacy, SP '11*, 431–446. Washington, DC: IEEE Computer Society, 2011. https://doi
.org/10.1109/SP.2011.24.

Levin, Carl. Deter Cyber Theft Act, Pub. L. No. S. 884 (2013). https://www.govtrack
.us/congress/bills/113/s884/text.

Libicki, Martin C. *Conquest in Cyberspace: National Security and Information Warfare*.
1st ed. New York: Cambridge University Press, 2007.

Liptak, Kevin, Theodore Schleifer, and Jim Sciutto. "China Might Be Building Vast
Database of Federal Worker Info, Experts Say." *CNN*, June 6, 2015. http://www.cnn
.com/2015/06/04/politics/federal-agency-hacked-personnel-management.

Long, Matt. "Department of Revenue Chief: No Security Officer for Nearly a Year
before Breach." *South Carolina Radio Network*, November 28, 2012. https://www
.southcarolinaradionetwork.com/2012/11/28/department-of-revenue-chief-no
-security-officer-for-nearly-a-year-before-breach.

Lowrey, Frank. *The Home Depot Inc. v. Visa Inc.*, No. 1:16-cv-01947-MHC (District
Court Northern District of Georgia June 13, 2016).

Markoff, John, and Nicole Perlroth. "Online Dispute Becomes Internet-Snarling
Attack." *New York Times*, March 26, 2013. https://www.nytimes.com/2013/03/27
/technology/internet/online-dispute-becomes-internet-snarling-attack.html.

Mason, Gary E. *American Federation of Government Employees, AFL-CIO vs. OPM*, No.
1:15-cv-01015 (District Court for the District of Columbia June 29, 2015).

Mason, Josephine, and Alastair Sharp. "Hacker's Ashley Madison Data Dump Threatens Marriages, Reputations." *Reuters*, August 18, 2015. http://www.reuters.com
/article/us-ashleymadison-cybersecurity-idUSKCN0QN2BN20150819.

Messaging, Malware, and the Mobile Anti-Abuse Working Group. "Comments on
Implementation of CSRIC III Cyber Security Best Practices," September 26, 2014.
https://www.m3aawg.org/node/354.

Morgan, Richard. "Ashley Madison Is Back—and Claims Surprising User Numbers."
New York Post, May 21, 2017. http://nypost.com/2017/05/21/ashley-madison-is-back
-and-claims-surprising-user-numbers.

Motion Picture Association. "CyberBunker Prohibited From Providing Internet
Access to The Pirate Bay." MPA press statement, May 13, 2010.

Moyer, Justin. "Why North Korea Has Every Reason to Be Upset about Sony's 'The
Interview.'" *Washington Post*, December 16, 2014. https://www.washingtonpost
.com/news/morning-mix/wp/2014/12/16/why-north-korea-has-every-reason-to-be
-upset-about-the-interview/.

Nakashima, Ellen. "Chinese Government Has Arrested Hackers It Says Breached OPM
Database." *Washington Post*, December 2, 2015. https://www.washingtonpost.com
/world/national-security/chinese-government-has-arrested-hackers-suspected-of

-breaching-opm-database/2015/12/02/0295b918-990c-11e5-8917-653b65c809eb
_story.html.

Nakashima, Ellen, and Adam Goldman. "CIA Pulled Officers from Beijing after Breach of Federal Personnel Records." *Washington Post*, September 29, 2015. https:// www.washingtonpost.com/world/national-security/cia-pulled-officers-from-beijing -after-breach-of-federal-personnel-records/2015/09/29/1f78943c-66d1-11e5-9ef3 -fde182507eac_story.html.

Newitz, Annalee. "Ashley Madison Code Shows More Women, and More Bots." Gizmodo (blog), August 31, 2015. http://gizmodo.com/ashley-madison-code-shows -more-women-and-more-bots-1727613924.

Newman, Jon O. *U.S. v. Morris*, 928 F.2d 504 (Court of Appeals for the Second Circuit 1991).

Novetta Threat Research Group. "Operation Blockbuster: Unraveling the Long Thread of the Sony Attack." Novetta, November 24, 2016. https://www.operationblockbuster .com/wp-content/uploads/2016/02/Operation-Blockbuster-Report.pdf.

OPM: Data Breach, House of Representatives Committee on Oversight and Government Reform (2015).

Ortiz, Carmen. *United States v. Gonzalez*, No. 1:08-cr-10223-PBS (United States District Court, D. Massachusetts March 18, 2010).

Ou, George. "TJX's Failure to Secure Wi-Fi Could Cost $1B." *ZDNet*, May 7, 2007. http://www.zdnet.com/article/tjxs-failure-to-secure-wi-fi-could-cost-1b.

Pereira, Joseph. "How Credit-Card Data Went Out Wireless Door." *Wall Street Journal*, May 4, 2007. http://www.wsj.com/articles/SB117824446226991797.

Perlroth, Nicole, and David E. Sanger. "North Korea Loses Its Link to the Internet." *New York Times*, December 22, 2014. https://www.nytimes.com/2014/12/23/world /asia/attack-is-suspected-as-north-korean-internet-collapses.html.

Peterson, Andrea. "The Security That IRS Provided Tax-Fraud Victims Just Got Hacked." *Washington Post*, March 3, 2016, sec. The Switch. https://www.washingtonpost.com /news/the-switch/wp/2016/03/03/the-security-the-irs-provided-tax-fraud-victims-just -got-hacked.

Peterson, Elliott. "Declaration in Support of Application for an Emergency Temporary Restraining Order and Order to Show Cause Re Preliminary Injunction." United States District Court for the Western District of Pennsylvania, May 27, 2014.

Prabhu, Jay V. Indictment in *U.S. v. Dennis Owen Collins et al.*, No. 1:13-cr-383. District Court for the Eastern District of Virginia, 2013.

Prince, Matthew. "The DDoS That Almost Broke the Internet." Cloudflare Blog, March 27, 2013. https://blog.cloudflare.com/the-ddos-that-almost-broke-the-internet.

Prince, Matthew. "The DDoS That Knocked Spamhaus Offline (And How We Mitigated It). Cloudflare Blog, March 20, 2013. https://blog.cloudflare.com/the-ddos-that-knocked-spamhaus-offline-and-ho.

Ragan, Steve. "Ashley Madison Self-Assessments Highlight Security Fears and Failures." CSO Online, August 19, 2015. http://www.csoonline.com/article/2973575/business-continuity/ashley-madison-self-assessments-highlight-security-fears-and-failures.html.

Rayman, Noah. "New Research Blames Insiders, Not North Korea, for Sony Hack." Time, December 30, 2014. http://time.com/3649394/sony-hack-inside-job-north-korea.

Rid, Thomas. Cyber War Will Not Take Place. 1st ed. Oxford: Oxford University Press, 2013.

Riley, Charles. "Insurance Giant Anthem Hit by Massive Data Breach." CNN, February 6, 2015. http://money.cnn.com/2015/02/04/technology/anthem-insurance-hack-data-security/index.html.

Rogers, Katie. "After Ashley Madison Hack, Police in Toronto Detail a Global Fallout." New York Times, August 25, 2015. https://www.nytimes.com/2015/08/25/technology/after-ashley-madison-hack-police-in-toronto-detail-a-global-fallout.html.

Romanosky, Sasha, and Alessandro Acquisti. "Privacy Costs and Personal Data Protection: Economic and Legal Perspectives." Berkeley Technology Law Journal 24 (3) (2009): 1061–1101.

Romanosky, Sasha, Rahul Telang, and Alessandro Acquisti. "Do Data Breach Disclosure Laws Reduce Identity Theft?" Journal of Policy Analysis and Management 30 (2) (March 1, 2011): 256–286. https://doi.org/10.1002/pam.20567.

Rosen, James. "S.C. Gov. Nikki Haley Takes Blame for State's Data Breach." McClatchy DC, November 28, 2012. http://www.mcclatchydc.com/news/politics-government/article24740893.html.

Ross, John A. Memorandum and Order in RE: Ashley Madison Customer Data Security Breach Litigation, No. MDL No. 2669 (District Court Eastern District of Missouri Eastern Division April 6, 2016).

Salas, Esther. FTC v. Wyndham Order Denying Wyndham Hotels and Resorts LLC's Motion to Dismiss, No. 13-cv-01887-ES-JAD (District Court for the District of New Jersey April 7, 2014).

Sanger, David E. "With Spy Charges, U.S. Draws a Line That Few Others Recognize." *New York Times*, May 19, 2014. https://www.nytimes.com/2014/05/20/us/us-treads -fine-line-in-fighting-chinese-espionage.html.

Sarko, Lynn Lincoln, Michael Corona, Christina Mathis, et al. vs. Sony Pictures Entertainment, No. 2:14-CV-09600-RGK-SH (District Court, Central District of California March 2, 2015).

Saville, Julie, and Nancy Loomis. "Why Wait for EMV to Solve Your Fraud Problems? One-Time Use Card Numbers Can Reduce Debit Fraud Now." First Data White Paper, December 2010. https://www.firstdata.com/downloads/thought-leadership /one-time-card-star-cert-wp.pdf.

Schneier, Bruce. "Did North Korea Really Attack Sony?" *The Atlantic*, December 22, 2014. https://www.theatlantic.com/international/archive/2014/12/did-north-korea -really-attack-sony/383973/.

Schwirtz, Michael, and Joseph Goldstein. "Russian Espionage Piggybacks on a Cybercriminal's Hacking." *New York Times*, March 12, 2017. https://www.nytimes.com /2017/03/12/world/europe/russia-hacker-evgeniy-bogachev.html.

Seal, Mark. "An Exclusive Look at Sony's Hacking Saga." *Vanity Fair*, March 2015. http://www.vanityfair.com/hollywood/2015/02/sony-hacking-seth-rogen-evan -goldberg.

Shackelford, Scott J. *Managing Cyber Attacks in International Law, Business, and Relations: In Search of Cyber Peace*. Revised ed. Cambridge: Cambridge University Press, 2014.

Shah, Paras. *NTEU v. Cobert*, No. 1:15-mc-01394-ABJ (District Court for the District of Columbia June 3, 2016).

Shain, Andrew. "S.C. Hack Victims to Get Lifetime ID Theft Resolution Aid." *The State*, October 30, 2012.

Shain, Andrew. "S.C. Tax Data Hacked: What's Known Three Weeks Later." *Beaufort Gazette*, November 17, 2012. http://www.islandpacket.com/news/local/community /beaufort-news/article33488127.html.

Shain, Andrew. "Security Contractor Didn't Detect Hacker from SCDOR Website." *The State*, November 14, 2012. http://www.goupstate.com/news/20121114/security -contractor-didnt-detect-hacker-from-scdor-website.

Sidel, Robin. "Home Depot Files Antitrust Lawsuit Against Visa, MasterCard." *Wall Street Journal*, June 15, 2016. http://www.wsj.com/articles/home-depot-u-s-credit -card-firms-slow-to-upgrade-security-1466000734.

Sieniuc, Kat. "OPM Calls For Dismissal Of Government Workers' Data Breach Suit." Law360 (blog), August 4, 2016. https://www.law360.com/articles/824965/opm-calls -for-dismissal-of-gov-t-workers-data-breach-suit.

Sleevi, Ryan. "Intent to Deprecate and Remove: Trust in Existing Symantec-Issued Certificates." Chromium Forum (blog), March 23, 2017. http://groups.google.com/a /chromium.org/d/msg/blink-dev/eUAKwjihhBs/rpxMXjZHCQAJ.

Smith, Jada F. "Cyberattack Exposes I.R.S. Tax Returns." *New York Times*, May 26, 2015, sec. Technology. https://www.nytimes.com/2015/05/27/business/breach-exposes-irs -tax-returns.html.

Smith, Tim. "Experts: Link Possible between 2012 Hacking, Tax Fraud." *Greenville Online*, March 8, 2015. http://www.greenvilleonline.com/story/news/politics/2015 /03/08/experts-link-possible-hacking-tax-fraud/24499699.

Smith, Tim. "Four Years Later, Case Still Open in DOR Data Breach." *Greenville Online*, August 12, 2016. http://www.greenvilleonline.com/story/news/crime/2016 /08/12/four-years-later-case-still-open-dor-data-breach/88453548.

Smith, Tim. "State Sending Some Tax Refunds by Mail." *Greenville Online*, March 2, 2015. http://www.greenvilleonline.com/story/news/politics/2015/03/02/state-sending -tax-refunds-mail-deter-fraud/24275417.

Solove, Daniel, and Danielle Citron. "Risk and Anxiety: A Theory of Data Breach Harms." 96 *Texas Law Review* 737 (2018). https://papers.ssrn.com/abstract=2885638.

Solove, Daniel J., and Woodrow Hartzog. "The FTC and the New Common Law of Privacy." *Columbia Law Review* 114 (4) (2014): 583–676.

Sorkin, Aaron. "The Sony Hack and the Yellow Press." *New York Times*, December 14, 2014. https://www.nytimes.com/2014/12/15/opinion/aaron-sorkin-journalists -shouldnt-help-the-sony-hackers.html.

Stempel, Jonathan. "Ashley Madison Parent in $11.2 Million Settlement over Data Breach." *Reuters*, July 14, 2017. http://www.reuters.com/article/us-ashleymadison -settlement-idUSKBN19Z2F0.

Stolfo, Sal, David Evans, and Steven M. Bellovin. "Measuring Security." *IEEE Security and Privacy* 9 (3) (2011): 60–65.

Stone, Brad. "Global Trail of an Online Crime Ring." *New York Times*, August 11, 2008. https://www.nytimes.com/2008/08/12/technology/12theft.html.

"Stophaus Chat Transcripts: March 2013." Krebs on Security (blog), August 26, 2016. http://krebsonsecurity.com/wp-content/uploads/2016/08/Spamhaus-2013-DDoS -chat-log1.txt.

Szathmari, Gabor. "Credentials in the Ashley Madison Sources." Rainbow & Unicorn (blog), September 7, 2015. https://blog.gaborszathmari.me/2015/09/07/credentials -in-the-ashley-madison-sources/.

Talbot, David. "Cyber Espionage Nightmare." *MIT Technology Review*, June 10, 2015. https://www.technologyreview.com/s/538201/cyber-espionage-nightmare/.

Taylor, Brad. "Fighting Phishing with eBay and PayPal." Official Gmail Blog, July 8, 2008. http://gmailblog.blogspot.com/2008/07/fighting-phishing-with-ebay-and -paypal.html.

Tharp, Jr., John J. *Amber J. Strautins v. Trustwave Holdings, Inc.*, No. 1:12-cv-09115 (District Court for the Northern District of Illinois Eastern Division March 12, 2014).

TJX Companies Inc. "Form 10-K." Securities and Exchange Commission filing, March 28, 2007.

Valeriano, Brandon, and Ryan C. Maness. *Cyber War versus Cyber Realities: Cyber Conflict in the International System.* 1st ed. Oxford: Oxford University Press, 2015.

VASCO Data Security International, Inc. Form 8-K. Securities and Exchange Commission filing, September 2, 2011.

Verini, James. "The Great Cyberheist." *New York Times*, November 10, 2010. https:// www.nytimes.com/2010/11/14/magazine/14Hacker-t.html.

"Verizon 2016 Data Breach Investigations Report." Verizon, April 2016. http://www .verizonenterprise.com/resources/reports/rp_DBIR_2016_Report_en_xg.pdf.

Waddell, Kaveh. "Feds Expect to Spend at Least $500 Million on the Next Five Years of Data Breaches." *The Atlantic*, August 13, 2015. https://www.theatlantic.com /politics/archive/2015/08/feds-expect-to-spend-at-least-500-million-on-the-next -five-years-of-data-breaches/458358.

Walker, Shameka L. *Federal Trade Commission v. Ruby Corp. Complaint for Permanent Injunction and Other Equitable Relief*, No. 1:16-cv-02438 (District Court for the District of Columbia December 14, 2016).

Walker, Shameka L. *FTC v. Ruby Corp. Stipulated Order for Permanent Injunction and Other Equitable Relief*, No. 1:16-cv-02438 (December 14, 2016).

Weisbaum, Herb. "CryptoLocker Crooks Launch New 'Customer Service' Website for Victims." *NBC Today*, November 14, 2013. https://www.today.com/money /cryptolocker-crooks-launch-new-customer-service-website-victims-2D11586019.

Weisman, Jonathan. "After an Online Firestorm, Congress Shelves Antipiracy Bills." *New York Times*, January 20, 2012, sec. Technology. https://www.nytimes.com/2012 /01/21/technology/senate-postpones-piracy-vote.html.

Whalley, Andrew. "Distrusting WoSign and StartCom Certificates." Google Security Blog, October 31, 2016. https://security.googleblog.com/2016/10/distrusting-wosign -and-startcom.html.

Wheeler, Tom. "Remarks of FCC Chairman Tom Wheeler." American Enterprise Institute, June 12, 2014. http://www.fcc.gov/document/chairman-wheeler-american -enterprise-institute-washington-dc.

Williams, Katie. "Lawsuits against Government over Hack Are Adding Up." *The Hill*, August 17, 2015. http://thehill.com/policy/cybersecurity/251326-lawsuits-against -government-over-hack-are-adding-up.

Wilson, Kathleen. "Distrusting New WoSign and StartCom Certificates." Mozilla Security Blog, October 24, 2016. https://blog.mozilla.org/security/2016/10/24 /distrusting-new-wosign-and-startcom-certificates.

Wilson, Kathleen. "Revoking Trust in One CNNIC Intermediate Certificate." Mozilla Security Blog, March 23, 2015. https://blog.mozilla.org/security/2015/03/23/revoking -trust-in-one-cnnic-intermediate-certificate.

Wolff, Josephine. "How a 2011 Hack You've Never Heard of Changed the Internet's Infrastructure." *Slate*, December 21, 2016. http://www.slate.com/articles/technology /future_tense/2016/12/how_the_2011_hack_of_diginotar_changed_the_internet_s_ infrastructure.html.

Wolff, Josephine. "Ransomware and the New Economics of Cybercrime." *The Atlantic*, June 7, 2016. https://www.theatlantic.com/business/archive/2016/06/ransom-ware-new-economics-cybercrime/485888/.

Wolff, Josephine. "Why Is the U.S. Determined to Have the Least-Secure Credit Cards in the World?" *The Atlantic*, March 10, 2016. https://www.theatlantic.com /business/archive/2016/03/us-determined-to-have-the-least-secure-credit-cards-in -the-world/473199.

Index

Acquisti, Alessandro, 8–9
Allegheny Technologies Incorporated, 107
Anderson, Ross, 3, 8
Andrews, Rick, 91, 94
Anthem breach, 53
Anti-Bot Code of Conduct, 250–252, 255
Apple iCloud breach, 46–47
Archuleta, Katherine, 123–137, 269–270
Ashley Madison breach, 185–203
Avid Life Media. *See* Ashley Madison breach

Barnes, Richard, 93
Beaconing, 104, 128
Bennett, Bruce, 176
Biderman, Noel, 189–195
Bitcoin. *See* Cryptocurrency
Bogachev, Evgeniy, 59–78
Boies, David, 182
Boiko, Vitalii, 154
Bonavolonta, Joseph, 75
Brewer, Jason, 35
Bryant, Kevin, 46

Certificate authority, 81–99
Certificate Authority/Browser Forum, 94
Certificate pinning, 95
CFAA. *See* Computer Fraud and Abuse Act

Chaffetz, Jason, 132, 135
Chip-and-PIN payment cards. *See* Microchip-enabled EMV cards
Chip-and-signature payment cards. *See* Microchip-enabled EMV cards
CIA, 138
CISA. *See* Cybersecurity Information Sharing Act
Citrix, 41
Citron, Danielle, 9
Clapper v. Amnesty International, 56–57, 179
Class action lawsuits, 55–56, 137, 178–179, 197–200 (*see also* Standing)
Cloudflare, 147–163
CNNIC, 96
Coleman, Gabriella, 6
Communications Decency Act, 116–117, 272–273
Communications Security, Reliability and Interoperability Council, 251
Computer Emergency Readiness Teams, 260
Computer Fraud and Abuse Act, 48–49, 212–214, 244–245
Computer Misuse Act, 245
Computer Security Incident Response Teams, 260
Consolidated Appropriations Act, 136–137
Cryptocurrency, 63–65

Cryptolocker, 63–78, 141–142
CyberBunker, 145–147
Cybersecurity Information Sharing Act, 260, 263, 273
Cylance, 130–131

DDoS attacks, 147–163
Deep Panda, 128–129
Deibert, Ronald, 9
Department of Homeland Security, 131–132, 265–266
Department of Justice, 139
Department of the Interior, 124, 129
Deter Cyber Theft Act, 118, 246–247, 256–258
DigiNotar, 81–99
Digital certificate. *See* Certificate authority.
Digital Millennium Copyright Act, 181–182, 198, 244
Digital signature. *See* Certificate authority.
DNS hijacking, 92–93
DNS reflection attack, 153–154
DNSSEC, 92–93
Domain Generation Algorithm, 61–62

Edler, Marcel, 151–152
Esser, Michael, 125
Etter, Jim, 45–46
Excellus Blue Cross Blue Shield breach, 53
Exfiltration (data), 117–118, 235–238

Federal Communications Commission, 250–252
Federal Information Security Management Act, 124–125
Federal Trade Commission, 27–28, 50–51, 187–190, 194–197, 226–228, 252–253, 270
FedRAMP, 133, 253
FireEye, 165

Foreign Intelligence Surveillance Act Amendments Act of 2008, 56
Forum of Incident Response and Security Teams, 260

GameOver ZeuS, 59–78
General Data Protection Regulation, 11
Gillmor, Daniel Kahn, 95, 99
Gonzalez, Albert, 19–37, 63, 73
Google, 81–99
Government Accountability Office, 136
GOZ. *See* GameOver ZeuS
Guardians of Peace, 169, 172–178

Haley, Nikki, 40, 44–46, 52
Health Insurance Portability and Accountability Act, 51
Hice, Jody, 134
Hickton, David, 102–103
HiKit (malware), 125–126
Home Depot, 36–37
Hoogstraaten, Hans, 87–88
Huawei, 123

ICANN, 160
Identity theft, 53–57
Impact Team, 185–190
Information Sharing and Analysis Centers, 260
Insurance, 264–268
Intermediary liability protections, 116–117, 247–268, 271–276
Internet Corporation for Assigned Names and Numbers. *See* ICANN
"The Interview" (movie), 176–177
Iran, 81–99
IRS, 45, 49, 52, 54

James, Jonathan, 22
JPMorgan Chase breach, 46–47

Kamphuis, Sven Olaf, 146–163
Kill chain, 3, 277

King, Jeremy, 34
Klausner, R. Gary, 179–180

Lazarus Group, 174
Levchenko, Kirill, 4
Libicki, Martin, 10
Linford, Steve, 148, 159
Lynch, Stephen, 122
Lynton, Michael, 165, 176

MacCall, Kevin, 192
Mandia, Kevin, 165, 170, 172, 175
Mandiant, 40, 43, 102–110, 165–166
Man-in-the-middle attack, 91–92
Marshalls breach. *See* TJX Companies
   Inc. breach
MasterCard, 34–37, 54
McDonagh, Sean Nolan, 149–161
MD5, 193
Messaging, Malware and Mobile
   Anti-Abuse Working Group,
   251–252
Microchip-enabled EMV cards, 33–37
Morris, Robert, 212–213
Morris worm. *See* Morris, Robert
Mozilla, 93–94

National Institute of Standards and
   Technology, 49, 52, 249, 266
Network and Information Security
   Directive, 11, 226–228
Newitz, Annalee, 195
Newman, Jon, 213
NIST Framework for Improving Critical
   Infrastructure Cybersecurity, 266
NIST Special Publication 800-53. *See*
   National Institute of Standards and
   Technology
North Korea, 73, 166–167, 172–177

Obama, Barack, 167
Office of Management and Budget, 133,
   209

Office of Personnel Management.
   See OPM breach.
Open Resolver Project, 156
Operation Get Right or Die Tryin'.
   See TJX Companies Inc. breach
Operation Stophaus, 145–163, 187
Operation Tovar, 59–78
OPM breach, 121–142
Optik, Alex, 149–150
Ozment, Andy, 132

Pascal, Amy, 165, 177
Payment Card Industry Data Security
   Standards, 30, 49, 200, 227, 254
Payment card industry liability shift.
   See Microchip-enabled EMV cards
Payment Card Industry Security
   Standards Council. *See* Payment Card
   Industry Data Security Standards
PayPal, 214, 216–217
Peterson, Elliott, 65, 232–233
The Pirate Bay, 146
PLA Unit 61398, 101–119, 122, 167
PlayStation breach, 177
PlugX (malware), 127–130
Prince, Matthew, 155
PROTECT IP Act, 247–248

Ransomware, 63–78
Reflection attack. *See* DNS reflection
   attack
Romanosky, Sasha, 8–9
Ross, John, 199–200
Ruby Life. *See* Ashley Madison breach
Russell, Steve, 135

Saulsbury, Brendan, 126–127
Scott, Christopher, 19, 25
Section 230. *See* Communications
   Decency Act
Seymour, Donna, 123–126
Shackelford, Scott, 10
Silva, Doriana, 195

Snowden, Edward, 112, 123
Solove, Daniel, 9
Sony Pictures Entertainment breach,
    165–184
Sorkin, Aaron, 182
South Carolina Department of Revenue,
    39–57, 211–212
Spam e-mail, 4, 216–217
Spamhaus Project, 145–163
Standing (legal), 55–57 (*see also* Class
    action lawsuits)
Stephens, Andrew Jacob, 149–151
Stop Online Piracy Act, 247–248
Stuxnet, 6
Sun Kailiang, 101, 106
Surma, John, 101–102
Sykes, Trevor, 192
Symantec, 91, 97–98
Szathmari, Gabor, 191–192

Target breach, 226–227
Tax fraud, 53–57
Taylor, Brad, 217
TJX Companies Inc. breach, 19–37
Toey, Damon Patrick, 19

UglyGorilla. *See* Wang Dong
US-CERT, 127, 131–132
U.S. Steel, 101–104

Visa, 34–37, 54

Wagner, Jeff, 133
Wang Dong, 106, 110–111
WannaCry, 72–73
War driving, 19
Watt, Stephen, 22
Wen Xinyu, 107
WEP, 20–21
Westinghouse Electric Company, 103,
    108–110
Wheeler, Tom, 250–253
WHOIS database, 160

Williams, Jonathan, 25, 69
WinXYHappy. *See* Wen Xinyu
Wiper (malware), 168–169
WPA, 20
Wyndham Hotel Group breaches,
    50–51, 195, 238–239, 252–253,
    270–271

Yahoo, 115–116
Yastremskiy, Maksym, 24–26, 60, 69, 73
Yelp, 214

Zaman, Humza, 24